GROUP PROCESS, GROUP DECISION, GROUP ACTION

SECOND EDITION

Robert S. Baron and Norbert L. Kerr

OPEN UNIVERSITY PRESS

Open University Press
McGraw-Hill Education
McGraw-Hill House
Shoppenhangers Road
Maidenhead
Berkshire
SL6 2QL
United Kingdom

Email: enquiries@openup.co.uk
World wide web: www.openup.co.uk

and
Two Penn Plaza
New York, NY 10121-2289, USA

First published 1992
Reprinted 1993, 1996, 1999
First published in this second edition 2003
Reprinted 2004

A catalogue record of this book is available from the British Library

ISBN   0 335 20697 2 (pb)   0 335 20698 0 (hb)

Library of Congress Cataloging-in-Publication Data
Baron, Robert S.
    Group process, group decision, group action/Robert Baron and
Norbert L. Kerr. – 2nd ed.
        p.   cm. – (Mapping social psychology series)
    Includes bibliographical references and index.
    ISBN 0-335-20698-0 – ISBN 0-335-20697-2 (pbk.)
    1. Social groups.   2. Performance.   3. Influence (Psychology)
4. Group-decision making.   5. Conflict (Psychology)   I. Kerr,
Norbert L.   II. Title.   III. Series.

HM716.B37 2003
301–dc21   2002030418

Typeset by Graphicraft Limited, Hong Kong
Printed in Great Britain by Biddles Ltd, King's Lynn, Norfolk

Dedicated to our families

CONTENTS

Preface   xii
Acknowledgements   xiv

ONE   **Introduction**   1
        Key concepts   1
        Initial considerations   1
        The defining of a group   1
        Explaining human reliance on groups: some theoretical
        perspectives   2
            Conditioning and social comparison theories   2
            Social identity and self-categorization theories   3
            Exchange theory   3
            Sociobiological theory   4
            Optimal distinctiveness theory   5
        Group characteristics   6
            Group norms   6
            Group size   7
            Group structure   7
            Group cohesion   11
            Leadership   15
            Stages   17
            Group entitativity   18
        Summary   18
        Suggestions for further reading   19

TWO   **Social facilitation**   20
        Key concepts   20
        Background   20
        Drive theory and social facilitation   21
        Zajonc's mere presence hypothesis   23
            Cottrell's learned drive view   24

Distraction/conflict (D/C) theory   25
Drive theory on trial   27
Self-based theories of social facilitation   29
  Self-presentation theory   29
  Self-efficacy theory   30
Attentional theories   31
Summary   34
Suggestions for further reading   34
Note   35

THREE   **Individual versus group performance**   36
          Key concepts   36
          Introduction   36
          Early research   37
          Task, resources and potential: Steiner's model of group
            performance   38
          The experimental analysis of process loss   43
            Group member characteristics   43
            Brainstorming   44
            Group size and performance   47
          Summary   49
            Solution to the Husbands & Wives problem   50
          Suggestions for further reading   50

FOUR   **Task motivation in groups**   51
          Key concepts   51
          Introduction   51
          Group motivation losses: social loafing   52
            Identifiability-mediated motivation losses   53
            Free riding   55
            Inequity-based motivation losses   58
          Group motivation gains   60
            The Köhler effect   60
            Social compensation   63
          Summary   66
          Suggestions for further reading   66

FIVE   **Social influence and conformity**   68
          Key concepts   68
          Background   68
          Social comparison theory   69
          Ostracism   71
          Conformity   73
            Classic studies   73
            The benefits of conformity   75
            Conformity data   76
          Recent research on conformity   78
            Priming   78
            Task importance   78
            Group identification   79

Minority and majority influence 83
   The afterimage study 84
   Summing across studies 86
   Variables affecting minority influence 86
   The two-process model 87
   Alternatives to conversion theory 89
Summary 91
Suggestions for further reading 91

SIX   **Extremity in groups** 93
Key concepts 93
Introduction 93
Groupthink 94
   Janis' initial model of groupthink 94
   Laboratory research on groupthink 95
   Historical case study reports of groupthink 96
   Revised versions of groupthink 97
   Avoiding groupthink 97
Group polarization 98
   Early research on group polarization 98
   Competitive social comparison and persuasive arguments ... 99
   A self-categorization view of group polarization 100
   Group polarization with real consequences 103
   Biases in information sampling 104
Intense indoctrination 108
Mob action 111
   Some causes of mob behaviour 111
   Deindividuation research 113
   Emergent norm theory 115
   The ID model 117
Summary 118
Suggestions for further reading 119

SEVEN   **Social combination approaches to group decision-making** ... 120
Key concepts 120
Introduction 120
Social combination approaches to group decision-making ... 122
Jury decision-making 125
   Jury size and decision rule 125
   Juries' leniency bias 127
An SDS analysis of group performance 129
Group versus individual susceptibility to judgmental biases ... 131
Complex group problem-solving: collective induction 133
Social communication and social combination: toward
   integration 135
Summary 136
Suggestions for further reading and viewing 137
Note 138

EIGHT   **Social dilemmas** 139
Key concepts 139

Background   139
The nature of social dilemmas   140
Cooperation in social dilemmas: motives and determinants   143
Dilemma features   144
Individual differences   146
Others' choices   147
Communication and commitment   149
Structural solutions to social dilemmas   150
Privatizing   150
Group size   151
Supplementary payoffs/costs   151
Changing the structure of the dilemma   152
Summary   153
Suggestions for further reading   154

NINE   **Intergroup conflict and aggression**   155
Key concepts   155
Introduction   155
Intergroup conflict and aggression   155
Research on realistic conflict theory   156
Frustration, aggression and scapegoating   156
Perceived injustice   157
Triggering events   159
Generic sources of intergroup conflict: minimal
groups research   160
Ingroup favoritism in minimal groups   160
Other perceptual and cognitive biases in intergroup relations   163
Outgroup homogeneity   163
The discontinuity effect and schema-based distrust of outgroups 164
Illusory correlation   164
Bargaining with the enemy: the carrot vs. *the stick*   166
The ultimate attribution error   166
Reducing intergroup conflict and aggression   166
Intergroup contact: the contact hypothesis   167
Superordinate goals   168
Manipulating social categorization   169
Gradual and reciprocal concession technique   171
Summary   172
Suggestions for further reading   173
Note   173

TEN   **Stress and social support**   175
Key concepts   175
Background   175
Affiliation research   176
Social support   178
The broken heart effect   179
Social support research   180
Explaining the relationship between social support and health   183
Control and self-esteem   183

Self-disclosure 183
Immune function 184
The buffering hypothesis 184
Can social support be harmful? 185
Matching theories of social support 186
Random assignment and social support research 187
Studies with healthy humans and primates 187
Research with patient populations 188
Social skills training 190
Summary 191
Suggestions for further reading 192

ELEVEN **Electronic groups** 193
Key concepts 193
Background 193
Unique features of computer groups 194
Attenuation of information exchanged 194
Loss of non-verbal and paralinguistic information 194
Loss of status information 195
Computer-mediated communication and anonymity 197
Group cohesion and identity 197
Social corroboration, social support and loneliness 198
Electronic violence on and off the internet 199
Similarities between computer groups and face-to-face groups 200
Social facilitation in electronic groups 201
Social influence in electronic networks 201
Working with virtual partners 202
Summary 203
Suggestions for further reading and links 204

TWELVE **Concluding thoughts** 205

Glossary 207
References 215
Index 260

PREFACE

Groups are a key element in human experience. Whether the group is a family, a street gang, a work group, an ethnic minority or a network of friends, group membership and influence represents one of the most powerful forces shaping our feelings, judgments and behaviours. Although group processes can lead to destructive and aggressive outbursts, they are also the source of some of our most noble actions, such as love, achievement, nurturance, loyalty and sacrifice. Despite the ubiquity and importance of groups for human existence, scholarly research on group topics is a relatively recent phenomenon. Although some of the earliest research in social psychology focused on how groups affected task performance (Triplett 1898; Ringelmann 1913), for the most part systematic research on other topics did not become widespread until the 1940s and 1950s. Therefore, it is not surprising that group research is still an emerging field. As such, it provides the excitement that derives from new theory and fresh empirical phenomena as well as the challenge (and frustration) that stems from the fact that there still is a good deal of ambiguity and uncertainty regarding many fundamental aspects of group process.

This book is designed for advanced undergraduate students in courses such as group dynamics and social psychology. In this volume, we try to share with the reader both the excitement and the challenge of conducting research on group phenomena. Where possible, we try to provide a historical context for the research (what inspired it, what obstacles were overcome, what controversies stimulated continued research), as well as the applied significance of what these laboratory findings mean in terms of our everyday life. Our primary objective, however, is to familiarize the reader with the theoretical perspectives and data that provided researchers with a means of interpreting group phenomena. We place special emphasis on several aspects of group experience that we feel are of particular significance. These include processes of social influence (Chapter 5), group productivity (Chapters 2, 3 and 4), extreme group behaviour (Chapter 6), group decision-making (Chapter 7) and intergroup conflict and prejudice (Chapter 9).

The book is organized historically, with early chapters presenting those research areas that first captured the attention of researchers and later chapters (social dilemmas, group decision-making, social support, electronic groups and group aggression) depicting areas that became active more recently. Chapter 1 introduces several basic concepts (e.g. group structure, norms, status) fundamental to understanding group research. Chapters 2, 3 and 4 then address one of the earliest and most basic areas of group research – how groups affect the task performance of individuals. Chapter 2 focuses primarily on non-interacting groups (i.e. where one simply works in the presence of others without any need for coordination), while Chapter 3 focuses on groups that work together for some common goal. Chapter 4 discusses how group contexts can alter productivity by affecting motivation. Chapter 5 covers basic issues of social influence and conformity, while Chapter 6 (new to this edition) focuses on some causes of extreme behaviour in groups. Chapters 8–11 examine several distinctly applied topics that have captured the interest of group researchers in recent years. It is our hope that this organizational structure will aid the reader in appreciating the complexities, challenges and insights that have characterized group research since its inception.

ACKNOWLEDGEMENTS

We would like to acknowledge the invaluable assistance of the secretarial and other personnel who contributed to this project, specifically Lynn Jennings, Becky Huber, Joyce Paul, Sondra Higbee and Jennifer Hogoboom. In addition, we would like to thank the many students who, over the years, have helped us to maintain our enthusiasm for group research. Finally, we would like to thank Professor Robin Martin for comments on an earlier draft and Professor Tony Manstead for his thoughtful comments on the draft and his encouragement on this project.

ONE

INTRODUCTION

KEY CONCEPTS

- What is the formal definition of a group?
- Why are humans drawn to groups?
- What theoretical approaches are used to study human affinity for affiliating with others?
- What characteristics do groups have?
- What theories exist regarding leadership and group cohesion?

INITIAL CONSIDERATIONS

Groups play a crucial role in human affairs. They shape our perceptions and attitudes, provide support in times of distress and affect our performance and decision-making. Group processes can produce everything from destructive mob behaviour to selfless loyalty (e.g. Paulus 1989). In this introductory chapter, we consider how social scientists define the term 'group'. Then, we discuss several important group characteristics that provide us with a means of both understanding and describing different forms of group experience.

THE DEFINING OF A GROUP

A mob of football (soccer) fans in Brussels runs amok just before the World Cup; seventeen die. A squad of inexperienced infantrymen are coached to spread out when moving along a roadway. Shelling begins and they group together, huddling against each other for comfort. A group of environmental activists meet to discuss their next group action. As the discussion progresses, the group comes to embrace a more radical position than they did previously and, eventually, they agree to commit an act of eco-terrorism.

These instances all illustrate principles of group dynamics. Yet the groups in question vary widely in their characteristics. These differences illustrate the difficulty of deriving a single definition of 'group' that is entirely satisfactory. Not surprisingly, many definitions have been proposed. Some stress that groups must have some permanence, structure and psychological meaning for members, thereby creating a feeling of belonging. In contrast, others are far more flexible in their definition, arguing only that some form of communication or mutual social influence occur if a collection of individuals are to be viewed as a group. For example, Forsyth (1999) defines a *group* as 'two or more interdependent individuals who influence each other through social interaction' (p. 5).

Many other definitions of 'group' exist, but it is clear that over the years researchers have tended to feel more comfortable with the more flexible conceptualizations, such as the one offered by Forsyth (1999). Thus, much of group research has focused on temporary groups that have no clear structure or lasting relationship to each other but whose members are bound only by some brief period of mutual influence or subtle communication. The research we discuss in later chapters on mob action, bystander helping, audience impact and 'minimal' groups illustrates such work.

EXPLAINING HUMAN RELIANCE ON GROUPS: SOME THEORETICAL PERSPECTIVES

Conditioning and social comparison theories

Theorists have proposed several reasons why groups play such a strong role in human affairs (Baumeister and Leary 1995). One straightforward view – the *conditioning* perspective – is that from infancy we learn to depend on others for comfort, food, aid, information, love, friendship and entertainment. Social approval, in particular, comes to be associated with a wide array of positive outcomes and, therefore, comes to be highly desired (i.e. reinforcing), as explained by processes of classical conditioning. *Social comparison theory* suggests a less obvious view. According to this theory (Festinger 1954), we feel very strong pressure to have accurate views, both about our environment and our abilities. One way to verify our views is to compare our opinions and ability-related performances to those of others. In other words, if physical reality is ambiguous, we create a social reality. Therefore, according to a social comparison perspective, at least one reason we group together is to gain comparative information. Presumably we do this in an attempt to protect ourselves from inappropriate decisions and judgments (Suls and Wheeler 2000; Suls *et al.* 2000).

Social identity and self-categorization theories

A somewhat different view of group benefits is offered by *social identity theory* (e.g. Tajfel and Turner 1986). According to this theory, our self-image and self-esteem are heavily dependent upon the groups we identify with. Therefore, group membership will often serve the purpose of helping us establish or maintain a satisfactory sense of self. It is easier to see oneself as, say, a rebel, if one belongs to or identifies with some form of counterculture group, be it a gang, an artistic clique or a rock band. According to the social identity view, then, we affiliate with groups in part as a means of feeling good about ourselves. A closely related view, *self-categorization theory* (see Hogg *et al.* 1990; Turner 1991; Turner *et al.* 1989), also holds that the group categories we belong to can affect our sense of identity. According to this perspective, however, these group categories must be salient or noticeable to have this effect. Thus, if we are representing our occupation at a job fair, our occupational affiliation will be highly salient to us. As a result, we will tend to think of ourselves in terms of our professional identity as opposed to the many other aspects of our selves that we could consider (e.g. our ethnicity, our role as son or daughter). Both social identity theory and self-categorization theory suggest that one benefit of group membership is that such membership helps us clarify who we 'are', what we believe and who our allies and enemies are (Sherman *et al.* 1999). This uncertainty reduction benefit is stressed by such proponents of self-categorization theory as Michael Hogg and Dominic Abrams (e.g. Hogg and Abrams 1993), who also point out that group norms prevalent in most groups (see below) also reduce uncertainty by providing guides for thought, customs and activity (e.g. Hogg 2001).

Exchange theory

One theoretical perspective, *exchange theory*, provides a broader view of group formation that encompasses all of the benefits discussed above. It argues that people gain certain advantages through group membership and, therefore, individuals will try to join those groups that provide them with the greatest 'gains'. According to this theory, group membership involves exchanging both rewards and costs with other group members. Rewards are positive elements gained through social exchange. They can be material goods or psychological goods, such as love, approval, improved self-identity or social comparison information. A key feature of group interaction is that we can only obtain many of these psychological rewards by affiliating with others. For example, being accepted by individuals of high status represents a very powerful, rewarding consequence of group interaction, as does having our important values and beliefs confirmed. Indeed, social stimulation often itself becomes an important resource that one can exchange ('Hey, let's party tonight!'). According to exchange theory, group membership also has costs. These include the resources that we give to the group, time and effort spent on group activities, opportunities lost by belonging to the group and emotional costs associated with group activity.

This emphasis on rewards and costs allows one to think about the 'profit' one achieves through group membership (where profit = reward – costs). Because exchange theory considers psychological sources of reward as well as material rewards as a source of profit, we can view such diverse groups as friendships, family groups and romantic couples as exchange relationships. The notion that even loved ones exchange resources among themselves has been most useful to family therapists and marriage counselors seeking to improve the quality of such relationships. Thus, for example, therapists might have couples 'negotiate' so that they may lower each of their respective costs and heighten each of their rewards, thereby elevating the mutual profit each gains from the relationship ('I'll happily do more of the kitchen chores, if you agree to keep me company at the pub on Friday nights'). According to a well-known exchange theory developed by Harold Kelley and John Thibaut, we can explain such things as our satisfaction with a group and our dependency on it by considering this notion of *profit*. If our profit is greater than the profit we think is fair or normal for such a relationship, we will be satisfied. Thibaut and Kelley (1959) refer to this standard of fairness as the 'comparison level' (CL). According to Thibaut and Kelley, our dependency on a relationship is primarily a function of what our other options are – that is, the 'profit' we can anticipate in our 'next best deal'. They refer to this value as 'comparison level for alternatives' (or CLalt). As an example, we might be quite dissatisfied in a particular relationship (this implies our profit is well below our CL), but if our other options are far worse, we will be unhappily quite dependent on the relationship (our present profit is well above our CLalt). Thus, according to Thibaut and Kelley, the further your present profit exceeds your next best option (CLalt), the greater your dependency on the group. Thibaut and Kelley's analysis explains many seemingly puzzling situations, such as individuals who remain in unfulfilling marriages or jobs. Although the satisfaction of such individuals is low, they must perceive their other options to be even worse.

Another interesting feature of this theory is that one's satisfaction with a social relationship will depend heavily on what we use as our standard of 'fairness' (i.e. our CL). For example, the communist regime in East Germany fell, in large part, due to strong feelings of economic deprivation on the part of the East German people. Interestingly, according to most economic indicators, East Germany had a higher standard of living than Italy, England or the remaining Warsaw Pact nations. This did little to assuage feelings of dissatisfaction, however. The key issue was that West Germany was apparently the most psychologically relevant comparison group for East German citizens and, by this comparison, their own economic circumstances appeared bleak. (Note that key changes occurred only after escape or migration to West Germany became possible, thereby providing an extremely attractive CLalt to remaining in East Germany.)

Sociobiological theory

Another theoretical view explaining the social tendency of human beings derives from theories of *sociobiology* (e.g. Bowlby 1958). These theories, which draw heavily on the work of Charles Darwin, basically argue that, on balance, grouping together has survival value for humans as well as many other species. Thus, when humans group together they are more able to protect themselves from predators and enemies and are also able to cooperate for the purposes of farming, child-rearing, hunting and caring for the sick and injured (Baumeister and Leary 1995). There are various ways in which genetic components might influence this tendency to congregate. For example, more intelligent organisms are probably more likely to recognize the survival benefits of affiliation. If this is the case, genetic influences on intelligence could explain why 'survival of the fittest' results in the pervasive human tendency to affiliate. Another example is that humans could have a genetic predisposition to bond – that is, to respond positively to contact and nurturance. In either case, the material and psychological rewards that we gain through group membership are seen as a strong contributor to the pervasive presence of group arrangements. Indeed, our desire to establish satisfactory, stable relationships with others and to be deeply appreciated by others can be described as one of the most fundamental of human needs (Brewer 1991; Baumeister and Leary 1995).

Optimal distinctiveness theory

The need to belong, discussed just above, must be balanced against another important human desire – the desire to see ourselves as unique and special individuals. This perspective is emphasized by *optimal distinctiveness theory* (Brewer 1991; Brewer and Gardner 1996). This view recognizes that, at times, certain aspects of group membership can make us feel uncomfortably anonymous, unimportant and more or less interchangeable with other group members. As a result, optimal distinctiveness theory contends that human beings need to find a comfortable balance between their desire to be distinctive and their need to belong and to be socially cherished. One prediction of this model is that if, for some reason, one's feelings of uniqueness are threatened, one will try to find a means of reasserting one's individuality. This might involve non-conformity to the ingroup (Brewer and Weber 1994) or identifying with a group that one feels is special or distinctive. This, of course, can explain why young people in their adolescent years often reject the norms of their family or the larger society and instead identify with particular youth subgroups that have very distinctive dress, slang, attitudes, and so on. On the other hand, if individuals feel isolated, unaccepted or unloved, one would expect very different group behaviours and membership choices. Thus, optimal distinctiveness theory, like several of the theories above, assumes that we often select the groups we identify with or join to provide us with certain psychological benefits. From our discussion so far, it should be obvious that people find groups essential for several different reasons. As a result, groups are likely to vary on a number of key dimensions. In the next section, we consider some of these dimensions.

GROUP CHARACTERISTICS

Group norms

A major feature of group experience is the nature of its *norms*, those behaviours, attitudes and perceptions that are approved of by the group and expected – and, in fact, often demanded – of its members. Such socially established and shared beliefs regarding what is normal, correct, true, moral and good generally have powerful effects on the thoughts and actions of group members. Indeed, failure to adhere to such norms often leads to some form of social penalty. As we will see when we discuss the conformity literature in Chapter 5, the nature of group norms has been shown in laboratory research to affect a wide range of judgments. These include artistic judgments, visual perception and auditory perception. For example, in one classic study, Sherif (1935, 1936) led individuals to a totally dark room and turned on a tiny bulb. This procedure creates the illusion that the stationary light is actually moving. This is referred to as the 'autokinetic effect'. (*Note*: To maximize the illusion, the room must be pitch black and the participants should be unfamiliar with the room's size.) Sherif exposed the participants to several trials, each time asking them to indicate when the light began to move, when it stopped and how far it moved. The participants were strongly influenced by the opinions of those around them. Indeed, Sherif was able to dramatically increase or decrease individuals' estimates of movement if he had confederates offer particularly large or small estimates. What was most impressive was that once participants changed their estimates in response to group influence, they maintained similar estimates on subsequent judgments, even when they were no longer accompanied by group members. From this it would appear that the participants had truly changed their private perceptions about the amount of light movement they were seeing and were not simply going along with the group to avoid conflict.

As this implies, norms can have impressive effects. Consider the case of The Symbionese Liberation Army (SLA). The SLA was a group of about ten men and women dedicated to the unusual goal of provoking a socialist/communist revolution in the United States. In February 1974, they kidnapped Patricia Hearst, the daughter of newspaper magnate William Randolph Hearst, from her college apartment in Berkeley, California; previously, they had assassinated a local city official in Oakland, California. This group had several norms that exerted great influence on members. Indeed, the members' acceptance of them was so deep that they often adhered to them unthinkingly. In several cases, this put the group at great risk. For example, they shared a strong normative belief that, as a group, they were admired and supported by the 'common people'. Acting on this belief, members were often quite frank regarding their SLA affiliation. Donald Defreeze, the group leader, went as far as canvassing the nearby neighbourhood for recruits and supporters, even checking with people living in the SLA's own apartment building. ('Hello. I'm with the SLA. You know, the wanted fugitives who kidnapped Patty Hearst. We're conducting a recruitment drive. Interested?') These actions are noteworthy not only because they obviously put the group at risk, but because they were so at variance with the group's paranoid but understandable concern about security in most other matters. Clearly, the group's belief in their popular support was a very deeply felt conviction.

Norms evolve in groups for several reasons. First, norms are often crucial for the group's survival or success. Thus, norms favouring bravery, sacrifice and loyalty (i.e. never informing) have obvious utility for groups involved in conflict and armed struggle, such as the Symbionese Liberation Army. Second, norms provide codes of behaviour that render social life more predictable and efficient. Imagine the chaos that would result if people ignored the codified norms governing driving. Finally, norms serve to reduce uncertainty and confusion when the environment appears unpredictable, unusual or threatening. In times of stress, we seem to be particularly upset by uncertainty. A group consensus or the opinion of a group leader regarding such things as 'what's going on' and the 'best way to cope' seem to be particularly comforting and persuasive.

Group size

Group size is an obvious enough group dimension, but it has several important ramifications. Larger groups are more likely to include individuals with a wide range of skills. Therefore, specialization of labor is more likely to occur. Larger groups also allow us to feel more anonymous. As a result, we may exhibit less social responsibility in larger groups, which, in turn, can lead to less task involvement and lower morale on the part of many group members as group size increases. In addition, size has a strong impact on group communication. One particularly well-documented effect of increasing group size is that, in larger groups, a smaller percentage of individuals contribute to group discussion. This is apparently due both to the members' heightened fear of participation and that there is less chance or time for individuals to express themselves in large gatherings.

Group structure

A third and most crucial dimension of groups is structure. Group structure is most likely to be well developed in permanent groups such as families, work groups, clubs, and so on, where there will generally be status differences among members, well-established norms of conduct and thought, leaders, followers and various cliques and subgroups. These factors comprise some of the basic elements of group structure. That is, structure refers to the way groups are organized and how various positions in the group are related. Most writers describe group structure as consisting of several key elements:

Roles

In almost all long-term groups, members will occupy different *social roles*. These are the expected behaviours associated with a given position within a group. Social roles may be formal or informal. Thus a street gang might have formal officers (e.g. club president, war counsellor) as well as a variety of informal roles (clown, tough guy, etc.). Often these informal roles evolve because of psychological needs within the group. Thus, the clown role will often serve to relieve group tension and to provide subtly veiled social criticism and commentary through satire that otherwise might be too controversial to air. That individuals often fill multiple roles can lead to *role conflict* in which the demands of one role are incompatible with the demands of another. Such conflicts have been the source of history's more dramatic episodes. The Wild West tale of how Sheriff Pat Garrett shot down his friend, the famous outlaw Billy the Kid (William Bonney), exemplifies this process. Garrett's role as an officer of the law served to direct his behaviour, despite it conflicting with his role as friend. This tale illustrates that roles can have a powerful influence on our actions, often leading us to act contrary to our private feelings or vested interest.

This type of role conflict can lead to a good deal of intellectual and psychological discomfort. Sir Thomas More, Lord Chancellor of England, experienced psychological agony when asked to sanction the dissolution of King Henry's VIII's marriage to Queen Catherine. More's roles as friend and advisor to the king conflicted with his role as a devout Catholic. Sir Thomas remained true to his religious conscience even when imprisoned and sentenced to death in 1535. Milgram's famous obedience studies (Milgram 1974) provide a second example. In these experiments, paid adult participants learned that as part of a study on punishment and learning, they as 'teachers' would be asked to shock a learner (actually a confederate) every time he committed a memory error. The experimental setting was extremely realistic, complete with a buzzing, blinking shock machine. The entire point of this study was to determine when the 'teacher' would refuse to comply with the requirements of his role as obedient research participant. Thus, in this setting, the role conflict entails the conflict between one's role as sympathetic and humane fellow citizen and one's role as responsible and cooperative research participant. Almost all 'teachers' began to express reluctance and show signs of stress as the intensity of the shock they administered increased and the 'learner' cried out in pain. If they refused to administer a shock, however, the experimenter urged them on by saying such things as 'please continue' or 'you must go on'. Only if the 'teacher' persisted in his reluctance despite the experimenter's urgings and demands was he excused from the study. In this study, it is clear that most participants were quite disturbed and concerned about the shock they thought they were administering. Some broke out into nervous laughter, while others bit their lips or dug fingernails into their palms. But this generally did not disrupt their role compliance, despite the learner appearing to be in pain. Over 60 per cent of 'teachers' administered the maximum shock voltage (450 volts) to the learner. Indeed, even when the 'teacher' was required to hold the victim's hand to the shock plate by force, the figure only dropped to 30 per cent. Milgram's results have now been replicated in several countries (Milgram 1974), showing how reluctant we are to confront authority when we are placed in a subordinate role. For those of us concerned about our susceptibility to authoritarian political regimes, or about how we would react when role requirements demand immoral action on our part, these data are most provocative and disturbing. It would be nice to think that we personally would act honorably under such role pressure, but the data imply that many of us could be pressured into committing a variety of costly, harmful or even immoral actions if role pressure is severe enough.

Status

Different social roles are usually associated with different degrees of *status*, which can be defined as the amount of respect and privilege accorded a group member. Although roles often provide a source of status, it can be based on other individual characteristics as well, such as physical attractiveness, intelligence, sense of humour and skill. Status is generally a function of the extent to which an individual's contribution is crucial to the success and prestige of the group, and how much power (control over group outcomes) that individual has. Thus, in many groups – especially infrahuman ones – status is determined by which individual is physically most dominant. Although status and power ordinarily go hand in hand, they need not. The British monarchy, for example, has exceptional status but relatively little power.

Our status can also be based on the extent to which we embody some idealized or admired characteristic. Status of this last type is often not based on our achievements or contributions. Thus, in high school social groups, physically attractive individuals tend to have unusually high status. Similarly, in most cultures, racial identity is unfortunately an important determinant of status, often completely overshadowing an individual's achievements, efforts and contributions. Differences in status have several important effects on group process. Individuals of high status are likely to be valued by the group and treated more tolerantly. As a result, they will often be less affected by group norms and peer pressure than members of lower status, in part because they are less likely to expect punishment for their actions. Thus, a common feature in many cults is that the group leader has materialistic and erotic privileges that violate the otherwise chaste norms of the group (Baron *et al.* in press). In a laboratory demonstration of such status-based privilege, Harvey and Consalvi (1960) used young male offenders, all from the same clique in a youth home. These young men were shown a stimulus (a line) and asked to estimate its length. All three friends thought they were seeing the same stimulus, but in fact in each group one young man ('the deviate') saw a stimulus line that differed from that seen by the others. Harvey and Consalvi then assessed the extent to which this young man's estimate was affected by hearing the very different estimates made by his mates. In line with our discussion, the group opinion (the group norm) had substantially less impact on those deviates who were highest in status (clique leaders), corroborating our assertion that high status often reduces the power of peer influences.

The opposite side of this coin is that those high in status generally have a disproportionately strong impact on group decisions and judgments, whereas those low in status tend to be ignored, even when they offer intelligent and creative advice. In a classic group study, Torrance (1954) examined the decisions made by aircraft bomber crews. Across a variety of problems, the crew was influenced to a greater extent by the opinions and answers offered by the pilot than they were by the opinions and answers offered by the tail gunner (a lowly enlisted man). This held true even when the tail gunner's opinions were correct and the pilot's views were not. These results illustrate the powerful effects status can have on group functioning.

Subgroups

The structure of many groups is dramatically affected by the existence of cliques and subgroups. Subgroups can be based on such things as similarity of age, place of residence, social role or vested interest. For example, the youth gang referred to above had several subgroups. One subgrouping had to do with age. Those over the age of 18 formed the gang elite. Another subgroup had to do with neighbourhood. Those from the poorest neighbourhood viewed themselves as being 'tougher' and more daring than those from the slightly less deprived neighbourhood, who, in turn, thought of themselves as more sophisticated and attractive to women. Subgroups can, of course, produce conflict. Older gang members were more interested in partying in bars where they could encounter more women and generally more excitement. The younger gang members, however, were too young to drink legally in bars, so they pressured the group to hold parties in motels and homes so that they could be included in the festivities. The group's general reluctance to spend group funds in this way was a source of friction between the older and younger subgroups.

Communication networks

A final element that defines group structure is the type of communication patterns that characterize the group. In most small groups, there are few restrictions on who communicates with whom. However, in larger groups and organizations, unrestricted communication becomes unwieldy and inefficient, if not impossible. Consequently, communication networks become established. In his classic work on communication networks, Leavitt (1951) pointed out that a variety of communication networks are possible. Some communication networks are depicted in Figure 1.1. Note that, in Figure 1.1A, all messages are routed through a centralized individual; indeed, other individuals can only speak with the person in this central location. In Figure 1.1B, each individual can only communicate with the two individuals adjacent to them in the network. Figure 1.1C provides something of a combination of Figure 1.1A and Figure 1.1B. Finally, in Figure 1.1E, the lower an individual's status, the less communication options he or she will have. This situation is a common one, since it insulates the leaders from undue demands on their time. A good deal of experimentation indicates that, in more centralized communication nets (for example, 1.1A, 1.1C, 1.1E), individuals who happen to end up in the central position are most often named as leaders. Not surprisingly, those who are not in centralized positions and who, therefore, are restricted in their communication options, are less satisfied with their group experience (Leavitt 1951).

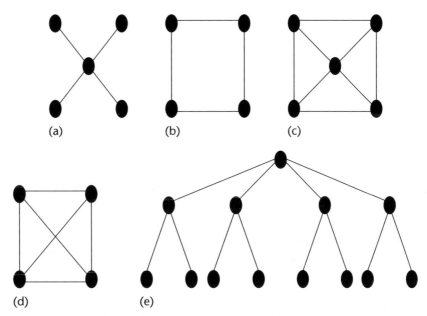

Figure 1.1   Some possible communication networks. People in each
network are denoted by solid ovals (•). Networks A, C and E are
centralized. Network B is partially decentralized. Network D is completely
decentralized. Network E is hierarchical.

These various aspects of group structure tend to serve key functions for
the group. Roles encourage specialization of labour by providing a clear
delineation of who should do what within the group and even specify
how particular group assignments should be executed or accomplished.
This reduces confusion and controversy and facilitates the group's ability to
respond to crises decisively. Differences in status establish lines of authority and control and also provide the means of rewarding and encouraging
behaviour that benefits the group. Subgroups often provide a power base
for individuals who share a common attitude, orientation or vested interest,
thereby increasing the probability that even minority positions get considered by the group. Finally, communication networks reinforce and
reflect the status and role characteristics of the group and often serve to
protect group leaders from being overloaded with requests and information
and allow for rapid and efficient transmission of news, goals, information
and commands throughout the group.

Group cohesion

Lewin's multi-factor view

The next group characteristic we will consider is *group cohesion* – that is, how
attractive the group is, as a whole, to its group members (for a review, see
Dion 2000). Kurt Lewin, one of the 'fathers' of group dynamics research,

characterized cohesion as the sum of all pressures (or forces) acting to keep individuals in a group (cf. Patnoe 1988). Thus, according to Lewin, cohesion is loosely conceived of as group solidarity that can result from a variety of causes (Dion 2000). Back (1951), one of Lewin's students, for example, created cohesion in three ways. In one group, people were told that they were likely to be emotionally compatible ('our tests indicate that you will like these people'). Another group was told they all had high ability on the key task in the study. A third group was told that if their group succeeded, they would win a valued prize. Despite the differences between these various sources of cohesion, they all produced increased conformity to group norms (but see McKelvey and Kerr 1988). These results are generally congruent with Lewin's views that cohesion can result from various causes. Attraction to the group may occur simply because group members like each other. Alternatively, group membership may be the best or only means of achieving some crucial goal. Finally, belonging to the group may provide individuals with status, a key sense of identity or some other equally important reinforcement.

The social identity view

In contrast to Lewin's multifactor view, Hogg and his associates (e.g. Hogg and Hardie 1992; Hogg and Hains 1996, 1998) have suggested that the social identification process alluded to by Lewin is a particularly crucial basis of group cohesion. Hogg and his team draw a distinction between interpersonal attraction (liking a person based on their personal characteristics) and *social attraction* towards other group members. According to Hogg, social attraction is based on the extent to which the other group members are viewed as a good 'embodiment' of the group's values, attitudes and behaviours. Thus, if you care a great deal about being an ecological mountain climber, you will feel attraction for groups that contain a high proportion of others who exemplify the norms and behaviours associated with this particular subculture regardless of whether these members have other likeable characteristics. Such individuals are referred to as *prototypic group members*. This term alludes to the fact that prototypes are thought to be abstract models that best illustrate or embody a category.

Hogg argues that social attraction is particularly important in groups that people strongly identify with. Hogg and Hains (1996, 1998) suggest that groups that elicit such strong feelings of identification from members will have certain characteristics. Such groups will elicit high levels of conformity from members, who, in turn, will hold stereotypes of outgroups and will make strong distinctions between (and favouring) ingroups versus outgroups. Hogg and his associates provide several sources of data that are congruent with the view that social attraction is important in such groups. One series of studies indicated that when group membership is made quite noticeable and salient to members, more attraction is felt for those (prototypic) group members who best embody the 'spirit' of the group (Hogg and Hardie 1992; Hogg *et al.* 1993). For example, Hogg and Hardie (1991) found this to be true with an Australian football team, while Hogg *et al.* (1993) found related effects averaging across five separate work groups in a university setting. This tendency to express attraction to, or liking for, those who most closely matched the group prototype was also stronger among those individuals who reported that they identified strongly with the group. These results indicate that, at least in salient and important groups, one source of attraction for others is how prototypical they are as group members.

However, this work does not demonstrate that our interpersonal (or individual) liking for others based on their personal traits and behaviours is an irrelevant factor in creating group cohesion. Neither does it indicate that social attraction is a more important source of our loyalty to a group (i.e. a more crucial form of cohesion) than interpersonal attraction. Two types of studies would help establish these points. One line of research could explore whether group allegiance, or group attraction, is higher in those groups that have a higher proportion of prototypical group members as opposed to groups that have fewer such individuals. That is, it would seem to follow from Hogg's view of cohesion that when we identify with a group, cohesion (attraction towards the group) will be higher in those groups in which most members have prototypic characteristics and lower in groups in which there is more variability. We know of no such studies of this type at this time. A second line of research could examine whether specific effects expected from highly cohesive groups are more likely to occur when the cohesion is based on social rather than interpersonal attraction. Hogg and Hains (1998) recently reported just such a study. As we will see in the chapter on group extremity (Chapter 6), there is reason to believe that people should be more reluctant to express their personal doubts and objections about a proposed group solution in highly cohesive groups. Hogg and Hains (1998) found that groups that were high in social rather than interpersonal attraction were indeed more likely to provoke this form of self-censorship. If this initial finding is replicated in subsequent research, it would do much to verify Hogg's (1993) notion that social attraction is a particularly crucial basis of group cohesion. At present, however, the data only suggest that social attraction (the extent to which others are prototypical) is one of several important sources of attraction for individuals within a group. Before this issue can be settled, several questions remain to be answered.

According to Hogg's model, social attraction is presumed to be a key basis for cohesion only in groups with which members strongly identify. However, such social identification is itself a source of cohesion. That is, the group is attractive because it provides us with a valued view of ourselves ('Wow, I'm on the Olympic team'). As a result, social attraction could only add to the strong cohesion that would already exist if most group members strongly identified with the group. Second, the social identity research on this topic to date has focused not on how we feel about the group as a whole, but rather on how we feel about specific group members. For example, most of the research by Hogg and his team uses as its key dependent variable ratings of, and reactions to, individual group members (based on the extent of their prototypical behaviour). Perhaps a more accurate view of this model is that it describes what factors affect interpersonal attraction in highly cohesive groups. An alternative view is that the degree of social attraction in a group (i.e. the proportion of members who exhibit prototypical behaviour) is a reflection – or a result – of the proportion of group members who deeply identify with the group. If most members deeply identify with the group, then most will work hard to maximize their prototypical behaviour. If so, social attraction would just be a *result of* the high degree of identification across members, which, in turn, would be the true cause of cohesion rather than social attraction. The answers to such issues hopefully will be clarified as research continues on this provocative and innovative perspective on cohesion.

Modern multidimensional views of cohesion

Recently, several writers have considered the possibility that cohesion is affected by factors other than simple friendship or respect among group members (see, for example, Cota *et al.* 1995; Dion 2000). One key factor may be *vertical cohesion*, or the extent to which group members trust and respect their superiors. Another factor is *horizontal cohesion*, or the good feeling that exists between peers within a given layer of organizational structure. These feelings can refer to social/personal issues ('I like these people') or to task-related issues ('My team is very effective'). Yet another factor is the extent to which the group member feels accepted and integrated into the group ('My team likes me'). Dion (2000) suggests that these are primary dimensions of cohesion that apply to most groups. A secondary set of such dimensions might be appropriate only for certain types of groups. For example, in therapy groups, the amount of trust and honesty may be more important than in, say, a sports team. Although research is still actively evaluating these various notions, it is safe to conclude that whether cohesion is based upon friendship, task effectiveness, group identification or vertical cohesion, high cohesion is a key group characteristic.

Cohesion can have several very powerful effects on group functioning. Thus, Evans and Dion (1991) found, in a meta-analysis of 27 studies, that highly cohesive groups were more productive than less cohesive groups. Another strong effect of cohesion is that it contributes to the loyalty, commitment and sacrifice exhibited by its members. These elements of loyalty and sacrifice were graphically illustrated in a dramatic incident from the history of the Symbionese Liberation Army (SLA). Several months after Ms Hearst's kidnapping, the main SLA group was surrounded in a house in Los Angeles by hundreds of heavily armed police officers equipped with riot gear and helicopters. The group had a clearly stated doctrine (or norm) to fight to the death.

Although dramatically outnumbered, not one of the SLA defenders agreed to surrender, even after the house was in flames and the police again offered to hold their fire. Instead, the SLA continued the spectacular firefight which was televised on local stations and which ended in their deaths. Indeed, when the remaining members of the SLA learned of their comrades' predicament, their first reaction was to reach the surrounded house to join their obviously doomed comrades (Hearst 1982). Although the SLA may have been unrealistic in its group goals, it is clear it was a highly cohesive group.

Finally, cohesive groups are generally a source of pride and respect for group members. Crocker *et al.* (1994) examined the effects of such *collective self-esteem*, or the amount of pride that members have in their group membership. They found that when individuals feel that their ethnic group affiliation is a source of self-esteem, they are more likely to report several forms of psychological well-being, including greater life satisfaction and less hopelessness, than other participants. These effects were especially pronounced for African-Americans and Asian-Americans than European-American participants. This finding is congruent with the idea that group membership should be far more salient and important an issue for members of ethnic minorities than for members of the dominant cultural majority (see also Bat-Chava 1994). In contrast, when collective self-esteem is low, group members have been found to disparage outgroup task efforts (Long *et al.* 1994). Apparently, this represents an attempt to feel better about the ingroup by comparison, thereby increasing collective self-esteem. This study is noteworthy in that other studies focusing on individually based self-esteem ('I feel good about myself') have not reliably reported such effects (for reviews, see Long *et al.* 1994; Rubin and Hewstone 1998).

Leadership

The style in which the group leader manages the group's affairs is another important group characteristic. Early theoretical treatments distinguished between task-oriented leaders and people-oriented leaders (cf. Shaw 1981). The former are primarily concerned with group performance and maintaining the group's competitive position; the latter are more concerned with group members' feelings, needs and problems. Not surprisingly, person-oriented leadership generally produces better morale than a task orientation (Shaw 1981). But which produces superior performance? Several writers have suggested that, despite its poor effect on morale, a strong task orientation is useful in times of stress, time pressure or lack of structure (Fiedler 1967). Here a powerful autocratic voice can impose order, set priorities and make rapid decisions. This is often seen in sports. In the closing minutes of a tight athletic contest, a successful coach cannot worry unduly about the egos of his players or take time to consider all opinions. Rather, confidence and decisiveness are necessary. Several studies have supported the view that task-oriented leadership is used more frequently (Fodor 1978) than people-oriented leadership and is more productive (Rosenbaum and Rosenbaum 1971) in times of stress. A rigid autocratic leadership style is not always wise, however. A survey by Suedfeld and Rank (1976) of the writings of revolutionary leaders indicated that some of history's most successful leaders varied their leadership style to fit the circumstances. Most revolutionary leaders used a rigid autocratic approach during the crisis period of the revolution. Those leaders, however, who left office because of political or military defeat or disgrace (e.g. Trotsky, Che Guevara) were far more likely to continue this rigid approach after the revolution than those who remained in power until voluntary retirement or death (Mao Tse Tung, George Washington, Oliver

Cromwell). The latter, in contrast, were more likely to become far more flexible and less doctrinaire once the crisis period had passed. In short, a leadership style that suits one set of circumstances may be poorly adapted for another.

Recently, theorists have suggested several additional perspectives on leadership emergence and leadership style. Lord *et al.* (1984) proposed *leader categorization theory*, which holds that leadership emergence is often affected by our person-schemas (expectancies and templates) about leadership. That is, we have expectancies that particular types of groups require particular types of individuals as leaders. Those individuals who happen to have such preferred characteristics are far more likely to be chosen as leaders. Thus a religious group might choose a bearded, older man with a serious demeanor as a church deacon if this profile closely matches their stereotype of church leader. Moreover, because of the biasing effects of schemas on our judgment, perception and memory, we will be positively biased when evaluating the performance of such leaders.

Social identity theorists offer an alternative view of leader emergence in groups that provoke a good deal of social identification from members. Hogg (2001), for example, argues that among individuals who identify socially with their group, those who come closest to embodying the norms and preferred behaviours of the group will be seen as group leaders. In addition, such individuals will be admired, thereby allowing them to lead others, because such admiration will heighten their persuasive powers. Hogg and his associates report several studies that are generally consistent with this view (Hains *et al.* 1997; Hogg *et al.* 1998b). Regardless of how leaders are selected or why they emerge, several theories describe a charismatic leadership style that is presumed to elevate group functioning. Bass (1998), for example, describes a tranformational style that involves such a charismatic factor. Bass's model assumes that leaders and followers both exchange resources. Followers receive direction, structure and, in some cases, expertise from their leader, while leaders gain power, privilege and control by taking on the obligations of leadership. *Transformational leaders* also provide the rank-and-file membership with inspiration and a sense of purpose that can lead followers to put aside their own short-term self-interest to work for some greater cooperative group goal. This requires the leader to have the ability to conceive of goals that capture the imagination and idealism of the rank and file, as well as the persuasive skills needed to convince followers that they are capable of reaching such goals. Bass contends that such transformational leaders tend to consider their subordinates' individual needs and reward them based on their individual merits. Moreover, transformational leaders encourage innovation and exploration by their subordinates. They also focus on rewarding correct behaviour rather than punishing incorrect action and avoid manipulative, deceptive strategies. Initial research with groups as varied as business and military organizations suggests that this style of leadership, while difficult to achieve, can provoke high rates of creative productivity in groups (House and Shamir 1993; Bass 1998). Bass points out, however, that not all leaders act so benignly. Some follow a pseudo-transformational style that also involves intolerance of non-conformity, threats, manipulation, punishment and selfish, self-aggrandizing behaviour on the part of the leader.

This type of twisted transformational style provides a good match for the leadership style seen in many extremist cults (Baron *et al.* 2003). Thus, in totalist groups as varied as Synanon and the People's Temple, while the leader had a very charismatic communication style and provided the group with transcendent goals, as well as a feeling of deep, cooperative purpose, he was extremely punitive towards dissenters. Moreover, the leaders in these two groups, Jim Jones and Chuck Dederich, both used ruthless power, a system of spies and various debilitating indoctrination procedures to maintain their position and exert control over the group (Baron *et al.* in press; Pratkanis and Aronson 2000).

Stages

Another characteristic is the *stage* of the group. Several writers have argued that groups can proceed through a variety of changes over time. Tuckman and Jensen (1977), for example, argued that in the earliest stages of group development, group members are most concerned about being accepted and learning more about the group and its circumstances. This stage of group interaction (called *forming* by Tuckman and Jensen) is marked by polite and inhibited behaviour and information-seeking. As the group matures and individual members come to feel more secure, there is a period of conflict (*storming*) in which members confront their various differences and vie for power. If the group survives this 'storming' stage, it will reach a stage (*norming*) in which it develops some consensus about roles, status and procedures. As a result of compromising during this stage, hostility and conflict will be lower and group cohesion should increase. Following this 'norming' stage, the group can begin to address more effectively its various group goals. During this period (the *performing* stage), there will be generally less conflict and emotion associated with the internal working of the group than in the previous stage. Finally, the group will reach a stage of disbanding (termed *adjournment* by Tuckman and Jensen) in which group activities drop, group goals are reached or given up and the group experiences the emotions associated with separation. These stages are offered as a general rule of thumb. Some groups avoid certain stages, whereas other groups may reverse certain stage sequences or, indeed, recycle through the stages as new problems emerge (Wheelan 1994; Arrow 1997).

As sensible as these group stages might appear, their importance is often neglected. If you have ever left a 'dead' party early, only to find out the next morning that it later turned into a wild romp, you can appreciate this fact. The first hour of a big social occasion is generally in the earliest stages of group development when social interaction is constrained. As the 'ice breaks' and individuals get to know each other, they feel more free to engage in the kind of uninhibited behaviour normatively appropriate at celebrations. Not all groups necessarily go through all of the stages outlined by Tuckman and Jensen (1977). Using our party example, many social gatherings obviously avoid the conflict or storming stage. But after reviewing a great many studies on group process, Tuckman (1965) concluded that the stages he outlined often represent an accurate portrayal of developmental stages within groups.

Group entitativity

The group characteristics we have described in this chapter refer for the most part to features that differentiate one group from another. One last issue to consider is what it is about a collection of people that leads them to be considered as a distinct entity (i.e. as a group), whether by the group members themselves or by onlookers. In thinking about this, Donald Campbell (1958) suggested that such factors as proximity (being physically close together), similarity of appearance or of belief, and sharing a common fate, collective movement and a common purpose were crucial variables affecting such perception of entitativity. Other writers have suggested that group organization and structure and the lack of diversity among group members also contribute to perceptions of 'groupness' (McGarty *et al.* 1995; Hamilton *et al.* 1998). Subsequent research indicates that the strongest inferences regarding entitativity occur for family and friendship groups, with smaller work groups also scoring high on entitativity (Lickel *et al.* 1998). Large ethnic and nationality categories are less likely to be viewed as distinct entities, while brief, geographically localized collections of individuals (e.g. a group waiting at a bus stop) are seen to be lowest in such entitativity (Lickel *et al.* 1998). As these ratings imply, the importance of groups for their members plays a strong role in how they perceive the entitativity of the groups they belong to, with ingroups receiving stronger entitativity ratings than outgroups ('We have a more distinct group than "they" do'). Group differences in entitativity may prove to have interesting consequences. Sherman *et al.* (1999) suggest that distinctive (highly entitative) groups will be more likely to be viewed as extreme and highly potent. They also suggest that such groups will be more likely to evoke stereotypes about the group, with group members being judged and perceived in light of such stereotypes (see also Brewer and Harasty 1996). These suggestions offer some very interesting possibilities for future research.

SUMMARY

Groups have a dramatic impact on human attitudes, decisions and actions. Group researchers tend to embrace a flexible working definition of 'group', often including temporary, unstructured groups in their investigations. There are several theoretical explanations for the pervasive influence of groups in human affairs. These include social comparison theory, social identity theory, exchange theory, optimal distinctiveness theory and sociobiological theories. Groups can be distinguished on the basis of several group characteristics, such as size, prevalent norms, structure, stage of development and their degree of entitativity. Group structure, in turn, is based on several components, including the nature of roles and status within the group, the number and types of subgroups that exist, and the communication network that characterizes the group. Our discussion of these various group features has touched upon a number of interesting psychological phenomena, including obedience (Milgram 1974), status biases (Torrance 1954), conformity in times of fear (Darley 1966) and the continuation of unsatisfactory relationships (Thibaut and Kelley 1959).

SUGGESTIONS FOR FURTHER READING

Baron, R.S., Crawley, K. and Paulina, D. (2003) Aberrations of power: leadership in totalist groups. In D. van Knippenberg and M.A. Hogg (eds) *Identity, Leadership, and Power*. London: Sage. Several case histories of leadership in cults.

Dion, K.L. (2000) Group cohesion: from 'field of forces' to multidimensional construct. *Group Dynamics: Theory, Research, & Practice*, 4(1): 7–26. An excellent recent review of work on group cohesion.

Milgram, S. (1974) *Obedience to Authority*. New York: Harper & Row. A full review of Milgram's classic work in which individuals are ordered to shock another.

Suls, J. and Wheeler, L. (eds) (2000) *Handbook of Social Comparison: Theory and Research*. New York: Kluwer Academic/Plenum Publishers. Up-to-date coverage of work on Festinger's influential theory.

Torrance, E.P. (1954) The behavior of small groups under the stress of conditions of survival. *American Sociological Review*, 19: 751–5. Examines how aircraft crews solve problems as a means of studying highly cohesive, intact groups.

Tuckman, B.W. and Jensen, M.A.C. (1977) Stages of small group development revisited. *Group and Organizational Studies*, 2: 419–27. Presents a classic model of group change.

TWO

SOCIAL FACILITATION

KEY CONCEPTS

- Do competitors always increase our performance?
- Why might the mere presence of other people affect us?
- What is social facilitation and how might it be explained?
- How have explanations for social facilitation changed over time?

BACKGROUND

In 1969, Zajonc and his associates performed what to most people would appear to be a bizarre experiment. They found that cockroaches ran faster down a runway to escape a light source if the runway was lined with an 'audience' of onlooking fellow cockroaches (each in its own plexiglass cubicle). This research team was re-examining one of the oldest questions in modern experimental social psychology: how the simple presence of others affects individual performance. As we will see, this study contributed to an important theory about this issue. To appreciate this fact, however, one needs some history. About 100 years ago, Milton Triplett, an American psychologist, became interested in the impact of the simple presence of fellow performers after noting that bicycle racers always achieved faster times if they had a live competitor. Triplett (1898) soon found similar results when he asked children to reel in line as quickly as possible on a fishing reel. In reeling as in cycling, *social* conditions were found to *facilitate* task performance. This effect has come to be called *social facilitation*.

Early social facilitation results attracted attention because the groups used in many of these studies represented very elemental social units, having no history, norms or structure and in which social interaction and cooperation appeared minimal. As such, this research focused attention on one of social psychology's most elemental questions, namely how the mere presence of other people affects our behaviour. A second reason early results were intriguing is that the earliest reports indicated that social facilitation effects occurred in a wide range of species. For example, researchers found that when conspecifics (or 'species mates') were present, dogs ran faster, chicks ate more grain, terns and fruit flies preened their bodies more often, and ants moved more sand while nest building (e.g. Palestis and Burger 1998). In one provocative study, Larsson (1956) even found that sexual behaviour among mating rats occurred more often if the couples were in the presence of other sexually active pairs of rats.

In humans, social facilitation has been found on many tasks, including those as diverse as jogging, word associations, amount purchased in a discount store, food consumption, emotional expression and computer use (e.g. Robinson-Staveley and Cooper 1990; Buck *et al.* 1992; Sommer *et al.* 1992; Redd and de Castro 1992; for reviews, see Guerin 1993; Aiello and Douthitt 2001). Moreover, such task facilitation has been found both in *audience paradigms*, in which the participant is observed by other students or by the experimenter, as well as in *co-action paradigms*, in which the participant works on the task while others (i.e. co-actors) work on the same task nearby. The early parallels between the human and non-human data suggested that social facilitation might be a basic and widespread social phenomenon. It soon became apparent, however, that the presence of others did not invariably lead to facilitated performance. In humans, for example, Allport (1924) found that social facilitation occurred on certain tasks such as simple multiplication problems, but on others (such as writing refutations of Greek epigrams) working in the presence of co-actors impaired performance. Results such as these produced a good deal of confusion. Why should social facilitation occur on some tasks and not others? The earliest attempt to answer this question was a provocative theory of social facilitation offered by Robert Zajonc (pronounced like science with a Z).

DRIVE THEORY AND SOCIAL FACILITATION

Zajonc (1965) argued that social facilitation and social impairment both occur because we are excited and aroused by the mere physical presence of species mates. According to Zajonc, when we are around others, whether co-actors, audiences or just bystanders, we are more physically excited and motivated. As a result, we try harder at the tasks we attempt. Psychologists generally refer to such feelings as a heightened state of drive.[1] States such as hunger, fear and frustration are typical examples of drive states. What may remain unclear to you is how this theory accounts for the fact that social conditions facilitate some tasks and impair others. If people are aroused and try harder, why do they perform worse on some tasks?

To explain this puzzle, Zajonc referred to a well-established set of results (e.g. Spence 1956) that indicate that increasing drive increases the speed, strength and probability of an organism's dominant response. A dominant response refers to the action that an animal is most likely to emit in a given set of circumstances. This dominant tendency may be due to training, habit, personal preference or innate factors. This fact is directly relevant to social facilitation because on well-learned, easy or instinctual tasks, the correct response tends to be dominant. Therefore, on easy tasks, correct responses should be facilitated or enhanced by high drive. In contrast, on counter-instinctual or difficult (i.e. poorly learned) tasks (e.g. writing one's name upside-down and backwards), the correct response would not be dominant. In such cases, increasing drive should impair performance by enhancing the tendency to perform the dominant (and incorrect) response (e.g. writing normally). In short, according to Zajonc, whether social facilitation or social impairment occurs is primarily a function of the type of task.

Direct tests of Zajonc's arousal/drive view were quite encouraging. In this research, investigators carefully manipulated task features so that dominant responses were either correct or incorrect. This work generally found, as predicted, that social facilitation occurred when dominant responses were correct and social impairment occurred when dominant responses were incorrect. For example, in Zajonc and colleagues' (1969) cockroach study, the dominant response among such insects was to run from a sudden light source. Zajonc and his co-workers arranged things so that, in one condition, the cockroaches could escape the aversive light by 'doing what comes naturally' – that is, running down a straight runway as quickly as possible. Here, an audience of onlooking cockroaches facilitated this dominant response. In a second condition, however, the cockroaches could only escape by making a sharp right-hand turn midway down the runway. This response required the insects to inhibit their dominant response (running fast), since they had to slow down for the turn. In this case, the audience impaired correct performance. Why? Because the audience strengthened the dominant and incorrect response of escaping at high speed. The results of this study and many others soon made it apparent that Zajonc was fundamentally correct in arguing that task characteristics play a crucial role in whether social facilitation or social impairment occurs. Consider some of the social facilitation studies performed in sports settings.

Studies have shown that social facilitation affects weightlifting (Meuman 1904), jogging (Strube *et al.* 1981; Worringham and Messick 1983), pool shooting (Michaels *et al.* 1982) and treadmill walking (Kohlfeld and Weitzel 1969). But nothing is uncomplicated in social facilitation research. Paulus and Cornelius (1974) found that gymnastic performance of trained gymnasts was impaired by spectators, whereas novices were unaffected. Kimble and Rezabek (1993) found very similar results when examining performance on a simple video game, and Forgas *et al.* (1980) found that spectators were more likely to impair the performance of experienced than novice squash players. These results flatly contradict the predictions of drive theory and may arise because experienced players feel more audience pressure to perform well and are more disturbed by the possibility of public failure (see the discussion on 'choking' below in the section on 'Attentional theories'). In a related study, Sokill and Mynatt (1984) found that, in sold-out basketball arenas, free throw shooting became *less* accurate among collegiate players, a highly skilled group. In explaining these results, some have argued that, even for accomplished intercollegiate athletes, high scoring gymnastic manoeuvres and accurate basketball shooting are not 'dominant' responses but instead require careful concentration on several subtle details. This view, then, would predict that social facilitation will most reliably occur on tasks that are relatively simple, primarily involving response speed and strength, in which the dominant response is completely mastered (e.g. sprinting, arm wrestling). Other sports that require precise form and accuracy (e.g. tennis, baseball, figure skating) might not necessarily benefit according to such a view. This analysis assumes that some aspect of the task determines whether social facilitation will occur. This assumption is accepted by most researchers in this area. Here the agreement ends, however, for there is still a very active debate about why social facilitation occurs. Since Zajonc's (1965) theoretical statement, a surprising number of theoretical notions have been suggested as explanations for social facilitation. Some examples are presented below.

ZAJONC'S MERE PRESENCE HYPOTHESIS

Zajonc's (1965, 1980) argument that the mere presence of species mates elevates drive/arousal remains one of the more provocative social facilitation theories. Zajonc (1980) argued that species mates have this effect because they are generally important and unpredictable stimuli that elevate uncertainty. This uncertainty can concern any number of issues. Will these people ridicule me, ignore me, evaluate me negatively? According to Zajonc, this increase in uncertainty will generally elevate arousal even in settings where others do not represent any obvious threat. For example, they need not be competitors or evaluators to elevate arousal. This mere presence notion has some alarming implications. In a world where crowding and overpopulation are continuing problems, the idea that arousal increases just because other people are present suggests that crowding could be a serious source of physical stress. Not surprisingly, several studies have addressed this 'mere presence' issue.

For example, Schmitt *et al.* (1986) asked participants to type their names on a computer in two ways – normally and then backwards, interspersing numbers among the letters (ostensibly to provide an identification code for the computer). This key activity was performed before the study began to minimize concerns about evaluation. Some participants performed this action in the presence of a person who was blindfolded and fitted with earphones. This individual was supposedly preparing for an upcoming study in perception. In this condition, normal typing ('the dominant response') was enhanced and difficult typing was impaired compared with participants who typed alone. Others have also found that working in the presence of either an inattentive audience or a blindfolded 'audience' produces social facilitation effects (e.g. Rajecki *et al.* 1977; Robinson-Staveley and Cooper 1990). Because such studies minimize the possibility of

competition from and evaluation by others, their results are usually interpreted as favouring the mere presence hypothesis.

Although these studies may indicate that mere presence can affect responding in some settings, other studies have suggested that the issue is a
complex one. As we will see in the chapter on social support (Chapter 10),
the presence of others in stressful settings usually results in a reduction
rather than an increase in arousal. Thus, mere presence cannot be viewed
as always increasing arousal. Moreover, several studies have shown that on
certain tasks, performance is only facilitated by the presence of an audience if it is evaluating or closely attending to the performer (e.g. Cottrell
et al. 1968; Guerin 1983; Worringham and Messick 1983). Clearly, mere
presence does not always trigger social facilitation or impairment. Guerin
(1986) offers one explanation for why this might be so. He expands on
Zajonc's assertion that social uncertainty is what leads to arousal. Guerin
states that uncertainty may not be strong in certain social contexts. He
believes that when we are performing in the presence of others, uncertainty should be strongest when we cannot monitor these persons. The
reason for this, according to Guerin (1986), is that we cannot reassure
ourselves that others in the setting are acting in a predictable and non-
threatening manner. Guerin (1983, 1986; Guerin and Innes 1982) has
presented some evidence favouring this *social monitoring* view, but the
data are too sparse to permit strong conclusions (cf. Geen 1989).

This is an area that requires continued research, since it is clear that we
do not yet fully understand when the mere presence of others will affect
individual task performance. The results of a study by Cacioppo *et al.*
(1990) suggest that Zajonc's notions regarding mere presence may require
some revision. They found no evidence of increased physiological arousal
when participants thought they were being observed periodically as they
waited for a study to begin (i.e. in a non-evaluative setting). However,
mere presence did have another effect. Those individuals who were observed
showed stronger momentary changes in skin conductance when mild
tones were played, suggesting that they were more alert and sensitive to
changes in their environment. These results suggest that, while Zajonc
may be wrong about how mere presence affects 'arousal', his more general
point that mere presence has some impact on how 'keyed up' or 'fresh'
our attention is receives some support. Certainly such results support the
view that subtle forms of social presence have interesting, albeit complex,
effects on behaviour, perception and problem-solving.

Cottrell's learned drive view

One alternative to Zajonc's mere presence/uncertainty view is Cottrell's
learned drive position. Cottrell (1972) suggested that species mates elevate
drive/arousal because, through learning, we have come to associate species mates with a variety of rewards (e.g. sexual satisfaction) and punishments (e.g. competing for food). As a result of this conditioning, we often
experience anticipatory excitement due to the mere sight of other individuals, provided that the situational cues remind us of these past associations. An example of this process would be getting nervous seeing someone

at a business meeting who reminds you of a past business rival. Cottrell would argue that the sight of this person at a party (a different setting) might produce little agitation. However, seeing the same person in a setting resembling your usual battleground should produce substantial arousal.

Cottrell's position is interesting in that it can explain both animal and human social facilitation. The theory also holds that, in humans, social facilitation should primarily occur when the setting is competitive or evaluative, because such settings should have the strongest past associations with rewards and punishments from others. Anyone who has experienced nervousness on stage or before an athletic contest will appreciate this view. This commonsense notion has a good deal of support. In one of Cottrell's own studies (Cottrell *et al.* 1968), social facilitation effects were found not to occur if the audience was blindfolded (these blindfolded individuals were supposedly preparing for another study). In a similar vein, other studies have indicated that, when audiences appeared disinterested in the participant, little social facilitation occurred (e.g. Guerin 1983). In one inventive study, Strube *et al.* (1981) placed a confederate in the stands at a jogging track and found that jogging speed only increased in the condition in which the confederate appeared to be focusing on (evaluating) the runner (see also Worringham and Messick 1983). In addition, several studies have found that competition from co-workers heightens social facilitation (cf. Geen and Gange 1977).

Despite these results, there is still controversy about the role of evaluation and competition. In an extensive meta-analytical review, Bond and Titus (1983) found little statistical evidence that varying the amount of evaluation altered social facilitation phenomena when one 'averaged' over studies. Whether this result is due to averaging across different types of manipulations or to problems in the experimental procedures in certain studies is hard to say. However, most social facilitation researchers believe that, at the very least, evaluation and competition can contribute to social facilitation effects (Harkins and Szymanski 1987a, 1987b; Sanna and Pusecker 1994; Gagne and Zuckerman 1999; Guerin 1999). A key link in this argument is that, in several studies, social facilitation effects were found to be strongest in people who tested high in trait anxiety (e.g. Geen 1985, 1989) or who were particularly concerned about achievement and competition (Gastorf *et al.* 1980). Clearly, however, enough nagging questions remain to encourage continued research.

DISTRACTION/CONFLICT (D/C) THEORY

According to this theoretical perspective, social facilitation occurs because audiences, co-actors and even bystanders often lead performers into *attentional conflict* – conflict about whether to attend to their species mates or to their ongoing task. The original version of D/C theory assumed that when the performer wishes to pay attention to more than he or she can manage, the resulting conflict leads to drive/arousal and stress, which, in turn, produces the social facilitation/social impairment effects described earlier. As we will see below, in a later version of the theory, Baron (1986) revised this model by arguing that attentional conflict affected people more by creating cognitive overload than by creating high drive. Imagine a scenario in which you are frantically trying to meet some typing deadline for a course, when at the same time the phone rings, the coffee begins to boil over in its pot and your puppy begins to chew on a book you borrowed from your professor. This dilemma should give you a feeling for the stress that attentional conflict can entail. According to the authors of this theory (e.g. Baron *et al*. 1978; Sanders *et al*. 1978), others can be distracting for a variety of reasons. In task settings, a key reason will often be the desire to socially compare our performance with that of others or to check the audience's reaction to our performance.

In lower organisms, attention to others may be caused by a concern about attack, competition for scarce resources, sexual attraction or simply herding instincts. This distraction often leads to attentional conflict in animals. Since conflict is a well-established source of drive, this theoretical view can account well for the facilitation of dominant responding in both animals and humans that so strongly characterizes the social facilitation literature. Distraction/conflict theory is provocative, however, in that it suggests that distraction during a simple task will improve performance if it triggers attentional conflict. The results of several studies support this view (for reviews, see Baron 1986; Huguet *et al*. 1999b). For example, as early as 1933, Pessin reported that distracting participants with lights and buzzers improved their performance on a well-learned memory task. Similar increases in performance occurred if participants were simply observed by the experimenter. In short, an audience had precisely the same effect as a mechanical distraction. Much later, Sanders and Baron (1975) added to these results by reporting that distracting participants produced precisely the facilitation/impairment effects usually produced by the presence of others. As we will see, no other model of social facilitation can easily explain such results.

Moore *et al*. (1988) found that an audience and a visual distraction produced similar patterns of heart rate and skin conductance during a reaction time task. In short, their results suggest that audiences are distracting. But distraction/conflict theory goes beyond the assertion that others are distracting. First, it contends that in most co-action studies, others are distracting in large part because we are tempted to compare our performance with that of others. The results of several studies support this view (e.g. Sanders and Baron 1977; Sanders *et al*. 1978; Seta *et al*. 1991). Sanders *et al*. (1978) and Sanna (1992) found that social facilitation/ impairment only occurs when individuals work on comparable tasks. Second, D/C theory assumes that an attentive and evaluating audience will provoke greater conflict and task effects. As noted above, there is much support for this view as well (e.g. Strube *et al*. 1981; Guerin 1983). Third, D/C theory argues that *conflict* is the crucial cause of social facilitation. This is not an easy hypothesis to test directly, but there is one relevant study. Groff *et al*. (1983) reasoned that one way to prevent attentional conflict from occurring in an audience experiment is to give participants the task of *attending to the audience*. In the low conflict condition, participants were told to record periodically whether a face on a TV screen was reacting positively or negatively. In this condition, the TV image was a live camera transmission of a confederate sitting several feet away from the TV screen, presumably evaluating the participant. In the high conflict condition, the facial image on the TV screen was not the face of the evaluating confederate but instead a recorded video. As a result, in this high conflict condition, if participants wished to examine the confederates (seated several feet from the TV), they had to glance away from their primary task. In a third condition, participants performed the rating task with no evaluator present. In all conditions, the participants were asked to squeeze a plastic bottle whenever they made a rating. As predicted, Groff *et al.* only found evidence of social facilitation on this squeeze response in the high conflict condition. In short, the presence of an evaluating audience only had an impact on responding if attentional conflict was likely.

The results of this study strongly suggest that attentional conflict contributes directly to social facilitation phenomena. If so, this may explain some of the puzzling inconsistencies in the social facilitation literature. Sometimes the mere presence of others produces social facilitation, whereas on other occasions it does not. Sometimes blindfolded audiences lead to social facilitation, but not always. In many studies, evaluation, competition or direct attention from the audience appear crucial to produce social facilitation; however, others report that evaluation manipulations have little effect on social facilitation phenomena. It is possible that at least some of these contradictions may be due to distraction differences. Seeing others in blindfolds is curious, unusual and thought-provoking and could well distract participants from their task. In some settings, however, the cover story explaining why blindfolds are needed may be so persuasive and skillfully administered that curiosity (and consequent distraction) is minimized. Similarly, in some settings the mere presence of bystanders may provoke distraction (the bystanders could be physically attractive, extremely well dressed, or perhaps ill at ease), whereas in others bystanders may be so ordinary that there is little distraction. Even evaluation pressure may produce 'internal' distraction if individuals are distracted from the task by worrying about how well they are doing (for a similar argument, see Geen 1989). These variations may explain why social facilitation results are sometimes inconsistent from study to study.

DRIVE THEORY ON TRIAL

All the theories discussed above share the assumption that social conditions produce drive/arousal which then facilitates dominant responding.[1] However, several authors have questioned this view (e.g. Manstead and Semin 1980; Carver and Scheier 1981; Bond and Titus 1983; Moore and Baron 1983; Geen 1989; Blascovich *et al.* 1999; Hugeut *et al.* 1999b). One reason for these doubts is the results of studies that measured whether physiological arousal (e.g. blood pressure, pulse, skin conductance) is increased by the presence of others. Moore and Baron (1983) reviewed 29 tests of the notion that audiences or co-actors elevated arousal and found that it did so in 11 but not in the remaining 18. Using a different analysis strategy, Bond and Titus (1983) found evidence that audiences increased physiological activity during complex tasks, but not during simple tasks. These results are supplemented by those of Cacioppo *et al.* (1990), who found that mere presence does not elevate arousal. Such data are not congruent with Zajonc's (1965) argument that the presence of others increases the individual's general arousal or drive level.

An additional reason to doubt the classic drive/arousal view of social facilitation is that, in certain studies, audiences have failed to increase dominant responding. Manstead and Semin (1980), for example, conducted five sub-studies using four different tasks and found no evidence that audiences heightened dominant responses. Glaser (1982) listed some 61 instances of such failures occurring between 1965 and 1982. On the other hand, it should be borne in mind that more than 200 studies have been conducted on social facilitation over the years and, consequently, some variation in results is to be expected. Indeed, in their extensive meta-analytic review of both published and unpublished work involving more than 20,000 participants, Bond and Titus (1983) found 'on average' reasonable evidence of social facilitation on simple tasks and social impairment on complex tasks. Nevertheless, the inconsistencies in this database, particularly regarding the physiological data, have encouraged researchers to consider the possibility that the physiological effects of co-actors and audiences are more subtle and complex than Zajonc suggested.

As we have seen, Cacioppo *et al.* (1990) found that participants who thought that they were being viewed by others showed stronger physiological orienting responses to soft sounds than non-observed participants. Thus, the presence of others may provoke greater attentional alertness rather than greater overall arousal. Alternatively, Blascovich *et al.* (1999) contend that Zajonc's description of arousal is too general to be completely useful. They offer a more specific physiological interpretation based on the notion that social conditions provoke different physiological reactions depending upon participants' feelings of mastery and control. Blascovich and his associates reported several studies (for a review, see Blascovich *et al.* 1999) which indicated that when we feel that we do not have the resources or ability to complete a task successfully, or deal with a problem, we show a *threat pattern*. This is marked by a moderate cardiac increase (from baseline) with either no change or a slight increase in vascular resistance. This combined reaction leads to heightened blood pressure under threatening conditions. When instead we feel optimistic about our ability on a task, we produce a *challenge pattern*. This pattern is marked by pronounced cardiac output with *lowered* vascular resistance; a reaction marked by little change in blood pressure but an increase in blood flow to our muscles and brain. Blascovich and his colleagues argue that when working on a simple or well-learned task, the presence of an audience or co-actors is likely to provoke a challenge reaction (e.g. 'I can do well despite this audience'). In contrast, a threat reaction is likely to occur when people are required to work on difficult, poorly learned or complex tasks under social conditions. Blascovich *et al.* had participants practise with care one of two tasks and then had them perform either the well-learned task or the 'new' task while a two-person team observed them. As predicted, social facilitation was seen with the well-learned task and social impairment with the new task. More crucially, when these participants worked in the presence of the observers, they showed classic physiological challenge patterns on the well-learned task and threat patterns on the new task. As Blascovich *et al.* are careful to point out, their results do not demonstrate that these different physiological patterns *cause* social facilitation/impairment. However, they provide us with a far more precise picture of the physiological changes that may be associated with social facilitation effects. In addition, the results strongly suggest that the classic drive/arousal view of social facilitation is too simplistic. Indeed, Blascovich and co-workers' findings complement several non-drive theories that we discuss below.

SELF-BASED THEORIES OF SOCIAL FACILITATION

Self-presentation theory

Charles Bond has argued that audiences and co-actors affect performance by increasing our concerns about projecting a positive self-image to onlookers (Bond 1982). Bond contends that our desire to look good to others often leads individuals to work harder when others are around. On difficult tasks, however, social impairment is presumed to occur because initial failures produce the expectancy of failure, which leads to reactions such as embarrassment and stress, which, in turn, disrupt performance. Several findings are consistent with this view. Bond and Titus (1983) observed that, in general, social conditions are more likely to provoke arousal on complex tasks. Bond and Titus argued that this higher arousal reflects the embarrassment that participants feel on complex tasks. This finding is complemented by that of Blascovich *et al.* (1999) that threat reactions are marked by heightened blood pressure, a common index of arousal.

Similarly, Bond (1982) reported social impairment on tasks in which simple items were embedded in a string of complex problems. Bond argued that when participants worked on these complex items, it led them to form generally negative performance expectancies that produced embarrassment and low performance when working in front of an observer, even on the occasional simple items they encountered. Unfortunately, contrary to Bond's prediction, complex problems were not socially facilitated when they were embedded in a larger group of simple problems (see also Sanders 1984). In a related study, Geen (1979) reported that, on a complex task, the poor performance usually induced by experimenter observation did not occur if participants were given early positive feedback about their performance. Task impairment did occur, however, when participants received negative feedback. Collectively, these results appear to be consistent with the view that our performance expectations do somehow affect our performance, as Bond suggests. A clearer picture of how expectancies alter performance emerges from a series of studies conducted by Larry Sanna and his associates evaluating a *self-efficacy* view of social facilitation.

Self-efficacy theory

Like Bond (1982), Sanna (1992; Sanna and Shotland 1990) proposed that social facilitation might depend on whether performers expect to receive positive or negative evaluations on the basis of their task performance. Sanna pointed out that such positive evaluations depend on two elements: high *self-efficacy* (a feeling of confidence and mastery) and high *outcome expectancy* (the belief that good performance will be positively evaluated by others). As we will see, however, Sanna's theory is not just a theory of self-presentation involving looking good to others. Sanna argues that, on easy tasks, the performer is likely to anticipate success. As a result, performers should expect positive evaluations from audiences, experimenters, co-actors and, under certain circumstances, from themselves. This expectancy of social reward, in turn, is assumed to heighten the person's motivation and persistence and thereby increase performance. In contrast, on difficult tasks, the performer would have generally negative expectancies regarding mastery (i.e. low self-efficacy) and, therefore, should expect negative evaluations (low outcome expectancy). Sanna assumes that such low expectancies should lower motivation and persistence, thereby impairing performance. One can envision several reasons for such low motivation and poor performance. Sanna and Pusecker (1994) point out that negative expectancies may trigger anxiety that interferes with performance, perhaps due to distraction. Another view is that individuals faced with the prospect of public failure disparage the importance of the task in an attempt to 'save face' and feel better about themselves (Steele 1997).

In one test of this model, Sanna and Shotland (1990) gave participants early feedback that either raised or lowered their expectancies as they worked on a memory task. As expected, observation by another person increased performance only when the participants expected to perform well. Moreover, negative expectancies tended to impair performance when participants were observed. Sanna and Pusecker (1994) gave participants either positive or negative performance feedback to manipulate efficacy expectancies (study 1) or simply had participants report their efficacy expectancies as they developed spontaneously (study 2). The experimental task involved easy and difficult word associations (e.g. what word is associated with the words 'shelf–read–end'? *Answer*: book). As predicted, those participants with high efficacy expectancies performed better if they thought the experimenter was going to evaluate their performance. Moreover, those with negative expectancies performed worse if they expected personal evaluation from the experimenter. Note that these instances of social facilitation/impairment occurred irrespective of task difficulty. Instead, it was participants' performance expectancies that affected whether facilitation or impairment occurred. Sanna (1992) reports similar results using co-actors rather than audiences to create social conditions.

Sanna and Pusecker (1994) reported another intriguing result. Some of their participants were given very clear evaluation standards that allowed them to evaluate their own performance. These participants showed the same 'expectancy' effects as those who were being evaluated by the experimenter. Thus those with high efficacy expectancies performed better when they could evaluate themselves, while those with low efficacy expectancies performed worse. Thus, it would appear that efficacy expectancies affect performance whenever one thinks about evaluation, regardless of whether that evaluation comes from the self or from others. As a result, this version of self-efficacy theory integrates the self-awareness view and the self-presentational view by suggesting that expecting to look good – or bad – either to oneself or to others can affect performance. These results, together with those of Bond (1982) and Geen (1979), suggest that this self-efficacy interpretation may represent an important partial explanation of social facilitation effects (Sanna and Pusecker 1994). Moreover, this theoretical perspective fits well with Blascovich and co-workers' (1999) challenge/threat view in that high self-efficacy under public conditions appears to be fairly synonymous with challenge, whereas low self-efficacy under public conditions is similar to threat. Thus, it is possible that these two physiological patterns provide markers that distinguish high efficacy expectations from low ones in public settings. Indeed, it is possible that these different physiological patterns can explain why high efficacy improves performance, whereas low efficacy impairs it, although the precise nature of this link is not yet clear.

ATTENTIONAL THEORIES

Yet another alternative to the drive/arousal view of social facilitation is provided by theories that emphasize how the presence of others affects information processing and attention. For example, Baron (1986), in a revision of distraction/conflict (D/C) theory, pointed out that attentional conflict can evoke *attentional overload*, a state created when an organism is trying to attend to more things (such as the task and the audience) than it has the capacity to process. According to Baron, such attentional overload can be provoked when the individual is tempted to split their attention between task demands and such 'distractions' as social comparison needs, internal worries about evaluation, or any other provocative or interesting feature of others who are present. How does this overload notion account for social facilitation? The key fact is that when we are bombarded with attentional demands, our focus of attention shrinks (e.g. Geen 1976). In such circumstances, individuals attend to a narrower range of stimuli. This can lead to facilitation of performance when a task requires us to process only a very few stimuli. A narrow focus allows an individual to 'screen out' irrelevant stimuli and concentrate on the key task features. In contrast, a narrow focus will impair performance if the task requires the individual to attend to a wide range of cues, because the narrow focus will screen out cues that are essential to the task. Given that most simple tasks involve attending to only a few stimuli, whereas complex or poorly learned tasks require us to attend to a wider range of stimuli or cues, attentional overload may be the cause of simple task facilitation and complex task impairment.

Manstead and Semin (1980) also offer an explanation that involves narrowed attentional focus. These writers suggest that task facilitation effects occur primarily on tasks that have become more or less *automatic*. Such tasks are thought to be so well learned that they have become 'second nature' to individuals and require little capacity and can occur with little conscious effort. Manstead and Semin (1980) reason that with such tasks the presence of others will improve performance by increasing attention to task-related cues and by making participants more aware of minor errors. On non-automatic tasks, however, a narrow attentional focus screens out necessary cues. An implicit assumption here is that with automatic tasks we have chunked the aspects of a task into larger stimulus–response segments. Thus we need to attend to fewer cues on such tasks. Thus, once tying our shoelaces has become an automatic response, all we need do to perform this task is to find the ends of our laces and 'do it'. A young child, however, has to look at the laces and think about each step of the procedure – finding the ends, pulling them tight, crossing one over the other, and so on. This perspective suggests that social facilitation effects may be limited to tasks where the correct response is more than just 'dominant', but instead more or less 'second nature' to the performer. Indeed, cases of choking under pressure observed occasionally in sports and in other public performances appear to arise because individuals pay too much attention to the various subtasks involved in the overall performance sequence. As a result, essentially, they 'unchunk' their well-learned 'automatic' skill, thereby turning a smoothly flowing automatic sequence into a more segmented series of microtasks. This effect arises apparently when paying too much self-focused attention to the control of the components of the overall task (Baumeister 1984; Lewis and Linder 1997; Beilock and Carr 2001). Interestingly, this form of *performance choking* is more likely to occur when we are particularly conscious of the high expectations others have of us. When Cheryan and Bodenhausen (2000) subtly reminded Asian women of the high expectancies others had regarding their skill at mathematics, their performance suffered. Perhaps this is why Butler and Baumeister (1998) found that choking was more likely to occur when individuals were observed by supportive rather than indifferent or hostile audiences.

Some preliminary findings support the idea that audiences lead to the narrowed attentional perspective that is thought to result from overload (Bruning *et al.* 1968; Geen 1976). For example, Bruning *et al.* (1968) had participants try to find a target stimulus (the letter 'o') that was hidden by a row of seven 'masking objects'. The participants did this over 15 trials or rows. In some conditions, additional cues were presented (i.e. consecutive numbers on the masking objects), which provided the participants with a useful hint regarding how to solve this problem over trials. In other conditions, these additional cues were not useful in solving the task (the numbers were not consecutive). Bruning *et al.* found that the presence of the experimenter (an evaluative audience) improved performance when the additional cues were *irrelevant*; in contrast, the presence of the experimenter impaired performance when the additional cues were *helpful*. Why did this occur? The most straightforward interpretation is that the presence of the experimenter induced a narrowed attentional focus in the participants. This focus 'screened out' the additional 'number' cues. This would help performance when the cues were irrelevant, by eliminating distractions, but would hurt performance when the number cues were useful. In short, these results are precisely what one would predict if social conditions provoked attentional overload and a narrowed range of attention.

Attentional theories are usually presented as alternatives to the classic drive/arousal view first expressed by Zajonc and his associates. However, few studies provide a critical test between the drive and attentional perspectives. A recent paper by Huguet *et al.* (1999b) is an exception. Huguet's team had their participants complete the Stroop colour–word task either alone or under various social conditions (i.e. with either an attentive or inattentive audience, a faster co-actor, etc.). The Stroop task requires participants to describe the colour of ink used to print words. Different colours are used for different words. The trick is that on key trials the words themselves are colour names (RED, GREEN, etc.). Such colour names slow progress on the task if we make the assumption that literate people have a dominant (indeed, automatic) tendency to read words and think about their semantic content. On this task, such a dominant 'reading' tendency interferes with (slows) the correct response, that is naming the colour of the ink. This sets the stage for a critical test of the drive and attentional viewpoints. If social conditions heighten dominant tendencies, as Zajonc contends, or heighten automatic processing as Manstead and Semin suggest, then when others are present, we should see slower performance on the Stroop task due to more reading and semantic processing. If, instead, social conditions provoke a narrowed range of attention, this greater focus should help participants to 'zero in' on just the colour of the ink while screening out the semantic content of the words. Thus social conditions should lead to both improved performance in colour naming and poorer memory for the content of the words, since their semantic meaning is presumed to be screened out. This latter result is what Huguet *et al.* found in studies using both audiences (study 1) and co-actors (study 2). Moreover, they only found these results in social conditions in which people should be most attentive to the audience (e.g. where the audience is paying close attention to them, or the co-actor is performing a bit better). These results are complemented by earlier reports that either co-actors (MacKinnon *et al.* 1985) or mechanical distractors (O'Malley and Poplawski 1971) provoke similar outcomes. Taken together, these results offer encouraging support for the view that overload and attentional focusing may underlie cases of social facilitation/impairment.

The attraction of this view is that it helps integrate several of the theoretical perspectives we have already discussed. First, this attentional view can explain social facilitation in non-human species, whereas the self-based theories appear less plausible in such cases. In addition, social uncertainty, self-consciousness, evaluative anxiety and attentional conflict are all states that should provoke overload because they are likely to absorb attention (Geen 1989). Indeed, overloaded capacity may, in turn, lower our feelings of self-efficacy (Sanna 1992) and heighten our feelings of threat (Blascovich *et al.* 1999). It remains to be seen whether this integrated view will be supported by the research that is conducted in the years to come, or whether several complementary explanations will be needed to explain in full the social facilitation phenomenon (Geen 1989; Sanna and Pusecker 1994).

SUMMARY

After more than 100 years of research on social facilitation, several conclusions can be drawn. In most cases, having others around us appears to facilitate simple tasks and impair performance on complex ones (Bond and Titus 1983). These phenomena have been observed across a wide range of species and tasks. Most researchers believe that evaluation and competition enhance such effects; however, in a few 'mere presence' studies, social facilitation has been shown to occur when evaluation and competition appear to have been kept low. Such 'mere presence' effects, however, do not always occur. In some circumstances, social facilitation has only been found in the presence of competition, evaluation, distraction or careful scrutiny from others (e.g. Groff et al. 1983; Worringham and Messick 1983). Inconsistencies such as these have prompted several theoretical explanations in an attempt to integrate existing findings. Certain theories argue that when we are near others, our drive and arousal are stronger, thereby strengthening our dominant responses. Despite many behavioural findings to support this view, studies that employ physiological measures (e.g. heart rate, skin conductance) do *not* consistently show higher physiological activity (i.e. high arousal) when audiences and co-actors are present. This suggests that some revision of a strict arousal view may be necessary. A second group of self-related theories emphasizes such elements as self-consciousness, concerns about public self-image and feelings of self-efficacy. Here, most support is for the self-efficacy perspective, suggesting that participants' early expectancies about success and failure probably influence social facilitation effects but do not completely explain everything associated with the social facilitation (e.g. it is unlikely that Zajonc's cockroaches felt more efficacious about escaping a light when fellow cockroaches were nearby).

A third theoretical direction holds that attentional mechanisms are responsible for social facilitation phenomena. Attentional theories are appealing. They apply to animal as well as human research and can explain many of the conflicting results and provide a means of integrating many of the theories that already exist. There is growing evidence that both audience conditions and co-actor conditions provoke the narrowed range of attentional focus that is thought to result from attentional overload. Moreover, these conditions provoke the same type of focusing effects produced by non-social distractions. Future research should focus on integrating these various diverse approaches to the study of social facilitation.

SUGGESTIONS FOR FURTHER READING

Baron, R.S. (1986) Distraction-conflict theory: progress and problems. In L. Berkowitz (ed.) *Advances in Experimental Social Psychology*, Vol. 19. New York: Academic Press. A thorough summary of the work on D/C theory and the introduction of an attentional view of social facilitation.

Blascovich, J., Mendes, W.B., Hunter, S.B. and Salomon, K. (1999) Social facilitation as challenge and threat. *Journal of Personality and Social Psychology*, 76: 68–77.

Geen, R.G. (1989) Alternative conceptions of social facilitation. In P. Paulus (ed.) *Psychology of Group Influence*, 2nd edn. Hillsdale, NJ: Lawrence Erlbaum Associates. A very complete review of the literature on social facilitation.

Huguet, P., Galvaing, M.P., Monteil, J.M. and Dumas, F. (1999) Social presence effects in the Stroop task: further evidence for an attentional view of social facilitation. *Journal of Personality and Social Psychology*, 77: 1011–25. Very recent evidence supporting the attentional view.

Zajonc, R.B. (1980) Compresence. In P. Paulus (ed.) *Psychology of Group Influence*, 2nd edn. Hillsdale, NJ: Lawrence Erlbaum Associates. Presents Zajonc's view that uncertainty accounts for 'mere presence' effects.

NOTE

1 In the early theories of drive (e.g. Spence 1956), states of heightened drive were not equated with physiological arousal. For this reason, some have argued that the physiological data are irrelevant to Zajonc's assertions regarding drive (Sanders 1981). Zajonc (1965), however, in his classic paper, did not draw a distinction between drive and arousal, often using the terms interchangeably. Clearly, his views draw heavily on those who argue that arousal and drive should have similar effects on behaviour (cf. Moore and Baron 1983: footnote 5). As such, we regard the physiological data to be crucial to the 'drive' view of social facilitation.

THREE

INDIVIDUAL VERSUS GROUP PERFORMANCE

KEY CONCEPTS

- Generally speaking, how do groups compare with individuals in their performances?
- What are the implications of comparing group performance not with individual performance, but rather with group potential productivity?
- What role do task demands play in analysing group performance?
- What are some of the sources of group process loss?

INTRODUCTION

In the previous chapter, we were concerned with the effects of the presence of others on individual performance. This discussion applied to such cases as individuals learning in a classroom, sewing machine operators working on individual garments in a factory room, and track athletes running in a group heat. But there is often more to being in a group than just being in the presence of others. This is especially true for groups that are trying to accomplish something – complete a lab report, plan a party, elect a candidate, and so on. Members of such task groups typically interact with and influence one another, and perceive themselves to be a group with a shared objective and a shared fate. One of the most impressive examples of such collaboration was the Manhattan Project, which resulted in the creation of the atomic bomb during the Second World War. The Manhattan Project used cooperative team problem-solving to achieve most of its aims and eventually involved over 100,000 individuals working under the supervision of many senior scientists in locations as varied as Los Alamos, New Mexico and Hanford, Washington (Gonzales 2000; Groueff 2000). One could ask whether progress towards this goal would have been better if the various scientists had worked wholly independently or competitively. Indeed, in some cases, both cooperative and competitive approaches were used on the Manhattan Project. Thus, the project director, J. Robert Oppenheimer, had one team racing to develop a plutonium device, while another group attempted to develop a rival, hydrogen bomb. This raises questions regarding the factors that are likely to make cooperative team efforts a more effective problem-solving strategy than individual or competitive efforts. In this chapter, we examine factors that affect group performance and the ways in which individual and group performance are related. One important theme in our discussion is that the link between individual and group performance cannot be understood without careful attention to the nature of the task. In this chapter, we focus on what McGrath (1984) called *cooperative tasks*. For such tasks, group members have a shared interest in working together toward some group goal. Such tasks also typically have some standard for evaluating performance.

EARLY RESEARCH

In many ways, early research on group performance paralleled early research on social facilitation. In both instances, rather simple questions were posed initially. For group performance, that simple question was, 'which is more productive, groups or individuals?' One well-known study in this tradition was done by Shaw (1932). In a classroom setting, both individuals and four-person groups attempted a series of intellectual puzzles. On one such puzzle, three married couples were trying to cross a river. A boat was available, but it could hold only three passengers. However, there were additional constraints, which reflected the sex and marital attitudes of the day. First, only the husbands could row and, second, no husband would allow his wife to be in the presence of any of the other husbands unless he was also present. (See whether you can solve the problem with such constraints. If you have trouble solving the problem, the answer is provided at the end of the chapter.) This is an example of what Lorge *et al.* (1958) call a *eureka task*. If a correct solution for an eureka task is proposed, it should be clear immediately (or, at most, only after a quick confirmation check) that it is indeed correct. The Husbands & Wives problem turned out to be fairly difficult for individuals in Shaw's study; only three of 21 were able to solve the problem correctly. However, three of the five groups solved the problem. Shaw obtained similar results for the other puzzles she examined. Why did groups do better than individuals? Shaw suggested that it was largely because of certain unique advantages the groups had – group members could catch one another's errors and reject incorrect solutions. This sounds plausible, but as we shall soon see, may be incorrect.

Shaw's basic finding summarizes the pattern obtained in many early comparisons of groups and individuals, not only for problem-solving tasks, but also for production, learning and memory tasks. Although there were exceptions to the rule and the differences between groups and individuals were not always large, groups generally learned faster than individuals, made fewer errors, recalled better, and were more productive with a higher quality product (for reviews, see Davis 1969; Laughlin 1980; Hill 1982). However, there was one way in which groups were typically inferior to individuals – the productivity per person. For example, if instead of simply comparing groups and individuals on the time needed for a solution (which tends to favour groups in most studies), we compare the number of *person-minutes* required (i.e. solution time × size of the group), groups usually required more person-minutes. At least on a practical level, where an employer's payroll ultimately depends on the number of person-minutes required to complete some task, this could be an important advantage of individual performance. On the other hand, if costs or person-hours are less important than rapid or accurate goal attainment, as was the case with the Manhattan Project, a group-based effort would generally be better. In summary, groups were generally more *effective* than individuals, whereas individuals were usually more *efficient* than groups.

TASK, RESOURCES AND POTENTIAL: STEINER'S MODEL OF GROUP PERFORMANCE

If you think for long about the simple question, 'which is more productive, individuals or groups?', you are likely to come to the usual and correct answer to any such overly simple question – 'it depends'. It clearly depends upon how capable the group members are at the task. Groups with incapable members may often perform worse than a skilled individual (e.g. a skilled lumberjack could undoubtedly cut, trim, split and load more timber on his or her own than any given group of, say, three psychology professors). Less obviously, it also depends upon the kind of task being considered. Certainly, if the task allows group members to pool their efforts (e.g. pulling on a rope in a tug-of-war), groups should do better than individuals (with comparable abilities). But there are also tasks for which the reverse should be true. For example, tasks that require extremely precise coordination of action (e.g. splitting a diamond, driving a car) will probably be performed better by an individual than by a group. A well-trained individual can carefully control and coordinate his or her actions better than a group, which has more limited capacities for close coordination of the actions of its members. Indeed, the success of the Manhattan Project depended on the exceptional skill of Dr Oppenheimer, who served as an able coordinator of this complex project, thereby overcoming this serious potential pitfall of collaborative group work. If the above analysis is correct, then the general conclusions to have emerged from the early study of individual versus group performance (tending to favour groups) may have as much or more to do with the types of tasks that were selected for study than with any general superiority of groups. But where does this leave us when we have to decide whether to assign a job to individuals or groups? Steiner (1966, 1972) proposed a model to help reduce much of this confusion. The central concept in Steiner's model is the notion of a group's *potential productivity*, the group's maximum possible productivity at a task. He suggests that this depends on two factors – *member resources* and *task demands*. Let us consider each of these in turn.

Member resources 'include all the relevant knowledge, abilities, skills, or tools possessed by the individual(s) who is attempting to perform the task' (Steiner 1972: 7). What makes a particular resource relevant, of course, depends on the task – physical strength is a resource at a tug-of-war, but not at an anagram task. A task's demands encompass several task features, the most basic of these being the task performance criterion – what aspect of performance is being measured. Asking a group to read a page as fast as possible with no concern for comprehension is a rather different task than asking it to read for maximal comprehension. Steiner suggests that if one knows a group's resources and the demands of its task, one can estimate the group's potential productivity. For example, if you knew how hard each of four members of a tug-of-war team could pull the rope individually, you could estimate the team's potential as the simple sum of those pulls. It would be rare, though, for a group to achieve its potential. Like machines that can never achieve 100 per cent efficiency, we would expect groups also to fall short of their potential. Steiner called this shortfall *process loss* and proposed that actual productivity = potential productivity – process loss. Process loss reflects a group's failure to act in the most productive way possible. Steiner suggested that there are two general sources of process loss. *Coordination losses* occur when group members do not organize their efforts optimally. For example, if members of the tug-of-war team pull at different times, the force that the group exerts on the rope is diminished. On the Manhattan Project, certain teams worked on basic problems and assignments that had to be completed before other teams could proceed with more advanced issues. As we noted above, Oppenheimer's expertise at coordinating these tasks was important for the group being able to meet the strict war-time deadlines involved (Groueff 2000). The second source of process loss concerns motivation. If group members are not optimally motivated, *motivation losses* result. So, if the members of the tug-of-war team do not try as hard when working together as when working alone, motivation losses would contribute to process loss.

With this simple equation, Steiner shifted attention away from the old, simple question, 'are groups more productive than individuals?' Because actual group productivity depends upon many factors (member resources, task demands, coordination, group processes), it became clear that there could be no general answer. Instead, Steiner posed new, more interesting questions: 'Are groups as productive as they can be and, if not, why not?' In one form or another, those questions will concern us through the remainder of this and the next chapter.

Steiner also provided another useful tool for tackling these questions – a task classification or taxonomy. Steiner argued persuasively that the nature of the task is crucial for any analysis of group performance. Steiner suggested three basic task features that enable us to classify tasks in meaningful and useful ways. One is whether the task can or cannot be subdivided into subtasks, each of which may be performed by different individuals. Tasks that can be subdivided he termed *divisible*; those which cannot be called *unitary*. The Manhattan Project as a whole was a divisible task with a series of components (how to initiate the reaction, deciding which and how much fissionable material to use, etc.). Indeed, one of Oppenheimer's major contributions was deciding how the task could best be divided and who should work on which components. The nature of the performance criterion constitutes Steiner's second task feature. *Maximizing* tasks make success a function of how much or how rapidly something is done; our familiar tug-of-war task is a good example. *Optimizing* tasks make success a function of achieving some correct or optimal solution; the Husbands & Wives problem is one such example, and the work of the Manhattan Project is another.

The final task feature identified by Steiner concerns how task demands link individual resources to potential group productivity. He identified four types of unitary tasks. In a *disjunctive* task, the group must select the answer or contributions of a single member. That being the case, it should select the best or most proficient member's contribution. The Husband & Wives problem is a unitary, disjunctive task; only one answer can be given and the group should select the answer of its most capable member. In a *conjunctive* task, the group's level of productivity is necessarily that of the least capable member. A good example of a conjunctive task is a mountain-climbing team connected to one another by ropes; the team can go no faster than its slowest member. In an *additive* task, the group product is the sum – or, occasionally, the average – of group member contributions. The tug-of-war task is clearly an additive task. Finally, in *discretionary* tasks, group members may combine individual inputs in any manner they choose. For example, in a blues band, the group could combine the contributions of the various musicians in any way it liked from performance to performance.

To understand better this task taxonomy, imagine three track teams each with four runners competing in the 400 m. Suppose that the runners' finishing times are as follows: Team A, 46 s (seconds), 47 s, 47 s and 49 s; Team B, 44 s, 45 s, 49 s and 53 s; and Team C, 45 s, 45 s, 46 s and 51 s. Which team wins the event? It depends on how team performance is defined – that is, on the demands of the groups' task. If the winning team is the team with the first runner to cross the finish line (disjunctive task demands), then Team B wins. However, if every member of the team must cross the finish line before the team has finished the race (conjunctive task demands), then Team A is the winner. And if the team score is the simple sum of the times of its four runners (additive task demands), then Team C has the best (i.e. lowest) score. The Manhattan Project was a combination of conjunctive and disjunctive tasks. Given the strong interdependence among the various teams, the project as a whole was limited by the progress made by the slowest team. On the other hand, many of the esoteric and complex scientific insights were disjunctive tasks that were solved by relying on the breakthrough solutions offered by the most gifted scientists. Clearly, many real-life tasks do not fit neatly into this taxonomy. But complex, divisible group tasks can often be broken down into parts that can be identified with one of Steiner's task types. More importantly, Steiner's taxonomy has proved to be a useful tool for much basic research on fundamental processes in task-performing groups.

To illustrate the application of Steiner's ideas, consider the Husbands & Wives problem used by Shaw (1932). To determine a group's potential productivity, one needs to specify the task's demands. First, since the goal is to come up with the unique correct answer, this is an optimizing task. Second, since the task cannot be subdivided (i.e. you cannot assign the first group member the job of getting Husband 1 across; the second, Wife 1; etc.), the task is unitary. And it would also appear to be disjunctive; in theory, if any group member is capable of solving the problem correctly, the group should similarly be capable of solving the problem. What is the group's potential productivity? One can intuitively see that groups have the potential of being more productive than individuals; a random sample of four persons (a group) appears more likely to include at least one person who can solve the problem than a sample of only one person (an individual). Shaw found that 3/21 or 14.3 per cent of individuals could solve the problem. Others (Taylor 1954; Lorge and Solomon 1955) have shown that, with this rate of individual solution, the probability of randomly composing a four-person group that contains at least one solver is 0.46. This figure is not significantly different than the real rate of success Shaw observed in her four-person groups (i.e. 3/5 or 0.60). This kind of analysis leads us to rather different conclusions than those reached by Shaw. She thought the superiority of her groups was largely due to better error-checking in groups. But Taylor's and Lorge and Solomon's analyses suggest that one should attribute the superiority of her groups entirely to their greater likelihood of containing at least one solver (i.e. to the greater resources the group possessed) rather than to any cooperative social process like error-checking. If this is correct, the superiority of Shaw's groups did not result from better problem-solving in the groups, but from the fact that the groups simply had a larger pool of resources available (Kerr 2000).

However, as noted above, groups do not generally operate without process loss. Most studies that have made the comparison find that groups perform below their potential (i.e. there is considerable process loss; for reviews, see Davis 1969; Steiner 1972; Lauglin 1980). A good example, which illustrates how such comparisons of potential and actual group productivity can teach us something about group performance, is Davis and Restle's (1963) study. They considered intellective problems similar to the one used by Shaw (1932), but rather than focusing solely on whether a solution was reached, they studied how long it took individuals and groups to reach a solution. The basic idea was similar to the 'best member' approach of Taylor and of Lorge and Solomon. One first estimates how fast individual solvers reach their solution. Then one estimates the speed of group solution on the assumption that the group should solve at the speed of its fastest solver. Davis and Restle called this a *hierarchical model* of problem-solving. They found that groups were consistently slower than one would expect given this hierarchical model. Thus there was process loss, but what might the source of this process loss be? Davis and Restle (1963; Restle and Davis 1962) suggested that the groups may have been too egalitarian; that is, every member might seek or be allotted part of the group's interaction time, even when they had little to offer (e.g. they might not be able to solve the problem). If you have ever been in a meeting where you and everyone else politely waited while some dimwit carefully elaborated on an obviously silly proposal, you have witnessed this in action. One of Dr Oppenheimer's challenges on the Manhattan Project was to negotiate among the eminent scientists in the group regarding key scientific conclusions and project decisions. Thus, although some breakthroughs on the project were quickly obvious to all, others required discussion and persuasion before generating enough consensus to allow progress (Gonzales 2000). In short, even on the Manhattan Project the more 'non-solvers' there were, the longer it took the group to reach a correct solution. To account for this type of process loss, Davis and Restle modified their original hierarchical model, which assumed the groups could operate as fast as the best member, by assuming that the rate of progress a solver could make was inversely related to the number of non-solvers in the group. This modified, *equalitarian model* of potential productivity fitted the groups' actual productivity speed-of-solution data very well. Thus, rather than simply concluding that groups were more productive than individuals, Restle and Davis's analysis provided more direct insight into the sources of their groups' effectiveness and ineffectiveness.

Steiner's model implies that there is a single, unique potential productivity baseline that constitutes an upper limit on group performance. This may be true for certain simple tasks, but, in many instances, there may even be more than one way of defining a group's potential productivity. For example, it makes sense to assume that a group can do no better than its most capable member at the Husbands & Wives problem. But what if Shaw was right; what if groups could catch and correct errors in ways that individuals could not? Groups might not only solve the problem if they contain at least one solver; they might also not pursue or submit an incorrect solution if there is at least one member who can recognize that it is incorrect.

Or consider a simple analogies task, like those you have probably seen on tests of verbal ability – 'is it true that A is to B as C is to D?' How might you define a group's potential productivity in terms of the resources (vocabularies, verbal reasoning abilities) its members possess? You could think of this as a disjunctive task and assume that the group should get the correct answer if any group member is correct. [It has been shown, by the way, that groups usually fall short of this baseline (e.g. Laughlin *et al*. 1975, 1976).] But this task may also be considered divisible. A four-person group may contain no person who knows the meaning of all four words (A, B, C and D), yet the group may still reach the correct answer if the meaning of each word is known by at least one member.

Steiner's analysis also implicitly assumes that individuals cannot be any more motivated in groups than they are when working individually. However, people are often more motivated in group settings than they are when working alone (Hackman and Morris 1975); think of the exceptional efforts people often make for comrades in combat, for team-mates, for family members, and so on. That is, it is possible that people in groups exhibit *motivation gains* as well as motivation losses. As one example, social facilitation research suggests one feature of group settings (i.e. the presence of others) that can enhance motivation. The desire to perform well for team-mates or close friends represents a second source of greater motivation in groups. The point of this discussion is that when thinking in terms of Steiner's theory, there may be more than one reasonable way of defining a group's potential. As a result, there are various ways of thinking about possible theoretical baselines of potential performance. By seeing how far group performance falls below such baselines, we can derive estimates of how much process loss, if any, is occurring in problem-solving groups (as Davis and Restle illustrated). Each such baseline makes different assumptions about how a group functions and, by comparing different baselines against actual group behaviour, we can get a better idea of which set of assumptions is psychologically reasonable and which is not.

THE EXPERIMENTAL ANALYSIS OF PROCESS LOSS

We have been discussing one way of analyzing and understanding group process losses, through testing the goodness-of-fit of theoretical models. Another approach is to identify an instance of process loss and then to analyze it experimentally. That is, one can determine whether certain variables or processes contribute to the process loss by carefully varying or assessing the conditions of group performance and seeing whether the level of process loss is affected. Below we describe a number of such analyses.

Group member characteristics

A series of older studies was reinterpreted by Steiner (1972) using this approach. All of the studies utilized the Horse Trader Problem, which asks, 'A man bought a horse for $60 and sold it for $70. Then he bought it back for $80 and sold it for $90. How much money did he make in the horse business?' (Maier and Solem 1952). This is a unitary, optimizing, disjunctive task. Any group containing a solver should be able to come up with the correct answer, which is $20. Not surprisingly for this type of task, a group is more likely to solve the problem correctly than a single individual, but what is surprising is that many groups that potentially could solve the problem fail to do so. For example, in Maier and Solem's (1952) original study, less than 80 per cent of the groups that contained at least one person who had correctly solved the problem while working individually ended up solving the problem. Why?

Part of the answer may be that it is not enough that a group member can solve a problem. He or she must share that solution with the rest of the group and this solution must then be accepted by the group. Many factors unrelated to the quality of one's ideas can interfere with these steps in the group problem-solving process. For example, a group member who can solve the problem but who has low status in the group may be less willing or able to present their solution. Furthermore, that solution may be undervalued by the rest of the group because of that individual's low status (Berger and Zelditch 1998). Torrance's (1954) study of bomber crews dramatically illustrates this process. Only 6 per cent of high-status pilots failed to persuade their crew they were correct; for low-status tailgunners, the figure was 37 per cent.

Another factor that is likely to affect solvers' behaviour is their confidence in their solution. The less confidence you have in your solution (even if it is the correct solution), the less likely you are to propose, let alone defend, that solution in the group. Johnson and Torcivia (1967) had students work on the Horse Trader problem individually. They reached solutions and indicated their confidence in those solutions. Then dyads (i.e. two-person groups) consisting of one solver and one non-solver were formed. Potentially, all these dyads should have solved, but only 72 per cent did so. As suggested above, the relative confidence of the two members in their solution was strongly related to whether the group solved. When the solver was more confident than the non-solver, the group solved 94 per cent of the time, but when it was the non-solver who was more confident, the group only solved 29 per cent of the time (cf. Hinsz 1990).

Of course, unless the task is a eureka task, simply presenting a solution to the group may not be sufficient to lead the group to accept it. It must usually be defended – its rationale must be presented, arguments against it must be refuted, the incorrectness of alternative solutions must be pointed out, and so on. This can not be done without taking part in a vigorous group discussion of the problem. Thus, all else being equal, we would expect greater process loss if a solver says little than when he or she says much. A subset of the groups studied by Thomas and Fink (1961) speak to this question. In each of their 18 groups, there was only one solver. Potentially, every group could solve but only six actually did so. But in every one of these six groups, it was the solver who was the most talkative member of the group. A non-solver was the most talkative member in 11 of the 12 groups that failed. So we see that groups sometimes fall short of their potential because the most capable member in the group is not always the most confident, talkative or highest status member.

Brainstorming

Other sources of process loss are constraints or distractions arising directly from the process of interaction in groups. A good example is the process loss that occurs in brainstorming groups. Brainstorming is a group performance technique designed to facilitate creative thinking (Osbourn 1957). Group members are instructed to generate as many ideas as possible, to build on others' ideas when possible, and not to criticize any ideas. The group task of generating as many creative ideas as possible does not fit simply into Steiner's task taxonomy. The task of coming up with any particular idea is disjunctive – as long as one member has the idea, the group should too. But the task of accumulating such ideas is additive – the more unique uses a member generates, the better the group's performance. An average n-person group's potential productivity (in terms of the *number* of ideas) should be equal to the performance of a *nominal group* (i.e. the total number of unique ideas that n separate individuals can generate). Osbourn (1957) suggested that brainstorming groups can even exceed this potential: 'the average person can think up twice as many ideas when working with a group than when working alone' (p. 229).

However, nearly all the studies that have made this comparison have found that brainstorming groups usually produce fewer (sometimes less than half as many) ideas as nominal groups (Lamm and Trommsdorff 1973; Diehl and Stroebe 1987). One important reason for this process loss appears to be *production blocking* – only one group member can talk at any one time in a brainstorming group. Diehl and Stroebe (1987) illustrated this by having four isolated individuals generate ideas, out loud, under special conditions. Although these four people were working alone, the experimenters prevented them from speaking out their ideas if one of the other individuals in that experimental session was already speaking (in another room). Diehl and Stroebe demonstrated that this set of conditions lowered the performance of these individuals so that it was as poor as that of a real interacting four-person group. Both performed far less well than four-person nominal groups where there was no production blocking. It is unclear at this point exactly why this is true. One possibility is that it may be hard to think of or remember ideas while waiting for a turn to talk; however, providing a memory aid (e.g. a notebook to record one's ideas) or making interruptions more predictable (e.g. by having group members speak in a fixed order) does not appear to reduce the amount of process loss (Diehl and Stroebe 1991). A more promising explanation may be that the delays and mutual interference that result from production blocking make it harder to come up with ideas – listening to others, waiting for a turn to speak, trying not to interrupt others, and so forth can interfere with our ability to get a productive train of thought started, or can 'derail' an ongoing train of thought (Nijstad 2000). As one indication of this, Nijstad (2000) required individuals to wait a few seconds before recording each new idea on a problem-solving task and found that this interruption reduced both the number of ideas and the 'flow' of ideas (i.e. how much each new idea was connected to the last idea) these individuals generated.

Besides production blocking, at least two other processes also appear to contribute to process loss in brainstorming groups. Although brainstorming groups are told not to be critical of one another, people are more likely to be nervous about how others might evaluate their performance in face-to-face groups than in nominal groups. Such *evaluation apprehension* could lead them to 'clam up' and not offer ideas in the groups. Some evidence for this comes from a study by Comacho and Paulus (1995). They found that when all the members of a group had low interaction anxiety (i.e. were generally less nervous about interacting with other people), they did just as well as nominal groups, whereas groups composed of members with high interaction anxiety showed the usual process loss.

The other process is one of *social matching* (Paulus and Dzindolet 1993). The idea here is that groups try, especially when they begin a task, to establish a social norm about just what level of performance is reasonable and appropriate. Because of factors like those we have already discussed (e.g. production blocking, evaluation apprehension), the initial rate of production in real groups is likely to be lower than in nominal groups.

Moreover, if the task is not intrinsically interesting or of high importance to group members, the group is likely to rely more on the least capable group members to define their common standard (members are likely to ask, 'just how little can one get away with doing?'; cf. Stroebe *et al.* 1996). If group members set their own goals to match such relatively low levels of performance, process loss should result. Paulus and his colleagues have made several observations that are consistent with this explanation: (a) groups that are less productive at their first brainstorming task tend to be less productive in subsequent brainstorming tasks, as one would expect if the initial experience with the task set the standard for subsequent occasions (Paulus and Dzindolet 1993: experiment 4); (b) if you replace the group's implicit performance standard by telling brainstorming groups that they can and should reach a relatively high level of performance, they do tend to do better (Paulus and Dzindolet 1993: experiment 5); and (c) groups with mixed interaction anxiety (i.e. containing members with both high and low scores) do as badly at brainstorming tasks as groups with uniformly high anxiety, just as you would expect if the group paid more attention to those who perform poorly than those who perform well in setting their group standard (Camacho and Paulus 1995).

By analysing and identifying the sources of process loss in brainstorming groups, we can come up with remedies to help such groups get closer to their potential. One such remedy is having a well-trained group leader or facilitator who can reduce production blocking (e.g. by pushing people to state their ideas quickly and to build on others' ideas) and evaluation apprehension (e.g. by discouraging criticism of each others' ideas). Some studies have shown that giving brainstorming groups such a facilitator can reduce or even eliminate their process loss (Offner *et al.* 1996; Oxley *et al.* 1996). Another very effective way of reducing process loss is for group members to interact via computers rather than face-to-face. This is not like a chat room where production blocking would still be a problem. Rather, the computer software allows individuals to type in their ideas without interruption (so there is no production blocking), to be anonymous (so there is low evaluation apprehension) and to be able to see copies of other group members' ideas on the screen whenever they like (so that they can jump-start new trains of thought). Such computerized brainstorming groups have been found to perform as well as nominal groups (e.g. Gallupe *et al.* 1991) and, when fairly large ($n > 9$), even outperform them (Dennis and Valacich 1993; Valacich *et al.* 1994). The latter result is quite striking, although not yet well understood. One interesting possibility is that the opportunities for stimulating one another's thinking are better in larger groups. The original, optimistic claims for the value of group brainstorming assumed that such mutual cognitive stimulation can and does occur. If so, then the true potential of a brainstorming group is more than the simple sum of the ideas the individual members could come up with on their own. What would Professor Steiner say about this superior performance? Have these large computerized brainstorming groups exceeded their 'maximal potential'? Well, not really. It does appear that in the Dennis and Valacich studies, computerized brainstorming conditions led to process gain over nominal group conditions. But such gain only leads us to revise our estimates of what such groups are capable of. Thus, according to Steiner's model, the best we can expect from a performing group is to meet its maximal potential rather than exceed it. In this case, the results of the computerized brainstorming studies lead us to reject a theoretical baseline which assumes that the only ideas we can come up with in the group setting are those that we would come up with when working alone. Rather, these studies provide some of the best evidence that, under some circumstances, there is a group synergy that leads us to produce more ideas when we learn the thoughts of others. One good piece of evidence that this might be so is the fact that when groups are composed so that the members have very diverse ideas, they end up generating many more new ideas (per person) overall than groups with members whose ideas overlap one another (Stroebe and Diehl 1994). We are more likely to be stimulated to think up wholly new ideas if the others in the group do not start with much the same set of ideas that we start with.

Group size and performance

In a way, the study of group size is just an extension of the old 'individual *vs.* group' comparison, except now the comparison is between smaller and larger groups. So it is not surprising that early research on group size, like the individual *vs.* group research, often paid little attention to task features and did not define potential productivity. Thomas and Fink (1963) reviewed this early work. Although a few studies found no effect of group size on group performance, most did. In a study that competes with Triplett (1898) for the distinction of being the first experiment in social psychology (Kravitz and Martin 1986), Ringelmann (1913) obtained typical results. Ringelmann had individuals and groups of two, three or eight males pull on a rope as hard as possible. The average force (in kilograms) was individuals 63 kg, two-person group 118 kg, three-person group 160 kg and eight-person group 248 kg. Clearly, group performance increased with group size, but the rate of increase was negatively accelerated; that is, the addition of another person to the group increased group productivity, but the size of that increase was less than the increase due to the last person added to the group. Similar results have been observed for groups working on intellectual puzzles (Taylor and Faust 1952), creativity tasks (Gibb 1951), perceptual judgments and complex reasoning (Ziller 1957).

Steiner's (1972) model suggests that, to understand the effect of group size on actual productivity, one needs to understand the effect of group size on potential productivity and on process loss. And these both require careful attention to task demands. The effects of group size should be very different for different tasks. For example, consider a disjunctive task like the Husband & Wives puzzle. Potential productivity for such a task depends on the probability of having a solver. As Lorge and Solomon (1955) have shown for disjunctive tasks (e.g. intellective puzzles, complex reasoning), the probability of the group containing at least one solver, and hence the group's potential productivity, is an increasing, negatively accelerated function of group size.

However, if the group is working on a conjunctive task (e.g. a tethered climbing team), larger groups should generally have a lower potential productivity. The larger the group, the greater the chance of containing a low-ability, non-solving group member. However, if the group is performing an additive task, like a tug-of-war, potential productivity ought to increase linearly with group size. In principle, on this type of task, a well-synchronized randomly composed four-person team ought to be able to do roughly twice as much as a randomly composed two-person team, assuming minimal process loss. The moral should be clear – how well large *vs.* small groups *can* perform depends on the nature of the group's task.

The relationship between group size and group process loss is less clear. Steiner (1972) speculated that, for most tasks, coordination losses increase with group size and often do so in an accelerating manner. The number of ways in which a group can organize itself (e.g. divide responsibilities, combine contributions, coordinate efforts) increases rapidly as a group gets larger. For example, in a tug-of-war task with n-person groups, the total number of pairings of members who must coordinate their efforts (i.e. pull at the same time and in the same direction) increases rapidly with group size; specifically there are $n(n - 2)/2$ such pairings (Steiner 1972). Again, task demands are crucial. For some tasks, coordination problems do not increase with size (e.g. group members working simultaneously but independently on anagrams). For other tasks, coordination problems quickly become severe as the group gets larger (e.g. a human pyramid crossing a tightrope).

For such high-coordination tasks, we might expect coordination losses to increase faster with group size than potential productivity does; this would mean that actual productivity should drop as the group gets larger. This was demonstrated by Kelley *et al.* (1965), who simulated an important group task – evacuating a burning building. Group members were placed in separate booths. Each booth contained a switch. By pressing this switch for 3 seconds, one could escape an electric shock. But there was a catch – if more than one person pressed the switch at the same time, no-one could escape (just as an exit may be blocked if too many people try to squeeze through at once). Signal lights in each booth indicated whether others were pressing their switches. Clearly, group members had to coordinate their actions for everyone to escape. Groups were all given ample time to escape – 6 seconds per member – so potential productivity was uniformly high for groups of every size. However, Kelley *et al.* (1965: study 2) found that actual productivity dropped as group size increased; for example, in a four-person group, the number of persons escaping per second was 0.16, whereas this figure was 0.04 for a seven-person group. Since potential productivity was constant across group sizes, this means that process loss (most likely coordination loss) increased with group size for this task. In huge collaborative efforts such as the Manhattan Project, lack of coordination is likely to be a serious problem but, as we have seen, it was kept within reasonable limits through the efforts of an accomplished administrative leader. Another contributing factor was the intense motivation produced by the patriotic fervour that marked the allied efforts in the Second World War. However, such motivation will not always be present. Indeed, Steiner (1972) speculates that, in many task settings, motivation losses as well as coordination losses may increase with group size. For example, when the reward for successful group performance is fixed, adding more people to the group clearly reduces each member's share of the reward and thereby the incentive to exert effort on the group's behalf. We will consider several other sources of motivation loss in the next chapter.

Recall that Davis and Restle (1963) found that groups did not solve disjunctive intellective puzzles as quickly as the hierarchical (i.e. 'best member') model would predict, but that the equalitarian model (which linked solvers' rate of progress to the proportion of solvers in the group) predicted group solution times well. Bray *et al.* (1978) obtained similar results in contexts comparable to those examined by Davis and Restle (small groups considering fairly challenging puzzles). But when the problems became easier or the groups became larger, groups took longer to solve the problems than either of these models predicted. A new model was needed, one that provided for an even slower rate of progress than the equalitarian model.

What might slow down such groups? There are several possibilities. Maybe a certain amount of time is needed to organize a group that is unnecessary for individuals (Bales and Strodtbeck 1951), or perhaps non-solvers act as even more of a drag on solvers' progress than the equalitarian model assumes. Bray *et al.* (1978) suggested another possibility. Stephan and Mishler (1952) found that the proportion of active speakers in discussion groups declined with group size. Perhaps the proportion of active participants in task groups also drops as group size increases. Even though there may be ten persons in the group, if only a few people are actively trying to solve the problem, the group's *functional size* might be much smaller and, as we have already noted, smaller groups would be expected to solve more slowly. In fact, Bray *et al.* found that, in most instances, groups were solving about as fast as the fastest solver in 'groups' of one or two persons. When ten-person groups are functioning like individuals, there is clearly considerable process loss. This could reflect coordination losses, such as the production blocking noted earlier for brainstorming groups. For example, if group interaction simply consisted of one group member at a time thinking out loud about the puzzle, it could be distracting and interfere with anyone else's thinking. In such a case, the group would function like a single individual. Or it could reflect increasing motivation losses in larger groups. Research to be considered in the following chapter bolsters this second possibility.

SUMMARY

Early research comparing individual performance with group performance generally favoured groups: groups tend to be more accurate, faster and more productive, albeit less efficient. Steiner's analysis of this question stressed the importance of task demands and suggested that clearer insights into group processes resulted from comparing groups' actual productivity with their potential productivity. Such comparisons suggest that groups routinely fall short of this potential. According to Steiner, thinking about task features provides us with one means of understanding how group performance differs from individual performance. Steiner offers a task taxonomy to help us to categorize better such task features. His model also suggests several sources of group process loss. For example, when the most capable members of a problem-solving group are not confident, have low status or are not talkative, the group is likely to underutilize its resources. The inability of everyone in an interacting group to talk and think at the same time can similarly impede optimal group performance. Such process losses can be avoided through modifications of the group's task; for example, computerized brainstorming groups can avoid many of the sources of process loss that arise in face-to-face groups. Such process losses also tend to increase as the group gets larger. This means that a larger group's functional size may often be much smaller than its actual size. As we gain knowledge about such group process losses, we may be more able to minimize them and thereby help task groups achieve their full potential.

Solution to the Husbands & Wives problem

Let us denote the three couples as H1–W1, H2–W2 and H3–W3. H1 rows across the river with his wife, W1. He leaves her on the other side and rows back. Then he picks up the other two husbands, H2 and H3, and rows with them across the river. H1 gets out and the other two husbands row back. They pick up W2, leaving W3 behind, and all (i.e. H2, W2 and H3) row across. H2 and W2 get out of the boat. H3 rows back, picks up his wife, W3, and then returns with her.

SUGGESTIONS FOR FURTHER READING

Davis, J.H. (1969) *Group Performance*. Reading, MA: Addison-Wesley. An excellent introduction to the topic.

McGrath, J.E. (1984) *Groups: Interaction and Performance*. Englewood Cliffs, NJ: Prentice-Hall. A thoughtful and provocative discussion of the connections between how group members interact and how they perform.

Parks, C.D. and Sanna, L.J. (1998) *Group Performance and Interaction*. Denver, CO: Westview Press. A good overview of recent work on group performance, with special attention given to research on more applied topics, like groups in the workplace.

Steiner, I.D. (1972) *Group Process and Productivity*. New York: Academic Press. A scholarly and incisive analysis of the psychology of task groups.

FOUR

TASK MOTIVATION IN GROUPS

KEY CONCEPTS

- What group performance conditions give rise to motivation losses among group members?
- What group performance conditions give rise to motivation gains among group members?
- What importance do the demands of the group's task have on such motivation losses and gains?

INTRODUCTION

As we begin working on this chapter, it is mid-September 2001, a couple of days after terrorists have crashed commercial airplanes into the World Trade Center in New York City and the Pentagon building in Washington, DC. Writing is punctuated with long periods of sitting in front of the television, following the news that swirls as dizzyingly as the dust and debris in lower Manhattan. One television interview is with an officer of an association of firefighters. The interviewer notes that hundreds of New York firefighters are missing and presumed dead. They had been trying to rescue people in the World Trade Center towers as those towers collapsed. And now their colleagues were lining up to re-enter the still very dangerous site and work lengthy shifts to help rescue and recover their fallen comrades and other victims. The admiring and puzzled interviewer asks the officer to explain such behaviour. He answers that it is difficult to explain, but suggests that those who do this work together form bonds that make them willing to go to extraordinary lengths to do their jobs, especially when they share the responsibility or the danger.

Most likely, there are many reasons. Such behaviour is partly how well-trained and dedicated professionals react when there is a vitally important job to do. But part of the explanation lies, as the officer suggests, in the dynamics of groups. When groups face collective tasks, their members often work differently than when they face similar tasks alone. Also, as the officer suggested, these differences can be difficult to understand and explain. But in the last few decades, some fascinating beginnings have been made in understanding them.

GROUP MOTIVATION LOSSES: SOCIAL LOAFING

The behaviour of the New York firefighters suggests that group members sometimes bring their very best efforts to their collective tasks. Ironically, though, most of the research to date has focused on how group settings can lower motivation. The main reason for this, we think, is not that the example of the exceptionally highly motivated firefighters is the exception to the rule, but rather that some fascinating early research on motivation loss captured many social psychologists' attention.

In the last chapter, we discussed Ringelmann's (1913) early study in which he observed a nearly linear decline in the average pull-per-member as the size of a rope-pulling team increased. If there had been no process loss, of course, the pull-per-member should have remained constant across groups of different sizes. Both Ringelmann (1913) and Steiner (1972) speculated that the resultant process loss was probably due to the greater coordination difficulties seen in larger groups. But it is, of course, possible that such suboptimal productivity was due to motivation loss, as well as, or instead of, coordination loss. That is, perhaps individuals in groups just did not care that much about maximizing their performance. Several of Steiner's colleagues at the University of Massachusetts, Amherst (Ingham et al. 1974) decided to find out. Their plan was simple – to estimate motivation losses, first eliminate all coordination losses. And their means of achieving this was elegant – to eliminate group coordination loss, eliminate the group. As in Ringelmann's classic study, several persons were in the laboratory; on different trials, between one and six individuals pulled on a rope as hard as possible. The key difference was that, in Ingham and co-workers' study, seven of the persons were confederates of the experimenter. Whenever the true participant was working, it was contrived that he was always ahead of any other persons on the rope, closest to the gauge that measured performance. Every person was also blindfolded, allegedly to eliminate distraction. During these trials, the confederates did not pull on the rope; in effect, there was no group, only the performance of an individual who believed he was part of a group. Ingham et al. found that as the apparent group size increased, performance fell; this was particularly evident for the smallest group sizes (i.e. one to three persons). Thus, the Ringelmann effect appeared to be at least partially due to motivation losses; as the group got larger, people tended to pull less hard.

Many years later, Latané et al. (1979a) replicated this result with a new task – cheering as loudly as possible. The experimental approach was similar – on key trials, participants thought that they were cheering as part of a group, but in reality only they were cheering. As both Ringelmann and Ingham *et al.* had found, individual motivation declined with apparent group size. Latané *et al.* called this motivation loss *social loafing*, a term that has come to be synonymous with Steiner's notion of group motivation loss. They also speculated that it might be a common 'social disease', doing widespread harm in many collective performance contexts.

Identifiability-mediated motivation losses

Subsequent research confirmed that the social loafing effect was genuine and reliable (Karau and Williams 1993). It is not restricted to motor tasks like rope-pulling or cheering; it can also occur when groups are performing cognitive or perceptual tasks (e.g. Petty *et al.* 1980; Szymanski and Harkins 1987; Weldon and Gargano 1988). It has also been demonstrated in many different countries, including India (Weiner *et al.* 1981), Japan (Williams and Williams 1984), Jordan (Atoum and Farah 1993), China (Earley 1989) and Taiwan (Gabrenya *et al.* 1981). Furthermore, all else being equal, it appears that the effect is somewhat stronger in western than eastern cultures (Karau and Williams 1993). Since differences between people in western and eastern cultures are often attributed to stable differences in a more general individualist–collectivist personality disposition, it is thus not surprising that social loafing appears to be relatively stronger among individualists (Wagner 1995; Erez and Somech 1996) or among those who see themselves as better than others (Charbonnier *et al.* 1998; Huguet *et al.* 1999a). Finally, men appear somewhat more prone to socially loaf than women (Karau and Williams 1993; Kugihara 1999).

But research has also suggested that the effect may not be nearly as universal a feature of group (as opposed to individual) performance as originally suspected. For example, it can be attenuated or eliminated by introducing into the performance setting any of the following factors known to enhance motivation: if the task is sufficiently involving (Brickner *et al.* 1986), attractive (Zaccaro 1984) or intrinsically interesting to group members (Smith *et al.* 2001); if group cohesion is sufficiently high (Everett *et al.* 1992; Karau and Williams 1997; Karau and Hart 1998; Worchel *et al.* 1998); if group members will be punished for poor performance (Miles and Greenberg 1993); or if the group sets performance goals (Brickner 1987). In general, then, social loafing is more likely to occur when there is no strong incentive to perform the task for individuals or for groups. Similarly, conditions that increase the cost of effortful task performance, such as fatigue (Anshel 1995; Hoeksema van Orden *et al.* 1998), or reduce one's sense of responsibility to the group (Kerr and Stanfel 1993) tend to increase social loafing.

More importantly, follow-up research has also revealed the underlying cause of the original social loafing effect (Kerr and Bruun 1981; Williams *et al.* 1981). When part of a group performing a rope-pulling or cheering task, one may feel less identifiable. These are additive tasks that combine all member contributions to produce a single group product. There is no way of identifying any individual member's contribution. Thus, if one chose to reduce one's effort at such a task, perhaps because it was fatiguing, uninteresting or unrewarding, no-one would be able to tell. This anonymity would be enhanced by increasing the size of the group, since the more inputs there were to the group product, the more difficult it would be to attribute any process loss to any particular member. But because the biggest difference in anonymity occurs between working alone (when one is fully identifiable) and working in a dyad (a two-person group), when one is no longer personally identifiable, this explanation also suggests that the biggest drop in effort should occur as one moves from individuals to dyads, with ever smaller drops in effort as group size increases. As noted above, the original social loafing studies found just this pattern.

There is a straightforward way to do a more direct test of the identifiability explanation. One can alter the task so that participants believe that every group member's contribution *can* be identified. For example, Williams *et al.* (1981) examined two variations of the cheering task. In one, the version originally used by Latané *et al.* (1979a), people sat in a circle around a single microphone. When groups cheered, only an overall sound level could be measured and each person's contribution was non-identifiable. For this version, Williams *et al.* observed the usual social loafing effect; member effort declined with group size at a negatively accelerated rate. But in the other version of the task, each person had his or her own individual microphone on a headset. No matter what the group size, a sound level reading could be taken for each person. For this version, there was no social loafing effect (cf. Kerr and Bruun 1981).

This result re-illustrates what should now be a familiar theme – task features are crucial in analysing group performance. The original social loafing effect turned out not to be a universal social (i.e. group) problem. Rather, it is a problem that only arises for certain group tasks, those tasks which combine member contributions so that no individual member's performance can be identified, what Davis (1969) terms an *information-reducing* task. However, on tasks for which individual member contributions are always identifiable, there is no such social loafing effect. Moreover, as we have noted, even when identifiability is low, group members do not invariably take advantage of the situation and loaf with impunity – if the task is interesting enough, if the group is cohesive enough, if there are special costs for poor group performance, and so on, little or no social loafing may occur. Thus, even for those firefighter tasks which are information-reducing (e.g. directing water on a fire from several fire hoses), we would not expect highly cohesive and dedicated groups of firefighters to show much social loafing.

To be more precise about the basis for the social loafing effect, it seems not to be identifiability *per se*, but rather the potential for evaluation that comes with identifiability (Harkins 1987; Harkins and Szymanski 1987b). That is, even if my contribution to the group product can be identified, I might still loaf if I felt that no-one could or would evaluate my performance. This was demonstrated in a clever study by Harkins and Jackson (1985). The task was to generate as many uses for an object as possible. Half of the participants were led to feel identifiable; the experimenter would collect each group member's ideas separately. The other half were not identifiable; all group members' ideas were placed in a single receptacle, making personal identification impossible. When participants thought that everyone in the group was generating uses for the same object, the usual social loafing effect was obtained – people generated fewer uses for the object in the non-identifiable condition. But when participants thought that every person generated uses for a unique object, so that person-to-person comparison and evaluation was not meaningful, loafing occurred *even when everyone was clearly identifiable*. It was the possibility for evaluation, not identifiability, which was crucial for producing social loafing. In subsequent work, Harkins and his colleagues showed that it is not just evaluation of personal performance by someone outside the group (e.g. the experimenter, a supervisor) that concerns and motivates a group member. Rather, the possibility of evaluation by other group members or even by oneself (Harkins and Szymanski 1987b; Szymanski and Harkins 1987) has similar motivating effects. Furthermore, an opportunity for group members to evaluate the group (but not individual members') performance can similarly motivate group members to work (Harkins and Szymanski 1989). Thus, the original social loafing effect appears to be restricted to a fairly narrow range of group task settings where evaluation of member or group performance by anyone is unlikely.

At first blush there would appear to be a contradiction between social loafing and social facilitation effects. We saw earlier that having co-actors present facilitates performance, at least on simple well-learned tasks (like rope-pulling or cheering). Yet here we see that people work less hard and, therefore, accomplish less, when working together than when working alone at such tasks. But having learned how group processes depend so much on the demands of the group's task, we should quickly observe that the tasks are not the same. In the social loafing setting, one works together with others, while one works for only oneself in the social facilitation setting. But is it this difference in task demands that holds the key to the apparent contradiction and, if so, why? Harkins (1987; Harkins and Szymanski 1987a) has examined these questions. He noted that Cottrell's learned-drive theory of social facilitation gave a central role to the evaluation implicit in others' presence, at least for humans. Harkins' own work suggests that evaluation also underlies the social loafing effect. The difference between the two settings is the effect that others have on the possibility of evaluation. In a social facilitation setting, the (mere) presence of others *increases* the likelihood of evaluation, since one's performance can be compared with that of others. In the social loafing setting (viz. group performance at an information-reducing task), having co-workers *decreases* the likelihood of evaluation (since one cannot be sure who did what). The key point is that being in a 'social' as opposed to an individual setting does not have a single, simple effect on the likelihood of evaluation and on performance; depending upon task demands, it can have quite opposite effects.

Free riding

You may have noted our recurrent use of the term 'the *original* social loafing effect'. This is because subsequent research has indicated that there are other types of group motivation losses, with different underlying causes, than those documented in early social loafing studies. One such loss arises from the opportunity for shared responsibility in many group tasks. When one works alone, success or failure usually rests entirely on one's own shoulders. But when one works in a group, the responsibility for the group's success or failure is shared among group members. So, for example, if one considers a collection of bystanders at an emergency to be a group, the responsibility for helping is diffused among group members. Such diffusion of responsibility has been shown to result in a kind of social loafing – the larger the group of bystanders at an emergency, the less likely it is that any particular individual will provide help (e.g. Darley and Latané 1968; Latané and Nida 1981).

Similarly, for certain group tasks there also exists the possibility that others in the group can and will do most or all of the work necessary for the group to succeed. For example, if I share an apartment with others, I can enjoy the benefits of a clean apartment as long as someone – not necessarily me – cleans the place up. If I am working in a group on an intellectual puzzle like the Husbands & Wives problem, as long as there is someone in the group able and eager to solve the problem, I could exert no effort at all and still be part of a successful group. As this last example illustrates, this is especially likely for disjunctive tasks, where the group can succeed if only a single member succeeds.

It is reasonable to assume that we would be less willing to exert ourselves when such possibilities exist to *free ride* (Olson 1965); that is, to benefit from the task efforts of other group members. Kerr (1983; Kerr and Bruun 1983) has suggested that group members are sensitive to the *dispensability* of their efforts. When they perceive their contributions to be dispensable, such that group success (or, for that matter, failure) depends very little upon whether they exert any effort, and when that effort is costly, they are less likely to exert themselves on the group's behalf. This was demonstrated in an experiment by Kerr (1983), in which participants worked in isolation either as part of a dyad or as an individual performer. The task was to pump air using a rubber sphygmograph bulb. If a participant reached a certain performance threshold on a trial, he or she was deemed to have succeeded. For individuals, this meant a 25¢ cash reward per trial (and a potential $2.25 payoff for the nine trials in the study). The group task was defined disjunctively; if either group member succeeded, the dyad succeeded and both members would receive 25¢. Regardless of condition, the participant received accurate feedback on his or her own performance after each trial. But in the dyads, the feedback on the partner's performance was false and designed to encourage free riding. After each and every trial, the participants learned that their partner had succeeded. It should have soon become evident to participants that they could free ride on their partner's efforts, since the partner was willing and able to do the unpleasant work required to ensure the dyad's success. And, indeed, dyad members worked significantly less hard than the individual control participants.

It should be emphasized that this type of social loafing was different from the original social loafing effects discussed above. As we have shown, the latter effects depended upon low identifiability and the resulting low evaluation potential. However, in the experiments demonstrating free riding

(Kerr 1983; Kerr and Bruun 1983), *every* group member's performance was individually monitored by the experimenter and completely identifiable, conditions under which the original social loafing effect is eliminated (Kerr and Bruun 1981; Williams *et al.* 1981). The opportunity to free ride – to get something for nothing – is not quite the same thing as the opportunity to socially loaf – to 'hide in the crowd'. Although both processes link social conditions (e.g. group size, group task demands) to the instrumentality of task effort, they are concerned with somewhat different outcomes: reductions of effort have a less direct impact on the chances of *group success* when free riding is possible; reductions of effort have less direct impact on the chances of receiving *salient personal and social evaluations* when social loafing is viable. Like social facilitation and identifiability-mediated social loafing (and, for that matter, nearly every other group performance phenomenon), the extent of free riding depends on task demands. For example, we might expect less free riding on an additive task, when group performance depends on every group member's contribution, than on a disjunctive task, when only one member's contribution counts, and we would be right (Kerr and Bruun 1983). What is important is how dispensable the group member feels; this judgment can depend on many factors, including task demands, group structure and member resources. Consider, for example, the effect that self-perceived task ability might play. If your group is working on the disjunctive Husband & Wives problem, the less capable you consider yourself to be, the more dispensable your efforts would appear: 'There's bound to be someone more capable than me who can solve this problem for the group'. But if the task is conjunctive, so that it is the least capable member's performance that defines the group score, exactly the opposite relationship should hold – it is the high ability member who should believe that it is unlikely that his or her performance will affect the group's score. Thus, perceived ability should, and does (Kerr and Bruun 1983), have exactly opposite effects on perceived dispensability and effort for disjunctive and conjunctive tasks.

Earlier we learned that social loafing depends on a key task feature, whether individual contributions can be identified and, therefore, evaluated. Identifiability also turns out to be relevant to free riding, but in a somewhat different way. Harkins and Petty (1982: experiment 3) gave group members a vigilance task, watching for dots flashing on a computer screen. In one condition, each group member had their own portion of the screen to monitor; they bore complete responsibility for detecting the dots than flashed in that portion. In another condition, all group members monitored the same portion of the screen; they shared the responsibility for detecting the dots that flashed there. The former task is essentially additive and gives little opportunity for free riding. But the latter task is essentially disjunctive (if any member saw the dot, the group would get credit) and presents an opportunity to free ride. The interesting thing, though, is that this opportunity was only taken when participants thought their individual performances could *not* be personally identified. When everyone could be identified, people took little – in fact, in contrast to the study of Kerr (1983) described earlier, practically no – advantage of the opportunity to free ride. Thus, not only does identifiability underlie or mediate the original social loafing effect, it also alters or moderates free riding.

Why? Probably because free riding violates a number of familiar and salient social norms. Although free riders might be saving themselves work and may not even be hurting the group's chances of success, by not doing their best at a group task, they may risk social sanctions for breaking certain social rules or norms, such as the norm of reciprocity (cf. Gouldner 1960) or the norm of social responsibility (cf. Berkowitz 1972). If group members are anonymous, though, there is no way of telling who has violated the norm. This effectively removes the threat of social sanction for norm violation and leaves one free to free ride.

Inequity-based motivation losses

How might you react if you discovered that a group member was free riding on your efforts; that is, was reducing his or her efforts, allowing others to 'carry' the group, and then was receiving the same rewards as every group member? For example, the group could be two people who share an apartment and whose task is to keep the apartment clean. How would you react to a flat-mate who never made any attempt to help keep the apartment clean, yet regularly enjoyed the benefits of your cleaning? As we noted above, this free-riding behaviour violates several social norms. You would be likely to remind the free rider of the norms and, if necessary, begin to apply social sanctions (e.g. express your irritation, ask him or her to move out).

One of the norms that such free-riding behaviour violates is the equity norm, which prescribes that ratios of inputs (e.g. effort) to outcomes (e.g. one's share of group reward) should be equal across comparable individuals (e.g. group members) (Adams 1965). For the problem we have been considering, equity theory (Adams 1965; Walster *et al.* 1978) suggests another solution. If my free-riding partner has lower inputs (i.e. less effort) but gets the same outcomes (e.g. same reward), one way in which equity could be restored would be for me to reduce my inputs too (e.g. reduce my effort). For example, I might simply refuse to clean the apartment. Earlier we discussed a study by Kerr (1983) in which free riding was demonstrated. It required dyads to pump air in a disjunctive task (success by either person ensured group success and reward). In another condition in that study, participants first learned during practice trials that both they and their partner were quite capable of succeeding at the task. The participants then received false feedback about their partner's performance following each of a series of performance trials which suggested that the partner was free riding – namely, the partner failed consistently. Under the disjunctive task demands, the partner still received the same 25¢ reward every time the group succeeded through the participant's efforts. As equity theory predicts, participants reduced their own efforts rather than carry this free rider. Drawing on the terminology of *social dilemmas* (which we consider in more detail in a later chapter), Kerr (1983) christened this the *sucker effect*; participants chose to reduce their own effort (and thereby, their own rewards) rather than 'play the sucker' and be exploited by a free-riding partner.

There is also some evidence that we apply a *means rule* when evaluating a person's inputs for equity calculations. For example, a $100 charitable contribution will be viewed as a more generous gift when it comes from a poor person than when it comes from a rich one (Gergen *et al.* 1975). Thus, when deciding whether things are equitable or fair, we take more into account than our partner's objective level of performance – we also take into account his or her means to be productive (e.g. ability, skills). In another condition of Kerr's (1983) study, the partner again consistently failed. However, in this condition, the practice trial performance indicated that the partner had very low task ability. Under these conditions, participants maintained high performance, willingly 'carrying' the failing partner. Apparently, one does not feel like a sucker when carrying a partner who cannot succeed, but does when the partner can, but will not, work.

The sucker effect is but one of a family of group motivation-loss effects that stem from the equity norm. In each case, there is an inequity among group members that can be removed effectively by reducing one's efforts and thereby lowering one's level of inputs. For example, if you are much more qualified than a co-worker, you are likely to feel inequitably treated if you receive exactly the same pay. Several studies (e.g. Kessler and Weiner 1972) have shown that people sometimes resolve this inequity by reducing their effort; presumably, this makes their total input (including both qualifications and effort) more comparable to that of their co-workers. A more obvious case is one in which co-workers receive different levels of pay for doing the same job based on such factors as time on the job or gender.

We have been careful to say that group members only 'sometimes' reduce effort in the face of inequity because, in most real group task contexts, there are many different types of outcomes and other inputs besides effort. It is not necessary that adjustment of effort be the only or the most likely means of restoring equity. So, for example, an underpaid worker might reduce the quality rather than the quality of his or her work to restore equity (e.g. Evan and Simmons 1969). Or an underpaid worker could simply quit rather than work on at reduced levels of effort (e.g. Valenzi and Andrews 1971). Furthermore, equity may also be restored by distorting reality (Walster *et al.* 1978); in some instances, it may be more feasible to alter one's perceptions and interpretations (e.g. the reason I get paid more is that my contribution is more important than others) than one's actual inputs or outcomes (e.g. Gergen *et al.* 1974). People are likely to use the means of equity restoration that is most convenient and least costly (Adams 1965); whether this involves motivation/effort reduction is likely to depend upon many features of the task and the individual.

It should also be evident that, at times, inequity might be reduced through *increases* in effort. For example, if one is overpaid relative to others in the group, one way to restore equity would be to increase one's effort – one would feel deserving of the higher pay if one actually did work harder (e.g. Pritchard *et al.* 1972). Or, if one were less qualified than others in the group, one might compensate for lack of qualifications by working harder (e.g. Adams 1963). Thus, as far as motivation in groups is concerned, the equity norm is a double-edged sword that could produce motivation gains as well as motivation losses.

GROUP MOTIVATION GAINS

Both our early example of the efforts put in by New York firefighters and the possibility of trying harder to reduce perceived inequities illustrate the potential for group motivation gains – greater effort by members of performance groups than among otherwise comparable individuals or co-actors. And in the last decade, social psychologists have documented a number of such motivation gain phenomena (Matsui *et al.* 1987; Erev *et al.* 1993; Kerr 2001b). We will examine two such phenomena here, the *Köhler effect* and the *social compensation effect*.

The Köhler effect

The study of group motivation losses was triggered by Max Ringelmann's (1913) seminal studies of group performance. Similarly, a series of old, nearly forgotten (Witte 1989) studies of group performance conducted by Otto Köhler (1926, 1927) has stimulated recent interest in group motivation gains. Köhler asked male rowing-club members in Berlin to perform a simple motor persistence task either as individuals or in dyads. In the individual condition, a rower held a bar connected to a 41 kg weight through a series of pulleys. His task was to do standing bicep curls for as long as possible, paced by a metronome with a 2 second interval. In the dyad condition, the weight was doubled (to 82 kg) and one member of the dyad gripped each side of the bar.

Two of Köhler's findings are of interest to us. First, across all dyads there was a significant motivation gain (see Hertel *et al.* 2000); on average, the dyads lasted longer at the task than one would expect based on the individual performances of the two dyad members. Second, this motivation gain was largest when the two dyad members were moderately different in their abilities (relative to when they were nearly equal or extremely discrepant in their abilities). The former effect was recently replicated by Hertel *et al.* (2000) using a less demanding physical task (cf. Stroebe *et al.* 1996), attaching a weight to one's arm and then holding the arm horizontally for as long as possible. A trial was considered to have ended when the arm was lowered and it hit a tripwire. In the dyad condition, two participants held their arms above a single tripwire. As we shall see, it is important to note that this task preserves the conjunctive task demands of Köhler's original task. That is, for both tasks, the group score is determined by the first dyad member to quit – the group can only do as well as its less capable member. In Hertel and co-workers' (2000) dyads, the groups, on average, lasted 14.25 seconds longer than their less capable members had performed as individuals – clear evidence of motivation gain.

Interestingly, Hertel *et al.* (2000) found that the magnitude of this motivation gain did not depend upon how similar in abilities the two group members were, contrary to Köhler's findings (also see Stroebe *et al.* 1996; experiment 1). Why not? Messé *et al.* (2002) suggest that Köhler's rowers were very familiar with one another's capabilities; they routinely trained

and competed together and were also able to observe one another perform Köhler's task individually. The participants in the study of Hertel *et
al.* on the other hand, were (like most people in laboratory experiments)
strangers to one another and had never observed each other's individual
performance before working together in a group. Messé *et al.* (2002) showed
that when group members knew just how capable their partners were, the
largest motivation gains at the arm-lifting task occurred when there was a
moderate discrepancy in capabilities between group members, just as in
Köhler's studies.

How might this motivation gain phenomenon be explained? One
explanation may be derived from theories developed to explain the
motivation loss phenomena we considered earlier in this chapter (Karau
and Williams 1993; Shepperd 1995). These are *expectancy-value* and *instrumentality* theories (e.g. Vroom 1964), which argue that one's choice of effort
is governed by how instrumental that level of effort is perceived to be for
achieving an outcome (i.e. whether or not one sees greater effort as leading to something), weighted by the value placed on that outcome (summed,
typically, across all possible outcomes). Thus, for example, the decline of
task motivation as group size increases, which Ringelmann (1913) initially
observed, can be understood as stemming from the decreased risk of identification and evaluation of one's contribution to certain group tasks (cf.
Kerr and Bruun 1981; Williams *et al.* 1981). That is, in these social loafing
contexts, high effort is not as instrumental in obtaining a valued outcome
(a positive evaluation by others or oneself; or, conversely, in avoiding the
disvalued outcome of a negative evaluation) as it would be if one were
working individually. Note that there is nothing in the structure of these
models that limits their application to instances of group motivation loss.
That is, in principle, it is quite possible that either high effort is more
instrumental or that the resultant outcomes are valued more (or both) in
the group performance context than in the individual performance context, in which case we would expect to see higher levels of effort in groups
– that is, group motivation gains.

The Köhler motivation gain effect can also be explained by such instrumentality models. The conjunctive nature of Köhler's task makes the performance of the less capable member crucial for the group's success. Hence,
the less capable member is likely to see his or her efforts as particularly
indispensable for the group's success or for other salient outcomes (e.g.
not being seen as responsible for a poor group performance). Such a
theory can also account for the effect of the discrepancy in member
abilities on the Köhler motivation gain. When dyad members' abilities are
nearly equal, they both want to quit at the same time, so neither is seen
as 'holding back' the other (or the group). When the discrepancy is very
large, it should become apparent to the less capable member (from one
another's apparent level of fatigue or perhaps from foreknowledge of one's
partner's strength) that there is little chance that they could match the
performance of the much more capable partner, and so they give up. But
when the difference in ability is moderate, the less capable member can
entertain hopes of matching their stronger partner and they should, therefore, persist as long as possible (to maximize group performance and to
avoid the stigma attaching to the person who quits first).

Another explanation has been suggested by Stroebe *et al.* (1996). When there is no clear standard of good performance, group members may engage in social comparison of one another's level of performance to decide on reasonable performance goals. When task accomplishment is important or valued by group members, there should be an upward bias in this social comparison process – that is, those performing less well should set goals closer to the performance levels of the most capable group members. Stroebe *et al.* plausibly argue that the weight-lifting task used by Köhler's rowers was an important training activity for the club, and thus the less capable members should have set higher goals in the dyad conditions, producing genuine motivation gains by the less capable dyad members on Köhler's conjunctive group task.

Hertel *et al.* (2000: experiment 2) suggested that these two explanations could be tested competitively by varying the group task demands. For the arm-lifting task, they contrasted two conditions. One was the conjunctive task demands used by Köhler – the dyad members held their arms above a single tripwire and the trial ended if either dyad member's arm hit it. The other condition employed additive task demands. Here, the dyad members again sat next to each other but each member of the dyad was given his or her own tripwire. The trial was not over when one dyad member quit; the other dyad member could continue as long as possible, and thereby earn more points for the team. According to the instrumentality explanation, motivation gains should only have occurred in the conjunctive condition, because it is only in this condition that the weaker member was indispensable for dyadic performance and other salient outcomes. However, as long as one could see and compare one's performance with one's partner, the processes of social comparison and goal setting should operate equally well under both additive or conjunctive task demands. Hence, the goal-setting explanation predicted that motivation gains by the weaker dyad member should have occurred in both the conjunctive and additive conditions. The results of Hertel and co-workers' (2000: experiment 2) study were clear. There was a significant overall motivation gain (of 45.7 seconds) in the conjunctive condition, but no significant gain under additive task conditions. These preliminary findings suggest that the Köhler effect is probably not simply a result of social comparison and goal setting, but is at least partially due to greater instrumentality of high effort for valued outcomes under certain task conditions.

Subsequent studies have shed more light on the psychological processes underlying the Köhler motivation gain. For example, the identifiability of group member contributions – the mediator of the original social loafing effects (Williams *et al.* 1981) and a moderator of free riding (Harkins and Petty 1982) – also seems to be an important moderator of the Köhler effect. When group members believe that their conjunctive task is information-reducing, so that even if the group score is knowable, no-one will be able to tell how well each group member performed, the Köhler effect disappears (Kerr *et al.* 2002). Thus, it would appear that it is not enough simply to know that the task is conjunctive and that the poorest performance will determine the group score; for weaker group members to push themselves beyond their normal limits at such a task, it must be possible for others to identify – and, presumably, to evaluate – their contributions to the group. Consistent with this line of argument, conditions that reduce but do not completely eliminate the possibility of evaluation (where it is possible to know *who* was the lowest performer but not how much worse they did than their partner) attenuate but do not eliminate the Köhler effect (Kerr *et al.* 2002).

The preceding results imply that the outcomes group members hope to obtain through their efforts when the Köhler effect occurs are not just group performance outcomes (e.g. whether or not the group gets a high score or succeeds at the task), but are also personal outcomes (e.g. how others evaluate you; what kind of impression you create on others). This, in turn, suggests that the Köhler motivation gain will depend, in part, on who the others in our group are and just how important their evaluation of us is. There are, of course, many ways of varying the identity of a group partner to check this out, but one apparently salient basis for evaluation, especially in performance contexts, is the sex of one's partner. There is evidence that, all else being equal, we care more about demonstrating our competence to members of the opposite sex than to others of the same sex (Kerr and Sullaway 1983; Kerr and MacCoun 1984). In all the Köhler effect studies examined so far, the groups have always been composed of people of the same sex. What would happen if the performance dyads were mixed sex? For instance, would a male who was the less competent member of a dyad push himself any harder when the other, more competent member was a female rather than a male? If all one was concerned with was maximizing the group's score, it should not make any difference. However, using an arm-lifting task, Lount *et al.* (2000) found that males persisted over a minute longer when their more capable partner was a female. Interestingly, these researchers found that females did not show any sensitivity to the sex of their partner – they produced the same magnitude of Köhler motivation gain with a male partner as with a female partner. However, subsequent research (Park *et al.* 2002) has shown that some women (those holding more traditional, non-feminist sex-role attitudes) do react to their partner's sex (they show a larger Köhler effect with a male partner than with a female partner).

Clearly, as the firefighter official quoted at the start of this chapter suggested, how hard one is willing to push oneself in a group depends a good deal on who is in the group and what kind of relationships they have with one another. So, for example, both the newer, 'rookie' firefighters and the more experienced, veteran firefighters might want to prove to one another just how capable they are and how well they can do their jobs, especially when it is an emergency that calls for the very best of all group members.

Social compensation

Suppose you are a pre-med student named Chris taking a laboratory course in organic chemistry. Chris believes that the admissions committee for the medical school she hopes to attend will give great weight to how well she performs in this course when deciding whether or not to admit her. Thus, doing well in the course is very important for her educational plans. Suppose further that, on the first day of class, the instructor randomly and permanently divides up the entire class into two-person lab teams. Each team is assigned to complete a number of lab projects. The projects have been designed to be challenging; both team members will have to work quite hard to complete the projects successfully. Furthermore, a single report is to be submitted for each team and both team members will receive whatever grade is given to the report. Finally, let us suppose that, by the luck of the draw, Chris' lab partner, Pat, turns out to be an art student who is taking the course to fulfil a general education requirement. Pat confesses to Chris that all he needs to graduate is simply to pass the course, and that he has no intention of doing any more than the absolute minimum amount of work required.

Certain aspects of this situation seem ripe for social loafing. First, because the contributions of the two team members cannot be identified, we might expect Chris and Pat to socially loaf much as Ringelmann's rope-pullers did. Second, because Pat stands to get the same grade as Chris, but is unwilling to do his fair share of the work, Chris might reduce her own efforts rather than 'play the sucker'. The only problem, of course, is that it is vital to Chris that the task be done very well. And unless some other solution can be found (e.g. getting into another section of the course; getting a new lab partner; persuading the instructor to allow individual lab reports and to grade students based on their individual performances), Chris may only have one choice to insure a good course grade – to work twice as hard, doing not only her own but Pat's work as well.

Earlier, we saw that the Köhler effect occurs when a low capability member recognizes that important outcomes depend upon them exerting exceptionally great effort at the group's task. Chris' hypothetical situation suggests yet another type of group motivation gain effect, *social compensation*. Here, it is the more capable or motivated group member's effort that is indispensable for important outcomes. Social compensation occurs when 'individuals increase their efforts on collective tasks to compensate for the anticipated poor performance of other group members' (Karau and Williams 1997: 158). In our example, Chris would have to increase her efforts to compensate for the anticipated poor performance of Pat.

To document such a social compensation effect, Williams and Karau (1991) compared pairs of co-actors with cooperative dyads working at a brainstorming task. In their collective condition, the idea generation task was additive (the group score was just equal to the sum of the individual members' contributions) and information-reducing (i.e. individual members' contributions could not be identified). Williams and Karau added two features that distinguished their dyads from most prior social loafing settings. The first was the value group members placed on group success. In their generic procedure, Williams and Karau told their participants that performance at the idea generation task was highly correlated with intelligence. Hence, poor group performance at the idea generation task would mark the group (and both its members) as low in intelligence, clearly a stigmatizing outcome. Thus, just like Chris and her chemistry grade, it was important to Williams and Karau's participants to do well at the brainstorming task. The second feature was the expectation of one's partner's performance. In the key conditions, participants expected rather poor performance from their partner, because the confederate-partner (a) asserted low ability (Williams and Karau 1991: experiment 1; Karau and Williams 1997: experiment 2), (b) asserted the intention to exert little effort, like Pat in our example (Williams and Karau 1991: experiment 2), or (c) the participant was chronically mistrustful of others (Williams and Karau 1991: experiment 1). Under these conditions, the participant should both have valued group success highly and have seen themselves as indispensable for that group success. As their analysis predicted, Williams and Karau (1991) found higher levels of performance in their collective condition than in the corresponding (i.e. with the same expectations about co-actor's performance) coactive condition (where each person worked individually).

Of course, if Chris suddenly decided to give up her ambitions to go to medical school, her dilemma would be solved; it would no longer be vital to do well in the chemistry course and she could simply follow Pat's example and take it easy in the course. This suggests that if it were not so very important to Williams and Karau's participants to do well at the group task, they would not feel compelled to compensate for their incapable partner. And, indeed, when the group brainstorming task was presented not as a valid test of intelligence, but rather as 'silly and trivial' (p. 576), the social compensation motivation gain effect disappeared (Williams and Karau 1991: experiment 3).

In certain regards, social compensation and the Köhler effect are similar. Both seem to stem from a combination of task demands, member abilities and valued outcomes that make the efforts of certain group members indispensable for obtaining those outcomes. But in other regards, they may be very different. For example, we know that the inequity inherent in social compensation – I have to do more than my fair share – is aversive. On the other hand, there are indications that the Köhler motivation gain is accompanied by positive feelings (e.g. less fatigue: Köhler 1926; greater enjoyment of the task: Hertel *et al.* 2000). The conditions giving rise to social compensation may foster resentment, whereas those giving rise to the Köhler effect may challenge group members to do better and they may enjoy meeting this challenge. Also, if making a positive impression on one's partner contributes to the Köhler effect, we might expect stronger motivation gains when one is more strongly attracted to one's fellow group members. Interestingly, Karau and Williams (1997: experiment 2) found social compensation for non-cohesive groups, but no such motivation gain for more cohesive groups. Rather, when the capable member (Chris, in our example) really liked the unmotivated member (Pat, in our example), she tended to reduce her effort rather than compensate for him. A challenge for future work on motivation gains will be to undrestand better how aspects of the group (its cohesiveness, its size), group members (their personalities, their concerns for various group and personal outcomes) and the group's task alter one's willingness to give one's very best effort to the group.

SUMMARY

The early studies of Ingham *et al.* (1974) and Latané *et al.* (1979a) gave rise to speculation that groups might be generally demotivating. For example, Latané *et al.* included a cartoon picturing hundreds of thousands of ancient Egyptian workers straining mightily on ropes to inch a pyramid block forward. The work foreman explains to an onlooker, 'Many hands make light the work'. The notion of social loafing gives a new meaning to these words – having many hands available (i.e. group performance settings) can lead us to make light of the work (to reduce our effort). We understand better now that there is nothing inherently demotivating about groups. Rather, only under certain very specific conditions will group members be less motivated than individual performers. As we have seen, under other conditions, group settings can even produce more motivation than individual performance settings. In this chapter, we began by focusing on some of the *de*motivating conditions arising in groups. These include: (a) when being in the group makes identification and evaluation less likely; (b) when being in the group creates opportunities that other group members may do the necessary work (free riding); and (c) when being in the group suggests that there are others who are not doing their fair share of the work (sucker effect). We then identified a couple of the settings that are capable of producing group motivation gains: (d) when one has lower capability than one's partner and the task demands are conjunctive (Köhler effect); and (e) when one has high capability, cares strongly about group performance, and must exert exceptionally high effort to compensate for the low capabilities of other group members (social compensation). Undoubtedly there are other, as yet unstudied, aspects of groups that also encourage reduced or enhanced task effort. However, if the effects we do know about are any guide, it is probable that motivation losses can be reduced or prevented, and motivation gains can be facilitated through proper modifications of the task. Group motivation losses and group motivation gains both follow from well-understood psychological principles, are limited in their occurrence and can be effectively controlled. As New York's firefighters have shown us, many hands can, but need not, make light the work.

SUGGESTIONS FOR FURTHER READING

Karau, S.J. and Williams, K.D. (1993) Social loafing: a meta-analytic review and theoretical integration. *Journal of Personality and Social Psychology*, 65: 681–706. Reviews 20 years of social loafing research and provides an instrumentality theory to integrate the findings.

Kravitz, D.A. and Martin, B. (1986) Ringelmann rediscovered: the original article. *Journal of Personality and Social Psychology*, 50: 936–41. Interest in group motivation can be traced back to the beginnings of scientific social psychology. This paper identifies Ringelmann's classic study as the discipline's first experiment.

Latané, B., Williams, K.D. and Harkins, S.D. (1979) Social loafing. *Psychology Today*, 13: 104–10. A discussion of some of the early findings and implications of work on this topic.

Witte, E.H. (1989) Köhler rediscovered: the anti-Ringelmann effect. *European Journal of Social Psychology*, 19: 147–54. An unearthing of Köhler's early studies of group motivation gains.

FIVE

SOCIAL INFLUENCE AND CONFORMITY

KEY CONCEPTS

- How do social scientists measure conformity?
- What are the different varieties of social influence?
- What factors increase or decrease social influence?
- What theoretical distinctions and controversies are currently being stressed?
- How does minority influence differ from majority influence?

BACKGROUND

When Christian missionaries first arrived in the South Pacific, they were shocked to find that Polynesian women often did not wear clothing above their waists. Almost as disturbing to the puritan sensibilities of these missionaries was the fact that Polynesians did not seem to disapprove of 'lazy pursuits' (e.g. Bingham 1988). Although the Polynesians fished for food and gathered fruits when necessary, survival on these South Pacific islands did not require long hours of arduous labour. The missionaries' concern about such violations of the puritan ethic led them to discourage the population from spending hours frolicking in the surf (Finney and Houston 1996) or engaging in idle romance (Bingham 1988).

The reactions of these missionaries illustrates one of the most fundamental insights of social science. This is that our beliefs regarding what is normal, correct, moral and good are social constructions – that is, norms – that derive power from the fact that they tend to be supported by most other people we encounter, especially in the groups we identify with (i.e. our *reference groups*). Such norms often evolve in response to demands of the physical or technological environment. The 'easy-going' Polynesian norms regarding clothing, hard work, romance, inheritance and family were well suited to a tropical environment in which food and other resources were plentiful, children could easily be raised communally and the need for elaborate shelter and private property was minimal. The missionaries, then, were trying to impose a set of cultural norms that had evolved in a very different and harsher environment.

Although some norms refer to broad cultural rules regarding thought, dress and behaviour, others evolve in smaller social systems. A study conducted over 50 years ago at a small women's liberal arts college in Bennington, Vermont illustrates the operation of such local norms (Newcomb 1943). Newcomb observed that students at Bennington, who generally came from politically conservative homes, became increasingly more liberal during their four years at college. The reason was that the opinion norms at the college were heavily influenced by the liberal views of the faculty, who strongly favoured the social reforms championed by President Franklin Roosevelt. Newcomb documented that this change in student opinion was closely associated with various forms of social reward (e.g. popularity, election to office, etc.). In this chapter, we examine processes and theories of social influence that underlie some of the phenomena illustrated by this study.

SOCIAL COMPARISON THEORY

Leon Festinger's (1954) theory of social comparison processes is one influential attempt to understand the effects of others on our own thinking. As we noted in Chapter 1, his starting point was that, for many of the issues that concern us, there are no right answers, no objective or physical source of certainty. Is dropping bombs on Afghanistan a sensible strategy to suppress international terrorism? Is a single currency for the European Union a good idea? Does Heaven exist? These are questions that are not easily answered by reference to universally accepted, objective criteria. When we do not have access to experts when assessing whether our own answers to such uncertain questions are correct (Suls *et al.* 2000), we can instead check the 'social reality' (Chapter 1) to establish whether there is some social consensus regarding the correct view. In short, our belief about the right answer or the correct view will often depend on the people with whom we talk and their positions in our group. If group opinion confirms our own view, our confidence in that view should increase (e.g. Orive 1988; Mullen and Hogg 1999).

Baron *et al.* (1996a) documented this process in several studies focusing on the effects of *social corroboration*. In one case, college students read some material from the Multiple Sclerosis Society. They were then asked whether they planned to contribute to the Society. Almost all these students planned to donate. However, in addition, some students were given the impression that the other students around them also planned to make a donation. This social corroboration heightened the students' confidence in the wisdom of their choice and, more importantly, led them to pledge more money than control participants. Baron *et al.* also found that young women in college pubs gave more extreme and confident final attraction/ repulsion ratings to photos of young men if the female experimenter briefly corroborated (e.g. 'oh him' – said with approval) the participants' first impression. Luus and Wells (1994) reported similar results when eye-witnesses to a staged crime discovered that other 'witnesses' agreed with their identification from a photo line-up. This corroboration raised the witnesses' confidence during their videotaped testimony. This confidence, in turn, heightened how believable these witnesses appeared when others (e.g. jurors) viewed the witness video. Note that this occurred despite the fact that, in all cases, the witnesses had identified the *wrong* individual. In short, when social comparison reveals that most others corroborate one of our beliefs, this belief acquires a 'social reality' that contributes to high levels of confidence, which, in turn, can lead to extreme attitudes and behaviour, even when the initial belief in question turns out to be incor-rect. Of course, feeling confident about one's beliefs and judgments is comforting as well. One can act decisively without exerting costly mental effort when one feels certain about one's preferences and attitudes. In-deed, there is a well-documented tendency for individuals to exaggerate the extent to which other individuals share their opinions or behavioural choices (e.g. Marks and Miller 1987). For example, if you agree to wear a sign advocating a cause, you assume most others would too. If you have refused, you assume most others would refuse (Ross *et al.* 1977). This *false consensus effect* represents a means by which we can manufacture or amplify social corroboration for our opinions and actions even when such corroboration may not be justified. This may be due to our desire to bolster both our confidence and our self-esteem ('I'm not weird. Most people agree with me or would do what I have just done').

Social comparison can have another conceptually distinct effect, how-ever, in addition to providing consensus information. Festinger argued that group members prefer to be in agreement. Our discussion of the false consensus effect above suggests several reasons why this might be so. Thus, when social comparison results in disagreement, various attempts are made to resolve matters. Festinger observed that group members will first try to persuade each other but, if this fails, rejection of group deviates will result. In some cases, this 'rejection' will be primarily intellectual or perceptual and, as such, will only take place 'in the heads' of the majority. Thus, group members may decide that some people are so different or unusual that they provide a poor or inappropriate basis for social com-parison. For example, the early missionaries in Hawaii did not have their confidence shaken by the fact that the native Hawaiians did not share their views. As non-Christians, the Hawaiians' views were considered irrel-evant for purposes of social comparison. Similarly, majority members may decide that an opinion deviate is 'not really one of us' or 'is really weird about this issue'.

In other cases, however, social rejection can involve more than just intellectual rejection. This was illustrated in a classic study by Schachter (1951). In this study, confederates purposely and steadfastly disagreed with the others in their group as they discussed the case history of a young delinquent named Johnny Rocco. At the end of the session, this deviate received lower ratings of desirability than others and was more likely to be chosen by the group for a low-status job. Schachter *et al.* (1954) reported similar results when observing European schoolboys as they discussed the desirability of model airplanes they planned to build as a group. Do other kinds of differences provoke such rejection? The answer here is clearly 'yes' (for a review, see Levine 1989). In one notable study, Freedman and Doob (1968) simply led participants to believe that one of them had a personality profile that differed from the rest. Later, the group was required to select someone to receive electric shock. Somewhat disturbingly, the deviate was disproportionately selected for this duty, indicating that just being different led to negative consequences even in the absence of any difference in opinion.

Why does disagreement and deviation from group norms so often lead to rejection and abuse? There are four plausible answers. First, occasionally group consensus and conformity will be necessary for groups to reach crucial goals. Here dissent threatens such goals and, at the very least, is time-consuming and socially disruptive. As a result, it is likely to evoke irritation and social sanctions. This notion is closely related to the notion, discussed in Chapter 1, that norms help establish an orderly and predictable social environment. Second, when deviates disagree with a majority, this disagreement often increases uncertainty among people who would otherwise have the security of social consensus for their views. Thus, deviates undermine 'social reality'. Given the important role that understanding plays in human survival and adaptation, such uncertainty is often particularly disturbing. Third, disagreeing with a clear majority is often insulting to the majority ('You guys are all wrong. What dummies!'). Finally, disagreement will often be viewed as disloyalty to the group and its worldview and thereby threaten feelings of group solidarity and group esteem. For example, imagine a cohesive group that learns that one of their fellow group members does not share their view that their group leader should be excused for some moral transgression. Such disagreement must lower the other members' confidence in their own views and, moreover, makes it clear that the group is not the united, supportive entity the members hoped it was. Creating such uncomfortable feelings will often provoke punishment and dislike. In accord with this analysis, conditions that heighten uncertainty, fear and needs for group solidarity have been found to increase the inclination to punish individuals who violate group or cultural norms. For example, several studies that have induced people to think about their own death have found that such manipulations increase hostility directed at such norm violations as engaging in prostitution, making unpatriotic statements (Greenberg *et al.* 1995) and injuring another person (Florian and Mikulincer 1997).

OSTRACISM

Recently, researchers have become interested in the effects of the social rejection just discussed. It is obvious that physical attacks, verbal abuse, criticism and ridicule serve as punishing events that affect our mood and behaviour (Kowalski 1997, 2000; Leary *et al.* 1998). But rejection does not have to be this extreme to have powerful affects on our actions and feelings. Social groups have long used simple shunning, or social non-recognition of others, as a means of punishment or of expressing disapproval. And few people have not felt the pain of being socially excluded, whether as a child, a teen or an adult. In the last few years, however, researchers have begun to examine the nature of this process more closely. In some research, confederates have simply ignored a specified individual during discussions or during laboratory games (e.g. Gardner *et al.* 2000). For example, in one very simple manipulation, Williams *et al.* (2000) had the research participant play a game of ring toss or ball toss with several confederates and varied how much the confederates included the participant in the game. In some conditions, individuals are largely excluded from the game. Interestingly, manipulations like these (i.e. brief non-verbal rejection on an unimportant task) have been found to have a variety of interesting effects. Following such simple rejection, individuals report such feelings as depressed mood, loneliness, anxiety and helplessness (e.g. Williams *et al.* 1998). These effects are more pronounced when individuals blame themselves for the rejections (Nezlek *et al.* 1997). In one intriguing study, Williams *et al.* (2000) used the Internet to recruit more than 1000 participants from across the world. Participants played a cyber version of a ring-toss game in which the flight of the ring from 'person to person' was depicted on the computer screen. By varying the computer display, Williams *et al.* were able to vary how included or excluded people were during the game. Here, too, being rejected, even by unknown others whom one would never meet, led to lowered feelings of mood and self-esteem. Indeed, just having individuals imagine they are being ignored can lead to more negative self-evaluations (e.g. Craighead *et al.* 1979).

Why do such simple acts of social exclusion have such strong effects? One answer is that social disapproval is a stimulus that has been associated with a wide variety of unpleasant events from the moment of our birth. In contrast, social approval has similarly been associated with an equally varied array of rewarding events. Skinner (1969) labelled such stimuli *general reinforcers* and argued that they serve as extremely powerful, long-lived conditioned rewards. This provides one explanation for the widely accepted belief that most individuals are deeply disturbed by social rejection of all types (Baumeister and Leary 1995). In addition, social exclusion can make it impossible for one to engage in social comparison. Social isolates, therefore, often find it difficult to gain social verification for their beliefs. This will often elevate their level of uncertainty, which, in turn, gives rise to anxiety and indecisiveness. Williams (1997) adds that ostracism threatens human needs to feel a sense of belonging, to feel in control, to have positive self-esteem and to live an engaged and meaningful life. As a result, Williams argues that ostracism leads individuals to compensate or reaffirm such needs, either through overt behaviour or through cognitive distortion. The former might involve such behavioural strategies as: stronger efforts at a group task (to bolster self-esteem or gain group acceptance); attempts at ingratiation, compromise and conformity (to foster belongingness); greater preparation, communication attempts and information-seeking (to heighten control); and identification with important or high-status reference groups (to bolster one's sense of meaningful existence). The alternative strategy is to use cognitive distortion or biased recall to bolster such needs. For example, people might make a special effort to remember the groups that have not rejected them.

At this point, there is tentative support for at least a few of these 'compensation' predictions. For example, Gardner *et al.* (2000) manipulated social rejection in a computer chat group and found that rejected individuals had better memory for the social events described in a diary as opposed to the individual events, perhaps reminding themselves of their own social life. Similarly, Williams *et al.* (2000) found that rejection in the ring-toss game heightened one's tendency to agree with others. Furthermore, Williams and Sommer (1997) found that women who were ostracized by the ball-toss procedure increased their efforts at a collective task (listing uses for an object). Interestingly, the opposite was found to be true with rejected men – males tended to reduce their effort at the group task after having been ostracized by fellow (male) group members. Perhaps these men were reacting to their rejection by disengaging from and devaluing the group. Further research is required to improve our knowledge of the psychological impact of actual or threatened social exclusion or ostracism. But in light of the existing research, corroborated by personal experience, there is little debate that ostracism and more extreme forms of social rejection represent potent forces of social control and social influence. Fear of such rejection is often a powerful force that induces individuals to accept influence from those around them.

CONFORMITY

Classic studies

One of the more dramatic examples of being socially influenced by the opinions, behaviours and performances of those around us is illustrated by conformity research. Conformity loosely refers to cases in which individuals change their attitudes, verbal statements or behaviours to adhere more closely to some salient social norm. In some cases, this can be in response to verbal arguments made by other group members but, in classic conformity studies, individuals change their actions or judgments just after hearing the judgments made by others without hearing any elaborate reasons. Sherif's study of the autokinetic effect, described in Chapter 1, was an early example of this approach. In this study, you will remember, individuals ended up agreeing about how far a stationary light point was moving after hearing each other's estimates. This effect is powerful and well replicated. One study by Rohrer *et al.* (1954) re-tested individual participants a year after their original exposure to the group norm and found evidence that the original norm still affected their judgments. In a slightly different version of this study, Jacobs and Campbell (1961) slowly rotated group members out of a group, replacing them with new group members. Original norms were manipulated through the use of confederates, who made relatively large estimates of light movement. This study and several others that followed (MacNeil and Sherif 1976) indicated that norms such as these could continue to affect the judgments of group members for up to eight 'generations' after the departure of original group members and confederates. Thus, the norm in a sense acquired a 'life of its own'.

The type of social influence seen in these classic conformity studies can stem from either or both of two forces: one based on group power (potential rejection and punishment) and the other based on trust in group opinion. The first, *normative* social influence, refers to influence caused by the rewards and punishments controlled by the group, whereas the second, *informational* social influence, refers generally to the tendency to rely upon social definitions of reality, especially those based on group consensus (Deutsch and Gerard 1955). Whereas both normative and informational influence may provoke changes in private beliefs, normative social influence is capable of provoking changes in behaviour even when the group has not changed the private attitudes of group members. This form of social influence is referred to as *compliance*. The term *internalization*, in contrast, refers to cases in which private belief change has occurred. Informational social influence is most likely to provoke this form of change. The term 'conformity' has been used to describe both forms of social influence.

The incoming freshmen Newcomb (1943) studied at Bennington College found themselves among strangers at a developmental stage in their lives when their intellectual and conceptual horizons were rapidly expanding and they were busy shaping their identities as young adults. For such young women, both informational and normative influence must have operated strongly to exert pressure toward conformity to the relatively liberal political views that characterized the campus milieu. At one level, these beliefs and the information that was associated with them simply concerned the laws of economics, political science and sociology as asserted by peers and authoritative teachers. In addition, however, if a student endorsed these views, it affected the approval and disapproval that would be received from others on campus. In turn, this approval or disapproval governed one's social status on the campus. In short, both informational and normative pressures produced conformity at Bennington College.

The social influence observed in Sherif's (1936) autokinetic situation is probably primarily due to just one of these two processes. Participants, literally, find themselves in the dark, lacking any physical standard against which to compare the position of the dot of light. Because they are uncertain, they are easily influenced by others' ideas and responses. In short, conformity here appears to be strongly affected by informational social influence. Although ambiguity, such as that in the study of Sherif, clearly does increase conformity, there is good reason to argue that it is not absolutely necessary. In another classic study of conformity effects, Solomon Asch (1956) asked groups of students at Haverford College to estimate which of three comparison lines matched a fourth 'test' line. Left to themselves, control students completed this task correctly 98 per cent of the time. Experimental participants, however, offered their estimates only after hearing the responses of several other students who, unknown to them, were confederates. The group judged many stimulus sets, on two-thirds of which (the 'critical' trials) the confederates systematically agreed on a clearly incorrect match. What did the participants do when faced with this collective madness? Despite the blatant incorrectness of the group choice, participants conformed with this norm on over a third of all critical trials. Indeed, with incorrect confederate feedback, 76 per cent of participants conformed with at least one of these blatantly incorrect group judgments despite the fact that, even after they publicly agreed with the group, most participants stated that the 'group choice' did not look 'correct' to them. On the basis of these self-report data, most theorists have assumed that normative pressures (concerns about not offending the group) played a strong role in provoking the social influence observed in this study. However, it would appear that conformity in such studies may involve more than normative influence. A recent meta-analytic review of over 90 Asch-type conformity studies by Bond and Smith (1996) indicated that, when one 'averages' over such studies, conformity is *not* higher when participants believe that their responses will be disclosed to the majority. If conformity in the Asch paradigm were completely a function of normative group pressure, one would expect such a lack of anonymity to heighten conformity. As a result, it would appear that informational social influence accounts for some of the change provoked in Asch-type studies. Perhaps the incorrect confederate feedback in such studies confuses participants to the extent that they become open to the idea that the confederates may be correct. Thus, informational social influence may play a far greater role in Asch-type studies of conformity than many researchers have previously recognized.

The benefits of conformity

These classic studies highlight the fact that conformity processes can often produce irrational or erroneous judgments. This stress on the irrational is due in part to a desire by researchers to determine whether conformity pressure is strong enough to undermine our confidence in our own powers of reasoning and perception. Although it is now clear that conformity can provoke errors in reasoning, we should not lose sight of the fact that conformity pressure for the most part serves crucial societal functions (Cialdini *et al.* 1991) and that conformity to social norms often is sensible and necessary. Thus, one reason why people fall back on the heuristic notion that 'all those people can't be wrong' is because, when a group of individuals agree collectively on some judgment, it is because that conclusion is justified more often than not. It is only in instances in which this heuristic is not justified that conformity leads to errors in judgment and perception. In addition, as noted in Chapter 1, conformity pressure insures social regularity and predictability that is essential for coordinated and efficient group action. Conformity pressure also provides one means of controlling group members, thereby increasing the likelihood that they will consider group interests as well as their own. This form of social control affects a wide range of behaviours, but is especially crucial for public-spirited actions such as water and energy conservation, not driving while intoxicated, providing aid to the unfortunate and conducting one's daily affairs with integrity. Consequently, it is not surprising that human groups place much emphasis on being able to elicit conformity from group members. In many cases, such conformity will be essential to group success and survival. As one extreme example, combat units would have little chance of surviving were it not for the very strong norms that call for loyalty and mutual support from squad members even in the face of intense danger.

Conformity data

Ally and group size effects

Conformity effects have been reported across such a wide range of judgments and participant groups that they represent one of the most substantiated and fundamental sets of phenomena in social psychology. For example, conformity has been observed on auditory judgments, aesthetic preferences, visual judgments and case-history decisions, to name just a few. Indeed, our reactions to everything, from wine to politics, is susceptible to conformity pressure. However, Asch's early studies indicated that conformity effects do not invariably occur when majorities pressure deviates. In one study (Asch 1955), conformity dropped to 10 per cent if two naive participants – as opposed to one – faced the incorrect majority. In short, conformity effects are undermined when the deviate finds that he or she is not alone in disagreeing with the majority. Indeed, Wilder and Allen (1977) found this to be true in an Asch-like context even when the two 'deviates' disagreed with each other, so long as they also disagreed with the majority. Thus, if a few brave souls are willing to stand up to a group majority, group pressure can be seriously weakened. As we have seen, however, being the person who takes the first step along this path can be perilous.

Another key finding in Asch's early work was that conformity increased as the size of the majority increased. However, this occurred only up to a point. When the majority contained approximately three members, conformity levelled off (Asch 1955). This result has been replicated many times (cf. Tanford and Penrod 1984). At least in part, these results stem from the fact that, after the majority has more than three members, participants begin to suspect that some of the majority are just going along with the group to avoid trouble (see below) and do not really share the majority view. As proof of this, Wilder (1977) demonstrated that when participants were sure that members of the majority were unaware of each others' views (and, therefore, independent of each other), majorities of size six caused more conformity than those of size three at least on certain judgments (e.g. how much a damage award should be). A second reason why conformity increases only slightly after the majority increases beyond three is that, as group size grows, each person added to the majority is noticed less; in social influence, as in many economic contexts, there appears to be a law of 'diminishing returns' (Latané 1981). Finally, Campbell and Fairey (1989) pointed out that the size of the majority is likely to have more impact on one's social influence when group influence stems primarily from group power (in that group size enhances such normative social influence) rather than from group persuasion (when even two confederates can create informational social influence). Thus, they found that the size of the majority was most important when the group norm was clearly wrong and social influence represented superficial public compliance.

A smorgasboard of other conformity findings

The findings discussed above represent just a small part of what we have learned about conformity over the years. Other critical results are listed below. People conform more when:

1 The judgment or opinion at issue is difficult (Bond and Smith 1996): social comparison needs are stronger under uncertainty.
2 They face a unanimous group consensus (Asch 1956; Wilder and Allen 1977): 'all those people cannot be wrong' and isolated deviates are most likely to be rejected and punished.
3 They value or admire the group (Back 1951; David and Turner 1996): rejection by one's friends or those we admire is particularly threatening.
4 They are scared (Darley 1966; Dolinski and Nawrat 1998): fear is thought to undermine confidence (Darley 1966), decrease our processing ability (Dolinski and Nawrat 1998) and heighten our desire to reaffirm our group allegiances (Greenberg et al. 1995; Florian and Mikulincer 1997).
5 They live in cultures in which cooperation, collectivism and harmony are highly valued, for example East Asia (Bond and Smith 1996; Cialdini et al. 1999; Kim and Markus 1999).
6 They are confronted by a majority that shows non-verbal signs of confidence (Baron et al. 1996b).

And people conform less when:

1 They have great confidence in their expertise on the issue or the judgement is quite easy (Deutsch and Gerard 1955): informational social influence is low.
2 They have high social status (Harvey and Consalvi 1960).
3 They are strongly committed to their initial view (Deutsch and Gerard 1955).
4 They do not like, respect or identify with the source of social influence (Hogg and Turner 1987; David and Turner 1996).
5 The majority shows non-verbal signs of low confidence (Baron et al. 1996b).

Gender and conformity

In several early studies, women were found to conform more than men. However, a careful review by Eagly (1978) of some 61 face-to-face conformity studies revealed that, in most, men and women conformed equally. In a minority of studies ($n = 23$), however, differences between the sexes did exist and, when they did, women were far more likely to conform than men [see also Bond and Smith's (1996) meta-analytic data]. This was due in part to testing conformity with materials on which men are more confident (sports as opposed to fashion). Second, men are also more concerned with appearing independent of others. Males do not conform less than women when their responses are anonymous. It is only under public scrutiny that males tend to resist social influence more than women. (Eagly *et al.* 1981). Third, women have been historically socialized to maintain social harmony in groups; this often involved assuming a deferential and submissive role. This, of course, would make them more vulnerable to conformity pressure. Interestingly, Eagly (1978) found more evidence of female conformity in older studies. It would appear, then, that changes in women's socialization is changing their susceptibility to social influence.

RECENT RESEARCH ON CONFORMITY

Priming

Several lines of research supplement the well-known conformity results listed above. In the last few years, various studies have indicated that conformity can be affected by the types of words, images or stories that people have recently encountered, especially when these images remind (or *prime*) the individual of such issues as conformity, independence or social rejection. For example, Epley and Gilovich (1999) had participants work on a sentence-completion task that involved generating several conformity-related words (e.g. agree, obey). They found that participants agreed more with others about the enjoyability of this task than individuals who had not been primed. Similarly, Pendry and Carrick (2001) primed individuals by showing them photographs associated with either rebellion (a punk rock fan) or conformity (an accountant). As expected, the conformity prime increased conformity in an auditory version of the Asch paradigm, whereas the rebellion prime reduced such conformity. Finally, Janes and Olson (2000) showed some participants a video of comedians ridiculing other people. Other participants saw comic routines based on self-ridicule or no ridicule. Participants were then asked to rate the humour of a printed cartoon after seeing the ratings of others. Conformity on this rating was greater among those who saw the 'ridicule others' video. In short, reminding participants of images related to conformity, rebellion and social ridicule have all been found to affect conformity. The 'ridicule-priming' results appear to reflect the greater likelihood that participants exposed to such primes will tend to think spontaneously about the social rejection that frequently is directed at opinion deviates. This, of course, could affect their willingness to disagree with others. It is still unclear, however, why thinking about 'accountants' or writing words such as 'obey' would make individuals more susceptible to social pressure. Perhaps these are socially approved images that legitimize the image of conformity. Further research on such topics is warranted.

Task importance

One limitation of almost all conformity research is that the decisions or judgments used are usually not very important to the participants. Who cares how far some light is moving or which line-length matches which? It is possible that, on more important issues, people will be more likely to ignore group influence and remain true to their own opinions. If this is the case, the laboratory research on conformity could overestimate the frequency of this phenomenon and the extent to which it has affected important historical decisions. Indeed, the rates of conformity previously reported (e.g. 80 per cent of trials by Sherif 1936) could be akin to laboratory 'hot house plants': obtainable only with the minimally important judgments collected in the typical social psychology laboratory.

Baron *et al.* (1996b) addressed this question by carefully manipulating the importance of their participants' conformity judgments. In the high importance condition, participants were told that people who finished an eyewitness identification task with the fewest errors would receive a $20 payment. They were also told that the eyewitness task was a well-regarded test of actual eyewitness ability. In the low importance condition, no money was mentioned and the task was described as a pilot test. In accord with the 'hot house' criticism, Baron *et al.* found that, when the task was made exceptionally easy (comparable to the task in Asch 1956), conformity dropped from 33 per cent of critical trials to 16 per cent when the task increased in importance. However, when the task was altered so that it was only moderately difficult, the results were quite different. In this case, when the judgment was important, conformity *increased* so that it occurred on more than 50 per cent of the critical trials, compared with 35 per cent when the task was less important. Moreover, so long as the confederates appeared confident, the more people conformed, the greater was their confidence in their incorrect final opinion. In short, given a modicum of ambiguity, conformity increased as it became more important to participants to offer an accurate judgment. Note that this occurred despite the fact that the group norm was incorrect. That conformity in this study occurred even when decisions were important to participants provides some support to those who argue that many important historical decisions were affected by conformity phenomena. Given that such decisions generally entail some ambiguity, Baron and co-workers' findings suggest that their importance actually might heighten the degree of social influence. Why is this? One plausible explanation is that if the judgment is difficult, individuals may lack the capacity to make a confident judgment by simply studying the problem. What else might they use to reach closure; closure that they deeply crave, given the importance of the issue? The answer would seem to be that, if others appear to be in agreement, this consensus is used as a hint or cue to settle the issue ('All those folks can't be wrong'). Thus, not only do we depend upon social reality to give meaning to situations, we are also especially prone to rely upon it when the judgment is difficult and important.

Group identification

Most social psychologists attribute conformity effects to informational and normative social influence. These forces can operate jointly or independently. Thus, you could be completely certain that you are right and the group is wrong (no informational social influence) and still conform because you really want to be accepted by the group (high normative social influence). As we have seen, such *compliance* describes adhering to a group norm despite harbouring strong private reservations about its legitimacy (as in Asch 1956; for a more elaborate discussion of varieties of social influence, see Nail *et al.* 2000). Given that compliance occurs because of group pressure, it is likely to persist only as long as such normative social influence is present. Internalized change, however, is thought to be more lasting. One means of provoking such lasting change is to have the group appeal to the logic, intelligence, vested interests and cherished values of the individual. Another source of such internalized change stems from circumstances in which the individual feels strong identification with the group – that is, has the desire to consider themselves as a loyal, typical and accepted group member. Kelman (1958) noted this almost 50 years ago, when he specified *identification* as an important source of social influence. In Kelman's view, social influence of this type occurs because it allows the targets of such influence to see themselves as being more like the individuals they admire and respect.

More recently, proponents of *self-categorization theory* have championed a modification of this view. These writers believe that classical explanations of conformity give too much consideration to the rational/intellectual processes of persuasion outlined above. Instead, they argue that group members process what the group has to say to figure out what norm the group favours, rather than why the norm might be sensible or in the individual group member's best interest (e.g. Hogg *et al.* 1990; Turner 1991). Self-categorization theory assumes that group members have strong needs to see themselves as 'solid' or typical members of the groups they find themselves part of. One of the best ways to accomplish this is to conform to *prototypic group norms*. Such norms are positions that allow the individual to be as much like other group members as possible, while at the same time being unlike members of competing outgroups. Thus, if members of an extreme leftist group donated $50 on average to support an immigrant rent strike, but more moderate liberals – the outgroup – donated $20 on average, the prototypic norm within the radical group might be $55. This norm is quite similar to the average amount donated within the group, but also maximizes the dissimilarity between the ingroup (we donate more) and the outgroup (they donate less). Thus, according to the self-categorization view, conformity occurs because ingroup members attempt to adhere to the prototypic norms that characterize and distinguish their group (e.g. Abrams and Hogg 1990; Turner 1991). Note that often the prototypic norms encourage group members to become collectively more extreme over time. But this is not always true. According to this view, compromise or averaging effects seen in such conformity studies as that of Sherif (1936) will occur if participants envision two or more outgroups, with one offering higher estimates than the ingroup and the other(s) offering lower estimates (Hogg *et al.* 1990).

There is some support for some of these predictions. Thus, Hogg *et al.* (1990) offer some evidence for the creation of prototypic norms. In this study, individuals were told that they had been assigned to a group that would soon debate with an outgroup on the topic of risk-taking. The participants were also allowed to hear a taped discussion of their own group on this topic. Some participants were told that their debate rivals endorsed very risky decisions, whereas others were told that these outgroups favoured very cautious decisions. In a third condition, participants were told about groups favouring both extremes. Before the discussion, participants predicted the position that their group would finally favour for the debate. This served as one measure of the ingroup prototype; that is, the norm that would mark the group as united and distinct. As expected, when the outgroup was depicted as very cautious, the participants predicted the final ingroup consensus (i.e. the prototype) to be more risky than the depicted group average. In contrast, when the outgroup norm was described as very risky, the predicted ingroup consensus was more cautious than the depicted group average. Finally, when two extreme outgroups were thought to be present, the predicted consensus did not differ from the group average. Moreover, the authors reported some results indicating that, after hearing a sample of group discussion, group members changed their opinions to agree more closely with the predicted consensus. These results suggest that individuals react to outgroup information when they hear about it. However, this does not establish that people think 'automatically' about such outgroups whenever they find themselves exposed to social pressure. This more extreme prediction from self-categorization theory has yet to be tested. We will discuss this study further in the next chapter, in our discussion of group polarization.

The above results are supplemented by the findings of several studies that various forms of social influence are more effective if they stem from ingroup rather than outgroup members (e.g. Abrams et al. 1990; David and Turner 1996). Thus, David and Turner (1996) found that environmentally oriented teenagers in Australia were not persuaded by a recorded message about environmental policy if it supposedly came from members of a non-environmental group (favouring logging); the opposite occurred among teenagers favouring logging. Although these results are congruent with self-categorization theory, they could also be due to the simple fact that ingroup members are viewed as more trustworthy and knowledgeable than outgroup members. However, these teenagers also shifted their position *away* from the outgroup after hearing the message, just as predicted by self-categorization theory. Moreover, these teenagers were in fact influenced by the same messages when they were said to represent the opinions of ingroup members. This movement away from the outgroup position certainly supports the idea that conformity and social influence are affected by group members' concerns about maintaining their distinctiveness from outgroup members.

A core assumption of self-categorization theory is that the groups we identify with contribute heavily to our self-image as individuals. If this assumption is valid, how might individuals react if they find that people with whom they strongly identify disagree with them on important issues? Alternatively, how might people react if they learn that they *agree* with members of a disliked outgroup? Several recent studies by Wendy Wood and her associates at Texas A&M University offer insights into such issues. This work capitalizes on the fact that many A&M students ('Aggies') feel intense loyalty and identification with the university and its conservative values. In one study, Wood *et al.* (1996) told A&M students that the average 'Aggie' disagreed with them on several attitudinal issues (e.g. regarding the use of marijuana). These students were more likely to change their attitude when told this than when told than an outgroup (foreign students at A&M) disagreed with them. In addition, when given the chance, the participants reinterpreted the meaning of certain key words in the attitude statements so that they could more easily agree with them. For example, these (anti-drug) students were likely to view the words 'I approve of marijuana use' as meaning 'I dislike marijuana use but tolerate it in others' when they learned that other 'Aggies' expressed such approval. Most crucially, these changes only occurred among the students who reported that they strongly identified with being an 'Aggie'. In a second, complementary study, Wood *et al.* informed students that a disliked outgroup (radical feminists) agreed with them on one such statement. Here, those who identified strongly as 'Aggies' reinterpreted key words in the statement so that they could justify *disagreeing* with this outgroup.

Buehler and Griffin (1994; Griffin and Beuhler 1993) also reported related reinterpretation effects when Canadian college students made decisions about such things as a risk-decision problem or a news story on possible police brutality after first learning of the responses of others. The reinterpretation effects in the Texas studies are consistent with the idea that individuals want to believe that they are, in fact, still similar to the admired ingroup and not similar to the rejected outgroup. The reinterpretation provoked by the desire to conform also indicates that, if people conform, they often need to feel there is some sensible reason for changing their opinion. This is congruent with the idea that conformity can have implications for sense of self, in that we want to see ourselves as sensible, rational individuals, not as easily swayed conformers. In accord with this view, Pool *et al.* (1998) found that when Texas A&M students discovered that they either agreed with a disliked outgroup or disagreed with other 'Aggies', they suffered a drop in self-esteem that was evident weeks later (*unless* they were encouraged to engage in the creative reinterpretation shown in the earlier study).

These studies document the important role played by group identification in provoking conformity and, more importantly, provide some of the most direct support for the view that conformity is linked to feelings about self-adequacy. As such, this work supports several key assumptions of self-categorization theory's account of social influence and conformity. This, of course, does not establish that all aspects of the theory are true. For instance, it is not clear from any of this research that individuals will generally ignore intelligent and well-reasoned arguments from outgroup members, or that they care little about perceptual accuracy and are concerned only about seeing themselves as loyal, prototypic group members, these being some of the more controversial predictions of self-categorization theory. In addition, the results of Pool *et al.* (1998) and Wood *et al.* (1996) indicate that self-esteem effects and re-definition effects only occur when individuals identify deeply with, or are strongly repulsed by, the groups in question. The strongest statements of self-categorization theory, in contrast, argue that such effects should occur even if we find ourselves in groups that we do not care that much about (Turner 1991). The results of Pool *et al.* and Wood *et al.* do not support that more extreme position. However, it would appear that concerns about being a loyal and typical group member do have important effects on conformity and social influence, at least in groups in which group identification is strong.

MINORITY AND MAJORITY INFLUENCE

The early years of research on social influence focused almost exclusively on how individuals were affected by group majorities. In the 1970s, however, some researchers essentially turned the tables (e.g. Moscovici and Lage 1976). If social influence always was directed from majorities to deviates, they asked, why was there ever any social change or innovation (Moscovici 1980)? Why did ideas about music, hairstyle, clothing and politics change? Why weren't we all still listening to Mozart (or jungle drums for that matter)? Why didn't we all still believe the world was flat? Obviously, majorities were not always successful in influencing deviates and, equally obviously, it is clear that, at least on occasion, minorities can have a dramatic influence on majorities. The first theorist to champion this (minority) position was Serge Moscovici, who conducted several studies of colour perception (e.g. Moscovici *et al.* 1969). In this research, Moscovici and his collaborators observed that when minorities (actually two confederates) offered unusual colour judgments (labelling blue as green), they were more likely to affect participants' private beliefs than when majorities offered these judgments. In this early research, individuals were more likely to agree publicly with the majority than with the minority, but in private sessions (away from the group) their beliefs were influenced most by minorities (for reviews, see Moscovici 1980; Maass and Clark 1984; Moscovici *et al.* 1994).

Why might this be true? Moscovici (1980) argued that because of the size and power of the majority, we primarily pay attention to *what* the majority demands of us rather than *why* they demand it. Thus, according to Moscovici's *conversion theory*, our public agreement with the majority is due to our desire to avoid ridicule and punishment rather than to any genuine private attitude change. This, of course, is a form of compliance. Stated differently, we are so focused on how the majority is reacting to us that we have little inclination to carefully process any logical reasons presented by the majority (Mugny and Perez 1991).

Minorities, on the other hand, are far less powerful. They are, however, unusual and provocative. In addition, minorities show courage when they disagree with a majority view. As a result, they may appear highly confident, committed and sincere. Moscovici (1980) argued that these qualities increase the likelihood that we will listen carefully to minorities as they express their views. And, as long as the minority actually has some good arguments (Kerr 2001a), this in turn makes it more likely that we will experience a genuine change in our beliefs in response to minority influence, a process Moscovici refers to as *conversion*. This 'conversion' is similar to the notion of internalized social influence described above. However, these converted beliefs will generally not be expressed publicly due to fear of rejection by the majority (Mugny and Perez 1991). Rather, they will be expressed privately or later in time or on related topics. Moscovici (1980) offered these ideas as very strong predictions. Thus, he stated that the *only* way of producing conversion was through minority group influence and that such conversion would only be expressed in private or indirectly. A complementary prediction was his assertion that our reaction to minority influence would *always* be a thoughtful one, whereas our reaction to majority influence would *never* involve such reflection. These strong statements were most probably made to encourage debate and research, but it is safe to say that Moscovici and his associates feel that, at the very least, minority influence is far more likely than majority influence to elicit careful thought and private belief change (Mugny and Perez 1991).

Moscovici's provocative predictions were bolstered by the results of several early experiments. In addition to the colour-naming studies conducted by Moscovici and his associates, Maass and Clark (1983), for example, had participants read passages on gay rights in which minority and majority positions were obvious. The participants then had to indicate how they themselves felt about these issues. In some cases, this was done quite anonymously; in other cases, however, the participants expected their responses to be made known to the others at their session. Regardless of whether the minority favoured gay rights (in some sessions) or opposed it (in other sessions), individuals tended to agree with the minority (and, therefore, oppose the majority view) when their opinion was to be kept private. In public conditions, however, just the opposite occurred. In brief, these and other related findings (for a review, see Wood *et al.* 1994) provided initial evidence that minorities can have substantial influence on opinions and judgments, even more than majorities under certain conditions (i.e. on delayed or indirect attitude topics; Crano and Chen 1998). Others have reported minority influence on topics as varied as a civil injury case (Wolf 1979), the Stroop colour/word task (Peterson and Nemeth 1996), abortion (Maass *et al.* 1982), foreign immigration (Mugny 1975), senior comprehensive exams (Trost *et al.* 1992) and college admission tests (De Dreu and De Vries 1993). In most of these cases, conversion occurred on private, delayed or indirect measures, as Moscovici predicted. However, this general outcome does not definitively confirm the very strong version of conversion theory that Moscovici outlined in his 1980 paper. That is, we need to examine whether minority influence always evokes more careful processing and more lasting private attitude change than majority influence. Similarly, we also need to evaluate Moscovici's contention that majority influence never, or rarely, provokes a careful consideration of the arguments, facts, and so on regarding the issue in question.

The afterimage study

Until recently, most research on minority influence focused on the contention that it is uniquely effective at producing private, long-lasting and indirect attitude change. Moscovici and Personnaz (1980, 1986) designed a particularly ingenious study to address this issue, which relied on the fact that, just after seeing a bright colour slide in a dark room, we tend to see the complementary colour as an afterimage. Specifically, a green slide should evoke a red/purple afterimage, whereas a blue slide should evoke a yellow/orange afterimage. Moreover, very few people know this fact. Consequently, Moscovici and Personnaz reasoned that if minority influence really was leading people to 'see' blue slides as green, they should be more likely to see a red/purple afterimage than people exposed to a majority. In addition, such a response would be unlikely to represent deliberate falsification by the participant (e.g. compliance) because most participants have no idea of what afterimages are caused by the various colours. The results of several of Moscovici and Personnaz' experiments were very encouraging. For example, in one, participants examined five blue slides. Before offering their own description of each, they heard a confederate describe the slide as green. This caused very little overt compliance. Only 5 per cent of participants said the slide was green. However, when this confederate was described as a minority, participants were more likely to report seeing the red/purple afterimage (that would be triggered by truly seeing a green slide) than when the confederate was part of a majority.

This remarkable result is particularly impressive when one considers that afterimages are caused by the pattern of stimulation of rods and cones in the retina. Thus, these results imply that minority influence actually led the eye to respond to the blue stimulus as if it were a green stimulus. Astounding! Astonishing! Implausible? And, unfortunately, not well replicated. Although Moscovici and Personnaz (1986) did report a successful replication of their 1980 result, at least four other attempts to replicate closely Moscovici and Personnaz's work have failed to corroborate their original findings (Doms and van Avermaet 1980; Sorrentino *et al.* 1980; Martin 1995, 1998). Martin (1998), in a particularly painstaking series of replication studies, found that people who were told that 'blue was green' did report a red/purple afterimage, as expected after a green slide. Moreover, these reports increased over trials, particularly among suspicious individuals. However, this 'afterimage-increase' occurred equally in the majority and minority conditions and, even then, only when a slide containing both blue and green hues was used.

Martin's (1998) finding that the 'afterimage effect' was pronounced among the most suspicious participants echoes an earlier report by Sorrentino *et al.* (1980). Thus, these afterimage shifts may well have occurred when surprise or suspicion led individuals to stare more closely at the greenish aspects of the slide, thereby heightening the predicted afterimage. But, contrary to Moscovici's claim, minority opinion does not appear more likely than majority influence to provoke such close examination; nor does this appear to be a case of getting individuals to see *pure* blue slides as green. Nevertheless, Moscovici's afterimage research represented a highly creative attempt to deal with an extremely slippery issue – that is, proving that a particular instance of social influence primarily reflects internalized belief change as opposed to some subtle form of compliance. Although this particular experimental procedure has been shown to be unreliable, experimenters continue to explore aspects of Moscovici's model. Subsequent research does indicate that, under certain conditions, minority influence can be an effective source of influence (compared with a no-influence control), can provoke more creative thinking in groups (e.g. Nemeth and Rogers 1996) and, in rare cases (Wood *et al.* 1994), can prove more effective than majority influence under specified circumstances (e.g. Maass and Clark 1983; Crano and Chen 1998).

Summing across studies

Wood *et al.* (1994) conducted a meta-analysis of 97 minority influence studies to evaluate Moscovici's assertions. *Meta-analyses* are used to estimate the 'average' strength of a treatment effect across several related studies. Wood *et al.* reported that, in accord with Moscovici's view and early conformity research, 'on average' majorities were more effective than minorities at producing change on publicly expressed opinions (e.g. Maass and Clark 1983). They also found that individuals exposed to minority views were most likely to change their opinions when they responded privately about topics that were only indirectly related to the focal topic originally addressed by the minority (e.g. Alvaro and Crano 1997). In fact, this indirect change has been found even when the direct and indirect attitudes have no logical link but are just part of a constellation of liberal or conservative beliefs. Thus, Alvaro and Crano (1997) found that, when individuals heard a conservative, anti-gay message from a minority (as opposed to a majority), they were more likely to increase their *opposition to gun control*, another conservative attitude. In fairness, however, Wood *et al.* found that this ability of minorities to provoke indirect attitude change varied from study to study. Thus, it is a rather unstable effect. Importantly, there was also some evidence that minorities were more persuasive than majorities when people were asked to express their views on indirect topics privately (e.g. Crano and Chen 1998). All of these trends are congruent with Moscovici's model. Contrary to Moscovici's prediction, however, 'on average' majorities were *more* persuasive than minorities on the primary 'focal' issue, even when people expressed their views privately (e.g. Trost *et al.* 1992; De Dreu and De Vries 1996). Thus, minority influence can be more persuasive than majority influence, but only in certain circumstances. We discuss these circumstances below.

Variables affecting minority influence

Recent research has clarified some of the conditions that either limit or enhance minority influence. Trost *et al.* (1992), for example, found that audiences were less persuaded by minorities than majorities when the audience began the study strongly opposed to the position advocated by the minority or majority. Trost and colleagues' preferred explanation for this was that strongly opposed individuals are highly motivated to defend their views and feel freer to reject and ridicule minorities due to their relatively low power. Several other studies have found that minority influence is only likely to be effective when it comes from ingroup members (e.g. David and Turner 1996; Alvaro and Crano 1997). For example, David and Turner (1996) found that minority influence had few effects on the private beliefs of pro-environmental high school students in Australia if they heard a minority message from students who were in sympathy with the logging industry. In fact, in this case, the audiences actually changed their private attitudes in an opposite direction (see also Wood *et al*. 1996; Pool *et al*. 1998). However, when David and Turner attributed the message to a minority of pro-environmental students, private change did occur. Apparently, not only are outgroup members often rejected as a source of social comparison, but they also appear to serve as negative reference groups from which we wish to distance ourselves. Findings such as these have led some writers to conclude that, for the most part, minority influence actually impedes rather than helps acceptance of the message (Wood 2000), with the exception being influence from ingroup minorities on issues of low importance to the target of influence (e.g. Trost and Kenrick 1994; Kerr, in press).

Within this context, it is interesting to examine studies that have focused on how to improve minority influence. This research suggests that the most effective form of minority influence occurs when the minority consists of more than one individual and they are in basic agreement. For example, Moscovici and Lage (1976) found that a minority of one exerted practically no influence over colour judgments when the minority asserted that blue was green, but that when two minority individuals made this judgment, minority influence was evident in both public and private responses of the majority. One key reason for these findings is that a minority of one can be dismissed by the majority as a 'weirdo' or a fool, but this reaction is more difficult to support when two or more people serve as the minority. Research on minority influence has also suggested that the minority should hold their position consistently over time to maximize their influence. Research by Mugny and Papastamou (1975–6), however, suggests that this consistency should avoid the appearance of rigidity and refusal to compromise. These researchers varied whether messages from minorities (on the topic of pollution) used flexible, moderate language or a more doctrinaire style. Only the former was effective in influencing listeners. McLeod *et al*. (1997) varied whether group members were face-to-face or in a computer chat group and found that minority influence was only significant in the face-to-face setting. Apparently, the majority appreciates the courage and commitment it takes to express dissenting views in a face-to-face setting. In short, there is much support for the notion that minorities can influence majorities, but there do seem to be some crucial limits to this phenomenon.

The two-process model

Although the initial research on minority influence focused on whether minorities were more persuasive than majorities on private and indirect attitudes, more recent research has focused on Moscovici's provocative contention that minority influence is the primary means of getting individuals to think carefully about the merits of an issue. The idea that minorities influence us by using reason, whereas majorities influence us by using their social power, has come to be known as the *two-process view of conversion*.

It is clear from several recent studies that Moscovici seriously over-stated his case regarding the mindlessness of majority influence (see Wood 2000). These studies indicate that majority influence will often provoke careful message processing; indeed, in most cases it triggers more careful processing than that evoked by minority influence (for a review, see Martin and Hewstone 2001). For example, despite some evidence of better recall of minority message content (Moscovici 1980), Mackie (1987) found that majority arguments were better remembered and generated more novel thoughts about the issue than did minority arguments (see also Tesser *et al.* 1983). Similarly, De Dreu and De Vries (1996) provided Dutch students with arguments favouring college entrance tests and found that both majority and minority arguments led the students to engage in thoughtful processing of the arguments, as measured by the time they spent reading the material. Moreover, on the focal issue, the cognitive activity triggered by majority arguments was positively correlated with attitude change on the topic, a sign of thoughtful attitude change (but see Maass and Clark 1983). In contrast, in the minority influence condition, these correlations were lower and non-significant. Crano and Chen (1998) report similar results. In addition, they varied the quality of the arguments used by the majority and an ingroup minority. This is a key manipulation, in that if individuals are processing the arguments carefully, they should react positively to an intelligent message and be unpersuaded by a weak message. This pattern is just what was found in *both* majority *and* minority influence conditions. Crano and Chen found that, on both the focal attitude (a mandatory student service requirement) and the indirect attitude (tuition increase), people reacted to these message quality differences more or less equally, irrespective of whether they were exposed to the minority or majority influence (indeed, on the focal issue, majority influence was more pronounced than minority influence). Several recent studies (e.g. Martin and Hewstone 2001; Kerr, in press) have presented results that suggest that this pattern arises when the relevance of the issue is high. These results offer strong evidence that majorities can evoke careful attention to message content and that such thoughtful attention may provoke greater persuasion than minority views. Collectively, these findings clearly contradict the strong version of Moscovici's conversion theory, which argues (a) that majorities *never* evoke such thoughtful persuasion, (b) that any social influence caused by the majority is unrelated to such thoughtful processing, and (c) that minorities are generally more likely to evoke such thoughtful elaboration than majorities. It is true that several of the cases reporting careful processing of majority arguments have focused on focal attitudes (where the minority is expected to be weak), but this still contradicts conversion theory. Conversion theory argues that, on such focal issues, the audience is unlikely to carefully and privately consider the arguments offered by the majority and is very likely to consider the minority's arguments, albeit not openly agree with them. The findings summarized above are hard to reconcile with that view.

Alternatives to conversion theory

Minorities and divergent thought

If Moscovici's conversion theory, at least in its strong form, does not fit the findings, how else might we explain the growing data on minority influence? Charlan Nemeth offers a more moderate two-process view of the minority influence literature. Nemeth (Nemeth and Kwan 1987) acknowledges that both majority influence and minority influence will provoke cognitive activity, but that the thinking provoked by minorities tends to be more creative and divergent. In short, such activity is presumed to consider a wider range of issues and solutions, including – but not limited to – the one advocated by the minority. This *divergent thought* pattern provides an explanation for why minorities are more likely to provoke change on indirect attitudes and topics (e.g. Alvaro and Crano 1997). Majority influence, in turn, is thought to provoke *convergent thought*. The latter is thought to be less creative and to focus on why the majority might be correct. Thus, they will be less likely to consider counterarguments, alternative solutions and alternative outcomes. In short, Nemeth does not argue that majorities never or rarely provoke careful processing, but only that this thought will tend to have a different character. Note that her model does acknowledge that the thought provoked by the majority's arguments will often cause persuasion. Nevertheless, given the different quality of the thinking, this model still represents a two-process view.

Several studies offer evidence that, at least on some tasks, minority influence does seem to spur divergent thought. For example, Nemeth and Kwan (1987) showed participants letter strings from which they had to form words. They were then urged by either a majority or a minority to deviate from their normal pattern and to solve the problem by reading the letter strings backwards. When this advice came from the minority, the participants showed more creative solutions to the word problem (e.g. reading forwards, backwards, every other word, etc.) than in the majority condition. Similarly, Peterson and Nemeth (1996) found that minority influence on the Stroop colour-naming task (name the colour of the ink rather than reading the printed word) provoked more integrated and multidimensional thinking. As a final example, Butera *et al.* (1996) found that high school students used more creative solutions and were more likely to explore disconfirming strategies when minorities, rather than majorities, offered suggestions about reasoning problems (see also Gruenfeld *et al.* 1998). These results are encouragingly consistent, suggesting that minorities will often provoke more creative thought. Presumably this is because individuals are more willing to challenge and object to minority views. One problem with this explanation, however, is that it does not explain directly some of the other findings in the literature, such as the greater persuasiveness of ingroup minorities and the fact that majorities seem to provoke more careful processing of persuasive arguments than do minorities when participants consider beliefs that are directly relevant to the group discussion (Wood *et al.* 1996; Martin and Hewstone 2001).

The expectancy violation view

A single-process model based on violation of expectancy fares somewhat better in this regard. Several writers have suggested that *expectancy violation* plays a key role in explaining many of the findings on minority versus majority influence (e.g. Mackie 1987). The idea here is that, when our expectancies are violated, we pay particular attention to the situation. This should lead to very careful message processing and consideration of the issue. Thus, minorities may provoke our attention due to our surprise at seeing individuals take the social risk of disagreeing with a majority (Baker and Petty 1994). Indeed, when people from our ingroup take a minority position, despite the possibility of social rejection, it is particularly surprising. This could explain the superior persuasiveness of certain ingroup minorities. Several writers have explored this possibility. Baker and Petty (1994) reasoned that finding out that a minority agrees with you may be surprising, in that it implies that the majority disagrees with you. In contrast, learning directly that a majority disagrees with you also should violate your expectancy. As Baker and Petty predicted, these situations provoked more careful scrutiny of message content, in that participants reacted more strongly to variations in message quality than did participants in less surprising conditions (e.g. those hearing a minority disagree with them). As noted above, Mackie (1987) also found evidence of very careful processing when a numerical majority disagreed with participants. Also in accord with this emphasis on 'surprise', Koszakai *et al.* (1994) found that minority influence was most effective if the majority was highly cohesive. Given that it should take particular courage for a minority to confront a cohesive group, this result fits nicely with the surprise explanation. In the same vein, McLeod and co-workers' (1997) findings that minority influence was more effective in face-to-face (as opposed to computer) groups are also congruent with this view, in that it is less surprising to learn of minority dissent when the minority is protected by computer anonymity.

In accord with the 'single-process' idea that both minority and majority influence are based on the same form of processing, Kruglanski and Mackie (1990) found that when examining the effect of various independent variables (e.g. message quality) on minority and majority influence, there is little evidence of any difference in the direction of effect as a consequence of minority/majority status. This is not what one would expect if these forms of influence represented different processes. Similarly, anecdotal evidence suggests that minorities can elicit compliance if they have some strong source of power, such as the ability to punish the majority. Such findings undermine the strong claims that minority and majority influence have little in common.

One must grant the expectancy violation view the advantage of simplicity. Only one simple construct is involved and it offers an explanation for why majorities occasionally provoke thoughtful change, whereas in other settings it is minorities that do so. What remains unclear with this explanation is why minority effects should be seen most often on indirect measures. Moscovici's original view regarding fears of social rejection may apply here. Individuals may not want to appear, *even to themselves*, to be aligned with minorities (David and Turner 1996). Thus, if they do encounter a surprising minority and it does provoke thoughtful change in beliefs, such change will only be manifest on indirect issues. These matters will obviously continue to attract a great deal of research attention, because research on the intricacies of minority influence is currently one of the most active areas of small group research.

SUMMARY

Conformity is a pervasive and useful social process, sometimes operating without our awareness, and at other times being instrumental to garner others' approval. Its opposite, resistance to influence, usually requires social support of other like-minded protestors. We have identified several factors that either heighten or minimize conformity and distinguished between two distinct causes of social influence: normative and informational influence. Consideration of factions or subgroups within a group discussion raised the issue of whether minority influence differs from majority influence, and whether the former elicits compliance whereas the latter produces thoughtful and true belief change. Research in recent years suggests that this characterization is too simplistic. It is now clear that, in many settings, majorities provoke more thoughtful attitude change than minorities. A possible exception is when influence comes from ingroup minority members. On the other hand, Moscovici's more basic point – that sometimes minorities are capable of evoking fundamental change in the views of the majority – is a perspective that is now generally well accepted and as such represents a fundamental contribution to our understanding of social influence. Researchers are currently attempting to specify the limiting conditions of minority influence and to arrive at an integrated theoretical explanation that can accommodate the complex findings in this area.

SUGGESTIONS FOR FURTHER READING

Baron, R.S., Vandello, J.A. and Brunsman, B. (1996) The forgotten variable in conformity research: the impact of task importance on social influence. *Journal of Personality and Social Psychology*, 71: 915–27. Demonstrates that conformity can increase as judgments become more important.

David, B. and Turner, J.C. (1996) Studies in self-categorization and minority conversion: is being a member of the out-group an advantage? *British Journal of Social Psychology*, 35: 179–99. An interesting study of ingroup versus outgroup influence.

Kerr, N.L. (2001) Is it what one says or how one says it? Style *vs* substance from an SDS perspective. In C. De Dreu and N. De Vries (eds) *Group Consensus and Minority Influence: Implications for Innovation*. Oxford: Blackwell. A key study on how communication style affects influence.

Martin, R. (1998) Majority and minority influence using the afterimage paradigm: a series of attempted replications. *Journal of Experimental Social Psychology*, 34: 1–26. Reports careful attempts to recreate the original results of Moscovici and Personnaz (1980).

Pool, G.J., Wood, W. and Leck, K. (1998) The self-esteem motive in social influence: agreement with valued majorities and disagreement with derogated minorities. *Journal of Personality and Social Psychology*, 75: 967–75. An inventive set of studies showing how conformity is linked to feelings of self-adequacy.

Williams, K.D., Cheung, C.K.T. and Choi, W. (2000) Cyberostracism: effects of being ignored over the internet. *Journal of Personality and Social Psychology*, 79(5): 746–62. How much does Internet ostracism bother us?

SIX

EXTREMITY IN GROUPS

- What elements of the groupthink model are well supported?
- What are the possible causes of group polarization?
- What factors heighten the power of intense indoctrination?
- What contributes to mob behaviour?
- What is deindividuation?

INTRODUCTION

One of the more disturbing instances of group action of the last century took place in Jonestown, Guyana in 1978 when over 900 members of a religious sect, led by the Reverend Jim Jones, elected to drink cyanide-laced fruit drink in an act of communal suicide. Audio tapes made by the group indicate that, when the members of the People's Temple discussed this decision, there was widespread support for the suicide (www.npr.org.archives). In fact, when one woman raised the idea that each person should be allowed to make this decision for himself or herself, she was collectively shouted down. This tragic and disturbing incident illustrates a well-documented and fascinating aspect of group life: individuals often will express stronger attitudes, and engage in more extreme actions, when acting together as opposed to alone. As a second example, the brutal mass killings and rapes that marked the ethnic strife in Rwanda, Algeria and the Balkans in the mid-1990s are usually attributed to the fact that these widespread atrocities were committed by gangs rather than by individuals. What is it about group action that occasionally leads to such intensity of belief and behaviour? Why do group members frequently end up making more extreme decisions and holding more extreme opinions after interacting with fellow group members? In this chapter, we discuss several theoretical perspectives that have been advanced to explain such events.

GROUPTHINK

Janis (1972, 1982) theorized that one reason groups may intensify attitudes and decisions is that group members, particularly those in selective, high-status groups, may inhibit their own private objections to group policy when in the presence of the group. Janis felt that this tendency was responsible for several policy blunders over the years. One such example was the NASA decision to continue with the launch of the *Challenger* space shuttle despite earlier reports that key seals on the launch vehicle would not function below certain temperatures. This error had fatal consequences for the crew of the mission, none of whom survived. According to Janis (1972), such fiascos could be explained by a phenomenon he called *groupthink*.

Janis' initial model of groupthink

Janis (1972, 1982) proposed the term 'groupthink' to refer to a kind of pathology, which, he argued, often occurs during group decision-making; a pathology that arguably contributed to high-stakes foreign policy disasters such as Argentina's decision to initiate the war in the Falkland Islands and Lyndon Johnson's escalation of the Vietnam War. Janis believed that groupthink was triggered by a number of antecedent conditions, including directive leadership style, intense group cohesion, similarity of ideology, pressure for unanimity, group insulation from critics, insecure member self-esteem and a sense of crisis. Janis argued that these forces combine to suppress dissent within groups to such an extent that group members end up supporting policies (norms) that may be extraordinarily ill-considered. Janis argued that groupthink usually occurs in very high-status groups because the opinions of the other individuals are extremely credible and the desire to be accepted is also 'sky high'. In such groups, a directive leader's favoured decision alternative often becomes established as the dominant group norm. Janis also theorized that a crisis atmosphere contributes to the problem by leading the group to push for a rapid consensus to the group norm and to stifle dissent.

This collection of features is said to provoke several inadequate decision processes. These include the following elements: (a) inadequate consideration of alternative options; (b) ignoring the implications of failure; (c) biased assessment of risks, costs and benefits; (d) poor information search; and (e) meagre contingency plans in the event that the group solution fails. This impoverished decision process, in turn, provokes several groupthink symptoms that can further perpetuate group allegiance to this decision. These symptoms include the illusion of consensus (members assume that they alone have doubts about the group's decision), stereotyping of the enemy as weak, immoral and stupid, and defending the group's favoured decision against doubts or criticism through rationalization, and overt attempts to stifle dissent.

It is important to note that according to the groupthink model, because other group members are viewed as being both powerful and wise in these groups, each member is especially likely to keep objections to him or herself. By not disrupting the group consensus, the individual accomplishes two things. He or she allows the group to 'solve' a threatening and demanding problem, thereby reducing any personal stress and uncertainty created by the decision ('All these smart people can't be wrong'; Callaway *et al.* 1985), and he or she remains in the group's good graces as well. The result of this process is that dissent becomes inhibited, the group tends to feel it is invulnerable, united and morally correct, doubts are 'explained away' and the enemy is disparaged as weak, stupid or immoral. For example, in the late 1960s, President Johnson and his advisors were able to delude themselves into thinking that the opposition to the Vietnam War in the USA was due to a small minority of misfits, weirdos and political extremists, when in fact it was a widespread reaction that eventually made it impossible for him to run for a second term as president.

Laboratory research on groupthink

Although this theory has a great deal of intuitive appeal, laboratory research on groupthink has been relatively sparse and has yielded uneven support for the specific predictions of the model (Esser 1998). For example, manipulations of high cohesion (e.g. telling participants that they will like each other) have generally not produced the poor quality of discussion Janis' theory predicts (for reviews, see Mullen *et al.* 1994; Esser 1998). Similarly, manipulations of threat (e.g. having experts evaluate the group's decision) have generally not triggered symptoms of groupthink (e.g. Fodor and Smith 1982; Turner and Pratkanis 1998a). In fairness, however, these laboratory manipulations do not produce either the extremely high level of ingroup feeling or strong levels of stress that characterize the policy-making groups in which Janis was interested.

Laboratory work does indicate support for the notion that, when groups are marked by such features as directive leadership, group insulation from critics and lack of systematic consideration of options, low-quality group problem-solving is more likely (e.g. Hodson and Sorrentino 1997; Esser 1998; but see Peterson 1997). But this is a less controversial set of predictions. When a group is hurried and dominated by the leader, discouraged from considering other options and insulated from critics, it is not very surprising that problem-solving suffers. Far more provocative are the predictions linking antecedent conditions such as cohesion or high status, similar ideology and stress with poor decision-making. For these predictions, the findings are, at best, weak (Aldag and Fuller 1993; Paulus 1998).

Mullen *et al.* (1994) reviewed much of the groupthink research and offered the tentative suggestion that all of the preconditions specified by Janis must be present before the various effects and symptoms of groupthink (suppression of dissent, poor consideration of options, feelings of superiority) become apparent. In one study, Turner *et al.* (1992)

raised stress levels by telling groups that their discussion would be videotaped and shown to others. Under these conditions, high cohesion did lead to poorer decisions. In short, simply finding that a single factor (high cohesion) fails to provoke symptoms of groupthink in a laboratory study could be dismissed as being due to the conditions necessary to provoke the phenomenon not being fulfilled. Nevertheless, laboratory evidence regarding the groupthink formulation does not provide strong support for all aspects of this model, leading some researchers to actively question the theory (Aldag and Fuller 1993; Paulus 1998) or suggest that extensive revisions are required (Longley and Pruitt 1980; Turner *et al.* 1992).

Historical case study reports of groupthink

Despite the inconsistent and fairly sparse laboratory data regarding groupthink, many social scientists still feel that this theory has much explanatory potential. Some of this continued confidence undoubtedly stems in part from a series of creative historical analyses that have been advanced to substantiate the model's various hypotheses (e.g. Schafer and Crichlow 1996; for a review, see Esser 1998). Although we must be careful of such historical analysis for several reasons – for example, we cannot be certain that contradictory examples have not been overlooked (Longley and Pruitt 1980) – such case studies do have the virtue of looking at cases where the antecedent conditions were strong enough to create the conditions deemed necessary by the model. In one such study, Tetlock (1979) conducted a content analysis of statements made by key decision-makers. This analysis showed that, for policy decisions that Janis had categorized as exemplifying groupthink, decision-makers' perceptions of the issues were much more simplistic and protective of their ingroup than for decisions that Janis categorized as non-groupthink. In a follow-up study, Tetlock *et al.* (1992) examined an expanded list of historical decisions (e.g. the Iran hostage rescue) using a careful rating system (Q sort). This sorting procedure reconfirmed Janis's (1972, 1982) earlier designation of these cases as instances or non-instances of groupthink. Interestingly, however, in this study, as in many of the laboratory studies on this topic, group cohesion and situational urgency had little impact on decision quality.

Although these two studies generally confirm Janis's original historical assessments of groupthink, Kramer's (1998) historical study is less supportive. Examining recently declassified documents relating to one of Janis's key cases, John F. Kennedy's decision to support an invasion of Cuba by Cuban exiles at the Bay of Pigs, Kramer finds that many of Janis's assumptions about that decision were in error. Contrary to Janis's analysis, these declassified documents reveal that Kennedy's decision was due more to political considerations and misleading information he received than to overconfidence, insulation or inadequate information search. Kramer's conclusions, of course, only bear on this one historical case. In another historical analysis of international decisions, Herek *et al.* (1987) asked both historians and psychologists to rate decision quality and number of groupthink symptoms for 19 national security decisions made in the USA.

Their conclusion was that the greater the groupthink, the more negative the outcome of the decision. Similar confirming reports based on historical case studies have also appeared (e.g. McCauley 1989). Therefore, although there is reason to doubt some of the specific details of Janis's model (e.g. the crucial role of group cohesion; his assessment of the Cuban invasion), there is still some basis to assume that certain elements of the model have validity.

Revised versions of groupthink

Several authors have offered revised explanations that define more narrowly the conditions for the groupthink phenomenon, in the hope of clarifying and improving the theory. One possibility is that group members primarily stifle their dissent when they feel insecure about their group status. For most individuals, this is more likely to be the case in early stages of their group membership or when the group itself is relatively new (Longley and Pruitt 1980; see also Chapter 1). According to this view, then, it is a desire to be accepted by an attractive group that provokes groupthink, rather than simple cohesion *per se*. Turner *et al.* (1992) discuss a second possible revision. This *social identity maintenance* (SIM) view suggests that groupthink occurs primarily when group members feel that their group has a distinct identity and, in addition, feel that the group is under attack. According to this view, groupthink results from members trying to defend the reputation and interests of a group they value and with which they identify. The SIM model, like Janis's model, considers cohesion to be a factor in groupthink but, as we noted in Chapter 1, social identity models focus on a particular kind of cohesion that is based more on social attraction than personal attraction. Thus, someone may not like many of his or her fellow members of an honorific society (e.g. the Academy of Science) and yet take great pride in his or her membership and feel respect for fellow members if they embody the prototypic features of the group (e.g. they all are productive and highly renowned scientists). Turner and co-workers' (1992) finding that cohesion impaired group decision-making only when the group was threatened offers initial support for this view. The results of a study by Stewart *et al.* (1998) are also consistent with the SIM model. In this study, a similar manipulation of stress (being held accountable to an audience) also decreased group discussion of dissenting views. Unfortunately, no manipulation of cohesion or social identity was included in this study. While it is too early to evaluate these revised views of groupthink, it is to be hoped that they inspire research that will help to clarify how to characterize the decision errors that mark classic cases of this phenomenon.

Avoiding groupthink

Several options have been suggested as strategies for avoiding the problems of groupthink. These include: (1) fostering open discussion of all alternatives; (2) considering 'worse case' scenarios; (3) creating contingency plans for failure; (4) advising leaders to avoid advocating any one plan early in discussion; (5) having group ideas reviewed by outside experts and devil's advocates (two being far better than one); (6) having several subgroups work on the problem independently (or give several independent groups a 'say' in the decision); (7) having formal 'second chance' meetings dedicated to reconsidering the wisdom of the initial decision; and (8) making groups and their members more openly accountable for their role in the decision (Janis 1982; McCauley 1989; Hart 1998). Future research should evaluate how effectively such strategies minimize the symptoms of groupthink.

GROUP POLARIZATION

The groupthink phenomenon illustrates how an emerging group norm, often one suggested by the group leader, can bias the content of discussion by suppressing dissent. Group polarization focuses on a related process whereby group discussion tends to intensify group opinion, producing more extreme judgments among group members than existed before discussion. This phenomenon provides a potent explanation for the escalation of attitudes and commitment that occurs when groups of like-minded individuals in groups as varied as Amnesty International, Hezbollah and Alcoholics Anonymous engage in mutual discussion. Unlike groupthink, however, group polarization is not thought to be limited to high-status or highly cohesive groups.

Early research on group polarization

Initially, researchers assumed that group discussion would have a mellowing influence on hotheads and extremists within the group. As a result, group discussion was expected to produce more moderate decisions than individual decision-making. Research soon made it apparent, however, that group discussion typically had just the opposite effect. Stoner (1961) was the first to report that group discussion led to riskier decisions on risk problems than did individual decision-making. Similar results have since been reported on a wide range of decision judgments. For example, group discussion led French students in the late 1960s to increase their disapproval of the USA (Moscovici and Zavalloni 1969) and prison inmates to heighten their approval of petty crime (Myers et al. 1974). Many other researchers have reported similar effects on other judgment and attitude dimensions. For example, group discussion also intensifies attitudes related to feminism, pacifism, equality, under-age drinking, and the guilt or innocence of a defendant (cf. Myers and Lamm 1976). Moreover, as noted by Dion et al. (1970), these effects have been found in different countries (e.g. England, France, Israel, Germany, USA and Canada) using a wide variety of participants (e.g. grade school children, industrial supervisors, etc.). Most theorists agree, however, that the group polarization effect does not occur invariably. One major requirement is that group members must basically agree, at least in a general sense, about what side of the issue they favor. For example, groups become riskier after discussion only when most members feel, before discussion, that taking some kind of risk in the setting is sensible. As another example, Myers and Bishop (1970) found that, in the USA, when people were grouped together with others who shared their views, discussion intensified racial attitudes, with liberals becoming more tolerant and 'traditionalists' becoming less tolerant following group discussion. In this sense, group polarization represents the intensification of a pre-existing initial group preference. Most of the research on this phenomenon has involved explaining the source of such polarization.

Competitive social comparison and persuasive arguments

Most theorists acknowledge that two previously discussed social influence processes, normative and informational influence, contribute to group polarization. If there is a pre-existing group preference or norm favouring risk, normative influence will make group members reluctant to deviate from that norm. In this case, those who are relatively least committed to the group norm are likely to be seen as deviates. Thus, if group members simply find out the positions taken by other group members, this information by itself can exert influence by initiating a subtle competition among group participants to be at least 'above average' in terms of their adherence to any group norm. For example, if the group favours risk, it is best to be above average on that dimension. In accord with this view, most individuals feel before discussion that they are better than average regarding their responses (Dion *et al.* 1970). Obviously, some individuals will learn that this self-serving presumption is incorrect during discussion, inducing them to change their responses.

On the other hand, informational influence will also affect group members when they hear the arguments and reasons that other group members provide when discussing decision preferences. For example, if most individuals are pro-risk before group discussion of a risk problem, group members are likely to hear numerous reasons favouring a risky position from other group members. This, in turn, might persuade others in the group to shift toward a riskier position. For a number of years, social psychologists debated which of the two basic influence processes was necessary and sufficient to produce the polarization effect. Burnstein and Vinokur (1977) contended in their *persuasive arguments theory* that group polarization was based solely on the arguments heard in discussion. Moreover, they argued that group discussion will lead to polarization *only* when the discussion contains arguments that are both compelling (logical, well thought out) and *new* to some of the group members. Although the research of Burnstein and Vinokur (1977) and others (Bishop and Myers 1974; Stasser and Titus 1987) shows a strong link between the flow of arguments during discussion (i.e. their number, valence and quality) and the degree of polarization, Burnstein and Vinokur's emphasis on the importance of *new* arguments was probably stated too strongly. Recent research indicates that polarization can occur when individuals do not hear new arguments during discussion but instead simply find out that others agree with their choices (e.g. Baron *et al.* 1996a) or learn that all members share the same reasons for their beliefs (e.g. Stewart and Stasser 1998). This polarization appears to be based on the increase in confidence created by such corroboration (Baron *et al.* 1996a).

In other studies stimulated by this theoretical debate, researchers have used experimental tasks in which no persuasive arguments are exchanged (e.g. Baron and Roper 1976; Cotton and Baron 1980; Myers 1982) to document that normative influence alone (i.e. competitive social comparison) is sufficient to produce polarization. Blascovich *et al.* (1975), for example, found that betting became more extreme during group play in a blackjack card game, even though players did not discuss their bets. On the other hand, proponents of persuasive arguments theory have used the opposite strategy to document the important role played by argumentation. In such studies, participants hear the arguments offered by others but are somehow prevented from knowing precisely what position these fellow group members favour. As a result, social comparison-based competition is difficult. Here, too, group polarization occurs (e.g. Burnstein and Vinokur 1973). In short, evidence exists to support the view that both competitive comparison and persuasive processes play a role in group polarization. As a result, it is safe to conclude that our tendency to polarize will be *stronger* when we hear lots of persuasive arguments during discussion that support the dominant point of view, as Burnstein and Vinokur suggest. On the other hand, it appears that hearing such arguments is not *necessary* to produce polarization, contrary to some of the early assumptions made by the persuasive arguments theorists.

One recent development in this research is the realization that polarization can be triggered by stating an opinion as well as hearing it stated. Brauer *et al.* (1995) documented that the more individuals repeated their opinions, the more likely they were to polarize in discussion of national issues (youth crime, nuclear power). This was particularly true when others repeated their arguments. In addition, the more people heard an opinion repeated – especially by different individuals – the greater the observed polarization. Given that group discussion often involves hearing others discuss commonly held beliefs, these findings provide us with insight about an aspect of group discussion that appears to produce extreme beliefs. Our hunch is that changes in confidence may mediate these effects. As we restate our beliefs, our confidence will grow stronger due to processes such as self-justification and selective attention to supportive information. Similarly, when we find that several others share our views, confidence should also be enhanced (McGarty *et al.* 1993; Baron *et al.* 1996a). Several writers suggest that such enhanced confidence should promote more extreme, persistent and strongly held attitudes (e.g. Baron 1996; for a review, see Gross *et al.* 1995).

A self-categorization view of group polarization

Although most recent research on group polarization has focused on the relative contributions of persuasive arguments theory and competitive social comparison theory, recently the advocates of *self-categorization theory* have suggested that group polarization is due to group members' desires to be seen as loyal and solid group members (e.g. Turner *et al.* 1989; Abrams *et al.* 1990; Hogg *et al.* 1990; Turner, 1991). According to this view, during discussion group members become more aware of their group affiliation (i.e. group salience increases) and, therefore, make more of an effort to adhere to *prototypic group norms*. These writers contend that this prototypic group norm is a position that maximizes similarity to the general positions of ingroup members while simultaneously minimizing any similarity to outgroup members. Thus, if one is in a risky group and knows about a cautious outgroup, the best way to differentiate oneself from such a group, thereby proving your group loyalty, is to endorse a position that is just a bit riskier than the average position in your own discussion group. According to self-categorization theory, this is not due to a competitive desire to be 'better' than average, but rather due to our desire to conform to an idealized group norm in a way that helps to distinguish us from outgroups. Thus according to the self-categorization view, group polarization is just a special form of 'conformity', a form in which group members are conforming to a 'polarized' group norm. This conformity represents a means of displaying and reasserting both the members' ingroup status and their non-membership of the outgroup. This is a provocative position to advocate, given that in most polarization experiments no outgroups were explicitly mentioned to group members. The self-categorization advocates argue, however, that group members tend to think of such 'implicit' outgroups on their own and work to differentiate themselves from the positions taken in such implicit groups. We now review some of the evidence bearing on this self-categorization view of polarization.

Ingroup/outgroup manipulations

First, there is growing evidence that we pay more attention to the arguments offered by ingroup members than by outgroup members. For example, Mackie *et al.* (1992) found that individuals were more likely to notice and react to the difference between good and bad arguments when they came from fellow group members (see McGarty *et al.* 1994; Alvaro and Crano 1996). This is a standard indication that people are paying close attention to the material. However, this was not true if these other group members opened their discussion with a clear statement of their final preference. According to self-categorization theory, under these conditions individuals do not need to listen carefully to the arguments to discover where the group norm is. As predicted by this theory, the participants in this condition conformed regardless of message quality. On the other hand, outgroup members generally failed to be persuasive, even when they offered high-quality arguments.

These results are congruent with the self-categorization view that group members are highly motivated to conform to ingroup norms and less motivated to carefully consider the intellectual merits of the issues. Presumably, the reason people listen carefully to ingroup members is their desire to discover the nature of the ingroup norm. If they learn this at the outset of discussion, they do not carefully process ingroup arguments. The results of Mackie *et al.* (1992) complement those of Mackie and Cooper (1984) and Mackie (1986: experiment 1) indicating that, when individuals listen to a tape-recorded discussion (about the fairness of college admittance tests), they polarize their opinions only if they are hearing the discussion of an ingroup as opposed to an outgroup. Indeed, in Mackie and Cooper's study, participants tended to shift away from outgroup positions when they learned of them. In Mackie's study (1986), the arguments presented on the tape provoked no polarization if they were described as just the comments of disconnected individuals. It is only when the tape was portrayed as a group discussion that it provoked polarization. (Note that this outcome is certainly not consistent with Burnstein and Vinokur's persuasive argument theory.)

Examining the role of ingroup and outgroup norms

In other research inspired by the self-categorization view, Hogg *et al.* (1990) manipulated whether a fictitious outgroup was described as being riskier or more cautious (on choice dilemma-risk decision items) than the participant. As noted above, the self-categorization assumption is that participants would want to differentiate themselves from the outgroup position whatever it is and would expect other group members to feel the same. In accord with this prediction, individuals faced with a more risky outgroup assumed that the ingroup norm would be relatively cautious, whereas those faced with a cautious outgroup assumed their ingroup norm would be relatively risky. Similarly, Mackie (1986) reported that people estimated that groups endorsed positions or norms that are more extreme than did isolated individuals. This is congruent with the self-categorization idea that groups are interested in differentiating themselves from others.

Group salience and degree of polarization

A final set of studies has examined the self-categorization prediction that group polarization should be greater if individuals think more about their group status. Spears *et al.* (1990) encouraged British students to think of themselves as a group (high group salience) by telling them they would be evaluated as a group and referring often to their group status. In other conditions, the participants did not have this group status emphasized (e.g. their own individual performance was emphasized – low group salience). Students then engaged in a computer chat regarding various topics they tended to agree on (e.g. nuclear power). As predicted by self-categorization theory, polarization only occurred when group salience was high. However, this occurred only when participants were anonymous and located in separate rooms. In contrast, when participants were in the same room, no polarization occurred, even when group salience was high. Given that most group polarization studies have participants engage in face-to-face discussion, this finding poses a challenge for self-categorization theory. It is hard to claim that social categorization explains the large array of face-to-face polarization studies if the group salience manipulation does not heighten polarization in face-to-face groups. This is not the only study to report such 'weird' group salience data. Mackie (1986: experiment 2) had people listen to taped discussions of groups which they thought they were about to join. In one condition, these individuals were told that their group soon would be competing with others, a condition designed to heighten awareness of group status. This manipulation did not heighten the amount of polarization that occurred. In short, group salience research has not consistently supported the self-categorization contention that heightened awareness of one's group membership will heighten group polarization. On the other hand, as we have seen, several other findings do support this view of group polarization. Research on this provocative theory is still active and we will undoubtedly learn more about its explanatory power and empirical limits in the years to come.

Group polarization with real consequences

Over 500 studies have examined the group polarization phenomenon using a wide range of judgments and participants. Relatively few of them, however, have studied decisions or judgments that have real and immediate consequences for the decision-maker. For instance, participants often are asked to make a series of hypothetical decisions in which they advise non-existent persons how much risk they should take (e.g. 'What would the odds of success at a new job have to be before you would advise Mr./Ms. Make-Believe to leave his/her present job for a new opportunity'). Given the powerful generality of the group polarization phenomenon, one might expect similar effects for both hypothetical and real decisions, but this has not always been the case. Several studies on gambling behaviour illustrate this complexity.

The most common finding from early work on hypothetical decisions was that group discussion elevated risk-taking. Thus, we should expect group interaction to elevate gambling behaviour. This indeed occurred in several studies conducted by Blascovich, Ginsberg and their associates (e.g. Blascovich et al. 1975). They found that participants bet more money playing blackjack if they discussed or otherwise knew the bets of fellow players. What complicates matters is that two race-track studies found just the opposite. McCauley et al. (1973) and Knox and Stafford (1976) recruited people making bets at a race-track by offering to pay for their next $2 bet. The participants' task was to decide which horse to bet on. This allowed the researchers to assess risk-taking by noting the betting odds of the horse the participants selected. In both studies, the participants tended to make *less* risky selections if they decided after group discussion rather than individually.

How can we resolve this inconsistency? A key procedural difference may be responsible for these apparently contradictory outcomes. In the race-track research, the group decision was to be *binding* on each group member in that the group's unanimous decision would determine what all group members bet. Here individual group members may have been reluctant to vote for or advocate a risky option in the group, since it might force someone who could not afford it to lose their money. In contrast, the blackjack research did not require a binding unanimous decision. As a result, group members could advocate risk without feeling that they were coercing others. In short, when groups make decisions that have binding, costly implications for all group members, the tendency to avoid coercion of those with fewer resources into committing more than they can afford may limit or even reverse group polarization effects.

Other research supports this view. Group discussion increased the willingness of college students to donate student fees to a hypothetical fund for Bengali refugees that was unlikely to be established by their student government (Baron *et al.* 1974). This corroborated other studies in which group discussion enhanced predominant individual generosity on hypothetical issues (e.g. Muehleman *et al.* 1976). When these same students were asked to make actual personal donations to an already existing on-campus Bengali relief fund, however, group discussion to full binding consensus reduced donations below participants' initial individual contributions. Thus, it would appear that while certain group pressures often lead us to become more extreme in groups, we also have a strong aversion to coercing others into making binding, high-cost decisions. Furthermore, it would appear that this aversion can inhibit group polarization effects when group decisions are binding on all group members. On the other hand, when such binding decisions are not required, within-group comparison and discussion has been found to polarize such behaviours as betting (Blascovich *et al.* 1975), contributing to charity (Baron *et al.* 1996a) and willingness to testify (Luus and Wells 1994).

Biases in information sampling

We have seen that there is good evidence that individuals are affected by the flow of arguments that they hear during group discussion. It is clear that, in such discussion groups, the information flow is biased so that it tends to justify the side of the discussion favoured by most group members and that this biased flow influences attitude extremity. Zdaniuk and Levine (1996) found that, even before discussion, the more support individuals expected for their opinion, the more they selectively thought about supportive ideas before discussion. In a similar vein, recent research on *information sampling theory* by Stasser and his associates (e.g. Stewart *et al.* 1998) indicates that group members have a strong tendency to emphasize the information that they share in common during group discussion. For example, Stasser found that important items of information that are known only to single individuals within the group are less likely to be mentioned during discussion than other items which are shared among group members (e.g. Stasser and Titus 1987).

Let us consider an example. Assume that committee members must choose between two political figures – Winston and Margaret – to endorse for office. Suppose further that all five members share the same three positive beliefs about Margaret (e.g. they all know of her loyalty, political skill and foresight), while each member holds a single, different positive belief about Winston (one member knows he is brilliant, another knows he is fearless, etc.). Since each member has three positive beliefs about

Margaret and only one about Winston, we would expect all five to favour Margaret initially, assuming that these traits are equally valued. However, if they pooled all their available information in a group discussion, they would have five positive beliefs about Winston and only three about Margaret and, as a group, should prefer Winston. Stasser (1988) labels this state of affairs a *hidden profile*. It describes a set of circumstances in which the information held in common by group members favours a particular choice, while the unshared information contradicts the choice.

What happens when groups discuss such profiles? If all information is discussed and considered equally during discussion, the rational group choice would be to prefer Winston. But, in fact, Stasser's research suggests that such a group would actually favour Margaret to Winston and that this opinion would grow *stronger* after discussion. Groups do not appear to pool unshared information efficiently, but rather dwell on shared information. In support of this interpretation, it has been shown that participants recall fewer unshared arguments from the discussion (Stasser and Titus 1987). Moreover, analysis of tape-recorded discussions document that unshared arguments are less likely to be expressed during discussion (Stasser *et al.* 1989b). Indeed, several studies have indicated that shared information is viewed as being more valid. Larson *et al.* (1998) found that teams of medical doctors dwelt more on their shared information when making a medical diagnosis and felt after discussion that the information that they collectively shared was a more valid basis for making the diagnosis than the information they possessed initially. In short, hidden profiles lead to biased information sampling during group discussion and this, in turn, has been found to lead to more extreme opinions following discussion (e.g. Stasser and Titus 1987). Sometimes, as in the purely hypothetical political example we just considered, this can lead to very poor group decisions. Stasser and Titus (1987) argue that this bias for shared information is most likely to occur when it supports the general initial sentiment within the group and when there is a relatively large number of 'shared' facts among members to discuss. In other words, if there is hardly anything to talk about, even unshared and unpopular views may get expressed during discussion. Thus the bias for shared information is less severe near the end of discussion (when the shared information is more likely to have been well covered) than near the beginning (Larson *et al.* 1998).

Why might hidden profiles lead to this selective bias in information sampling? One obvious explanation is that the more people who know about a given 'shared' fact, the more likely that it is to be expressed by someone. Although this 'law of numbers' almost certainly plays a role in suppressing discussion of unshared information, there is also evidence that normative group influence (i.e. fear of group rejection and a desire for social approval) make group members reluctant to offer unique and unshared views that contradict an emerging group consensus. Thus, in one key study, Gigone and Hastie (1993) had groups discuss and try to predict what grades other people were likely to achieve in their introductory psychology class based on various bits of information, such as attendance. Some of this information was shared and some unshared. The results indicated that the initial pre-discussion pattern of members' views (the initial group norm) was the key element affecting the final group prediction. In short, the bits of information that were actually discussed (which might be affected by the 'law of numbers') was less crucial than the position the group members initially favoured as they began the discussion – a clear case of normative influence. This is not all that surprising, in that a discussion of shared information is more pleasant than a consideration of differences. It permits group members to support and confirm each others' views as opposed to objecting (by presenting contrary information) or 'showing off' (with new information) (Wittenbaum et al. 1999). Not only is shared information more likely to be mentioned by members, it is also more likely to be re-mentioned and discussed (Stasser et al. 1989b). This pattern of results supports the idea that normative social influence is a key factor determining what information gets exchanged and emphasized during group discussion.

Remedies for biased information sampling

Even though the bias favouring shared information appears to be very strong, it can be countered, at least to some extent. Earlier in our discussion of group decision-making, we noted the distinction between intellective and judgmental tasks (Laughlin and Ellis 1986). In most of the early work by Stasser and his colleagues, the group's task was judgmental – there was no single, demonstrably correct alternative. However, if group members believe the opposite – that the task is intellective and that, given enough and the right information, it is possible to identify the 'correct' answer – we might expect group members to do better in seeking out all potentially useful information. This was confirmed in a clever experiment by Stasser and Stewart (1992). Groups considered a single murder mystery case. Members were given relevant information – some shared and some unshared – to create a hidden profile of the true culprit. Some of the groups were led to believe that there were no conclusive facts in the case (i.e. that the task was judgmental), whereas other groups were led to believe that they collectively possessed enough information to determine conclusively the guilty suspect (i.e. the task was intellective). Many more of the latter groups (67 vs. 35 per cent) managed to discover enough of the critical unshared information to discover the hidden profile.

Another factor that reduces shared-information bias is the belief that certain group members have special knowledge, expertise or responsibility. For example, Stewart and Stasser (1995) found that telling the group that some group members had special knowledge or expertise led the group to uncover and recall relatively more of the unshared information members possessed. It would appear that saying something that no-one else knows has a very different impact if group members think the speaker has special expertise ('Oh, I didn't realize that . . .') than if they do not ('That's probably just his opinion . . .'). It also seems to help the group if they know just which members are likely to have which unique pieces of information; groups were more likely to solve the murder mystery if they were told which members had the critical unshared information, but not if they simply knew that someone did (Stasser et al. 1995).

Even a minority of one who knows *all* the facts (shared and unshared) can do much to minimize the hidden profile effect, if the rest of the group has some inkling that useful, unshared facts exist (Stewart and Stasser 1998). McLeod *et al.* (1997) reported similar results, provided that the discussion involved a face-to-face group as opposed to a computer chat group. Of course, this work also points to the danger of the group falsely attributing expertise to members who are really not expert, thereby giving too much credence to such members' socially uncorroborated opinions.

Although some remedies have been shown to be effective, it is also important to note that many others have not. In one particular condition of Stasser and co-workers' (1989b) study, group members were asked to avoid stating their initial preferences and were encouraged to review all relevant facts. Groups discussed the political candidate problem for 30 minutes. These instructions did increase the amount of discussion that occurred, but the discussion again primarily favoured those facts initially shared by group members (67 per cent of all shared facts were discussed in contrast to 23 per cent of unshared facts). Similarly, Stewart *et al.* (1998) found that increasing how accountable people were to some external evaluator did not increase the extent to which they discussed unshared information. In short, such findings suggest that subtle pressures within groups increase the likelihood that individuals will talk about the issues they agree about, while decreasing the chances that they will consider issues they differ on.

Some effects of biased discussion

The tendency to focus group discussion on points of agreement and supportive arguments will have several effects that will heighten extremity of opinion and action within groups. First, as noted above, this biased flow of information provokes more extreme attitudes, in that discussion provides people with confirmation that others share their views. As we have seen, several studies have documented that corroboration of this type leads to more confident and extreme opinions (Stasser and Titus 1987; McGarty *et al.* 1993; Luus and Wells 1994; Brauer *et al.* 1995; Baron *et al.* 1996a). Second, this process of dwelling on commonly held ideas and arguments will create an inflated estimate of group agreement. Such feelings of consensus are associated with several outcomes in group discussion, including overconfidence (Sniezek 1992), underestimation of risk (Williams and Taormina 1993), less extensive generation of ideas during discussion of decision material (Crott *et al.* 1998) and poorer decision-making (for a review, see Shulz-Hardt *et al.* 2000). Indeed, Schulz-Hardt *et al.* (2000) found that the tendency to prefer supportive information before group discussion was only inhibited when groups had at least two individuals who did not share the group's initial decision preference.

Groupthink revisited

What is striking in reading this research on shared-information bias are the similarities to groupthink. This work documents that discussion among like-minded people commonly evokes selectively focused discussion, inappropriately high confidence, an exaggerated idea of consensus and a polarization of belief following discussion. Note, however, that we are not dealing with high-status, highly cohesive groups under stressful decision pressure. The only key ingredient here is that group members start out sharing a general preference on an issue. Perhaps the failure to corroborate some of the key hypotheses of groupthink theory has to do with the fact that the phenomena specified by groupthink occur far more commonly than Janis assumed and do not require the antecedent conditions of cohesion, stress, and so on. If so, the errors in attitude, perception and decision specified by groupthink theory could plague a much wider array of groups than was previously thought possible.

INTENSE INDOCTRINATION

As we have seen, the study of social influence raises several interesting theoretical questions for group researchers. Social influence processes, however, can have powerful and important real-life implications as well. This is seen quite dramatically in instances of intense indoctrination. In Chapter 1, we referred to Patty Hearst's abduction by the Symbionese Liberation Army (SLA). What was most startling about this incident was that, within weeks of her kidnapping, Ms Hearst had joined forces with her captors, participating in both a bank robbery and a shoot-out at a sporting goods store. A year later at her eventual capture, she proclaimed her occupation as 'urban guerilla'. Somehow the SLA had transformed Patty Hearst from a student into a revolutionary in a matter of weeks. This 'accomplishment' is somewhat less surprising, however, when one considers the psychological principles underlying such cases of intense indoctrination and the social influence process to which Ms Hearst was exposed (Hearst 1982), a process in which initial compliance slowly becomes transformed into internalized belief change.

If one examines classic cases of intense indoctrination, such as the 'brainwashing' of captured westerners by Chinese Communists in the early 1950s (Lifton 1961) or the treatment of political dissidents by the Soviet KGB in the 1930s and 1940s (Hinkle and Wolff 1956), a common pattern is evident. The indoctrination takes place in stages. Baron (2000) outlines an attentional capacity view of indoctrination that specifies four such stages. The first is referred to the *softening up stage*. This is marked by a variety of disorienting and stressful procedures commonly involving isolation from one's friends and family, inadequate sleep and nutrition, overstimulation (e.g. overwork) and various emotional manipulations (e.g. fear). Patty Hearst, for example, was held handcuffed in a dark closet for four weeks while being repeatedly threatened with death. In other cases, indoctrinees find themselves away from home in a dizzying round of activities, lectures, games, prayers, meetings and work, often leaving them scant time for sleep or private reflection (Baron *et al.* 2003).

This is followed by the *compliance stage*, in which the recruit tentatively 'tries out' some of the behaviours requested by the group, more or less

going through the motions or paying lip service to many of their demands. Often this is viewed as a period of exploration by the recruit to see
what such compliance nets him or her. In other cases, individuals comply
out of politeness or from a desire to not make a scene. In Ms Hearst's case,
her initial decision to 'join' the SLA was only a simple ruse on her part to
appease a group that was threatening to murder her (Hearst 1982). In this
stage, indoctrinees may change their appearance and may 'try out' various
novel behaviours (e.g. meditation, martial arts drill, learning new doctrine). This stage is not hard to understand. People are responding to
threat, curiosity or deeply ingrained norms of politeness.

It is in the *internalization stage* that things become interesting, in that
the compliance transforms itself into privately held belief change. Here,
the recruit or indoctrinee begins to consider the possibility that the group's
worldview is correct. In most cases of compliance occurring outside of
intense indoctrination, individuals conform due to some noticeable threat
or inducement. Once this pressure is removed, the compliance ends. In
intense indoctrination, however, a variety of subtle pressures serve to prolong the behaviour and these pressures often lead to actual belief change.
How can we explain this process? First, conformity pressure is likely to be
quite strong. Because of the experiences in the softening up stage, the
individual will often be confused, exhausted or scared. As Baron (2000)
points out, these conditions drain available attentional capacity, lower
self-confidence and leave the indoctrinee more dependent on others. Darley
(1966), for example, found greater conformity when participants were
frightened by the prospect of upcoming shock. Dolinski and Nawrat (1998)
also found that individuals were more easily manipulated by social influence manipulations after a fear induction. Additionally, by separating the
recruit from his or her friends and family, the indoctrinating group denies
the recruit access to allies who might bolster his or her original views. As
a result, the indoctrinating group becomes a more powerful influencing
agent, especially because they will generally be united. If there is one
lesson from the conformity research, it is that we do not realize how
susceptible we are to social influence if we have no social support and
everyone around us agrees on a given point. This is true not just because
group judgments are credible. As we have learned, groups are a key source
of approval. In these cases of intense indoctrination, the group is the only
source of immediate approval. This dramatically increases their power,
for we generally underestimate the extent to which we depend upon
positive relationships with others to maintain our self-esteem and sense of
well-being.

A second cause of internalization is that the stress of the softening up
period undoubtedly leaves us with less attentional capacity (Easterbrook
1959). As a result, we are less capable to consider carefully the wisdom, or
lack thereof, of the arguments and doctrine of the indoctrinating group.
Using such techniques, cults have persuaded their members to accept
beliefs that seem absolutely bizarre to outsiders. For example, one small
religious sect still active in the USA convinced members that, to transcend
'needs of the flesh', they should try to restrain themselves from bathing,
touching other people, urinating or defecating too often, and even from
wearing glasses (Martin and Young 1979). Another religious sect preaches

that the urge to sleep more than 4–5 hours a day is pressure from the devil, while several others have induced male group members to submit to vasectomies or castration (Pratkanis and Aronson 2000; Baron *et al.* in press). In short, because the stress of intense indoctrination reduces attentional capacity (Baron 2000), the indoctrinee is more susceptible than usual to flawed and illogical arguments.

A third mechanism that provokes private belief change is the individual's need for identity. Mass movements provide us with larger than life goals and a sense of purpose that can transcend the insignificant goals of our own lives. The dedicated follower can feel special, selfless and a part of history. Thus, many of the major existential dilemmas that plague modern man (e.g. 'Why is my existence important?', 'What is the meaning of life?', 'What is a good life?') evaporate if one totally accepts an indoctrinating group's message.

The final and perhaps most crucial mechanism producing internalization, however, involves cognitive dissonance phenomena. Put simply, we have a strong tendency to justify our behaviours. This tendency is particularly strong when our behaviours have been costly and unusual. One straightforward means of justifying an unusual action that we have committed (e.g. Patty Hearst's participation in the Hibernia Bank Robbery) is to think of reasons why the action was sensible, correct or necessary. This, in turn, will often lead the individual to further embrace the group's cause and doctrine ('I robbed that bank to finance and publicize a needed revolution'). From this perspective, it is not surprising that indoctrination procedures generally require indoctrinees to engage in increasingly public self-criticisms and attacks on their 'old' pre-group associates. Indeed, Ms Hearst was required early in her indoctrination to make radio announcements critical of her family. The public nature of these confessions increases their psychological cost, which, in turn, heightens the dissonance the indoctrinee feels. Many studies have found that cognitive dissonance procedures such as these are a powerful means of producing attitude change (Aronson 1968) and there is little doubt that they play a major role in intense indoctrination. Moreover, this process can produce a 'one step at a time' pattern of escalating commitment in which initial compliance triggers private belief change, which then leaves the indoctrinee susceptible to even more extreme requests from the group. This is a phenomenon known as the *foot in the door effect*.

The final phase of intense indoctrination can be described as the *consolidation stage*. In this stage, the recruit solidifies his or her newly acquired allegiance to the group by making various costly behavioural commitments that are hard to undo (e.g. donating one's personal possessions to the group; cutting ties to family and old friends; recruiting new members). This final stage of indoctrination is marked by totally accepting group doctrine and policy, with little critical examination. The primary reaction of the recruit to negative information about the group is denial and rationalization. Doctrine is accepted on the basis of absolute faith. At this point, it takes extremely dramatic evidence to shake the faith of believers. This almost total acceptance of doctrine on faith probably occurs in part because group members find it quite effortful to agonize continually over whether the group's ideology is correct or justified. As this implies, carefully evaluating group doctrine will often strain the members' attentional capacity, a capacity that already is depleted by the other rigours of indoctrination. The believer can avoid this painful process by simply deciding at some point that the group doctrine is correct, and henceforth *anything* the group requires or argues is accepted on faith as being justified and true. In a sense, the group member has adopted a biased perspective so that he or she can avoid confronting any doubts. For this reason, the indoctrinee who has reached the consolidation stage will be highly resistant to persuasion from those outside the group and highly susceptible to influence from inside the group. When this is coupled with the group polarization and cognitive dissonance pressures likely within such groups, we have the conditions to heighten the extreme behaviour and beliefs that are highly resistant to change.

MOB ACTION

A recent website posting (www.siamweb.org/news_culture/jakarta_riot/ – 2001) provided a wrenching eyewitness account of an incident during the 1998 anti-Chinese riots in Jakarta, Indonesia in which a gang of men invaded a Jakarta apartment, raping, stabbing and killing several of the inhabitants. Accounts such as this provide us with a close and uncomfortable look at evil. As noted earlier, some of the most disturbing examples of human behaviour have occurred when groups erupted into acts of violence and destruction, acts so vicious and senseless that they make us question how evolved we are as a species. Individuals in Europe, Africa and the United States have died in riots triggered by events as trivial as the outcomes of sporting contests. And, of course, the ethnic rioting that occurs periodically on every continent often has the effect of provoking retaliatory attacks, transforming a community into warring camps. How can we explain such savage and tragic behaviour?

Some causes of mob behaviour

Observers of nineteenth-century mass behaviour (Le Bon 1895; Tarde 1895) saw crowds as behaving more impulsively and irrationally than individuals. They thought that crowds undermine social restraints such as shame, fear and guilt. Why might this be so? One answer is that individuals often feel relatively *anonymous* in crowds because it is hard to keep track of who is doing what. This anonymity, of course, should lower feelings of fear – fear of detection, evaluation or retaliation. Le Bon also felt that crowds led people to ignore their own individuality, a process that has come to be called *deindividuation*. The gist of this notion is that rather than focusing on their own individual actions and responsibilities, deindividuated people focus on those around them and, indeed, view themselves as just a part of that group. In such a state, one is presumed to be less susceptible to feelings of fear and guilt and less concerned with one's ordinary standards and the consequences of abandoning them. In addition, as we will see in the chapter on social support (Chapter 10), a substantial body of literature suggests that being with others (e.g. acting as part of a group) does reduce fear (e.g. Amoroso and Walters 1969). Whether this fear reduction occurs due to conditioning, social comparison or the fact that often people are truly safer when acting within groups, the result should be the same, namely less fear-induced inhibition of aggression.

Le Bon's thoughts about deindividuation are closely related to the modern research on responsibility diffusion. The gist of this research is that people feel less responsible for their actions in many group settings. Thus, those who aggress as part of a group can often absolve themselves of much of the guilt by attributing primary responsibility to others. Much research indicates that individuals often *diffuse responsibility* in this manner when in group settings. Darley and Latané (1968), for example, found that bystanders acted less responsibly during a simulated emergency if they thought other people were also present and able to help. In short, one view of crowd action is that people in mobs often feel released from normal social restraints.

In addition to reducing fear, guilt and felt responsibility, being part of a large group of people often induces excitement and a flood of sensations. As we mentioned in our discussion of intense indoctrination, a substantial body of research indicates that such conditions of *arousal and sensory overload* inhibit careful reflective thought while heightening our tendencies to engage in simplistic, emotional and stereotypic problem-solving and responding (e.g. Eysenck 1977). In addition, as we saw in Chapter 2 on social facilitation, heightened arousal may increase dominant responding. In accord with this view, several studies have confirmed that, provided people are tempted or frustrated, they tend to engage in more uninhibited, aggressive or antisocial behaviour when arousal has been heightened by such things as white noise, exciting films, sexual stimuli or exercise. In a series of studies, Zillmannn and his associates (see Zillmannn 1979) demonstrated that participants administered more shock to someone who angered them in conditions in which the participants were recently aroused by sexual lures or exercise (e.g. Zillmannn et al. 1974; Cantor et al. 1978). In addition, Zillmannn found that individuals aroused by insult or exercise were more sexually 'turned on' by sexually exciting lures (e.g. films), a finding with clear implications for mob action, in that such groups frequently engage in acts of sexual aggression as well as other forms of anti-social behaviour (for a review, see Zillmannn 1998). In short, if we make the reasonable assumption that mob scenes generally elevate the arousal of people who comprise the mob, Zillmannn's work implies that such arousal will often heighten aggression, sexual activity and other impulsive mob activity.

Modelling also contributes to emotional and bizarre behaviour in mobs. When groups provide us with a good deal of anonymity and excitement, the larger the group, the greater the likelihood that we will encounter someone uninhibited enough to 'break the ice' by exhibiting, or modelling, aggressive or uninhibited action. Such *releaser cues* can serve several functions. First, they may suggest to others that such behaviour is called for or appropriate. This is especially true if the action evokes approval (e.g. cheers) from the crowd. In short, behavioural models can help establish norms that encourage wild, aggressive or impulsive behaviour (Wheeler 1966). Second, if the behaviour of the model goes unpunished or results in a positive outcome for the actor, it encourages similar action from others (Wheeler 1966). Finally, in some cases, the model's behaviour suggests novel behavioural options that never would have occurred to the others in the group. These notions are supported by research with both children and adults. Thus, it is well established that observers who watch aggressive models later exhibit more aggression than those who have not seen such models (e.g. Bandura *et al.* 1961).

Deindividuation research

Zimbardo (1969) developed a model of deindividuation that incorporated many of the ideas cited above. He was concerned about specifying the causes and consequences of a deindividuated state. He argued that 'antecedent conditions' such as arousal, anonymity, diffused responsibility and being in a group, in combination, all served to lower the extent to which we monitor our own actions. This lowered self-monitoring, in turn, was presumed to render individuals less susceptible to fear and guilt, thereby 'releasing' them to engage in such things as revelry or violence when so tempted. Prentice-Dunn and Rogers (1989) offer a very similar analysis, arguing that the combination of such antecedent conditions provokes less privately felt self-awareness, which lowers social restraints (fear, shame, guilt).

Zimbardo emphasized anonymity as a key component; most deindividuation studies have manipulated this construct in one form or another. Thus, some studies manipulate how identifiable the participant is to the victim by having participants wear hoods or masks, using dimly lit rooms or the like. The outcomes of these anonymity studies are not always consistent. In fact, in some studies anonymity has been found to *decrease* aggression (e.g. Diener 1976). For the most part, however, the research supports the notion that anonymity elevates aggression and other antisocial behaviours. Postmes and Spears (1998) conducted a meta-analysis of some 60 studies of deindividuation and concluded that, when one 'averages' across these studies, antisocial behaviour was significantly higher when participants could not be identified by their victims.

Another common strategy in this research is to combine several of the factors thought to trigger deindividuation and examine their effects. Thus, in deindividuated conditions, anonymity might be manipulated with dim lighting, group cohesion increased through the use group 'trust' exercises, arousal increased through the use of noise or music, and so on (e.g. Diener *et al.* 1976). Target behaviours in such research might be the extent to which participants take more than their share of candy, go over a time limit when being tested, harass a 'pacificist in training' or administer electric shock (for reviews, see Diener 1980; Prentice-Dunn and Rogers 1989; Postmes and Spears 1998). The results of Postmes and Spears' meta-analysis indicate that such combined manipulations significantly heighten various measures of antisocial behaviour. Also, as predicted by various views of deindividuation, Postmes and Spears found that antisocial behaviour was more likely to occur in those deindividuation studies in which participants were run in groups rather than as individuals. Indeed, they also found that deindividuation effects were significantly larger as the size of the group increased. For example, Mullen (1986) found that in 60 lynchings between the turn of the century and 1946, the larger the mob relative to the number of victims lynched, the more vicious and brutal was their murder of the victim. This was true even after controlling for severity or type of crime allegedly committed by the victim. Although the results of Postmes and Spears' meta-analysis indicate that several classic manipulations of deindividuation do affect antisocial and uninhibited behaviour as predicted, we must be cautious. The overall strength of the relationships they reported, although significant, were generally weak (much like a significant but low correlation) and often inconsistent across studies.

Some writers argue that lack of self-awareness, not anonymity *per se*, is critical to a deindividuated state (e.g. Diener 1980; Prentice-Dunn and Rogers 1989). In other words, the key issue might be whether the anonymity leads you to focus less on your own responsibility and individual role in an action. Some findings support this view. Several manipulations that increase self-awareness (e.g. the presence of mirrors) have been found to reduce such antisocial behaviour as cheating (Diener and Wallboom 1976), hostile aggression (Rule *et al.* 1975) and petty greed (Beaman *et al.* 1979). In the ingenious study of Beaman *et al.* (1979), groups of costumed children in the USA were observed as they arrived at a home to request candy on Halloween. One condition was designed to enhance self-awareness. In this condition, children gave their names at the door and found that the candy bowl was placed just before a large mirror. In all conditions, the children were asked to take only one candy each and were then left alone at the candy bowl. The self-awareness manipulations suppressed their illicit candy-taking. For example, when the mirror was present, only 12 per cent took extra candy, whereas with no mirror in sight 34 per cent exceeded the limit of one candy each. The mirror, however, had no such inhibiting effect when the children had not given their name at the door. In Diener and Wallboom's (1976) study, 71 per cent of their participants violated time limits on an IQ test under normal conditions, but only 7 per cent did so when made self-aware by working in front of a mirror and hearing their own voice.

Unfortunately, as with anonymity, the effects of such manipulations are inconsistent across studies. Indeed, Postmes and Spears (1998) concluded that, across studies, manipulations that increase private self-awareness (e.g. placing participants in front of mirrors or letting them hear their own voice) did not reliably decrease antisocial actions; that is, their meta-analysis showed that the overall effect of private self-awareness on antisocial behaviour was almost zero. However, the trick-or-treat study of Beaman *et al.* was for some reason not included in this analysis. In addition, manipulations in which participants were dressed alike were not considered by Postmes and Spears to be manipulations of (low) private self-awareness, despite the fact that many researchers interpret such manipulations in this fashion.

On the other hand, low *public self-awareness* (e.g. when the participant cannot be observed by others or by camera) does elevate antisocial action.

This public self-awareness, of course, is just another word for anonymity from outsiders and, therefore, supplements the studies cited above that indicate that anonymity elevates antisocial behaviour. Viewed as a whole, the findings from the deindividuation studies offer cautious support for Zimbardo's (1969) original suggestions regarding the role of anonymity, group cohesion and group action as triggers for antisocial action. What remains a matter of active debate (e.g. Postmes *et al.* 2001) is how important self-awareness is in this process. One possibility we may wish to consider is that anonymity, group support and responsibility diffusion all lower fear and guilt directly, even when self-awareness remains high. A second controversial issue is the extent to which mob action represents 'norm free action', as argued by classic views of deindividuation (e.g. Prentice-Dunn and Rogers 1989). These theories assume that mobs engage in wild behaviour because, in such groups, fear and guilt are lowered and this, in turn, makes the members more likely to ignore societal norms and rules. There are critics of this view, however (e.g. Turner and Killian 1972). These writers question why some crowd settings explode into aggression and anger, others provoke wild celebration, while yet others do little out of the ordinary? The emergent norm view of deindividuation addresses these issues.

Emergent norm theory

Although several studies have indicated that groups are more likely to trigger antisocial action, there is some evidence that these effects do not simply represent norm-free behaviour. For instance, Johnson and Downing (1979) reported that dressing participants in medical gowns decreased aggression, whereas having them wear Ku Klux Klan-like outfits increased it. Rabbie *et al.* (1985) found that anonymity decreased the aggressiveness of males but increased that of females (for a similar finding, see Lightdale and Prentice 1994). These outcomes suggest that situation-specific norms or gender norms may be affecting behaviour. In contrast to Ku Klux Klan outfits, medical uniforms bring to mind norms of helpfulness. Similarly, aggressive action is seen as normatively more appropriate for males than females (e.g. Eagly and Steffen 1986). Consequently, because people generally conform more to norms when observed, it makes sense that, when identifiable, males would aggress more and females less. In short, each group, when identifiable, conforms more to the norms that define their gender-linked role.

Such findings suggest that social norms might play an important role in determining the behaviour of a crowd. Several researchers (e.g. Turner and Killian 1972) suggest that an emergent norm can develop in crowds that may contradict broader societal norms. Thus, a pro-aggression norm may develop within a crowd despite the fact that, in the larger culture, aggression is anti-normative. Alternatively, a celebration norm may evolve in a different setting. According to this view, the stone-throwing of Palestinian youth during the Intifada occurs not because they are less responsive to norms, but because, in that group setting, stone-throwing is normative.

The SIDE model

The proponents of social identity theory (Spears *et al.* 1990; Reicher *et al.* 1995; Lea *et al.* 2001; Postmes *et al.* 2001) have recently offered a social identity view of deindividuation effects (the SIDE model). This view extends emergent norm theory in an interesting direction by suggesting that anonymity *from other group members* actually *increases* the extent to which individuals comply with aggressive/violent group norms. Thus, they argue that anonymity affects mob action not by lowering fear, but by increasing conformity to group norms. Most writers in the area of social influence and conformity assume that anonymity of this type *decreases* conformity because groups cannot easily punish non-conformers if the group cannot identify who the non-conformers are. Thus, anonymity within groups is usually presumed to lower conformity. But the SIDE model assumes that individuals in mob settings are conforming to mob norms voluntarily and with enthusiasm due to their desire to see themselves as loyal and well-established group members, not because they fear group sanctions. According to this perspective, the reason anonymity often elevates conformity to group norms is because anonymity lowers our focus on our own individual features and person-to-person differences and increases the tendency for individuals to view themselves as group members. As a result, these 'group-focused' individuals should care more about immediate group norms than broader societal norms. If those local group norms favour some violation of broader societal norms – whether it be euphoric celebration or violent destruction – anonymous group members will be more likely to conform to such action. In non-anonymous conditions, in contrast, people are reacted to as individuals and will think of themselves in that fashion. As a result, their concern about group norms will be lower and they will instead be concerned with general societal norms.

There is some emerging support for aspects of this SIDE view. Lea *et al.* (2001) found that, after a computer discussion of topics such as immigration and politeness, participants who were kept visually anonymous from each other reported that they felt more connected and attracted to their groups than did groups that could see a silent video feed of the other members of their group. It is conceivable, of course, that this occurred because in the anonymous discussion participants were more uninhibited and therefore had more fun. But this study offers some support for the interesting prediction that anonymity from each other leads to greater group identification. This report is complemented by Spears and co-workers' (1990) finding that members of a computer group conformed to student norms on topics such as nuclear power and affirmative action only when participants remained anonymous from each other and had their group identity emphasized. In a third paper in this series, Postmes *et al.* (2001) created norms using the inventive strategy of priming participants to think either about efficiency or social needs. Computer groups of three then discussed how to handle a problem in hospital administration. Groups that were provided with both visual and name-based anonymity were affected more by the nature of the dominant norm than groups who saw photos and names of their computer-linked partners. Thus, we have some initial evidence that anonymity increases group identification as well as conformity to group norms, as proposed by the SIDE model. Nevertheless, there is still reason to have reservations about this model.

Critique of the SIDE model

First, Postmes and Spears (1998) reported in their meta-analysis of prior studies that anonymity from other group members (the very treatments used in these last two studies) did not, 'on average', significantly increase the kind of antisocial behaviour of interest in studies of mob action. Rather, it was anonymity from those *outside* the group that was found to be most reliably linked to aggressive, destructive or antisocial action. In addition, the kind of anonymity created in the computer chat groups often used in the SIDE research is different from the anonymity that exists in face-to-face mobs. In computer groups, one cannot see the others but one can learn a lot about their opinions and backgrounds during group discussion. In contrast, in crowds and mobs, one can still see the other group members. Anonymity here stems from the fact that neither you nor any other participants or onlookers generally know the names, opinions or backgrounds of most mob members. These different forms of anonymity may well have different effects. Indeed, most of the research on the SIDE model focuses on how anonymity affects conformity on attitude topics and feelings of group identification. In contrast, research on earlier models of deindividuation focuses on such outcome variables as aggression, cheating and stealing. As a result, we cannot be sure that these two research traditions are indeed focusing on the same phenomenon. An additional difficulty is that mob action is often marked by intense emotion, be it elation, anger or a mixture of both. The SIDE model's view of mob activity as simple conformity to group norms does not provide a good explanation for the occurrence of such emotions. Thus, there are reasons to question the extent to which the specific interpretation offered by social identity theory fully explains the full range of deindividuation phenomena. However, a growing number of researchers are acknowledging that deindividuated behaviour does not necessarily involve release from social norms. This suggests that some combination of the classic 'lowered restraints' view championed by theorists such as Zimbardo, Diener, and Prentice-Dunn and Rogers and the emergent norm view favoured by the emergent-norm and the SIDE theorists may provide a more complete explanation for mob action.

The ID model

We offer an *integrated deindividuation* model (ID model) as a possible means of combining the lowered-restraint view offered by classic theories of deindividuation and the emergent norm view described above. This integrated model embraces the classic assumption that the arousal, group support, anonymity from outside scrutiny and shared responsibility of mob action does, in fact, lower fear and guilt. Note that such anonymity from scrutiny and group action were identified as reliable causes of deindividuated behaviour by Postmes and Spears in their meta-analysis. On the other hand, the same meta-analysis indicated that self-awareness was not a crucial variable. However, one need not postulate low self-awareness for this drop in fear and guilt. If people cannot identify you, and you have the power of a crowd behind you, you have a rational basis to have less fear of punishment, harm or failure, even if you remain self-aware. In addition, if other people are performing a given action (e.g. shouting insults, throwing rocks at riot police), it tends to legitimize the action, thereby further lowering guilt. Such group action also diffuses responsibility ('I just threw one rock; that didn't do much harm'), which also provides a rational reason to feel less guilt. Lowered levels of fear and guilt would 'release' the crowd members to violate restrictions imposed by society at large. But when would group members choose to take advantage of this freedom to act in an antisocial or impulsive manner? We contend that this will be likely only when norms encouraging such behaviour pre-exist in the group setting or emerge in the crowd. Without such norms, antisocial behaviour will be unlikely. This notion explains why anonymity has been found to increase antisocial behaviour in some but not all studies of deindividuation (e.g. Diener 1976). As noted above, aggressive or exuberant models may help establish such 'ingroup' norms, especially if such releaser cues meet with crowd approval. Note that our ID model does not assume that either lowered self-awareness or high social identification are necessary conditions for the provocation of extreme group behaviour. In short, we would agree that mob behaviour is guided by the ingroup norms that emerge, but that such behaviour is also facilitated by lowered fear and guilt, which permit participants to flaunt broader societal norms. Interestingly, several very disturbing and well-known photographs of lynch mobs in the USA depict the crowd as gloating and proud. Such a reaction is what one would expect if the situational norms of the setting legitimized the brutality of the mob, at least in their own view. This lowered fear and guilt, coupled with (a) the freedom of acting on one's desires and impulses and (b) the excitement provided by dramatic crowd action/confrontation, can also provide an explanation for the intense emotions that characterizes mob settings.

SUMMARY

The extreme attitudes and behaviours that often occur in groups can be attributed to several group processes. These include groupthink, group polarization, intense indoctrination and mob action. Groupthink in problem-solving groups produces the suppression of dissent as well as exaggerated notions of the ingroup's moral superiority and invulnerability. Groupthink appears to be due to our desires for social approval from the group as well as how much we trust group opinion when it takes the form of a consensus. Originally, groupthink was presumed to be limited to extremely high-status groups, but recent research suggests that it may occur in a variety of groups. This process of suppressing any ideas that diverge from the group's favoured solution can contribute to extreme decisions and attitudes.

Group polarization describes the fact that groups of like-minded individuals tend to endorse more extreme decisions and attitudes following discussion. This is due, at least in part, to the biased flow of arguments in such groups, which provide members with added support for their beliefs. It also can be triggered by finding out that others support your views, leading to an increase in confidence as well as the competitive desire to be at least as committed to the group's general position as the majority of other group members. Finally, there is some recent support for the notion that groups become more extreme to distinguish themselves from outgroups. Intense indoctrination can be a major cause of extreme behaviour in groups. This process involves a series of stages, generally beginning with a stressful period, and then moving to a stage in which the indoctrinee 'tries out' some of the ideas, policies and behaviours advocated by the group. The behaviour in this compliance stage occurs sometimes out of curiosity, sometimes out of politeness and at other times due to pressure. Over time, however, such processes as systematically orchestrated conformity pressure, cognitive dissonance manipulations and carefully censored messages begin to produce the privately accepted belief change that characterizes the internalization stage. These processes, coupled with procedures that isolate the person from dissenting opinion and exhaust the indoctrinee mentally and emotionally, can produce attitude change that is extreme and highly resistant to change, as seen in the consolidation stage of indoctrination.

Mobs, too, can provoke remarkably extreme behaviour. This appears to be due at least in part to factors such as anonymity, power and shared responsibility and their impact on social restraints. In addition to these factors, the behaviour legitimization provided by large co-acting groups also lowers feelings of fear, guilt and shame. If the crowd adopts norms favouring impulsive, destructive or antisocial behaviour, these large group settings can provoke extreme behaviour, disturbing to contemplate or to witness.

SUGGESTIONS FOR FURTHER READING

Baron, R.S. (2000) Attentional capacity and intense indoctrination. *Personality and Social Psychology Review*, 4: 238–54. An examination of why people become committed to extremist organizations.

Esser, J.K. (1998) Alive and well after 25 years: a review of groupthink research. *Organizational Behavior and Human Decision Processes*, 73: 116–41. A key overview.

Hogg, M.A., Turner, J.C. and Davidson, B. (1990) Polarized norms and social frames of reference: a test of the self-categorization theory of group polarization. *Basic and Applied Social Psychology*, 11: 77–100. Outlines and tests several key predictions of self-categorization theory.

Postmes, T. and Spears, R. (1998) Deindividuation and antinormative behavior: a meta-analysis. *Psychological Bulletin*, 123: 238–59. Examines variables affecting errant behaviour in large groups.

SEVEN

SOCIAL COMBINATION APPROACHES TO GROUP DECISION-MAKING

KEY CONCEPTS

- What are the *social communication* and *social combination* approaches to the study of group decision-making, and how do they differ?
- How are social decision schemes used to link individual group member preference with group preference?
- What does a social combination analysis reveal about how juries reach their verdicts?
- How are *intellective* tasks different from *judgmental* tasks, and why is this distinction important for explaining how groups reach agreement on tasks?
- In general, should groups be more or less susceptible to judgmental biases than individuals?

INTRODUCTION

At one time or another, you have probably been part of a decision-making group. It might have been a rather formal affair, such as a committee or club meeting with a formal agenda and rules of procedure. More likely it was an informal setting, such as a group of friends trying to decide what movie to see. A lot goes on in decision-making groups – many viewpoints are expressed; discussion may shift from topic to topic suddenly and without apparent reason; genuine persuasion may occur but so may capitulation to social pressure; common political processes (e.g. compromise, logrolling, coalition formation) may be observed; people form impressions of one another. It is to this rather complex but fascinating topic that we now turn our attention.

Group decision-making is not only a fascinating topic, it is an important one as well. We entrust groups to make many of our most important decisions. The US Congress declares war (in principle, if not in practice), boards of directors make business decisions that can affect thousands of workers and stockholders, the US Supreme Court decides whether and when women may end their pregnancies, and juries sometimes literally make life-or-death decisions.

In this chapter, we will not attempt to consider in detail all of the complex psychological processes involved in group decision-making. For example, we will not be concerned here with how groups generate decision alternatives (a key issue in the group problem-solving process); rather, we will address how groups choose among a set of well-specified and known alternatives on problems and decisions.

Nearly every decision-making group must achieve some level of agreement or consensus among group members to define a group choice. This required degree of consensus is called the group's *decision rule*. A good example is the familiar majority-rules criterion used in most elections; another example is the unanimity rule used by most juries (see Miller 1989). Decision rules may be explicit and formal (e.g. a two-thirds majority voting rule specified in an organization's bylaws) or implicit and informal (e.g. a chairperson's intuitive assessment that sufficient agreement exists in a meeting to consider the matter at hand settled). Such decision rules are one of several important aspects of group decision-making procedures. Other aspects include the voting rules that govern how individual preferences may be expressed and pooled (e.g. vote for your favourite option *vs.* rank order all options) and the group's formal agenda (e.g. sometimes the order in which issues are taken up affect the decisions reached). However, we will restrict our attention here to the typical, small, face-to-face decision-making group that has a rather simple agenda (viz. a single decision to make) and a simple, usually informal, voting rule (e.g. direct polling of first preferences).

In this chapter, we are concerned primarily with understanding the process by which a group moves from initial disagreement (i.e. failure to satisfy its decision rule) to agreement (i.e. satisfaction of the operative decision rule). Viewed in this light, group decision-making is fundamentally concerned with social influence processes, the topic of the last two chapters. The traditional approach to the study of group decision-making might be called the *social communication* approach. It assumes that the best way to analyse how a group reaches its decision is to listen to what the group members say to one another. Typical questions posed by someone taking this approach might include: 'Who talks to whom?'; 'Who says what?'; 'Do others agree or disagree?' This approach has yielded much useful knowledge (e.g. Strodtbeck and Mann 1956; Bales 1958). For example, it is clear from this type of analysis that groups often develop two kinds of leaders, those that focus on task demands and those that attend to the feelings and social needs of group members. Another interesting finding is that those who take on leadership roles tend to have very high rates of participation in the group (e.g. Sorrentino and Boutillier 1975; Mullen *et al.* 1989).

Here, we focus on a rather different approach to investigating the group decision-making process. It has been termed the *social combination* approach (Laughlin 1980; Davis 1982). Its basic unit of analysis is not a spoken thought or argument, but rather the actual preferences of the group members. Someone taking this approach might ask: 'How much support does each alternative have at the beginning of group delibera-tion?'; 'Are there regular patterns in the way preferences change?'; 'Can I predict what the group's decision will be if I know the members' prefer-ences?' This approach is called the social combination approach because it tries to specify how group members combine what they bring to the group (e.g. their personal preferences) into a single group product (e.g. a group decision).

SOCIAL COMBINATION APPROACHES TO GROUP DECISION-MAKING

The basic idea of the social combination approach is to find some recipe, rule or function for translating what group members bring to the group's task (e.g. their abilities, motivations) into what the group actually accomplishes (e.g. the group level of performance). A social combination approach to group decision-making asks, 'Is there a way of relating the preferences of individual group members (the input) to the final prefer-ence of the entire group (the output)?' The most ambitious attempts to answer this question have employed Davis' (1973) *social decision scheme* or SDS model (for other interesting social combination models, see Hastie *et al.* 1983; Crott and Werner 1994). Before describing the SDS model, we should perhaps warn the incurably math-phobic reader that a good under-standing of this approach requires the use of some mathematics. The good news is that the required math is not too hard to follow if you familiarize yourself with the terminology and work through the descrip-tion of the model carefully and step by step. More importantly, the basic ideas behind the math are fairly simple (Stasser 1999) and the utility of those simple ideas is fairly broad (Levine 1999).

The SDS model assumes that groups of a fixed size, r, must choose among a set of n alternatives, $A_1, A_2, A_3, \ldots A_n$. A simple illustration is a six-person jury that has to choose between a guilty and a not guilty verdict, for which $r = 6$, $n = 2$ and $(A_1, A_2) =$ (guilty, not guilty).[1] The SDS model does not try to predict the final decision of any particular group, but rather the overall distribution of group decisions, denoted as $(P_1, P_2, P_3, \ldots P_n)$. For example, if 65 per cent of the six-person juries considering the same case decided that the defendant was guilty, then the distribution of group decisions would just be $(P_1, P_2) =$ (65% guilty, 35% not guilty). The input for the SDS model is based upon the corresponding distribution of *individual* preferences (denoted $p_1, p_2, p_3, \ldots p_n$), and consists of all the possible ways that the r members of the group could possibly be distrib-uted across the n decision alternatives. For the example we have been considering, there are seven such 'splits', which are displayed on the left-hand side of Table 7.1. If each individual juror starts deliberation prefer-ring either a guilty or not guilty verdict, then each six-person jury must begin deliberation with one of these seven splits. In fact, for any particu-lar trial, one could estimate just what percentage of juries would begin deliberation with each possible split. A simple way to do this is to poll

Table 7.1 Some illustrative social decision schemes

Initial splits		(a) Majority/ otherwise hung			(b) Zeisel and Diamond (1978)			(c) Proportionality			(d) Kerr and MacCoun (1985)		
#G	#NG	G	NG	H	G	NG	H	G	NG	H	G	NG	H
6	0	1.00	0.00	0.00	1.00	0.00	0.00	1.00	0.00	0.00	1.00	0.00	0.00
5	1	1.00	0.00	0.00	0.95	0.02	0.01	0.83	0.17	0.00	0.81	0.00	0.19
4	2	1.00	0.00	0.00	0.83	0.13	0.04	0.67	0.33	0.00	0.31	0.26	0.42
3	3	0.00	0.00	1.00	0.42	0.46	0.12	0.50	0.50	0.00	0.11	0.46	0.43
2	4	0.00	1.00	0.00	0.12	0.85	0.03	0.33	0.67	0.00	0.00	0.84	0.16
1	5	0.00	1.00	0.00	0.02	0.97	0.01	0.17	0.83	0.00	0.00	0.89	0.11
0	6	0.00	1.00	0.00	0.00	1.00	0.00	0.00	1.00	0.00	0.00	1.00	0.00

Abbreviations: G, guilty; NG, not guilty; H, hung.

each jury before it begins deliberation. [Alternatively, one could poll a sample of individual jurors to estimate the overall distribution of juror verdict preference (p_1, p_2), and then, using some basic probability theory, one could calculate the probability of each possible split occurring in randomly composed juries.]

The challenge of the SDS model is to link group member input (viz. starting splits) to group output (group decisions). As noted above, the SDS model does this probabalistically. It does not assume that all groups starting from the same place (i.e. with the same starting split) end up in the same place (i.e. reach the same group decision). Rather, the model tries to identify d_{ij}, the probability that a group starting with the *i*th split will eventually decide on the *j*th decision alternative. If we allow that another possible jury 'decision' is to reach no decision at all (i.e. to 'hang'), then in the jury example we have been considering, there are 21 such values (7 possible splits × 3 jury decision alternatives). These values can be conveniently arrayed in a box or matrix form, as illustrated in panel (a) of Table 7.1. As you can see, this particular *D matrix* or *social decision scheme* is a way of expressing the simple idea that initial majorities will ultimately prevail in the jury. For example, if the majority does in fact rule, and if the jury begins deliberation with four jurors favouring conviction and two favouring acquittal (the third row), this *D* matrix predicts that the jury will eventually convict with certainty (i.e. with probability $d_{21} = 1.0$), and has no possibility of either acquitting or hanging (i.e. $d_{22} = 0.0$ and $d_{23} = 0.0$). When the jury begins deliberation with a majority favouring acquittal (see the last three rows of the matrix), this social decision scheme predicts jury acquittal with certainty. Remember that a social decision scheme has to make a prediction for *every* possible initial split; what happens when there is no initial majority [i.e. when the jury is initially split (three 'guilty', three 'not guilty') as in the middle row of the matrix]? In this particular matrix, it is predicted that such a jury will not be able to reach any agreement if majority rules – that is, the jury is certain to be hung ($d_{43} = 1.0$).

We will be discussing the other matrices in panels (b), (c) and (d) of Table 7.1 below, but their presence should suggest to you that there are many other conceivable decision schemes besides the simple 'initial majority wins' idea summarized by matrix (a). The whole idea of the SDS approach is to identify useful D matrices – useful in the sense that they can reveal patterns that illuminate the process and predict the result of group decision-making. Thus, for example, using this approach we can deduce which decision scheme is adopted most often in a given set of circumstances. A couple of general ways of doing this have been proposed (Kerr *et al.* 1979). One way is to estimate D directly. For any particular group decision task, one might simply count how often groups move from each possible starting split to each possible final group decision. This has been attempted, for example, with jury decision-making. Zeisel and Diamond (1978) interviewed real jurors after their trials to learn their verdict preferences at the start of deliberation. Knowing the juries' final verdicts, Zeisel and Diamond were then able to construct the estimated D for jury deliberation presented in panel (b) of Table 7.1. Take a careful look at this matrix. As you can see, it is a variation on the first decision scheme we considered. Zeisel and Diamond's results suggest that initial majorities usually but do not always prevail in juries, and that minorities very occasionally also prevail. [Apparently, Henry Fonda's accomplishment of reversing a large majority's position in the original version of the film *Twelve Angry Men* is not complete fiction.] The D matrix also suggests, unsurprisingly, that the more even the initial split, the more likely it is that the jury will be unable to satisfy its unanimity decision rule (i.e. that the jury will be hung).

A second way of identifying useful D matrices is to start with an idea or theory of how groups reach consensus and to translate this into a social decision scheme. For example, if you believe that all group members contribute equally to discussion and that the probability that a group adopts a position is simply equal to the *proportion* of all arguments expressed that are in favour of that position, then a proportionality D matrix like the one presented in panel (c) of Table 7.1 should accurately summarize group decision-making and predict group decisions. Thus, if two-thirds of your members begin the decision process favouring option A, then the proportion of groups deciding on that option would be predicted to be 66 per cent by this decision scheme. Or suppose you theorized that numerically larger majorities are usually able to persuade or pressure minorities into submission, and that the group would only have trouble reaching agreement if there was considerable initial disagreement. Davis *et al.* (1975) suggested several D matrices for describing jury decision-making that incorporated these assumptions. Of these, a D which held that an initial two-thirds majority would always prevail and that the jury was likely to be hung otherwise [embodied by the now-familiar panel (a) of Table 7.1] predicted their simulated juries' decisions best. As one can see, in most regards, it parallels the D obtained by Zeisel and Diamond [panel (b)]. The most glaring difference is the much higher rate of predicted hung juries in Davis and colleagues' D (in the middle row). This may be explained by the fact that deliberation time was limited in Davis and colleagues' simulated juries but not in Zeisel and Diamond's real juries; sharply divided simulated juries are less able to reach agreement before the available time runs out (Kerr 1981).

JURY DECISION-MAKING

As we have seen, one group to which the social combination approach has been applied is the jury. Juries are particularly fascinating decision-making groups. In those countries that use the jury system as the basis for determining matters of civil and criminal justice, such groups routinely make decisions with extremely important consequences – at times, literally life-or-death decisions. Juries also have attracted considerable research interest because they lend themselves well to experimental study. Their decision alternatives are explicit and usually small in number (e.g. guilty *vs.* not guilty). Furthermore, unlike many other important real-world decision-making groups (e.g. boards of directors, legislative committees), juries are typically composed of a few unacquainted laypersons who have no further contact after reaching their decisions. In these regards, typical laboratory groups of strangers may well simulate actual juries (Bray and Kerr 1982).

Jury size and decision rule

Another reason for special interest in the jury is that, over the past few decades, courts have raised basic psychological questions about jury behaviour. For example, in the early 1970s the US Supreme Court had to decide whether departures from the jury's traditional size and decision rule (viz. twelve persons and a unanimity rule) were proscribed by the US Constitution. The majority of the Court held that they were not (*Williams v. Florida*, 1970; *Johnson v. Louisiana*, 1972); under the Constitution, states could use juries that contained fewer than twelve persons and that followed a non-unanimous decision rule (e.g. simple majority).

The dissenting minority disagreed with the Court's decisions on several grounds. They rightly pointed out that smaller juries would be less representative of the local community. For example, suppose the local community contains an ethnic or racial minority group making up 5 per cent of the total population. Although 46 per cent of all randomly composed twelve-person juries would contain at least one member of this minority, only 26 per cent of all six-person juries would do so. When representation of a minority group viewpoint bears on the jury's task (e.g. the defendant belongs to the minority group), such differences could be important. The Court's dissenting minority also argued that convicting someone under a non-unanimous rule meant that one or more jurors could remain unconvinced of the defendant's guilt; has a prosecutor really proved a defendant's guilt beyond any reasonable doubt when there are jurors who harbour doubts that they feel are reasonable? Furthermore, under a non-unanimous decision rule, once the decision rule has been satisfied, there is no need for juries to continue to deliberate. It would even be possible, in principle, that a jury would have enough votes for conviction on its very first poll and would quit deliberation without listening to any of the opinions of the pro-acquittal minority.

The Court's majority dismissed these concerns. For example, they thought the majority would never simply outvote an unconvinced minority, but would continue to deliberate as long as necessary to give everyone his or her say and to reach unanimity if at all possible. (It is interesting to note that jurors are often minimally or wholly uncompensated for their time. The Court's theory suggests that jurors who might normally be earning $100 a day would voluntarily choose to listen, perhaps for days on end, to the views of someone whose judgment they question, while compensated for their time at the rate of, say, $10 per day.) An explicit assumption of the Court majority was that a jury's size and decision rule would not materially affect either the process or the product of group decision-making.

Early research findings (e.g. Davis *et al.* 1975; Nemeth 1977; Saks 1977) appeared to bear out this opinion: conviction rates were not affected by changes in jury size or decision rule. In addition, Davis *et al.* (1975) found that a single social decision scheme (viz. the two-thirds majority/hung otherwise *D* matrix) accurately predicted the verdicts of both six- and twelve-person juries and juries operating under both a unanimity and a two-thirds majority decision rule. Thus, there also appeared to be little effect of size or decision rule on the process of decision-making. But it would have been premature to conclude that the Court's majority was correct. It is always possible that jury size or assigned rule might have an effect under conditions not examined in those initial studies. One of the virtues of the SDS model is that, once you have validated a social decision scheme under particular experimental conditions, you can also predict what decisions groups should make under new and unstudied conditions (e.g. for different group sizes, for cases producing different juror conviction rates). The SDS model allows one to do simulations or 'thought experiments' (Davis and Kerr 1986) in which one can explore the possible impact of many variables by extrapolating from what is known to what is unknown. Such thought experiments (Davis *et al.* 1975) suggested that both jury size and assigned decision rule should exert effects on jury verdicts under certain conditions. Specifically, they suggested that the impact of these variables should be strongest for 'close' cases (i.e. ones for which the evidence for and against conviction was nearly equally balanced, producing a conviction rate near 50 per cent) and should be manifest primarily in the rate of hung juries.

As far as the effects of varying the assigned decision rule is concerned, this prediction is intuitively plausible. We would expect – and much research has confirmed (see Stasser *et al.* 1982) – that juries are most likely to be hung when they begin deliberation with large factions favouring both sides. Such initial splits are clearly more likely to occur for close cases than for lopsided ones (i.e. ones with conviction rates near 0 or 100 per cent). Furthermore, under a unanimity rule, to avoid a hung jury it is necessary that every single member of one of the opposing factions be converted to the other side, leading to greater agreement and accept-ance of the group's final decision (Kerr *et al.* 1976; cf. Mohammed and Ringseis 2001). Under a rule of non-unanimity, it is not only more likely that the jury will begin deliberation satisfying the rule, but if this does not occur, fewer conversions will be required to meet the decision rule.

The reason for the corresponding predictions involving jury size is only slightly less apparent. It is well known that pollsters always want to get as large a sample as possible to estimate the overall opinion of a population. The smaller the sample, the more likely it is that the sample results differ greatly from the population value. The same logic applies to the size of juries. In a maximally close case, half the individual jurors would convict and half would acquit (i.e. p(guilty) = 0.50). The conviction rate among jurors in a very small jury (as in a small polling sample) would be ex-pected to depart more from this population value than in a larger jury. The smaller the jury, the less likely that the jury will also be evenly split and, therefore, the less likely the jury is to be hung. It is interesting to note that these effects require no assumption of differences in the way in which different-sized groups seek consensus; rather, they are direct and simple consequences of sampling processes. Armed with the results of such thought experiments, subsequent studies confirmed these predic-tions. Switching from a unanimous to a non-unanimous decision rule (Kerr *et al.* 1976) or from twelve- to six-person juries (Kerr and MacCoun 1985) does not materially affect the ratio of convictions to acquittals, but such variations do decrease the rate of hung juries, especially for close cases. This is important because defendants consider a hung jury a relat-ively positive outcome. Because retrials are expensive, prosecutors will often drop charges or will plea-bargain more flexibly after a hung jury.

The reaction of the Supreme Court to the research evidence on the effects of jury size and assigned rule has been disappointing. In one ruling (*Ballew v. Georgia*, 1978), after reviewing much theoretical and empirical evidence that indicated that jury size affects many aspects of jury func-tioning, the Court allowed its previous endorsement of six-person juries to stand, contenting itself with prohibiting jury size to drop below six persons in criminal trials. The Court has held (*Burch v. Louisiana*, 1979) that unanimity is necessary in juries as small as six, but at the time of writing (2002) has not reconsidered this issue for larger juries. In this, as in many other areas (Saks and Baron 1980; Kerr 1986; Thompson 1989), the Court has ignored or misinterpreted relevant scientific evidence.

Juries' leniency bias

As we have seen, initial majorities usually prevail in juries. This pattern suggests that, as far as determining the final verdict is concerned, there is 'strength in numbers': numerically larger factions (e.g. majorities, pluralities) are more likely to prevail than their relative size would indicate (Stasser *et al.* 1989a; Kerr 1992a). Several social influence processes are consistent with this conclusion. Larger factions should be able to (a) generate more arguments for their position (Hawkins 1962), (b) exert greater power to entice or coerce conformity to their expectations (Asch 1956; Latané 1981) and (c) provide a more viable standard for defining social reality (Festinger 1954) than smaller factions.

Departures or exceptions to a rule, such as the 'strength in numbers' pattern, may be as informative about the nature of group decision-making as the rule itself. For example, if a faction's power to win converts is related to its size, as a simple strength in numbers rule might suggest, we might expect factions of equal size to have equal drawing power in groups. But research on criminal jury behaviour has revealed an exception to such a rule. It is well illustrated in the D obtained by Kerr and MacCoun (1985) and displayed in panel (d) of Table 7.1. As you can see, juries that began deliberation with equal splits (i.e. three guilty, three not guilty) were not equally likely to convict and acquit; rather, they were much more likely to acquit than to convict. Similarly, a two-person minority advocating acquittal was much more likely to prevail (26 per cent of the time) than a two-person minority advocating conviction (which, in this study, never prevailed). This *leniency bias* has been observed in many studies (Stasser *et al.* 1982; MacCoun and Kerr 1988). It suggests that, for close cases and all else being equal, juries would be less likely to convict than individuals (e.g. individual jurors or comparable judges). Interestingly, Kalven and Zeisel (1966) found that most disagreements about the verdict between the trial judge and jury are cases in which the jury would acquit but the individual judge would convict.

A possible explanation for this effect is that the college students who comprise nearly all of the simulated juries examined in this research area are politically liberal and lenient; however, MacCoun and Kerr (1988) also observed a comparable leniency bias in both non-student and student mock juries. The leniency bias effect appears to be attributable to the standards of proof used in criminal trials. Jurors can make two kinds of errors – falsely convicting an innocent defendant or falsely acquitting a guilty one. Common law has long emphasized avoiding the former of these errors, even if it would increase the chances of committing the latter type of error. This can be achieved through several means – instructing jurors to presume the defendant's innocence; placing the burden of altering this presumption on the prosecution; requiring proof of guilt beyond a reasonable doubt. This general prescription to give defendants the benefit of any doubts should functionally make pro-acquittal advocates more persuasive. Similarly, Nemeth (1977) suggested that pro-acquittal jurors have the easier task. They need only plant one reasonable doubt in opponents' minds. However, pro-conviction faction members must eliminate all reasonable doubts from their opponents' minds.

MacCoun and Kerr (1988) tested this explanation by varying the standard of proof under which juries deliberated. All of their four-person mock juries began deliberation with equal splits (two guilty, two not guilty). Half were instructed by the judge to apply the usual, reasonable doubt standard of proof. The rest of the juries were told to apply the 'preponderance of evidence' standard, which requires them to favour whichever side produces the stronger evidence. The latter standard is symmetric and should not give any advantage to either side. In the reasonable doubt condition, they found the usual effect: 74 per cent of all juries that reached a verdict acquitted the defendant. However, there was no leniency bias in the preponderance of evidence condition; their verdicts were split roughly equally between conviction and acquittal. Thus, the leniency bias appears to have its roots in demands of the jury's decision task.

AN SDS ANALYSIS OF GROUP PERFORMANCE

The SDS model was initially developed by Davis (1973) to analyse group decision-making. However, it may also be applied to group problem-solving. Instead of focusing on all the ways member preferences may be split or distributed, we may focus on all the possible ways members' task-relevant resources (e.g. knowledge, abilities) are distributed in the group. For example, in a simple task like an anagram task, we might simply classify each group member as a solver or a non-solver. Thus, in a six-person group, there again would be seven possible splits, as listed on the left-hand side of Table 7.2. The social decision scheme matrix D again summarizes what happens between the beginning and end of group inter-action; here, the output is the distribution of groups that manage to solve and not solve the problem. Again there are many possible social com-bination rules. In the chapter on individual versus group performance (Chapter 3), the Lorge-Solomon model was described; it predicts that a group will solve the problem if it contains at least one solver. This idea is translated into the 'truth-wins' D matrix in Table 7.2.

Again, the key issue is which of the many possible social decision schemes provides the most informative and predictively accurate description of how groups combine their members' inputs. In an extensive series of studies (Laughlin 1980; Laughlin and Ellis 1986), Laughlin and his col-leagues compared the predictive ability of a number of possible D matrices for groups' performance on several different group problem-solving tasks. The best-fitting D varied across tasks. More importantly, Laughlin

Table 7.2 Social decision schemes and group problem-solving

Initial splits		Group performance			
		(a) Truth wins		(b) Truth-supported wins	
#S	#NS	S	NS	S	NS
6	0	1.00	0.00	1.00	0.00
5	1	1.00	0.00	1.00	0.00
4	2	1.00	0.00	1.00	0.00
3	3	1.00	0.00	1.00	0.00
2	4	1.00	0.00	1.00	0.00
1	5	1.00	0.00	0.00	1.00
0	6	0.00	1.00	0.00	1.00

Abbreviations: S, solve; NS, not solve.

noticed a pattern: a faction that had the correct solution could persuade the rest of the group of its 'winning' solution with fewer people in its faction *if* the correct answer could be demonstrated to be correct (Laughlin and Ellis 1986). There are many tasks that have an 'objective' criterion for evaluating group performance. Simple arithmetic problems are good examples of what Laughlin terms *intellective* problems. In principle, group performance on an intellective task should be predicted by the 'truth wins' rule – having a single solver should guarantee the group's success. Of course, before truth can win, solvers need to be motivated to share their knowledge, and non-solvers must have the ability and motivation to recognize when a proposed answer is correct. When all these conditions are met, the correct response is fully demonstrable. These conditions are most likely to be met for simple mathematics or verbal intellective tasks. This is exactly what has been found (Laughlin *et al.* 1976; Laughlin and Ellis 1986). Moscovici's (1985) work on minority influence, discussed in Chapter 5, suggests that the power of a minority depends on its style of advocacy (viz. consistent, non-rigid) and its possessing at least some social support in the group. Here we see another route to minority influence – when the minority is advocating what can be persuasively shown to be the 'truth', even a minority-of-one can have considerable influence (Kerr 2001a).

At the other extreme, there are tasks with no objective basis on which to evaluate group solutions/decisions. Trying to decide many ethical, aesthetic or attitudinal issues represents what Laughlin terms *judgmental* tasks. On such tasks, since there is no objective basis for evaluation, potential group choices must, of necessity, be evaluated through social consensus (cf. Festinger 1954). Consequently, the most accurate social decision schemes for such tasks should be ones for which there is considerable 'strength in numbers', such as 'majority rules' decision schemes. Indeed, group decisions on judgmental tasks low on demonstrability (e.g. a group rating Billy Graham on a 7-point good–bad scale) appear to be described best by social decision schemes for which there is considerable strength in numbers (e.g. initial majority wins, averaging otherwise; Kerr *et al.* 1976).

Between these two extremes are tasks of intermediate demonstrability. Such tasks as verbal analogies (A is to B as C is to _____) and English vocabulary tasks are 'quasi-intellective' and relatively high on demonstrability. There is high but not complete agreement on the relevant conceptual system (i.e. the meaning of English words). Answers may be correct according to the dictionary, but they are often not obviously correct, especially to non-solvers. For such tasks, Laughlin (e.g. Laughlin *et al.* 1976) has shown that it is not enough simply to be right; one needs some support in the group to guarantee group adoption of a correct answer. The 'truth-supported wins' decision scheme is shown in panel (b) of Table 7.2.

How would we categorize the decision-making task of a jury? Jury decision-making appears to be 'quasi-judgmental'. There is generally much disagreement about what the facts in a trial are and what those facts really mean. It is extremely rare that a particular verdict is demonstrably correct. Thus, we might expect juries to accept the position of strong majorities and, as we have seen, they usually do. But there is fairly general agreement on one point – criminal defendants should be given the benefit of the doubt. In essence, when there is no clear majority to define the 'correct' verdict socially, an 'acquittal well supported wins' decision scheme seems to describe jury decision-making accurately. In a sense, if we agree to give the defendant the benefit of the doubt and enough jurors express such doubts, acquittal is the 'correct' verdict. Laughlin's research makes a point in the realm of group decision-making that we have stressed repeatedly – group behaviour depends strongly on the group's task. In the present case, we see that the demonstrability of a task determines which social decision scheme and, hence, which type of social influence processes occur in group decision-making and problem-solving.

GROUP VERSUS INDIVIDUAL SUSCEPTIBILITY TO JUDGMENTAL BIASES

One of the reasons why groups are entrusted with making very important decisions is the hope that they will also make better decisions than alternative decision-makers (e.g. individual judges, a single leader). We have already discussed several lines of research that belie that hope: (1) group discussion tends to polarize individual judgments; (2) groups with leaders that are too directive and that have too great a concern with maintaining harmony can become victim to groupthink; and (3) groups tend to be preoccupied with shared information and can neglect useful unshared information. Another aspect of this faith in group judgment is the belief that judgmental biases – departures from some idealized standard of judgment – will be less pronounced for groups than for individual decision-makers. An example is the claim that juries should be less susceptible than individual jurors to all sorts of judgmental biases (e.g. Kaplan and Miller 1978; Kerwin and Shaffer 1994). For example, Kaplan and Miller (1978) suggested that jury deliberation focuses attention toward the evidence, which all jurors have in common, and away from jurors' individual biases. Indeed, they found evidence that the biasing effect of one type of information – an attorney's obnoxious in-court behaviour – on verdicts was much greater among individual jurors than among those same jurors after they had deliberated the case as juries. There are other empirical demonstrations of such attenuation of bias by groups, including groups being less susceptible than individuals to the hindsight bias (Stahlberg et al. 1995), the fundamental attribution error (e.g. Wittenbaum and Stasser 1995), departures from rational economic choice (e.g. Robert and Carnevale 1997) and underutilization of consensus information in attribution (Wright et al. 1990).

Unfortunately, there are also many empirical demonstrations of groups amplifying judgmental biases: for paying too much attention to past losses versus the risk of future losses (Whyte 1993; Smith et al. 1998); for committing the conjunction error (i.e. estimating the probability of a joint event as being greater than the smaller probability of the two events; Tindale et al. 1996); for over-reliance on vivid, anecdotal information (e.g. Argote et al. 1990); and even juries' responses to information they are instructed to ignore (e.g. a prior conviction: Hans and Doob 1976; defendant attractiveness: MacCoun 1990; pretrial publicity: Kramer et al. 1990).

Furthermore, other studies have reported no overall difference in susceptibility to bias between individual and group decision-makers (for a review, see Kerr *et al.* 1996). How can this very inconsistent pattern of results best be understood?

As noted earlier, it is possible to do 'thought experiments' with social combination models like the SDS model, extrapolating from what is known or suspected to what is unknown. To do such thought experiments for groups and cognitive biases, we need to know two things. First, we need to know the magnitude of the bias among individuals. We can determine this by looking at the array of individual judgments (e.g. judgments of guilt) when people are given biasing information and when they are not. Second, we have to have a good hunch about how groups reach their decisions on such cases (summarized by the operative social decision scheme). With this information we can use the SDS model to predict what decisions groups should come to and, in turn, estimate the magnitude of bias among decision-making groups. This has now been done for a variety of judgmental biases (Kerr *et al.* 1996) and, in this way, it has been shown theoretically that the answer to the question, 'which is more biased, individuals or groups?', requires a complex response. The correct answer seems to be 'it depends', and upon many factors, including the size of the group, how biased individuals are, the nature of the bias, the group decision-making process (i.e. the social decision scheme, *D*) and even the extremity of individual judgment.

To show that this is more than a theoretical 'solution' to the question, one may check out the predictions of the SDS model by comparing individual and group decision-makers under different conditions, conditions that the model says should matter. So, for example, let us return to Kaplan and Miller's (1978: experiment 3) finding that juries were less affected by the personality of an attorney than were individual jurors. The trial materials that were used in Kaplan and Miller's study happened to result in individual verdicts that were fairly extreme (i.e. depending on trial, most jurors either strongly favoured conviction or strongly favoured acquittal; there were no 'close' cases). Those are precisely the conditions that should, under a majority-wins decision scheme [as in panel (a) of Table 7.1], result in less bias in groups than among individuals, which is precisely what Kaplan and Miller found. This is because a majority-wins scheme tends to polarize opinion (i.e. produce group decisions that are relatively more extreme than individual preferences). But if all individual opinion is already fairly polarized (i.e. extreme), then existing differences between individuals (e.g. those exposed *vs.* not exposed to biasing information) tends to get compressed together in groups as everyone shifts toward the same extreme pole or end of the dimension of judgment (e.g. a not guilty–guilty scale), thereby producing a form of ceiling effect. As a result of this 'squeeze', the differences between those who get biasing information and those who do not will be minimized compared to the bias effect seen among individuals. However, this same group decision-making process should have a very different effect if individual judgment is not extreme, but closer to the middle of the judgmental dimension. Here, it turns out, the polarizing effect of a majority-wins scheme tends to have the opposite effect, making existing differences between different sets of individuals even greater among groups. Thus, if an unbiased group starts out at an intermediate position of, say, 45 per cent favouring guilt, while a group with biasing information starts out at, say, 60 per cent favouring guilt, the first group may polarize towards not guilty while the second polarizes towards a guilty verdict. In short, Kaplan and Miller may have been testing for group exaggeration of bias using materials that were least likely to show such effects. These predictions were tested by Kerr *et al.* (1999).

Kerr *et al.* (1999) took two versions of the same criminal trial. One produced rather extreme (low) rates of conviction (about 34 per cent) among individual jurors; call this the 'weak case'. The other, which had slightly different evidence, produced a moderate juror conviction rate (57 per cent guilty; the 'moderate case'). Jurors for both trials were also exposed to biasing information in the form of pretrial publicity (biasing because ideally jurors would pay no attention to such information, presented outside of court and not subject to the usual rules of evidence). Some jurors saw publicity that implied the defendant's guilt (e.g. the defendant had been implicated in improper activities well before the crime); others saw publicity that was exonerating (e.g. the defendant had received public commendation for upright behaviour). Even though jurors were supposed to ignore such information, they did not (overall, the juror conviction rate was 8 per cent higher among those seeing the former, incriminating publicity). However, as the SDS model predicted, the effect of such biasing information on groups (i.e. juries) depended upon the extremity of the overall conviction rate. Just as Kaplan and Miller (1978) had found for their extreme cases, there was practically no bias effect among juries for the weak case. However, juries who had seen the moderate case showed a much larger biasing effect (a difference of 29 per cent between juries exposed to the two forms of publicity *vs.* the 8 per cent difference observed for individual jurors). Thus, the faith that juries are less biased than jurors seems to be justified under some conditions but wholly unjustified under others. The important point here is that social combination models have begun to tell us just what those critical conditions are.

COMPLEX GROUP PROBLEM-SOLVING: COLLECTIVE INDUCTION

In most research, it makes sense to start with simpler problems and then to shift gradually to more complex cases. Early work applying social combination models to group problem-solving has used this strategy, starting with simpler tasks (e.g. simple verbal or mathematical problems) and then considering relatively more complex group problem-solving tasks. One of the more complex tasks that has been the focus of considerable research is the task of collective induction (i.e. a group trying to infer or induce an underlying general principle from some more specific manifestation of that principle). Maybe one of the reasons that social scientists have become interested in collective induction is that induction is a staple of scientific research – the attempt to identify general laws in nature from specific observations – and much such scientific induction is carried out by groups of investigators.

In a typical collective induction experiment, participants (individuals or groups) are first given an exemplar of some to-be-discovered rule involving standard playing cards. So, for example, if the rule were 'even diamonds alternate with odd spades', participants might first be shown the 'four of diamonds'. They are then asked to choose a new card, are told whether or not the new card fits the rule, and then are asked to generate an hypothesis about what the rule might be. They then continue the process of card selection, feedback and hypothesizing for several rounds, until a final hypothesis is solicited. In these studies, the amount and type of information available to individual and group performers is carefully controlled, to analyse how group members select and combine information to perform this task.

Laughlin (1996, 1999) has proposed a set of postulates which both summarize this program of research and constitute a theory of how groups perform induction (and conceptually similar) problems. Some of his postulates incorporate ideas developed in earlier work on social combination processes, which should by now be familiar to the reader. These include the distinction between intellective and judgmental tasks, the criteria for a demonstrably correct solution, and the notion that the number of members in the group that is sufficient and necessary to determine a collective decision is inversely proportional to the demonstrability of the proposed response (cf. Laughlin and Ellis 1986). Other postulates are more specific to collective induction. One suggests that inductive tasks have both intellective and judgmental features. For example, determining whether a particular hypothesis is consistent with the available evidence is an intellective task, whereas choosing among plausible alternative hypotheses (all of which fit the available data) may be largely judgmental. Another postulate states that if at least two group members propose the correct or another plausible hypothesis, the group will always come to a collective decision using one of these 'supported' plausible alternatives. However, if this condition is not met, the group will select from all of the proposed hypotheses. Yet another postulate states that if the majority of members suggest the same hypothesis, the group will use a majority-wins social combination process (voting); otherwise, the group will follow a proportionality process (turn-taking) and may even propose a brand new, emergent hypothesis. Laughlin's model suggests that when the unique, 'correct' hypothesis is suggested in a group, the social combination process insures that it will be retained in the group through subsequent empirical trials and will eventually become the group's final hypothesis. Such processes makes it extremely unlikely that the correct hypothesis will 'emerge' somehow in a group where none of the group members has proposed it.

In a recent contribution to this program of research, Laughlin *et al.* (1998) compared the performance of four-person groups with the performance of four independent individuals on an information-rich induction problem. Specifically, group performance was compared to the performances of the best, second best, third best and worst individual performer. They found that the four-person group performed at the level of the best individual. These new findings may be contrasted with earlier studies comparing individuals and groups at induction tasks. For example, Laughlin *et al.* (1991) showed that when groups were presented with one, two, three or four arrays of cards, they performed at the level of the second ranked individual. However, when the groups were presented with five arrays of cards, the groups performed at the level of the highest ranking individual. Laughlin *et al.* (1998) have concluded that groups will perform at the level of the best individual on information-rich induction problems because of group's greater capacity to process large amounts of information. They further suggest that groups will therefore be increasingly effective relative to individuals as the amount of information and complexity of the problem increases.

SOCIAL COMMUNICATION AND SOCIAL COMBINATION: TOWARD INTEGRATION

Science is always caught between the desire for, and intuitive belief in, simple explanations and the apparent complexity of the natural world to be explained. So it is with the group consensus-seeking phenomena we have been considering in this chapter. It would be nice and simple if either the social communication or the social combination approach alone provided a complete understanding of how groups reach decisions. Each approach has contributed independently to our understanding. But there are good reasons to believe that the two approaches need to be combined to achieve a full understanding of group decision-making. It is not only true that member preferences and member comments both affect group outcomes, they also affect one another.

A simple illustration is Hawkin's (1962) finding that there is a simple linear relationship between the size of a faction and that faction's share of jury deliberation. One can easily imagine two interesting extremes for such a relationship. At one extreme, opposing factions would simply trade arguments, so that the pro-conviction faction and the pro-acquittal faction would each have roughly half of the speaking time, regardless of the size of those factions. At the other extreme, each juror would take an equal share of deliberation. This would make a faction's share of deliberation equal to its relative size (e.g. a nine-person faction would take up roughly 75 per cent of a twelve-person jury's deliberation time). But Hawkins found that the actual relationship fell in between these two extremes – larger factions took a larger share of deliberation, but less than their proportional share. This suggests an exchange of arguments between factions, but one in which larger factions give a bit more than they get.

The size of a faction or of a group also appears to affect which particular arguments are expressed, as we have already seen. Stasser and his colleagues (e.g. Stasser and Titus 1985, 1987; Stasser *et al.* 1989b) have shown that information which is shared by several group members is much more likely to be voiced during group deliberation than information which is unshared. Furthermore, the larger the group or faction, the stronger this tendency is. Moreover, when it comes to totally novel information, the larger the faction favouring an alternative in a group, the more the group prefers to discuss new information that supports, rather than opposes, that alternative (Schulz-Hardt *et al.* 2000). Faction size not only seems to affect the amount and content of speech, it also appears to affect the way we speak. Kerr *et al.* (1987) led mock jurors to believe that their own preferred verdict preference was favoured by either a majority or a minority of the jury. They were then asked to serve as spokespersons for their faction. Jurors, especially male jurors, who thought they were in the minority sounded more nervous, were less likely to raise novel arguments, and were less likely to identify personally with those arguments than jurors who thought they belonged to the majority. Thus, part of the power of majorities in decision-making groups may derive from their members' speech style.

There are also indications that, when it comes to describing what goes on in the group and what the group is likely to decide, the relative importance of what people say (the content of communication in the group) versus what they prefer (the distribution of preferences in the group) can vary across tasks and groups. For example, when groups have no clear majority (Parks and Nelson 1999) or are considering an intellective task (like a jury deciding on how much money is required to pay for someone's medical expenses; Kaplan and Miller 1987), group discussion tends to focus more on the exchange of factual information (e.g. 'how much does a hospital room cost per day?') and the content of group discussion is likely to become a better predictor of what the group will ultimately choose. But when the task is more judgmental (e.g. a jury deciding on punitive damages) or the group is operating under time pressure, group discussion focuses relatively more on non-factual, value judgments (e.g. 'how can you say that when we all disagree . . . ?'), suggesting that larger factions are exerting greater normative influence (Kaplan and Miller 1987; Kelly *et al.* 1997). Also, group decision-making procedures that force members to take sides early and publicly (e.g. asking for a show of hands before beginning discussion) seem to alter the style of group deliberation from an exchange and weighing of information (evidence-driven deliberation) to a battle of antagonistic factions (verdict-driven deliberation) (Hastie *et al.* 1983). One consequence of this change is that it is harder to get group members to compromise and agree on anything when they strongly identify with and become committed to a particular faction (Kerr and MacCoun 1985; Davis *et al.* 1993). Finally, as we saw when we discussed the social influence exerted by majorities versus minorities, the impact of arguments may depend upon whether they come from a majority than from a minority. Apparently, faction size affects not only what is said and how it is said, but also how it is heard and interpreted. Such research clearly demonstrates that member preferences and member arguments are complexly interrelated, and that both determine the path groups take to reach consensus.

SUMMARY

Group decision-making can be viewed as a process in which groups move from initial disagreement to a sufficient level of agreement to satisfy some decision rule. This process can be analyzed in several ways. The traditional approach has been to analyse the content of communication in the group. An alternative approach is to relate individual member preferences to group preference through some type of social combination function. One such function is a social decision scheme, D, which specifies for every possible initial distribution of individual preference the probability that the group will choose each possible decision alternative. The decision-making of juries in criminal trials, for example, appears to be summarized by a D in which strong initial majorities nearly always ultimately prevail. When there is no strong initial majority in the jury, the jury is more likely to be hung. Furthermore, pro-acquittal factions are relatively more likely to prevail than comparable pro-conviction factions. Thought experiments and actual experiments have confirmed a consequence of this social combination process – reducing the size of juries or not requiring unanimous agreement in juries reduces the likelihood of a hung jury, which constitutes a net disadvantage to defendants. Depending on several factors (e.g. the initial extremity of jurors' verdict preferences), juries can be both more and less susceptible to judgmental biases. Juries' leniency bias illustrates another principle – majorities to do not always prevail. For decision tasks with a demonstrably correct alternative, even a single correct member may be sufficient to insure that the group adopts that correct alternative. For more complex tasks, more complex social combination processes are required.

It has become increasingly apparent that neither the social combination approach nor the social communication approach alone can fully describe how groups reach decisions. Not only does what members say to one another change group member preference, the levels of support for various positions in the group appear to affect what is said, how it is said, how it is heard and what effect it has on others. An integration of alternative approaches to group decision-making holds the greatest promise for understanding this complex and important process.

SUGGESTIONS FOR FURTHER READING AND VIEWING

Hans, V. and Vidmar, N. (1986) *Judging the Jury*. New York: Plenum Press. A wide-ranging and readable overview of the scientific study of the jury.

Stasser, G. (1999) A primer of social decision scheme theory: models of group influence, competitive model-testing, and prospective modeling. *Organizational Behavior and Human Decision Processes*, 80: 3–20. A brief but comprehensive introduction to the social decision scheme model.

Stasser, G., Kerr, N.L. and Davis, J.H. (1989) Influence processes and consensus models in decision-making groups. In P. Paulus (ed.) *Psychology of Group Influence*, 2nd edn. Hillsdale, NJ: Lawrence Erlbaum Associates. Provides an overview of social decision scheme theory and research.

Twelve Angry Men (MGM/UA Video 1957 theatrical release, 2001 DVD release). Although a fictional rendition of a jury deliberation, this film illustrates several principles of group decision-making that emerge from research employing the social combination analysis.

NOTE

1 Recently, the basic logic of the SDS model has also been extended (see Davis 1996; Hinsz 1999) to analyse group decision-making on continuous responses scales, such as when a jury must decide upon what level of damages to award to an injured person (Davis *et al.* 1997).

EIGHT

SOCIAL DILEMMAS

KEY CONCEPTS

- What is the nature of the mixed motives that arise in social dilemmas?
- What kinds of people are relatively more or less likely to cooperate in a social dilemma?
- What role do social norms, such as reciprocity or commitment, play in social dilemmas?
- What structural features of social dilemmas have important effects on group member cooperation?

BACKGROUND

A basic feature of group life is that a group member's outcomes often depend not only upon his or her own actions, but also to some extent on the actions of others in the group. At times, this *interdependence* among group members strongly encourages mutually beneficial behaviour. For example, for an Olympic rowing team to have any chance of winning a gold medal, all members must do their best. Such *pure cooperation* situations provide a set of behavioural choices (e.g. every team member rowing as hard as possible) that can simultaneously maximize every group member's outcomes (e.g. all win medals); personal and group interests coincide. At the opposite extreme, termed *pure competition* or *zero-sum* situations, any gain by one person necessarily entails an equivalent loss by another person. An example would be the interaction between a buyer and seller; any change in the purchase price necessarily means a gain by one party and an equivalent loss by the other party. Here, one's own and others' interests are diametrically opposed.

Between these two extremes lie a variety of interesting *mixed-motive* situations, so called because one must choose between behaviours that serve different motives – personal interest versus the interests of others or of the group as a whole. For example, when a buyer and seller must reach agreement on several points (e.g. price, warrantee, interest rate on loan) which they value differently, the possibility exists of finding some agreement with which each person is content, although neither obtains his or her most preferred outcome. Research on bargaining and negotiation examines how such agreements are sought and obtained (e.g. Pruitt and Carnevale 1993). Another example is the wrangling that goes on at political party conventions. Sometimes, to win a nomination or to determine the party's position on some issue, two or more candidates may join forces and end up sharing a valued prize (e.g. patronage jobs, political power), which each, of course, would rather have all to themselves. Considerable research has also been devoted to studying such coalition formation processes (Stryker 1972; Kahan and Rapaport 1984). Although groups face many interesting mixed-motive situations, in this chapter we focus our attention on one particularly important type, the *social dilemma*.

THE NATURE OF SOCIAL DILEMMAS

The ecologist Garrett Hardin (1968) provides a vivid and well-known illustration of a social dilemma – the 'tragedy of the commons'. Suppose a community permitted any citizen to graze his herd on a commonly held pasture (the 'commons' that students of US history will associate with battles of the American Revolutionary War). Each individual herdsman is motivated to add additional animals to his herd, since his profit grows as his herd increases. But the commons is finite; it cannot accommodate additional animals without limit. If the number of animals becomes too large, the commons will be overgrazed, there will be no grass for any animals, and all the herdsmen will be ruined. Therein lies the dilemma – the pursuit of personal self-interest by individual herdsmen produces collective disaster.

In any social dilemma, one has to make a behavioural choice. One has to choose between behaviour that benefits the group and behaviour that benefits oneself. In the simplest case, where there are only two possible behavioural choices, the first alternative is typically designated C (for the 'cooperative' choice), while the latter is designated D (for the 'defecting' choice) (Orbell and Dawes 1981). In social dilemmas, the defecting choice (e.g. adding more animals to the herd) will always – or usually (Liebrand 1983) – result in better personal outcomes, at least in the immediate future; that is, one will be personally better off by defecting than by cooperating. So, for example, no matter what other herdsmen do, increasing my own herd (D) increases my own profit. *But*, in a social dilemma, universal defection (everyone chooses D) results in a poorer outcome for everyone than universal cooperation (everyone chooses C) – unrestrained pursuit of personal self-interest leads to collective disaster.

What makes social dilemmas so important? One reason is that they bear on some very fundamental questions about social life: Will humans always pursue their personal interest? If so, is this necessarily a bad thing for the group? Under what conditions will humans sacrifice personal interest for the common good? For example, advocates of *laissez-faire* economic theories often cite Adam Smith's (1776) argument that unrestrained pursuit of self-interest ultimately serves the welfare of the whole group (Orbell and Dawes 1981). The existence of social dilemmas challenges this viewpoint. Social dilemmas suggest (as have other political philosophers, e.g. Hobbes 1651) that unless some limits are put on the pursuit of personal goals, the entire society may suffer.

A second good reason for studying social dilemmas is that they are extremely common and have very important consequences. We provide several examples in Table 8.1. As you can see, many important environmental, political and social problems are social dilemmas (van Vugt *et al.* 2001). But social dilemmas do not only occur in very large groups or societies – small groups also routinely face social dilemmas. For example, in a previous chapter we considered the problem of keeping clean an apartment shared by a group. As long as there is some chance of somebody else cleaning the apartment, one saves time and effort by not doing any of the cleaning. But if everyone living in the apartment follows this reasoning, the apartment may become unlivable.

The most popular experimental simulation of a social dilemma is the *Two-person Prisoner's Dilemma* (PD) game. It gets its name from the scenario defining the earliest version of the game (Luce and Raiffa 1957). Two prisoners, let's call them Jake and Elrod, are suspected of being accomplices in a crime. The police question them separately and urge them to confess. The deal offered to the prisoners is summarized in the top matrix of Figure 8.1. Each prisoner must choose whether to confess (the defecting choice) or not confess (the cooperative choice – with respect to one's partner of course, not with respect to the police or to society). The deal offered by the police makes the prisoners interdependent; Jake's fate depends not only on his own decision, but also upon Elrod's. If Elrod refuses to confess but Jake does confess, thereby providing the evidence necessary to convict Elrod, Elrod will receive the maximum 10-year sentence, while Jake will go free for 'turning state's evidence'. Elrod has the same opportunity. If neither confesses, the police will only be able to get convictions on a lesser charge resulting in a 1-year sentence for each. Finally, if both confess, both will be convicted and receive intermediate 5-year terms.

What would you do if you were in Jake's shoes? If Elrod confesses, you would be personally better off confessing (5-year sentence) than not (10-year sentence). And if Elrod does not confess, again you would be personally better off confessing (0 years) than not (1 year). So no matter what Elrod does, Jake would be better off confessing (which is why the police made this offer). But if Elrod in the other room comes to the same conclusion and decides that it is in his personal best interest to confess, you both end up worse off (5-year sentence) than if you both made the other, personally costly choice of not confessing. You are caught in a social dilemma. As Figure 8.1 suggests, you do not have to use the prisoner

Table 8.1 Examples of social dilemmas

	Cooperative choice	Defecting choice	Nature of the dilemma
Commons dilemma	Conserve the resource	Consume the resource	It is rewarding to consume the resource (e.g. to keep your house heated to 70° F/21° C), but if everyone does, the resource may be exhausted
Population control	Have fewer children	Have more children	Large families may be personally better (e.g. by providing labour or old-age security) but over-population could lead to general misery
Public radio	Contribute	Do not contribute	Each listener saves money by not contributing, but if no-one contributes, all are denied the benefit of the station
Free trade	Allow full access to your markets	Restrict access to your markets	One's own national industries will profit if other, competing nations are denied access to local markets, but all nations suffer in a general trade war
Budget deficit	Give up personal entitlement, tax break, etc.	Cling to any personal entitlement, tax break, etc.	Each individual or special interest is personally better off if they retain their entitlements, but large and damaging budget deficits may result from too many such entitlements
Cartels (e.g. OPEC)	Limit production	Produce as much as possible	The larger each producer's output, the larger its personal profit, but when everyone produces as much as possible, the price is driven down to all producers' detriment
Soldier's dilemma	Face the dangers of battle	Avoid the dangers of battle	Each soldier is personally better off by avoiding the battle, but if no soldier in the army chooses to fight, the battle will certainly be lost and all may perish
Unionization	Join the union	Do not join the union	Each employee saves dues by not joining the union, but without member financial support, the union and its benefits are lost

scenario to play the prisoner's dilemma game. All that is important is that the basic requirements for a social dilemma be met – that is, the players' payoffs satisfy the inequalities presented in the bottom matrix (Rapoport 1973).

Experimental research has produced several consistent findings that give us some insight into how people behave in social dilemmas. Below we sample a few of these findings (for more detailed reviews, see Orbell and Dawes 1981; Stroebe and Frey 1982; Messick and Brewer 1983; Komorita and Parks 1994, 1995).

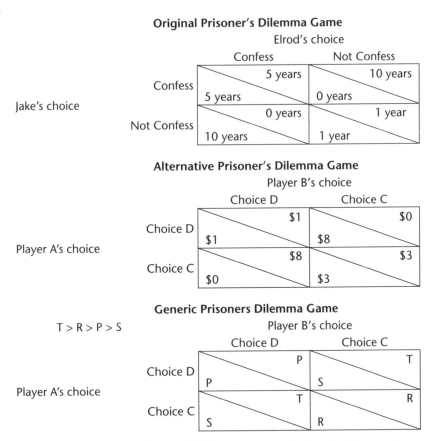

Figure 8.1 Two-person Prisoner's Dilemma games. Each cell of the matrix defines the outcomes of the two players choosing the alternatives indicated for that cell's row and column headings. The payoff below the diagonal is received by the row player. (For the purposes of applying the inequalities of the bottom matrix to the original Prisoner's Dilemma game, remember that years in prison are disutilities; the larger the number, the worse the outcome. So, after attaching negative signs to the entries in the top matrix, it also satisfies the inequalities.)

COOPERATION IN SOCIAL DILEMMAS: MOTIVES AND DETERMINANTS

In most settings, behaviour is multiply determined. That is, there are often many different motives underlying a particular behavioural choice. This is certainly true in social dilemmas (Messick 1984). The most obvious motive is self-interest – all other things being equal, you are likely to choose the alternative that yields the most positive tangible outcomes to you. However, that cannot be the only motive at work. If it were, people would rarely if ever cooperate in social dilemmas because, by definition, the defecting choice produces better objective outcomes in such situations, at least in the short term. Yet we know that people often do cooperate in social dilemmas like those listed in Table 8.1. Soldiers do fight, listeners do support their public radio stations, and at least some people do limit their consumption of scarce resources. Clearly, other motives also come into play.

Messick (1984) has suggested several such motives. One is the motive to solve the collective group problem – win the battle, preserve the radio station, save the commons. When one focuses one's attention on and places a high subjective value or *utility* on outcomes that benefit the entire group, cooperative behaviour becomes more likely. Another is the motive to comply with salient social norms; we may often cooperate because we are expected to. For example, Jake may refuse to confess and send Elrod to prison because this would violate the strong street norm against informing ('ratting' or 'grassing') on a pal.

Many factors can be expected to influence such motives. These include features of the dilemma itself, the person making a choice between defecting or cooperating, the other person(s) in the dilemma, and the nature of the interactions and relationships among the group members. Let us consider each of these in greater detail.

Dilemma features

The most obvious factors affecting cooperation are the specific payoffs offered in the dilemma. We would expect Jake to be more tempted to confess if, in addition to going free, he were to receive a $10,000 reward if his testimony resulted in Elwood's conviction. [Generally, in the generic PD game pictured at the bottom of Figure 8.1, we would expect cooperation to increase as R or S increases and to decrease as T or P increases (Rapaport 1973).] Such predictions have been confirmed experimentally (e.g. Rapaport and Chammah 1965; Komorita *et al.* 1980).

It is not only important what the actual payoffs for cooperating and defecting choices are; it also matters how such choices are presented or framed (Kahneman and Tversky 1984). For example, half of Brewer and Kramer's (1986) participants were allowed to *take* anywhere from 0 to 25 points (worth 2 cents apiece) from a shared replenishable resource pool (among researchers this is usually called a 'commons resources' framing; it might be clearer for us to refer to it as a 'withdrawal' framing). The rest of their participants were first given 25 points and then had to choose how many to put into such a pool (which is usually called a 'public goods' framing, but which we might refer to as a 'contribution' framing). Although the two versions of the task were functionally the same, with exactly the same payoff possibilities, participants cooperated more (i.e. left more in the shared pool) under the withdrawal frame than under the contribution frame (for a review of framing studies, see De Dreu and McCusker 1997). Apparently, it is harder to give up resources one already has than to forego equivalent resources never possessed (Kahneman and Tversky 1984; Thaler 1985). In a similar vein, van Dijk and Wilke (1997) have suggested that taking something that belongs to a group may be perceived as doing something bad, whereas not contributing the same amount to a group is perceived differently, as not doing good. Baron (1996) has shown that doing harm is widely seen as a greater moral fault than not doing good. Similarly, framing a 'contribution' problem in terms of the harm done by a defecting choice leads to greater cooperation on a subsequent game than framing exactly the same problem in terms of the helpfulness of a cooperative choice (Kerr and Kaufman-Gilliland 1997). And framing a problem so that it looks as though a cooperative choice rewards others is more likely to lead to cooperation than a functionally identical framing that looks as though a defecting choice punishes others (Komorita 1987).

One structural solution (see below) to Hardin's commons dilemma is to give a leader authority over group member choices. For example, the mayor of the village might be given the authority to decide just how many animals each villager can graze on the commons. Several early studies (e.g. Rutte and Wilke 1984) suggested that groups are more willing to accept such leadership when it is clear that the group cannot solve the dilemma with each member making his or her own, unrestricted choices. Van Dijk et al. (in press) note that giving up one's free choice to a leader may have very different implications depending on how the social dilemma is framed. In a 'contribution' frame (e.g. contributing one's own funds to a local public radio station), group members contribute their personal resources in the hope of providing something of value that is shared by all. In a withdrawal frame (e.g. Hardin's tragedy of the commons), on the other hand, group members take resources out of such an initially shared pool. Van Dijk et al. reasoned that, in general, we are more reluctant to give up control of our own personal resources to a leader than to give up control of our access to shared resources. So, they predicted (and found) that without feedback on how well the group was doing, group members were more reluctant to have an autocratic leader when a dilemma had a contribution frame than when it had a functionally identical withdrawal frame. On the other hand, if the group does get feedback that the group is doing poorly at solving the dilemma, van Dijk et al. suggested that alternative framings could have exactly the opposite effect. For example, if I receive feedback that my group is failing to meet its goal in a 'contribution' task, any personal contribution I am forced to make by an autocratic leader will be wasted (e.g. why contribute to the local radio station if that station is likely to go off the air?). In contrast, if I learn that my group is failing to manage a withdrawal dilemma problem, this suggests that, even if the group fails, I will personally profit by defecting (e.g. even if the commons is likely eventually to be overgrazed, I will profit from my large herds until this happens). The latter 'failure' should seem less personally costly than the former, and so one may be less willing to give up one's personal freedom to a leader who might prevent such selfish behaviour. Indeed, van Dijk et al. found that, when feedback was provided, groups failing at a dilemma with a contribution frame were more willing to have an autocratic leader than groups failing at a dilemma with a withdrawal frame – exactly the opposite of what they had found without failure feedback. These various lines of research demonstrate that how well a group can solve a social dilemma and how they react to difficulties in finding solutions can depend strongly upon the perspective with which group members view the dilemma.

Individual differences

If you think about the groups to which you have belonged and the social dilemmas your groups have faced, you will probably discover that there are real individual differences in willingness to cooperate. Some people will rarely free ride, even though they could easily do so, and will even continue to cooperate (for a while, at least) in the face of other group members' free riding behaviour. Others are likely to defect at every opportunity.

What distinguishes a cooperating group member from a defecting one? One element seems to be the person's level of *trust*. Given the options, most people recognize that mutual cooperation is preferable to mutual defection in a social dilemma, but it is rather risky to cooperate unless you can count on the rest of the group to cooperate as well. One needs to be confident '. . . that one will find what is desired from another, rather than what is feared' (Deutsch 1973); that is, one needs to trust one's partner(s). Of course, such trust could develop over the course of past interaction (e.g. Jake knows that Elrod never betrayed him all the other times they were arrested). But some people seem to possess a 'depersonalized trust' (Brewer 1981), a belief that other people can generally be counted on to cooperate. Such 'high-trust' people have been found to be more likely to cooperate than 'low-trust' individuals (Messick *et al.* 1983). The relative uncooperativeness of low trusters appears to be triggered by fear of exploitation by others – if you remove the risk of such exploitation (e.g. guarantee to refund contributions made if too few contribute to provide some public good), trust turns out to be unrelated to cooperation (Parks and Hulbert 1995).

How might we expect people with high versus low trust to react when others say they will act cooperatively? High trusters respond cooperatively; they even tend to be indifferent to others' assertions of competitive intent (Parks *et al.* 1996). Low trusters react very differently; they tend to ignore assertions of cooperative intent but decrease cooperation in response to assertions of competitive intent. When placed in a commons dilemma where the resource pool is dwindling, low-trust participants increase the size of their harvests (getting theirs while the getting is good), while high-trust participants decrease their harvests (persisting in the hope that others would see the need for mutual sacrifice to save the commons; Messick *et al.* 1983; Brann and Foddy 1988). However, if assertions are accompanied by sufficiently long periods of unconditional behaviour (e.g. the partner follows 'I plan to cooperate' with repeated cooperative choices), the 'blind spots' of both high and low trusters can be overcome (e.g. even low trusters will reciprocate the other's cooperative intent/behaviour; Parks *et al.* 1996). (In our discussion of the GRIT technique in the next chapter, we will see that de-escalating conflict between mutually distrustful groups also requires such consistently trustworthy action.)

There are also clear individual differences in the relative weight placed on one's own versus others' outcomes (Messick and McClintock 1968;

McClintock 1972). Some people, termed *individualists,* place no weight at all on others' outcomes; their behaviour is governed completely by personal self-interest. Others, termed *cooperators*, weigh both their own and others' outcomes, acting to optimize joint welfare. A precious few, termed *altruists*, put no weight on self-interest and complete weight on others' welfare. Finally, *competitors* strive to maximize the difference between their own and others' outcomes; their goal is to do better than others, even if that means getting somewhat less for themselves. With the possible exception of the altruist, you can probably think of particular individuals who hold each of these *social values* or *social orientations*. It is not surprising that the greater value one tends to place on others' outcomes, the more likely one is to make cooperative choices in social dilemmas (Kuhlman and Marshello 1975; Liebrand and van Run 1985; Kramer *et al.* 1986). How cooperatively or competitively a person behaves is affected by how they balance their own versus others' outcomes. For example, commuters with more self-focused orientations (competitors or individualists) tend to analyse transportation social dilemmas in terms of personal costs and benefits – for example, they would ask, 'just how efficient would car travel be for me?' (van Lange *et al.* 1998) or 'how convenient would a privatized railway system be for me?' (van Vugt 1997).

However, such individual differences in social motives seem to reflect more than just the relative importance of one's own versus others' outcomes. A competitor seems to have different expectations of others and to place different interpretations on others' behaviour than a cooperator does. For example, competitors are less trusting than cooperators (Cunha 1985; although see Parks 1994). Although nearly everyone sees defecting as worse than cooperative behaviour, competitors draw this distinction less strongly than cooperators (Liebrand *et al.* 1986b). On the other hand, there is a tendency to see someone who sacrifices self-interest for collective welfare (i.e. chooses to cooperate) as weaker, more naive and less purposeful than someone who looks out for his or her own interest (i.e. chooses to defect). But it is competitors who most strongly draw this distinction. Thus, cooperators are more likely to evaluate others' behaviour on moral grounds; competitors are more likely to interpret a partner's behaviour in terms of power (Liebrand *et al.* 1986b). Finally, both competitors and cooperators think that a smart person would choose as they would choose. That is, when asked to guess how another person would behave in a social dilemma, cooperators think that an intelligent person would cooperate more than an unintelligent one, while competitors expect that anyone with brains would defect (van Lange and Kuhlman 1994). Clearly, different social motives reflect profound differences in values, outlooks and beliefs.

Others' choices

In many simulations of social dilemmas, participants are asked not only to make a single defect/cooperate choice, but to make several such choices over repeated trials. One of the earliest questions to be examined was whether the apparent behaviour of the partner(s) has an effect on the participant's behaviour? We say 'apparent' because the experimenter could and usually did control the feedback participants received; typically, this feedback did not correspond to the actual behaviour of another player, but was preprogrammed by the experimenter.

One pattern is clear in this research – if my partner always defects, I am almost certain to defect, too. In multi-person social dilemmas, people seem to imitate what their partners do (Messick *et al.* 1983; Schroeder *et al.* 1983); it is as if the partners' behaviour establishes a norm for the group. However, in simple two-person contexts, things are not so simple. In these dilemmas, if the partner always chooses to cooperate, most participants will defect, exploiting the partner (Rubin and Brown 1975). Is there any way a partner can behave to encourage high rates of cooperation? One partner strategy does seem to work, the 'tit-for-tat' strategy (Rapoport 1973; Axelrod 1984). This is when my partner always mimics my last response; if I cooperate on one trial, he or she cooperates on the next trial. This even seems to work when most, but not all, of the other people in a larger ($n > 2$) group reciprocate (Komorita and Parks 1999). The larger the proportion of group members who use a tit-for-tat strategy, the greater the overall cooperation (Komorita *et al.* 1992). Also, a 'tough' reciprocal strategy (i.e. one which only reciprocates cooperation when a majority of others cooperate) is more effective than a 'soft' strategy (which reciprocates cooperation even if only a few others cooperate; Komorita *et al.* 1993). However, such reciprocal strategies tend to be less effective when the temptation to defect is very high (i.e. when one stands to gain a great deal by making the defecting choice; Komorita *et al.* 1993).

We noted earlier that cooperative choices were influenced by several motives: self-interest, effective problem-solving, conformity to norms. One norm that is particularly relevant in the present context is the *norm of reciprocity* (Gouldner 1960). This powerful norm prescribes that, for each benefit (or harm) received, an equivalent benefit (or harm) should eventually be returned. When my partner consistently defects, both self-interest and the reciprocity norm prescribe that I, too, defect. When my partner consistently cooperates, however, self-interest prescribes that I take advantage of them and defect, while the norm of reciprocity prescribes that I also cooperate. In the light of such competing forces, it is not surprising that a 100 per cent cooperative partner produces participant cooperation levels that are neither very high nor very low. Nor should it surprise us that people especially concerned with their own welfare – those with individualistic or competitive social orientations – lean toward exploiting such a situation, while those especially concerned with doing the moral, right thing – those with a cooperative social motive (Liebrand *et al.* 1986b) – are more likely to reciprocate a partner's uniform cooperation (Kuhlman and Marshello 1975). However, if the former, 'pro-selfs' can first be persuaded that the consistently cooperative other is honestly trying to be cooperative (and not just being stupid or trying to lure them into a risky, cooperative choice), they will, contrary to their usual reactions, reciprocate that other's cooperation (van Lange and Semin-Goossens 1998).

Why, then, is the tit-for-tat strategy so effective? There are several possible reasons (see Axelrod 1984), one of which is self-interest. When my partner uses a tit-for-tat strategy, I cannot exploit them. If I choose to defect, so will they and we are both worse off than if we both choose to cooperate. Thus, the situation becomes one of either both choosing to cooperate or both choosing to defect; in a social dilemma, mutual coopera- tion is always preferable. Another, related reason is that the tit-for-tat strategy makes the reciprocity norm very salient. If my partner mimics my last response, I should soon come to realize that the best way to get partners to cooperate with me is for me to cooperate with them.

Communication and commitment

Recall that Jake and Elrod were separated by the police and not allowed to talk with one another about their choices. Would it make any difference if they had been allowed to communicate? Many studies (e.g. Rapoport 1974; Dawes *et al.* 1977; van de Kragt *et al.* 1986) have indicated that it would – that each would be more likely to make a cooperative choice (i.e. not confess) if they had been allowed to talk it over first. Although com- munication could encourage cooperation in several ways (e.g. by clarify- ing the nature of the dilemma or by enhancing feelings of group solidarity; Brewer and Kramer 1986), it now appears likely that another social norm underlies at least part of the effect of communication – the norm of commitment. This norm prescribes that you carry out those actions that you have promised or committed yourself to perform. There is some clear evidence that communication leads group members to make and keep promises to cooperate. For example, Braver and Wilson (1984) gave every member of a nine-person group $5 and then told them that, if at least three members returned the money, each of the non-returning group members would get an additional $10. Groups were then allowed to dis- cuss the problem. Every group ended up holding a lottery to decide which three members should sacrifice their $5 for the others' sake. All decisions to keep or give up the money were made in private. Furthermore, each member left the laboratory separately, so there was no possibility of inter- action afterwards. Nevertheless, even though it meant surrendering $5 for no personal gain, 71 per cent of the group members selected in the lotter- ies kept their commitment and voluntarily returned their $5.

This commitment or promising explanation also implies that groups that discuss their shared social dilemma and make commitments to coop- erate will cooperate more even if they subsequently discover that their cooperative act has little impact on solving the dilemma ('a promise is a promise') and, indeed, it has been shown that they do (Kerr and Kaufman- Gilliland 1994). As one might also expect, when group discussion includes explicit promises to cooperate, members of those groups subsequently cooperate more (Orbell *et al.* 1988; Chen and Komorita 1994; Kerr and Kaufman-Gilliland 1994; Bouas and Komorita 1996). Furthermore, the cooperation-enhancing effects of group discussion are not affected by whether one's choice in the dilemma is made publicly or privately, sug- gesting that the promising norm may be internalized for most people (i.e. people feel personally bound to keep their commitments, even if others cannot tell whether or not they have done so; Kerr and Kaufman-Gilliland 1994; Kerr *et al.* 1997). Therefore, group members can be counted on more to 'do the right thing' and act on the group's behalf if they are given the chance to discuss a social dilemma and have committed themselves to solving it cooperatively.

STRUCTURAL SOLUTIONS TO SOCIAL DILEMMAS

The research reviewed above gives us some insight into the psychology of individual choice behaviour in social dilemmas. But, by and large, such research does not suggest direct ways to remedy uncooperativeness in such settings. For example, one could rarely restrict membership in real groups facing real social dilemmas to people with high depersonalized trust or with cooperative social motives. Nor could one plausibly lead real group members to believe that other group members will always operate under a tit-for-tat rule. Another general approach to solving social dilemmas is to apply *structural solutions* (Messick and Brewer 1983). Such solutions 'eliminate or alter the pattern of incentives that characterize social dilemmas' (p. 29). The basic idea is to change the pattern of payoffs so that defection is less attractive. One such structural solution is to give a leader or a governing body the power to reward cooperative choices and punish defecting choices or to simply require cooperative choices of the membership. Thus, in industrialized countries, regulations exist about such basic issues as garbage and waste disposal, medical research, school taxes, support of police and fire services that either insure that cooperative behaviour occurs or that uncooperative choices (cheating on one's income taxes) get punished. This strategy assumes that certain cooperative choices are so essential to long-term group survival that one cannot 'roll the social dilemma dice', an assumption made by a number of political philosophers who acknowledge that laws, and certain 'restrictions of freedom' (say the freedom to fling one's rubbish into the streets), are justified under such circumstances. In undeveloped countries where such regulations are often not in place, one can see that without such 'restrictions' individuals will often fail to make cooperative choices, much to the eventual cost of the group both in terms of their health and long-term economic security. Several other such structural solutions are described below.

Privatizing

A structural solution that is sometimes used in shared resource pools is *privatizing*. One converts the commonly held resource to a privately held one. For example, the community might divide up the grazing commons into privately held, fenced plots. Now if the size of a citizen's herd exceeds the carrying capacity of his plot, only he will be affected adversely. Under these conditions, each herdsman will be motivated to use his or her share of the resource responsibly. Research has confirmed the effectiveness of privatizing (Cass and Edney 1978: Messick and McClelland 1983) or approximations to privatizing, such as making energy or water consumers have personal meters, which requires them to pay for what they use, instead of paying a flat rate or an equal share of what the whole community uses (van Vugt and Samuelson 1999). Unfortunately, there are many social dilemmas, including commons dilemmas, where this solution cannot be used. For example, certain commonly held resources cannot easily be divided or reserved for individual use (e.g. the air we breathe, shared fishing grounds).

Group size

Several studies have suggested that cooperation is more likely in smaller groups. This would suggest, for example, that smaller communities would be better able than larger communities to provide needed public goods and preserve commonly held resources. Why should this be so? Perhaps because reducing group size affects each of the basic processes we discussed earlier – maximizing self-interest, conforming to norms, trying to solve the group's problem effectively.

First, people may more easily identify with a small group than with a large, faceless collective. Kramer and Brewer (1986) have suggested and shown that a strong sense of belonging or *social identity* leads to more cooperative behaviour. They suggest that the more you feel part of the group, the less strongly you distinguish between your personal welfare and the group's welfare. If I value the group as I value myself, cooperation becomes an indirect form of self-interested behaviour.

We have pointed out that groups can rely on formal rules (e.g. tax laws), informal local norms (e.g. a community standard for the proper herd size) or general norms (e.g. reciprocity) to encourage cooperative behaviour. But enforcement of any social norm requires two things: (1) the ability to monitor behaviour so that norm violations will be detected, and (2) that the social sanctions the group uses to punish norm violation are salient. Reducing group size may enhance each of these. As we learned in our discussion of social loafing, it is often easier to monitor the behaviour of members of small than of large groups. And if we generally feel a stronger attachment to smaller groups, their sanctions (e.g. rejection from the group) should also be more salient (Fox 1985).

Finally, when it comes to avoiding the tragedy of mutual defection, people may feel that their behaviour has little impact in large groups (Olson 1965; Messick 1973). For example, whether or not I decide to become a supporting member of my local public radio station seems to matter far less if I live in a community with one million listeners than a community of 1000 listeners. This belief seems to hold even if there is, in fact, no objective difference in how important our behaviour is for smaller and larger groups (Kerr 1989). Even when our behaviour really does have some effect on the group's fate, it tends to be much harder for us to discern that unique effect when the group is very large (Allison and Messick 1985).

Supplementary payoffs/costs

We all routinely enjoy many public goods; commodities which, once provided, are available to all, regardless of whether we actually helped to provide them. Examples are police protection, public highways, public parks and national forests. Why do citizens pay the money needed to supply these public goods if they could enjoy them whether they pay (cooperate) or not (defect)? The answer is as inescapable as death. Unlike the experimental scenarios we have been considering, the taxes used to provide such public goods are not paid on a voluntary basis; there are very substantial penalties for failing to cooperate. An alternative to adding such costs for defection is adding extra incentives for cooperation. For example, during fund-raising drives for public television in the USA, viewers are offered not only continued use of the station (a public good) but also various 'premiums' (i.e. prizes) for contributing to its support. Such tangible incentives can be effective in encouraging more cooperative behaviour (e.g. Wit and Wilke 1990). Of even greater interest to social psychologists are the intangible, social incentives that groups might use to the same end.

As we saw in Chapter 5 on social influence, one potent social incentive is social inclusion/exclusion. In most social dilemma experiments, such inclusion/exclusion is unlikely – participants make their choices anonymously and have very little interaction with one another. However, some recent studies have suggested that a threat of social exclusion for uncooperative behaviour can be a potent means of deterring defecting behaviour. For example, Ouwerkerk et al. (2001) found that there is a 'one bad apple will spoil the whole barrel' effect – one uncooperative group member can trigger widespread defection (e.g. Rutte and Wilke 1992). What would happen, though, if the group could remove the bad apple from the barrel – that is, could exclude its least cooperative member? When there was no such threat, the researchers found the 'bad apple' effect – group members were more likely to defect if there was one very uncooperative group member than if there was not. But if the group could vote to get rid of the bad apple, the existence of such a defector actually increased the overall rate of cooperation in the group (see also Kerr 1999). This suggests, for example, that one of the reasons why small communities often do manage to preserve valued shared resources is that community members do not want to risk the social exclusion that could result from taking more than one's fair share.

Changing the structure of the dilemma

We have just considered one structural change, adding additional rewards or punishments to the explicit payoff structure of a social dilemma. Another class of structural changes that seem to hold considerable promise for solving social dilemmas is altering group members' options regarding when they are interdependent and with whom they are interdependent. So, for example, what would happen if, instead of being randomly paired with another person to play the prisoner's dilemma game (effectively what happens in many laboratory studies), people were able to choose whether to continue to play with one person or to switch to another or not to play at all (which is a lot closer to the structure of many real social dilemmas)? The last option was explored experimentally by Orbell and

Dawes (1993). Members of groups of six persons either had to play the prisoner's dilemma against each other in a round-robin fashion (no choice condition) or they could sit out a round of the game whenever they liked (choice condition). As a group, the people in the choice condition ended up earning more money than those in the no choice condition. The reason was that those who were less inclined to be cooperative (e.g. those with competitive social motives) were especially likely to decline to play in the choice condition. To return to the original prisoner's dilemma scenario, let us suppose that I am the kind of untrustworthy, uncooperative criminal who would probably testify against my partner if I were ever confronted with the prisoner's dilemma. I probably would expect my partner to do much the same. With such expectations, it would make sense for me to be a lone criminal and avoid working with a partner at all. If relatively uncooperative criminals avoid working with others, this tends to leave relatively more cooperative criminals to work together. If and when they face the prisoner's dilemma, they are more likely to cooperate with one another and end up with a good mutual outcome. Not only are less cooperative folks less likely to join groups where they are interdependent on others, it appears that they are also more likely to bail out of existing interdependent relationships when things start going bad (Orbell et al. 1984; van Lange and Visser 1999).

Such research suggests that having the ability to pick and choose one's partners could – by altering the likely composition of such groups – improve the overall level of cooperation in social dilemmas. However, this can be a double-edged sword. If, contrary to the expectations of the more cooperative individuals, most other people are rather uncooperative, the trusting cooperators could end up being exploited by those others (e.g. the trusting villager limits his own flock size while his competitive neighbours destroy the commons). Also, there is a danger that one will only cooperate with very special 'chosen' others. For example, you could choose to be very concerned about the welfare of some single, special other (e.g. your child, your spouse), but find that you could take best care of that person only by exploiting the larger community (Batson et al. 1995).

SUMMARY

We learned in a previous chapter that, for most tasks, groups are potentially more productive than individuals. However, we also learned that group settings can sometimes undermine individual effort, for example through social loafing or free riding. In this chapter, we have seen another potential risk of group life – in social dilemmas, personally rewarding behaviour can hurt the group (and can, therefore, hurt me as a member of the group). As this chapter has shown, much has been learned about behaviour in social dilemmas. Although much more remains to be learned, there may be an even greater challenge than extending the scientific study of social dilemmas. It is applying our knowledge to the solution of actual social dilemmas. Besides the usual problems of disseminating and applying social science research, this topic poses a special problem. When a group realizes that it faces a social dilemma and wants to do something about it, it suddenly faces a new social dilemma (Yamagishi 1986). Its choices are to contribute time, energy, knowledge, and so on, to the solution of the original dilemma (cooperate) or to do nothing (defect). Everyone would prefer to let others solve the problem, but if everyone defects, the problem remains unsolved. Clearly, finding solutions to social dilemmas will be a very difficult and challenging task. However, the grave consequences of ignoring these problems also suggest that is a vitally important task.

SUGGESTIONS FOR FURTHER READING

Hardin, G. (1968) The tragedy of the commons. *Science*, 162: 1243–8. A classic illustration of a social dilemma.

Komorita, S.S. and Parks, C.D. (1994) *Social Dilemmas*. Dubuque, IA: Brown & Benchmark. The most comprehensive overview of research on social dilemmas.

Orbell, J.M. and Dawes, R.M. (1981) Social dilemmas. In G. Stephenson and J.H. Davis (eds) *Progress in Applied Social Psychology*, Vol. 1. Chichester: Wiley. An excellent introduction to theory and research on social dilemmas.

van Vugt, M., Snyder, M., Tyler, T. and Biel, A. (2001) *Co-operation in Modern Society: Promoting the Welfare of Communities, States and Organizations*. London: Routledge. An exploration of some of the problems facing those who would try to solve real-world social dilemmas.

NINE

INTERGROUP CONFLICT AND AGGRESSION

KEY CONCEPTS

- What aspects of the relationships that exist between groups contribute to intergroup conflict?
- What aspects of the way we perceive groups and group membership contribute to intergroup conflict?
- What are some of the ways to reduce intergroup conflict?

INTRODUCTION

The history of the twentieth century was darkly stained with blood. An estimated 100 million civilians were casualties of wars, ethnic conflicts, massacres and systematic attempts at genocide (Chalk and Jonassohn 1990). The striking thing about these horrors is that they are not, for the most part, based on conflict between individuals, but rather on conflicts between social groups – between an 'us' and a 'them'. The focus of this chapter is to explore the complex psychological causes and cures for such intergroup conflict.

INTERGROUP CONFLICT AND AGGRESSION

Analysis of intergroup conflict has tended to be based on two approaches. One is concerned with identifying sources of conflict that grow out of the relations between real groups, such as ethnic, neighbourhood, religious and political groups that have competing vested interests and/or a history of conflict. This approach is exemplified by *realistic conflict theory*. A second approach is concerned with identifying generic intergroup processes that arise in short-term groups that have no prior history and are not necessarily in competition. This second approach, exemplified by research on *minimal groups*, has revealed several intriguing perceptual, emotional, cognitive and motivational processes that have expanded our conception of intergroup behaviour and fuelled a good deal of modern research. In this section, we will begin by considering the first approach.

Reasearch on realistic conflict theory

Initial conceptions of intergroup conflict assumed that group hostility and aggression occurred primarily when groups were competing for scarce resources or otherwise had incompatible and mutually frustrating goals. For example, the conflict between Israelis and Palestinians might be attributed, at least in part, to their incompatible desires to possess a single piece of land. The best known research evidence for this *realistic conflict theory* is the classic 'Robbers Cave' study conducted by Muzafer Sherif and his associates (Sherif *et al.* 1961). The site of the study was a boys' summer camp located in the Robbers Cave State Park in Oklahoma (by legend, the outlaw Jesse James and his gang used the caves as hideouts). Sherif and his colleagues brought twenty-two 12-year-old boys to the camp and randomly assigned them to two groups, subsequently named the 'Eagles' and the 'Rattlers'. Initially, the two groups had no contact with one another, the intent being to nurture group formation and identity. When the groups were allowed to interact, the settings were carefully designed to maximize competition between them (e.g. tugs of war, football). The groups were in real conflict for things they valued, such as camp championships, various prizes (e.g. pocket knives) and the bragging rights that went with them. Name-calling, overt aggression and destruction of property was evident within days, culminating in food- and fist-fights on several occasions.

Frustration, aggression and scapegoating

When groups really are competing for limited resources (e.g. prizes, land, jobs), they tend to interfere or block each other's goal attainment – in short, their interaction may be mutually frustrating. This certainly was the case with the Eagles and the Rattlers. And such frustration can be a potent source of aggressive behaviour (Dollard *et al.* 1939; Berkowitz 1989). But much of the hostility and aggression we see between social groups takes place in contexts in which there is little such overt and frustrating conflict. In some cases, this might simply reflect how well group members can nurse old grievances; for example, some of the incidents that are blamed for current warfare between ethnic groups in the Balkans took place hundreds of years ago. In other cases, this might just reflect the fact that the conflict is covert, subtle or even imagined. Yet another explanation is suggested by the *scapegoat theory* (Dollard *et al.* 1939), which argues that hostility toward groups sometimes represents aggression redirected or displaced away from the original frustrating agent. When the true source of frustration is too powerful to aggress against or there really is no clear agent to blame (e.g. economic frustrations resulting from drought or faceless economic forces), the impulse to aggress can be satisfied by displacement to targets that are safe, easily identified and authorized by social norms. Members of social groups, especially groups that are distinctive, powerless and socially stigmatized, would meet these requirements. Interestingly, various groups that historically have been targeted as victims of intergroup hostility (e.g. Blacks, Asians, Jews, Gypsies) had either physical characteristics or clothing styles that provided distinctive markers of their group status. There is both experimental (e.g. Miller and Bugelski 1948) and non-experimental (e.g. Hovland and Sears 1940; Hepworth and West 1988) evidence that frustration in one setting can be followed by increased hostility toward members of stigmatized social groups. A classic example is Hovland and Sears' (1940) early report of an inverse correlation between the price of cotton (an important indicator of economic prosperity in the American South) and the number of racial lynchings. More recent research suggests that such displaced aggression is most likely when the scapegoat is in some way similar to the true frustrating agent and, as discussed more fully below, when there is some provoking, 'triggering' event involving the scapegoat (Marcus-Newhall *et al.* 2000; Pedersen *et al.* 2000). Thus, in the late 1990s, ethnic and racial violence in a section of New York City flared when an elderly orthodox Jewish man accidentally struck and killed a black child while driving his automobile. This provoked days of rioting by the poor black residents who, in general, were angry and frustrated about their traditional poverty and, in particular, resented the financially better off orthodox Jewish community that shared their neighbourhood and who provided a convenient scapegoat for their negative feelings. Eventually, these events resulted in the death of a Jewish student. In other times and places, of course, the death toll from such forms of ethnic violence have been far worse.

Perceived injustice

As the example above suggests, notions of fairness and equity will frequently play a key role in triggering aggression between groups. Sadly, groups in conflict rarely agree on these judgements, with each group generally feeling that their own group has been treated unfairly. For example, Hastorf and Cantril (1954) documented that football fans of two rival reams judged the 'enemy' team as being at fault after watching the unusually violent film of the contest. Similarly, Maoz *et al.* (2002) reported similar distortion when Israelis and Palistinians evaluated the fairness of peace proposals supposedly offered by the 'other' side (see Vallone *et al.* 1985). Equity is a circumstance in which the ratio of own outcomes to own inputs is equal to that of a relevant other. Lack of equity can cause several types of problems. If you work harder than me at the same job, but get paid less, I may feel guilty. If the situation is reversed, I may feel angry. What complicates this picture is that when people 'calculate' equity, they often differ in what they consider relevant inputs. Newly hired workers are less likely than long-time workers to consider seniority important. Those with high status or power readily convince themselves that they deserve bigger shares than others – their time is 'worth more'. Manual labourers will decide their sweat and toil is more valuable than the efforts made by the 'pencil pushers' who simply have to make decisions. A feeling of inequity can be a potent source of angry or instrumental aggression. Outcomes perceived as unfair elicit stronger aggression than those that are simply unpleasant. Even when the unpleasantness of two events is equal, a negative *social* experience (in which another person has intentionally caused the unfair outcome) leads to substantially more aggression than a non-social event. On average, across numerous studies, social provocation elicited twice as much aggressiveness as non-social negative events (Carlson and Miller 1988). And the experience of unfairness almost always results from the actions of another person rather than a non-social cause.

When inequity arises in interpersonal relations, as in an inequitable dating relationship, the relationship is often terminated (Berscheid and Walster 1978). In intergroup settings, however, short of secession or mass migration (e.g. as when Pakistan was created and Hindus migrated from the new country into India, while Moslems in India fled to Pakistan), such dissolution is much more difficult. As will be seen, inequity, often also described as *relative deprivation*, can contribute powerfully to intergroup hostility and conflict.

Relative deprivation

In our preceding discussion of equity, unfairness was seen as a strong contributor to anger. Fairness also strongly figures among the moral components invoked in ethnocentric comparisons. In a study by Liebrand *et al.* (1986a), participants were instructed to start each of an array of sentences with 'I' if it described something which they did more often than others. Other sentences were to be started with the word 'they'. Both Dutch and American participants began more sentences describing fair behaviours with 'I' than with 'they' and began more descriptions of unfair behaviours with 'they' than with 'I'. In other words, unfair action is seen as more characteristic of an outgroup ('they'). Behaviours of the they/unfair type were also rated as more salient and recalled substantially more frequently than behaviours in any of the other three categories (the they/fair, I/fair and I/unfair categories). Also, there was a strong negative correlation between rated frequency of a behaviour and its salience. The experience of unfair behaviour from others may occur infrequently but it stands out in memory. Not surprisingly, when ingroup members feel that they have been treated unfairly by outgroup members, ingroup/outgroup bias becomes intensified (Caddick 1982).

Intergroup hostility and aggression is especially likely to occur when there are perceived inequities, or *relative deprivations* (Runciman 1966; Crosby 1976), at the group level. In the United States, despite the recent progress of minorities with respect to employment, income and occupational distribution (Smith and Welch 1984), there are still noticeable gaps in income and privilege between racial and ethnic groups. To the extent that the plight of minority groups has improved, should they feel that much more content? Perhaps, but in periods when the low status of one's group is no longer seen as stable and intractable, attention tends to focus on the present inequality rather than on historical improvements (e.g. compared with the plight of one's grandparents). Moreover, when discrepancies between groups are seen by members of the relatively disadvantaged group as illegitimate or unfair, feelings of relative deprivation become an even stronger source of anger and fuel for intergroup conflict. And it is when one feels unfairly deprived both personally (as an individual) and collectively (as part of a group) that resentment is highest and protest is most likely (Vanneman and Pettigrew 1972; Foster and Matheson 1995). Like inequity, relative deprivation is caused by the gap between expectations and achievement – own input and outcome compared with those of others. With its emphasis on expectations, however, relative deprivation theory considers contributions to unfairness beyond those that stem directly from own inputs. Thus, it may be that a sense of deprivation will be stronger during periods of recent good outcomes paired with rising expectations than during periods of much poorer outcomes paired with low expectations (Davies 1969).

Triggering events

In the contemporary United States, perhaps especially on college campuses, most people know that it is wrong to be prejudiced. Consequently, they mask prejudice or negative behaviour toward blacks and other minorities. When put into a teacher–learner paradigm in which the learner is supposed to be punished for making mistakes, white students administered less shock to a black than to a white learner. However, when whites had been angered by the victim, they behaved quite differently, administering far more shock when angered by a black than a white victim (Rogers and Prentice-Dunn 1981). In other words, having justification for anger or aggression triggers bias toward outgroup members that is masked under other circumstances (Dollard 1938).

What we are arguing here is that intergroup bias can help to set the stage for intergroup aggression but it is not a sufficient condition for it. Also necessary are motivational forces. Perceptions of unfairness and group-level inequity (relative deprivation) can also contribute by providing motivational impetus. They too, however, are necessary but not sufficient. Such general social inequities typically have persisted over a period of time without eliciting collectively organized conflict. The critical issue is why group protest or rebellion becomes mobilized at any particular point during the period in which group-level inequity or unfairness exists. Even when social forces create an increase in relative deprivation, it is usually a gradual one, making it difficult for any single moment to be seized on as the time for action, rather than the preceding one or the next one. These considerations argue for the additional need for specific triggering events. These events can be a vivid, dramatic and specific instance of unfairness from an outgroup or an example of rebellion, defiance or aggression on the part of an ingroup member. This latter process has much in common with our discussion (in Chapter 6 on extremity in groups) of aggressive models serving as releaser cues in the case of mob action. Such triggering events can provide justification for social rebellion, as well as suggesting that such rebellion is normatively appropriate. In the example we discussed above, the African-American community felt that the slow medical treatment provided for the young black auto-accident victim symbolized their marginalized status in the community and justified their anger toward the driver, who received prompt ambulance service. Finally, these triggering events must also occur at a time when collective action and rebellion appear feasible or likely to succeed (Bandura 2000); the political, ideological or social climate must appear to be ripe for change.

GENERIC SOURCES OF INTERGROUP CONFLICT: MINIMAL GROUPS RESEARCH

It probably does not surprise us very much that factors like those discussed above (frustrating competition between groups; one group unfairly receiving more wealth or status than another; social norms permitting one to vent one's frustrations on members of certain groups, triggering events) can lead to intergroup hostility and aggression. But if such poor intergroup relations were the only elements contributing to intergroup hostility and aggression, we could (as we will later discuss), at least in theory, reduce such hostility by improving group relations (e.g. finding ways of reducing competition and conflict between groups, such as identifying common interests among groups; reforming our societies to reduce glaring inequities). Unfortunately, the roots of intergroup hostility may run deeper, arising from very basic human needs and modes of thinking.

Ingroup favouritism in minimal groups

The dramatic results of Sherif *et al.* (1961) in the Robbers Cave study are consistent with the idea that competition and incompatible goals contribute to intergroup conflict (i.e. dislike, distrust, hostility, etc.), although, as we have seen above, several additional situational features must be present if this distrust and hostility are to be expressed as overt aggression. However, about thirty years ago, several reports (e.g. Rabbie and Horwitz 1969; Tajfel 1970) suggested that competition for resources may not be a *necessary* condition for creating negative feelings about outgroups. For example, Tajfel and his associates (see Tajfel and Turner 1979; Tajfel 1982) found that British schoolboys tended to favour the members of their own groups over members of other groups (i.e. they showed *ingroup favouritism*), even in *minimal groups* in which the groups in question were quite arbitrary and temporary, with no history of conflict and no likelihood of future conflict. In minimal groups research, people are 'grouped' on the basis of such minor things as whether they over- or underestimate the number of dots on a slide or prefer a particular type of abstract artist. It is hard to imagine these newly defined and rather meaningless groups being very important to the boys. Nevertheless, when asked to allocate money among other participants, the boys tended to award more to anonymous others who happened to be in their own group than to anonymous others in the other group. Indeed, they seemed more intent on creating differences in payment between members of the two groups than on simply maximizing what ingroup members received. The clear and disturbing implication of this and many other such studies (for reviews, see Brewer 1979; Brown 1988; Mullen *et al.* 1992) is that simply creating minimal groups – mere social categorization – may be sufficient to trigger intergroup discrimination.

The most popular explanation for this effect has been advanced by *social identity theory* (Tajfel and Turner 1986), which suggests that favouring one's own group in this way reflects a need for positive self-esteem ('If my group is good, so am I'). This theory makes a couple of further predictions. First, if discrimination in the minimal group setting is undertaken to bolster one's self-esteem, then those who discriminate most ought to show the largest increase in esteem. Second, if entering the laboratory with low self-esteem means that one's need for self-enhancement is especially strong, then it should be those with lowest self-esteem who discriminate most. There have been a few confirmations of these predictions (e.g. Lemyre and Smith 1985; Hogg and Sunderland 1991), but overall the empirical support for them has been weak and inconsistent (see Abrams and Hogg 1988; Crocker and Luhtanen 1990; Hunter *et al.* 1997; Rubin and Hewstone 1998).[1] Nevertheless, the social identity explanation has been widely accepted, perhaps because, until fairly recently, there were few alternative theories. It would not really surprise or interest us much to discover that people prefer to reward themselves more than others (or, perhaps, that they apply their own positive attributes to fellow ingroup members – see Cadinu and Rothbart 1996). That is why it has been an important feature of the classical minimal group experiment that participants never can give money to themselves, only to others. But if people believed that by giving more to people in their own group they were somehow increasing the chances that they personally would be rewarded, then apparent ingroup favouritism might just be another instance of self-favouritism. Several researchers have suggested that something like this might well be going on in minimal group experiments – that we expect the good deeds we do to fellow group members to be reciprocated by them somewhere down the line. So giving more to an ingroup member could, in an indirect way, be perceived as doing oneself a favour. There is some interesting evidence that this might be true (e.g. Ng 1986; Rabbie *et al.* 1989; Yamagishi *et al.* 1999; Gaertner and Insko 2000). For example, Gaertner and Insko (2000: experiment 1) took pains to convince their participants that they would not be the recipients of any other people's allocations. This eliminated ingroup favouritism, at least for males. In another study, the same researchers showed that men discriminated when they were dependent on ingroup, but not on outgroup, members. However, the results of some studies seem to contradict this explanation (e.g. Platow *et al.* 1990; Gagnon and Bourhis 1996).

Tajfel's (1970) original explanation of ingroup favouritism was that there could be fairly general social norms that require us to do more for ingroup than for outgroup members, but he abandoned this explanation in favour of the social identity one. That might have been a mistake, because there is mounting evidence that a significant motive for ingroup favouritism is a normative one – I favour the ingroup, even a minimal ingroup, because I assume that this is what I am expected to do (Wilder 1986) or because I have been frequently rewarded for group loyalty in other settings. For example, Jetten *et al.* (1996) noted a positive relationship between how much one favours the ingroup and how much one thinks that fellow ingroup members expect such behaviour. And the magnitude of ingroup favouritism can be altered by making different norms more accessible (Jetten *et al.* 1997). So, for example, priming normative beliefs in loyalty produces stronger ingroup favouritism than does priming normative beliefs in equality (Hertel and Kerr 2001). The implication of such research is that discrimination may not be the inevitable consequence of social categorization – *if* the salient social norms prescribe non-discrimination.

There is another intriguing piece of evidence that social categorization on its own is not sufficient to trigger discrimination – people do not show ingroup favouritism when instead of allocating money or other positive outcomes, they have to allocate some negative outcomes (e.g. blasts of noise) among ingroup and outgroup members (Hewstone *et al.* 1981; Mummendey *et al.* 1992; Otten *et al.* 1996). This seems inconsistent with a social identity explanation – I can express the superiority of my group and myself just as easily by acting as if my group deserves less harm as by acting as if my group deserves more money. But this result is not inconsistent with a normative explanation. There seems to be a very general norm that prescribes 'do no harm' (Baron 1996). According to such a norm, immoral acts of commission (e.g. hurting someone) are seen as more blameworthy than are immoral acts of omission (e.g. not coming to someone's aid). Such a 'do no harm' norm might outweigh the usual 'take care of your own' norm, which encourages ingroup favouritism.

Such new theories and findings have had the beneficial effect of stimulating interest and debate about the causes and pervasiveness of ingroup favouritism. Old assumptions are being re-examined. It has been suggested, for example, that the ultimate goal of ingroup favouritism may not be to boost one's self-esteem, as originally maintained by social identity theory, but rather to achieve distinct and simple categories, as maintained by self-categorization theory, and thereby to minimize aversive uncertainty (Hogg and Mullin 1999). Doing simple things to reduce uncertainty (e.g. allowing participants to become familiarized with the allocation task) can eliminate the usual ingroup favouritism (Grieve and Hogg 1999). Also, new studies are being done to see whether old explanations can be salvaged. A particularly interesting example is Gardham and Brown's (2001) study, which offers a social identity explanation for the lack of favouritism when negative outcomes are being allocated. They argue that asking an experimental participant to actively do harm to other participants is indeed counter-normative, such that when an experimenter makes this request the result is that the participant no longer identifies with his or her ingroup, but rather with all participants (all of whom are potential victims of the nasty experimenter). In support of this idea, they found that when some students from a single school were asked to do harm (give negative outcomes or take away positive outcomes from fellow students), they showed no ingroup bias and also identified less with their minimal group and more with the school that they (and the remaining participants) attended.

The fact that people often discriminate between their own and other groups even when the groups are quite minimal is a striking and fundamental social psychological result. However, contrary to the implications of the initial minimal group experiments, there are now many indications that such ingroup favouritism is not an inevitable consequence of the simple formation of social categories. As we have just seen, such favouritism is more likely when positive outcomes are being distributed, loyalty norms are stressed, the individual feels that there is some possibility of being repaid by other group members sometime in the future, and there is no common enemy facing both ingroup and outgroup. It remains to seen, however, exactly what the full list of necessary and sufficient conditions are for such discrimination to occur.

OTHER PERCEPTUAL AND COGNITIVE BIASES IN INTERGROUP RELATIONS

In addition to factors such as competition (stressed by realistic conflict theory) and social categorization (stressed by the minimal group approach), intergroup hostility can be fuelled by several perceptual biases. These are discussed below.

Outgroup homogeneity

It is not uncommon to hear people describe groups to which they do not belong in very simple terms, as if '*they* are all alike'. This tendency to perceive greater uniformity in outgroups relative to one's own (in-) group is termed the *outgroup homogeneity* effect, for which there is considerable evidence (e.g. Miller *et al.* 1985; for a review, see Linville and Fischer 1998). For example, Quattrone and Jones (1980) told students at Rutgers University about the attitude of another student regarding a public issue. If this other student was described as an outgroup member (a student at Princeton University), the research participants were quite willing to assume that other Princeton students felt similarly about this issue.

Why should this be? It appears that a common aspect of human thought is to simplify our world by assigning the various stimuli we encounter into various 'generic' categories. Moreover, we have a tendency to exaggerate the similarity of stimuli that belong to the same category as well as to exaggerate the amount of difference *between* categories (Campbell 1956; Tajfel and Wilkes 1963). This last reaction makes the categories easy to remember and renders them more useful. For example, we might decide that we don't like the taste of 'hot sauce' and avoid any sauce that we consider to be in that category despite the various diffences between them. In this way, little time is lost making our recipe and grocery store decisions. This generalized reaction sadly applies to categorizing people as well as hot sauce. Thus, one dangerous dynamic in ethnic prejudice is to conclude that 'they are all alike' and also that 'they' are very different from us. The one exception to this general tendency to exaggerate the similarity within a social category occurs when reacting to our own ingroup members – in the study of Quattrone and Jones, another Rutgers student. According to Linville (1989), this exception occurs because, in our own groups, we tend to know a wider range of people, know them well and, therefore, cannot ignore the various complex personal differences that mark almost any collection of human beings. In short, we tend to hold more complex conceptions of the groups to which we, as complex people, belong (Park and Rothbart 1982). This still creates a problem regarding ethnic discrimination so long as 'they' are all the same and also very different from 'us'.

However, the notion that we always see outgroups in simpler terms than ingroups is itself an oversimplification. Any number of conditions can reduce or even reverse this outgroup homogeneity effect, including belonging to a small, minority group (Simon and Brown 1987), belonging to a low-status group (e.g. Boldry and Kashy 1999), facing some threat to the ingroup (which may call on us not only to pull together, but to see ourselves as more alike; Rothberger 1997) and focusing on traits that are defining for ingroup membership (Brown and Wootten-Millward 1993).

The discontinuity effect and schema-based distrust of outgroups

The minimal group research shows that simply categorizing people into 'us' and 'them' can lead to discrimination. A parallel finding is that, all else being equal, intergroup interactions tend to be less cooperative than interpersonal interactions. Insko, Schopler and their colleagues have compared the level of cooperation in a standard two-person Prisoner's Dilemma game (see Chapter 8) with the level of cooperation when the two players are in groups rather than individuals. The consistent finding (for a review, see Schopler and Insko 1992) is that competitive responses are much more likely in the intergroup situation, an effect so pronounced and robust that it was called the *discontinuity effect*, to signify that something qualitatively different happens when groups rather than individuals confront each other in mixed-motive settings. Part of that 'something different' seems to be the belief that, in such settings, a group is more likely to act in a competitive, exploitative way than is an individual (Insko and Schopler 1998). If we enter an intergroup interaction with such schema-based distrust – presuming that the other side cannot be trusted – it is not surprising that we act more defensively and aggressively.

Illusory correlation

The illusory correlation is another cognitive bias that promotes negative views about outgroups. Perceivers tend to overestimate the frequency with which members of a smaller, more distinct group engage in infrequent

Table 9.1 Number of desirable and undesirable traits attributed to members of each group

Desirability	Group A	Group B
Desirable	18	9
Undesirable	8	4

kinds of behaviours. In one illustrative study, participants read a series of 39 sentences. Each described a person by his first name, his membership of group A or B, and a moderately positive or negative behaviour that he performed (e.g. John, a member of Group A, raked the lawn before dinner; Harry, a member of Group B, sarcastically chided his secretary). Two-thirds of the desirable behaviours were ascribed to Group A (see Table 9.1).

The frequencies of *both* desirable *and* undesirable behaviours in Group A were double those for Group B. As a result, the ratio of good to bad behaviours was the same in the two groups; hence, there was no overall relationship between group and good/bad behaviour. Note, however, that Group B is smaller than Group A and that, in this setting, undesirable behaviours are less frequent than desirable actions. This relative infrequency makes both Group B and undesirable behaviours more distinctive. Apparently, this distinctive information 'sticks in our minds' and we tend to associate the two distinctive elements together (i.e. Group B with undesirable action). Therefore, participants overestimate the co-occurrence of instances of a Group B person performing an undesirable behaviour. That is, they perceive an illusory association between membership in Group B and the desirability of the behaviour of persons in that group, even though no such relationship exists in the information that is presented to them. Consequently, Group A was rated more favourably than Group B on various evaluative traits (Hamilton and Gifford 1976).

Such a misperception provides a cognitive basis for intergroup bias (for other reasons for such illusory correlations, see Stroessner and Plaks 2001). Most everyday human behaviours are positive. Because contact with outgroup members in everyday life is less frequent than with ingroup members, and because negative behaviours are less common, both the outgroup and negative behaviours are distinctive elements and, therefore, the ingredients for a negative stereotype based on an illusory correlation are in place. Even if whites and blacks behave negatively at the same low rate, the illusory correlation effect will act to augment negative valuation of blacks by whites. Moreover, the illusory correlation effect is stronger when the distinctive (infrequent) traits are negative rather than positive (Mullen and Johnson 1990). Even more disturbing is the finding that these stereotype-based errors are greater in times of arousal, fear and anxiety (Kim and Baron 1988; Wilder and Shapiro 1988, 1989; Baron et al. 1992) and, therefore, are likely to have greater impact in times of crisis. Finally, the effect generalizes to other negative trait dimensions in addition to those specifically observed, creating an overall devaluation of the outgroup (Acorn et al. 1988).

Bargaining with the enemy: the carrot *vs.* the stick

Suppose our group finds itself in a conflict – real or imagined – with another group. How can we change the minds or actions of the people in the other group to resolve the conflict? There are many possible tools of social influence available, ranging from the relatively more conciliatory (e.g. persuasion, compromise) to the relatively more coercive (e.g. threat, punishment). Which tools we use will, of course, depend upon which we expect to be effective. Here, too, it seems that our expectations are biased in intergroup contexts. We tend to believe that the outgroup will give in to more hostile, coercive strategies, but are equally certain that such techniques would backfire if applied to us (Rothbart and Hallmark 1988). If each side in an intergroup conflict overestimates the effectiveness of coercion when dealing with the other, it is not hard to see how intergroup relations can quickly sour.

The ultimate attribution error

A well-known attributional bias in social psychology is the *fundamental attribution error*. This is when we neglect situational factors that lead another person to behave in a certain way and, therefore, we attribute his or her behaviour to stable personal attributions. Something similar and pernicious can arise when people, especially those with negative attitudes toward an outgroup, are asked to explain the behaviour of members of that outgroup. When members of the outgroup behave in a negative way, it is relatively more likely to be seen to be due to features of their character or personality (Pettigrew 1979; Hewstone 1990). What makes this *ultimate attribution error* especially pernicious is that those ostensible character flaws may be seen as shared by all members of the group, as if they were inevitable, genetically determined stains – 'that's just their nature'. The opposite bias occurs with positively evaluated behaviours; good acts by ingroup members are believed to reflect their character, whereas the same acts by outgroup members are not seen as the result of lasting virtues, but are explained away (e.g. as being due to special circumstances).

REDUCING INTERGROUP CONFLICT AND AGGRESSION

One lesson from history is quite clear. Once intergroup hostility becomes established, it is no simple matter to reduce it. As we have argued, due to various cognitive biases, views of the outgroup will tend to be distorted and these selective perceptions are apt to be intensified by processes of group polarization. Add to this a history of mutual hostility and desires for revenge (e.g. for past inequity) and one faces a serious challenge if one wishes to de-escalate the conflict.

Intergroup contact: the contact hypothesis

Allport (1954), in his very influential book, *The Nature of Prejudice*, first advanced the argument that contact between members of antagonistic groups could help reduce that antagonism. His *contact hypothesis* suggested, though, that this contact must occur under certain critical conditions: those interacting from the different groups should have equal status (if members of one group are socially subordinate to members of the other, the contact will only reinforce existing stereotypes and perceived inequities); the contact should be supported by authorities, law and custom; the members of the different groups should have common goals and should work together to achieve those goals; and the contact ought to be extended in time. Allport felt that such conditions allowed the individuals involved to come to appreciate outgroup members as individuals and human beings. The futility of increasing contact without these conditions was illustrated by Sherif *et al.* (1961) in their Robbers Cave study. After hostility had been created between the two groups through competition, the Eagles and the Rattlers were brought together for several potentially positive interactions (e.g. viewing films). However, these brief and impersonal contacts served as opportunities for the expression – not the reduction – of intergroup hostility. Similarly, desegregation that merely places formerly divided groups into the same school or neighbourhood without also insuring the other, facilitating conditions, appears to have little benefit in reducing intergroup hostility (Gerard and Miller 1975; Miller 1981; Gerard 1983).

Pettigrew (1998) has suggested another critical condition for intergroup contact to reduce intergroup hostility – the contact situation must provide participants with the opportunity to become friends. This extends Allport's (1954) notion that reducing intergroup prejudice requires that individuals come to consider the common humanity and individuality of outgroup members. Indeed, many of Allport's suggested conditions may matter so much precisely because they are functional for achieving this key condition; friendships are unlikely to form under circumstances where there are competitive interactions, norms encouraging hostility, unequal status and brief, uncooperative encounters. When opposing group members become friends, their contact is likely to be varied, to be extended in time and to promote intimacy, the most effective way to contradict social stereotypes. In support of this argument, surveys (e.g. Pettigrew 1997) have shown that living in an integrated neighbourhood increases contact with outgroup members, but does not reduce prejudice toward the outgroup. On the other hand, when that contact results in friendships with outgroup members, prejudice wanes (Pettigrew 1998; Pettigrew and Tropp 2000). Moreover, the benefits of such friendships may extend well beyond the people who become friends. Wright *et al.* (1997) arranged for two members of hostile groups to engage in friendly interaction. It was gratifying to find that these new friends became less hostile toward their respective outgroups, but even more interesting to find that, after they returned to their groups, the fact that they had an outgroup friend helped reduce the level of outgroup hostility among other ingroup members.

Superordinate goals

Realistic group conflict theory suggests that intergroup hostility stems from groups' conflicting goals. The clear implication of this theory is that if the situation could be reversed, so that the groups have common goals, that hostility could be reduced. After the Eagles and the Rattlers in the Robbers Cave study had come to thoroughly dislike and mistrust one another, Sherif *et al.* (1961) introduced a series of *superordinate goals* that required the two groups to cooperate to achieve valued rewards (e.g. food and water). For example, it was arranged to have a truck that was supposed to get food for both groups to stall at the bottom of a hill. Neither group alone had enough boys to pull the truck to the top of the hill where it could be set rolling and be started, but, working together, it could be done. As a result of such cooperative episodes, intergroup aggression diminished, replaced by intergroup friendship in a matter of days (Sherif *et al.* 1961; Brown and Abrams 1986). Indeed, these boys ended their camp experience by sharing the competition prizes they won earlier with the very boys they had competed with. In fact, the two groups elected to ride home from camp on the same bus.

Aronson and his associates (1978) used related strategies to reduce racial tension in US high schools. Aronson *et al.* instituted what they called a *jigsaw technique*, which requires students of differing races to work cooperatively during class. Students would first master one part of an assignment working in one interracial group. They then would join a second interracial 'jigsaw group' in which each member would have information about different segments of the assignment and the information would be shared. In short, the students participated in several cooperative racially mixed groups. The results of this and similar cooperative learning procedures (e.g. Johnson and Johnson 1981; Slavin 1985) have been generally positive in terms of reducing racial hostility (Aronson *et al.* 1978) and encouraging learning (Johnson *et al.* 1981).

Such results are encouraging, but there are limits to the power of pursuit of superordinate goals. First, it may be important to have several successful episodes of mutual group cooperation, as happened in the Robbers Cave study; if there is a long history of intergroup conflict, single or isolated instances of cooperation between groups may have little impact (Wilder and Thompson 1980). Second, if previously hostile groups fail in the pursuit of their superordinate goals, even greater hostility can result (e.g. Blanchard *et al.* 1975; Worchel *et al.* 1977). Third, the benefits of cooperative learning often do not generalize beyond the students who are in the class (Slavin 1985), although, as noted above, Wright *et al.* (1997: experiments 3, 4) reported such generalization in a non-school context under conditions where such cross-group friendship occurred.

One reason why a positive experience with one or two outgroup members tends not to generalize to other outgroup members is that we are reluctant to give up our stereotypic opinions of social groups. This may be because rethinking such stereotypes entails a good deal of mental effort and because they provide us with a false sense of security and knowledge. One way of holding on to one's stereotype in the face of disconfirming evidence is to decide that the outgroup person whom we know and like is somehow atypical of the outgroup as a whole. For example, a person might decide that a level-headed, emotionally stable woman he knows has some characteristic that makes her atypical (e.g. she was raised by her father). This *exceptional case bias* would allow this person to maintain his view that women as a rule are impractical and emotionally volatile. Wilder *et al.* (1996) found that individuals who learned about a non-stereotypical outgroup member only changed their stereotype about that group if it was made clear that the person they were learning about was, in fact, a completely typical group member. Otherwise, their stereotypes remained unchanged. Finally, the benefits of limited cooperative contact are not permanent; if such contact is followed by a return to the same conditions that initially nurtured hostility, those benefits will dissipate (Schofield and Sagar 1977).

Manipulating social categorization

Sometimes, as we have seen, intergroup hostility stems from all-too-real conflict between groups. But we have also seen that it is sometimes more how we perceive and understand the distinction between 'us' and 'them' that leads to such hostility. By changing those perceptions of who belongs to what group, one can do much to reduce that hostility.

From 'us *vs.* them' to 'me and you': decategorization

One such change is to discourage thinking about people in terms of their group memberships and to encourage thinking about them as distinct individuals – to shift emphasis from intergroup to interpersonal, as Allport counselled as early as 1954. This shift in categorization has been called personalization or *decategorization* (Brewer and Miller 1984). Wilder (1981) describes several studies in which bias towards outgroup members is reduced if those members are somehow individuated. For example, in one study the usual ingroup/outgroup bias was much lower in conditions where the outgroup was described as being in disagreement on certain issues. Similarly, if people from different groups who are working together on a task are instructed to try to get to know each other as individuals, they subsequently show less ingroup favouritism (e.g. Bettencourt *et al.* 1992). Idealized conditions of intergroup contact (e.g. equal status, supportive norms) may reduce prejudice, in part, by simply undermining one's tendency to view outgroup members simply as interchangeable members of a disliked category.

Cross-categorization

People who belong to different groups (e.g. Muslims and Christians) typically have other group memberships in common (e.g. Muslim women and Christian women). Another route to reducing intergroup hostility is to increase group members' awareness of such *cross-categorizations*. It is harder to maintain the simple 'us *vs.* them' outlook when you realize that many of 'them' could just as easily be thought of as 'one of us' for some other, salient group membership (Urban and Miller 1998; Brewer 2000). Thus, for example, Bettencourt and Dorr (1998) placed Republicans and Democrats in work groups. In some cases, all Democrats were given one kind of role assignment while Republicans were given another type of assignment. In short, there was no cross-categorization. As predicted, in this condition, both Republicans and Democrats showed indications of intergroup hostility (e.g. low evaluations of the others and low point allocations to each other). However, in another condition, some Republicans and Democrats received the one group work assignment while the other assignment was also spread among Republicans and Democrats. In short, cross-categorization was present in this condition. In this case, intergroup hostility between individuals with political differences was far less pronounced. Indeed, in one study by Marcus-Newhall *et al.* (1993), a cross-categorization manipulation completely eliminated intergroup hostility (for a review, see Brewer 2000). Thus, this cross-categorization strategy appears to hold a good deal of promise regarding the reduction of prejudice.

From 'us *vs.* them' to 'us all': recategorization

The goal of decategorization is to eliminate or at least minimize group distinctions, to make people who formerly judged one another on colour to become 'colour blind'. The goal of recategorization is to replace old group distinctions with a new one, but a new one that includes everybody (e.g. regardless of skin colour, we're all human beings). Gaertner, Dovidio and their colleagues have developed this idea in their *common ingroup identity model* (Gaertner and Dovidio 2000). They show that there are many ways to encourage such recategorization, including stressing inclusive traits, eliminating physical distinctions (e.g. separate *vs.* mixed seating of group members), the use of more inclusive language (an inclusive 'we' rather than the exclusive 'us and them') and pursuing superordinate goals. On this last point, they have provided evidence (e.g. Gaertner *et al.* 1990) that a key reason why working together towards some shared goal reduces intergroup hostility is precisely because it prompts seeing former outgroup members as members of a more inclusive ingroup. They also have shown that the benefits of such recategorization are broad, including more cooperation, more willingness to help and more self-disclosure across old group boundaries. Such benefits tend to be far-reaching. When we help or self-disclose to others, they tend to reciprocate, and friendlier personal relationships result. One means of provoking such recategorization is the sudden presence of a common threat or enemy. For example, shortly after the terrorist attack of the World Trade Center in New York City in September 2001, it was common for New Yorkers and, indeed, all Americans to downplay their ethnic and racial differences and to instead act with greater friendliness and trust towards fellow Americans.

From 'us *vs.* them' to 'us, them, and us all': dual identities

There are, however, limits to the utility of the recategorization strategy. Sometimes the original group members are strongly attached to their group memberships and will resist abandoning them for some new, inclusive one. For example, even though many Europeans regard themselves as part of a new European Union, their national identities are unlikely to disappear quickly. A second limitation is the generalization problem. Experiences that prompt recategorization usually occur with specific outgroup members. How can the reduction in hostility toward those individuals be generalized to the rest of the outgroup? If one completely blurs the original 'us *vs.* them' distinction (the goal of recategorization), then it may be harder to generalize the more positive feelings toward certain of 'them' to the rest of 'them' (Hewstone and Brown 1986; Johnston and Hewstone 1992). A third problem with the recategorization approach is that there are some clear advantages of maintaining some level of cultural diversity: cities, cultures and countries are more exciting and interesting when there is some variety regarding food, customs, clothing, entertainment, and so on. A total homogenization of a culture would eliminate this excitement.

Such considerations have led to interest in a variation of the recategorization strategy – one that encourages perceiving inclusive group memberships, but acknowledges and to some extent encourages retention of older, less inclusive identities. For example, one can think of oneself as both English (inclusive category) and as someone with a particular ethnic, religious or racial heritage (e.g. Hindu, Muslim or Christian). As suggested above, such *dual identities* are particularly effective in encouraging the generalization of positive contact with a few outgroup members to the rest of the outgroup (e.g. Brown *et al.* 1999). Moreover, when people from different groups work together, it can be more beneficial for intergroup relations to give the groups different responsibilites, so that each group can feel that it had a vital role in achieving the superordinate goal (Brown and Wade 1987). However, if different groups have different responsibilities, it is important that no group is seen to be an inferior partner; if the groups' status is not equal, this promotion of dual identities loses its advantage (Dovidio *et al.* 1998).

Gradual and reciprocal concession technique

A somewhat different strategy, based more on equity and bargaining considerations, has been suggested by Osgood (1980). Termed the gradual and reciprocal concession technique (GRIT), this procedure, aimed primarily at de-escalating international conflict, also seems appropriate to intergroup problems on a smaller scale. The goals of this strategy are to increase communication and reciprocity between groups while reducing mistrust, thereby allowing for de-escalation of hostility and creation of a greater array of possible options. This strategy has two unique features. The first is that it can be initiated unilaterally. One group or country can decide to try GRIT even without agreement from the other. The second is that GRIT explicitly assumes that one group's initial, unilateral attempts to de-escalate conflict will be mistrusted and misinterpreted by the other as a deceptive and manipulative strategy. As a result, GRIT includes several features designed to deal with such mistrust. The GRIT strategy is as follows:

1 Announce your general intentions to de-escalate tensions and your specific intention to make an initial concession.
2 Execute the initial concession unilaterally, completely and, of course, publicly. Provide as much verification as possible.
3 Invite reciprocity from the outgroup. Expect the outgroup to react to these steps with mistrust and scepticism. To overcome this, continued concessions should be made.
4 Match any reciprocal concessions made by the outgroup and invite more.
5 Diversify the nature of your concessions.
6 Maintain your ability to retaliate if the outgroup escalates tension. Any such retaliation should be carefully calibrated to match the intensity of the outgroup's transgression.

Evidence on the utility of GRIT is scarce. Perhaps this is to be expected of a technique created to de-escalate international tension. Meaningful laboratory studies on such procedures would be hard to design. One exception is Wilder and Thompson's (1980) finding that attempts to de-escalate intergroup hostility are far more effective if the de-escalating group makes persistent attempts to reduce tension. There are, however, several rare historical 'case histories' that suggest that GRIT can be effective. For example, Mikhail Gorbachev's decisions as leader of the Soviet Union in the period 1986–89 closely follow the GRIT model. Gorbachev made several unilateral concessions that resulted in serious de-escalation of world tensions in this period. First, on two occasions, the Soviets postponed resumption of atmospheric nuclear tests despite being unable to extend the prior treaty with the Reagan administration who, at that point, referred to the Soviet Union as the 'Evil Empire'. They then agreed twice to summit meetings despite the Reagan administration's refusal to discuss the Star Wars defence system. They then agreed to the Intermediate and Strategic Range Nuclear Missile (INF) Treaty (exceeding US requests for verification), despite continued refusal by the USA to bargain about Star Wars. Next came agreements on the Berlin Wall and the unification of Germany. Eventually, even the staunchly anti-Communist/anti-Soviet Reagan regime had to take notice and the result was a reduction of tensions between the two superpowers. This eventually resulted in the end of the cold war that had dominated world politics for 50 years. It will be interesting to see whether group researchers begin to apply the principles of GRIT in attempts to improve our ability to reduce intergroup conflict. Then we should acquire suffcent exerimental data to more fully evaluate this interesting model.

SUMMARY

Intergroup conflict has many causes. Some of them stem from economic, political, religious or ideological disputes, which leave the contending groups frustrated, unfairly treated and primed to express their hostility. Once such anger is established, triggering events such as flagrant or symbolic abuses by outgroup members or acts of rebellion or aggression by ingroup members often serve to provoke overt acts of aggression from groups in conflict. For example, Ariel Sharon's inspection of the Temple Mount in Jerusalem, a sacred Muslim shrine, in 2000 was a symbolic action that sharply escalated intergroup conflict in Israel. Social norms and conventions can channel this hostility toward members of social groups that may or may not have any real responsibility for it. Besides these large-scale, macro causes, we should also recognize a number of small-scale, micro perceptual biases that can nurture intergroup hostility, discrimination and aggression. Mere social categorization – creating an 'us and them' distinction – can lead to ingroup favouritism. Fortunately, this is not an inevitable consequence of categorization – 'us and them' need not always lead us to 'us *vs.* them'. Other intergroup biases include the tendency to see the outgroup as more homogeneous than our ingroups ('they are all alike'), to see outgroups as exploitative and untrustworthy ('you just can't trust them'), to be too ready to attribute an outgroup member's undesirable behaviour to something inherently characteristic of the whole outgroup ('that's their nature'), and to see the outgroup as more effectively dealt with using coercive means of influence ('that's the only language they'll understand'). With so many and such a complex a set of causes, it is not surprising that there are no simple cures for intergroup conflict. Some must come at the 'macro' level – striving for greater justice and fairness for members of all social groups. But other important cures stem from changing the way we use and think about group membership. Any of several departures from a simple 'us and them' way of seeing the social world may help 'us' avoid making the present century as bloody as the last one.

SUGGESTIONS FOR FURTHER READING

Brewer, M.B. (in press) *Intergroup Relations*, 2nd edn. Buckingham: Open University Press. A very recent review of the prejudice literature.

Gaertner, S.L. and Dovidio, J.F. (2000) *Reducing Intergroup Bias: The Common Ingroup Identity Model*. Philadelphia, PA: Psychology Press. Presents new ideas about the reduction of prejudice.

Sherif, M., Harvey, O.J., White, B.J., Hood, W.R. and Sherif, C.W. (1961) *Intergroup Conflict and Cooperation: The Robbers Cave Experiment*. Norman, OK: Institute of Group Relations. A vibrant account of the summer camp study.

Tajfel, H. and Turner, J.C. (1986) The social identity theory of intergroup behaviour. In S. Worchel and W.G. Austin (eds) *Psychology of Intergroup Relations*. Chicago, IL: Nelson Hall. A nice statement of social identity theory.

NOTE

1 As one means of explaining these chaotic self-esteem data, Long and Spears (1998) suggest that the inconsistent relationship between self-esteem and discrimination may be due to differences between the effects of chronic

self-esteem and manipulated self-esteem on discrimination and ingroup bias. Long and Spears suggest that when self-esteem has been manipulated so that it is temporarily lowered, discrimination is more likely to provide an effective means of repairing this momentary drop in esteem. In contrast, people with chronic low self-esteem may be more likely to have accepted this state. If so, they would be less inclined to search for techniques to momentarily raise their self-esteem. This explanation would explain why Crocker's work on chronic self-esteem does not support the social identity prediction (of more discrimination with low self-esteem), while Hogg and Sunderland's research on manipulated self-esteem does provide such support. In addition, Long and Spears argue that low personal self-esteem is less likely to provoke discrimination than low collective self-esteem ('my group is bad'). Their own research provides initial support for this view. However, at the moment there are insufficient data to evaluate this possibility fully, nor is it immediately clear why a person would be willing to repair their collective self-esteem via discrimination but not be eager to do the same when personal self-esteem is low.

TEN

STRESS AND SOCIAL SUPPORT

KEY CONCEPTS

- Why do people gather together when frightened?
- What are the elements of social support?
- When will social support backfire?
- What role does social comparison play in social support?
- What is the broken heart effect?
- Do pets improve our health?
- Does it really do any good to talk about our troubles?

BACKGROUND

One of the most primitive human tendencies is for individuals to huddle together in times of fear, sorrow or extreme excitement. Baumeister and Leary (1995) go so far as to argue that our desire for attachment to others is a basic human need. Certainly, the tendency to seek out others in times of stress reflects one of the most documented psychological phenomena of recent years (cf. Wills 1997). Indeed, recent research indicates that those people who are strongly supported by friends and family are less devastated by a wide variety of stressors, including the death or illness of a spouse (Pennebaker and O'Heeron 1984; Baron et al. 1990), the loss of one's job (Linn et al. 1985), living with cancer (Fawzy et al. 1993) and learning that one's child has cancer (Morrow et al. 1984). One recent study even found links between social support and one's likelihood of contracting the common cold. In this study, Cohen et al. (1997) used nose drops to expose individuals to the common cold virus. These participants were then quarantined for five days. Those who reported having social support in many aspects of their life were less likely to develop cold symptoms.

AFFILIATION RESEARCH

Some of the earliest research to examine this group effect was conducted by Stanley Schachter. His interest in this topic was initially captured by reports that, after periods of prolonged isolation, individuals often experienced unexplained anxiety. Schachter reasoned that if isolation produces anxiety, perhaps the opposite is also true – that affiliation reduces it. Schachter's (1959) initial experiments were quite simple. He frightened participants with the threat of shock and then examined the extent to which they chose to be with others. As predicted, over 60 per cent of these people chose to wait with others before the shock began. In a low fear control group, the equivalent figure was 33 per cent.

After replicating and extending this phenomenon in several follow-up studies, Schachter argued that there were at least two reasons fear produced this desire to affiliate with others. First, he felt that fearful people were especially interested in information about the stressful situation ('how bad will this be?') and their response to it ('am I overreacting here?'). Other people are an important source of this type of information and, as a result, Schachter suggested that one reason we prefer to be with others in times of stress is to engage in social comparison. Social comparison, as you may remember from Chapter 1, involves comparing your feelings, behaviour and opinions to those of others to get a fix on the accuracy of your opinions and the relative strength of your reactions (e.g. 'how frightened am I compared to the others around me?'). Second, Schachter argued that having other people present served to reduce fear directly even when no direct communication or comparison was possible. Presumably, this direct fear reduction was based in large part on early childhood conditioning because, for most individuals, parents are often associated with the prevention or cessation of stressful stimuli during childhood.

Schachter's suggestions have received a good deal of support. In a dramatic series of case study reports, Lynch et al. (1974) closely observed the heart activity of three severely injured patients as a female ward nurse sat down and held the patient's hand. All three patients had been paralysed with the drug Curare for medical reasons. In some cases, the nurse spoke soothingly to the patient while holding their hand, but in others he or she was silent. These periods of human contact both with and without verbal reassurance produced a substantial reduction in heart rate in all three patients. For example, one patient reduced her heart rate from 125 to approximately 110 beats per minute while having her hand held (silently). Although these results are provocative, they are based on case study reports with limited participants and few controls. Fortunately, several carefully controlled laboratory studies have indicated that direct fear reduction does occur when individuals affiliate with others, particularly if the companions are themselves acting calmly (cf. Epley 1974). Probably the most compelling and carefully documented study of this type using human participants was conducted by Amoroso and Walters (1969). In the first stage of this study, women volunteers received a series of moderate electric shocks while they worked on a learning task. Not surprisingly, this shock elevated the participants' heart rate and self-reports of anxiety, and also interfered with their task performance. After the first series of shocks, one group of women waited alone for five minutes before the second series of shocks began. A second group of women waited silently with three other individuals. At the end of the five minutes, the experimenter assessed the participant's anxiety, heart rate and task skill. As expected, those who waited alone had a higher heart rate and self-reported anxiety, and performed worse than those who waited with companions. The soothing effects of affiliation could be inferred from the participants' physiological reactions and task performance, as well as their self-reports.

This use of multiple measures is important. The earliest research on this issue relied primarily on fear questionnaires. These can easily be falsified. Amoroso and Walter's results appear to be free of such problems. An additional strength of this study is that the participants did experience stress, whereas in earlier studies people were only threatened with shock, a threat they may have doubted. Moreover, Amoroso and Walters' results complement those of several other studies that also used exposure to shock as a stressor. Seidman *et al.* (1957) found that individuals tolerated more shock when in the presence of a non-shocked companion. Similarly, Ader and Tatum (1963) found that shock avoidance (i.e. fear) was more pronounced when people were tested as individuals rather than in pairs. Several studies, however, found that the soothing effects of companions are most likely to occur if the companions appear calm (e.g. Latané *et al.* 1966). Indeed, in some cases, openly fearful companions have been found to increase the fear of individuals. Imagine yourself in the study run by Shaver and Liebling (1976). First you learn that you will receive a series of painful injections. Then you are joined by a companion who reacts by muttering such things as 'Oh my God' and 'No'. Not surprisingly, participants in this condition made 40 per cent more errors on a maze task than those tested alone. Obviously, not all companionship is comforting. For the most part, however, calm companionship has been shown to be beneficial.

On balance, then, there is a lot of evidence for Schachter's argument that affiliation can reduce fear in human participants. Indeed, similar effects have also been widely reported among a variety of animals. For example, young goats are less upset by darkness and unpredictable shock if they are accompanied by their mother, chickens are less immobilized by a 'shock signal' when in the presence of a calm companion, and rats appear less stressed by exposure to a wide open space when they are with a partner (Epley 1974). This is due, at least in part, to the rats being distracted from the fearful situation by their companions (Moore *et al.* 1981).

But what about Schachter's arguments regarding social comparison? Remember, he argued that fear-based affiliation was caused at least in part by needs for social comparison information, in addition to the direct effect that groups had on fear reduction. Here, too, the data support his view. First, stress is more likely to provoke both affiliation and emotional contagion when the people around you are facing the same type of stress, thereby making them comparable (Gump and Kulik 1997). Second, the social comparison view assumes that fear produces a variety of uncertainties which the individual attempts to resolve by social comparison. In accord with this notion, Kulik *et al.* (1996) found that new surgical patients were particularly interested in affiliating with patients who already had experienced the surgery in question (as opposed to other new patients). It would appear that this preference for 'veteran patients' was because such veterans could provide the new patients with first-hand information about the procedure. Note that, according to the social comparison view, greater uncertainty should produce greater desire to be with others with whom one can make comparisons. Several studies have found this to be true. For example, Gerard (1963) gave people the impression that they were connected via electrodes to an 'emotion meter'. In one condition, the readings from this emotion meter were made to appear steady and, therefore, implied a consistent emotional reaction. In a second condition, the readings from the emotion meter varied a good deal. Since this made the reading hard to interpret, it elevated uncertainty. As predicted, those in this latter condition exhibited stronger desires to affiliate with others.

In another study, Mills and Mintz (1972) had participants ingest a strong dose of caffeine. Half were told that they had ingested a mild sedative, whereas the others were correctly told that the caffeine would arouse them. Mills and Mintz reasoned that those given the 'sedative' instructions would feel a good deal of surprise, confusion and uncertainty when they experienced the strong arousal caused by the caffeine. The question was whether this uncertainty would produce a stronger desire to be with others. This is just what Mills and Mintz observed, suggesting again that social comparison needs are an important reason for grouping together in uncertain, stressful circumstances. In summary, stress has generally been found to increase affiliative tendency and seems to do so because affiliation provides individuals with both direct stress reduction and an opportunity to gain useful information from others. What is noteworthy about most of the findings stemming from Schachter's affiliation work is that the research concerns the effects of affiliating with total strangers. Indeed, many studies did not even permit direct verbal exchanges between participants, although admittedly much information can be gained just by looking at one's companions in a stressful context. If total strangers are comforting in times of stress, the soothing effects of good friends and family should, if anything, be even stronger.

SOCIAL SUPPORT

Studies of *social support* (the soothing impact of friends, family and acquaintances) show just such results. Social support has been found helpful with a wide range of stressors and participants (for reviews, see Cohen and Syme 1985; Uchino *et al.* 1996; Umberson *et al.* 1996; Cohen *et al.* 2000). As we will see, social support can take a variety of forms. It can represent simple advice or material assistance. It can also be offered in the form of love, respect, acceptance or emotional support. The research described below illustrates these points.

The broken heart effect

Some of the most dramatic evidence concerns what happens when long-standing companionship is suddenly removed. Several studies have indicated that individuals are far more likely to suffer illness and death in the years just following the death of their spouse. In one study, this 'broken heart' effect reflected the fact that, averaging over all age categories, bereaved spouses were three times more likely to die than the members of a similarly aged married control group (Stroebe et al. 1982). Indeed, for those between the ages of 20 and 29, the bereaved were almost ten times more likely to die. No result this astounding should be accepted at face value without some form of corroboration. When we look at similar studies, the results are rather more modest but the differential death rate among bereaved and non-bereaved samples is nevertheless remarkable. For example, Rees and Lutkins (1967) found that, in one town in South Wales, 12.2 per cent of bereaved spouses died within one year of the original death, whereas only 1.2 per cent of controls passed away. Indeed, in this study even bereaved non-spousal relatives were more likely to die (4.76 per cent) than persons in the control group. Apparently, the impact of physical and psychologically based illness is much stronger for those who find themselves deprived of a major source of social support.

The surprisingly high mortality of people mourning the death of their spouse has prompted much careful analysis (e.g. Stroebe et al. 1993). Stroebe et al. (1982) documented some interesting facts. First, although there are differences from study to study, grief appears to have its major effect on health and mortality within the first six months of the partner's death. Second, younger people appear to be affected more by their spouse's death. Although widowers aged 50–54 are 1.66 times more likely to die than same-aged married individuals, those aged 25–29 are 6.27 times more likely to die than their married counterparts. Finally, males appear to be affected more than women by the loss of their spouse. The results of Reich (1983) verify the differences between the sexes found by Stroebe et al. (1982). Reich (1983) reported that the death rate among bereaved male widowers was 40 per cent higher than in a non-bereaved control group in the six months following the loss of a spouse, with most of these deaths being due to cardiovascular problems. No such pattern was found for women. The precise reason for such differences between the sexes is unclear. One possibility is that men are more likely than women to try and 'tough it out alone' when they are bereaved, which would be consistent with the fact that they are generally more reluctant than women to disclose their intimate feelings (Reis 1998). Another is that they may engage in unhealthy or high-risk behaviours in times of grief. In addition to these questions, researchers are currently exploring the basis of the 'broken heart' phenomenon. One strong possibility is that the immune and neuroendocrine (pituitary/adrenal) systems are less effective when one is recovering from the death of a loved one (Herbert and Cohen 1993). Another possibility is that one tends to neglect one's health more in the absence of strong social support or during periods of grief (Krantz et al. 1985). Future research will undoubtedly shed light on such explanations.

Social support research

Research on the loss of a spouse has some unique properties, since such a loss is in itself an extremely powerful stressor. Most social support research has examined how the presence of friends and family protect the individual and minimize the effects of other stressors, such as combat, illness, the loss of one's job, relocation, and so on. For example, Janis (1963) argued that belonging to a close-knit combat unit provided soldiers with soothing feelings of control and power. He felt that, in a real sense, the group served to replace the family unit as a source of security. Cobb (1976) also commented on the sense of control we may gain through group membership. The reason why this emphasis on control is important is that stress research indicates that simply thinking one has some control over stress renders that stress far more tolerable (e.g. Geer *et al.* 1970; for a review, see Thompson and Kyle 2000). For example, using severe noise as a stressor, Glass and Singer (1972) found that providing people with a 'cut-off switch' almost completely eliminated the negative effects of the noise. What was interesting is that individuals never actually used the switch. Simply knowing it was available was comforting enough. In short, if social support does raise feelings of control, we would expect it to reduce stress. However, Cobb (1976) also alluded to another factor. He reasoned that when we are accepted by a group, we are more likely to feel important, worthy and loved. As a result, we are likely to be more upbeat, optimistic and confident and this, too, may play a crucial role in adapting to stressful events. As we will see later in this chapter, there is a good deal of data to support this view (e.g. Linn *et al.* 1985).

Dimensions of support

The support we receive from friends, family and loved ones can be complex and multi-faceted. In one case a friend might provide us with temporary housing, in another crucial advice, and in yet another the knowledge that we are accepted, loved or cared for. All of these instances represent some form of social support and yet they are quite varied in nature. How can we integrate these different dimensions into an overall construct? Theorists differ in their analyses of social support, but certain common components can be identified (Weiss 1974; Cobb 1976; Cohen and McKay 1984). We list them here using the labels identified by Weiss (1974):

- *Attachment*: the feelings of emotional support, intimacy and liking that exist in a group. It is fostered by the love, caring and attention group members provide for each other.
- *Guidance*: information, advice and feedback provided by the group.
- *Tangible assistance*: material aid, whether it be financial or in the form of service.
- *Embeddedness in a social network*: feeling part of a cohesive or well-defined group. Often such feelings contribute to an individual's sense of identity.
- *Opportunity to provide nurturance*: the extent to which the individual feels that others are dependent on him or her for support. Note that

Weiss (1974) is the only major social support theorist to identify this component.

• *Reassurance of worth*: the acceptance, love and respect that we receive from others bolster our feelings of self-esteem and self-adequacy.

These components have been useful in developing measures of social support. For example, one can create a measure of social support by asking questions about these various dimensions. With such measures researchers have been able to examine the relationship between social support and various stress-related outcomes. This research clearly supports the arguments of Cobb, Janis and others that social support should improve one's ability to cope with stress.

Correlational research on social support and health

Nuckolls *et al.* (1972) examined the rate of complications among 170 pregnant army wives who had reported experiencing major life changes during their pregnancy. Those who had strong social support had a relatively low rate of complication (33 per cent). The rate was almost three times higher (91 per cent) for women who had low social support. Gore (1978) found that, among unemployed males, low social support was associated with higher levels of cholesterol and more illness symptoms. Indeed, in various studies over the years, low social support has been linked to such conditions as cardiovascular disease, tuberculosis, depression, low birthweight in children, arthritis and even death (see Uchino *et al.* 1996, 1999). Admittedly, most of these are correlational findings and it is, therefore, hard to be sure whether the lack of social support *causes* these effects on health. For example, it is possible that once someone is ill, they simply *report* fewer friendships because of depression or in an attempt to gain sympathy.

To partially address this problem, certain studies have utilized *prospective research designs*. This involves assessing social support at one point in time and then examining the extent to which it is associated with health outcomes in the years that followed. One of the earliest of these extensive projects was completed in California by Berkman and Syme (1979). Over 4000 individuals were first classified in terms of their degree of social support, as measured by their marital status, membership of clubs and church groups, and the extent of their contact with friends and relatives. A 9-year follow-up indicated that males with the least social support were 2.3 times more likely to die during the period than those with substantial social support. For women who lacked social support, this disadvantage ratio was 2.8. The researchers were careful to control for a wide range of variables, such as socioeconomic status, obesity, physical exercise, smoking and use of alcohol. These dramatic findings would be less plausible if they were not well corroborated by at least six similar reports from regions as diverse as Michigan and Georgia in the United States, Gothenberg in Sweden, and Eastern Finland (see House *et al.* 1988). In the Swedish study, for example, males who had least social support had death rates four times higher than those with high social support.

As just noted, Berkman and Syme (1979) controlled for many variables, such as smoking and obesity. These controls are crucial in research of this type because people are not randomly assigned to the high and low social support conditions, but rather 'select themselves' to these conditions. Consequently, individuals in these two conditions are not strictly comparable. For example, it is conceivable that it is easier to find social support if one is healthy, attractive, a non-smoker, and so on. If so, those high in social support may have been 'healthier' than others at the beginning of the study, suggesting that the health of these participants causes social support, rather than vice versa. Therefore, careful researchers assess such confounding variables as smoking and obesity so that statistical procedures can be used to control for their influence. Unfortunately, these statistical techniques have limits. No matter how many confounding variables are assessed for use as statistical controls, it is possible to omit some other key variable. For example, Berkman and Syme (1979) were unable to assess serum cholesterol as a control variable. On the other hand, when one reviews all the research on social support and mortality, a wide range of confounding variables have been considered and none has eliminated the relationship between social support and mortality. Thus, if there is a key confounding variable, it is not an obvious one. More importantly, we already know from laboratory research that people who are randomly assigned to receive social support (in the form of simple companionship) experience less distress during stressful procedures than those tested alone (e.g. Amoroso and Walters 1969). Note that the use of random assignment in experimental studies *does* make it highly likely that there will be initial comparability among the participants in various conditions. Therefore, combining these data with the large-scale field studies on mortality make it quite likely that social support does play a causal role in health status. Indeed, after an extensive review of this literature, House *et al.* (1988) concluded that the evidence favouring a causal link between social support and health status is at least as strong as that used originally to link smoking and cancer. Currently, researchers are examining which aspects of social support are most important in this relationship and how they have the effect they do.

Pets as sources of social support

Humans are not the only source of love and friendship. Who among us has not known someone who is devoted to a cat, a dog or a horse? Since love and friendship are key aspects of social support, researchers have begun to explore whether animal 'social support' has the same therapeutic effect as human social support. Research with children (Friedmann *et al.* 1983), terminal cancer patients (Muschel 1984), heart attack victims (Friedmann *et al.* 1980) and the elderly (Mugford and McComisky 1975; Garrity *et al.* 1989) supports the conclusion that contact with pets has therapeutic effects (for some exceptions, see Lago *et al.* 1983; Robb and Stegman 1983). For example, Friedmann *et al.* (1980) examined the survival of more than 90 individuals released from hospital after a heart attack. Ninety-four per cent of those patients who owned pets were still alive one year after their hospital admission. In the non-pet group, only 70 per cent were still alive. Similarly, Siegel (1990), in a carefully controlled field study, found that elderly pet owners made fewer visits to the doctor over a one-year period and responded to stress with less illness than non-pet owners. Interestingly, these effects were strongest when the pets were dogs. Other research has indicated that contact with pets reduces blood pressure, heart rate and skin conductance (e.g. Baun *et al.* 1984; Allen *et al.* 1991). Allen *et al.* (1991), for example, found that blood pressure and skin conductance of dedicated pet owners was lower during a stressful mental task if their pet was present. Indeed, physiological responding in this condition was lower than in conditions in which human friends were present. Thus it appears that pet ownership provides some of the same benefits produced by human social support and, indeed, may provide increased benefits under certain conditions.

EXPLAINING THE RELATIONSHIP BETWEEN SOCIAL SUPPORT AND HEALTH

Control and self-esteem

The dramatic impact of social support on mortality and other stress-related variables has prompted a great deal of discussion and research. Some has been directed at investigating *why* social support has this comforting effect. Research on this topic has focused on the role of advice and material aid, as well as how social support affects feelings of control and self-esteem. Not surprisingly, it indicates that those who report having more social support feel more capable and better about themselves. This has been found to be true for adult males (Linn *et al.* 1985), high school students (Cauce *et al.* 1982) and student nurses (Hilbert and Allen 1985), among others. This relationship between support and esteem is a two-way street. Being liked and accepted by others should lift self-esteem; at the same time, those with high self-esteem are probably more attractive to others, making it easier for them to obtain social support. It does appear, however, that self-esteem plays a key role in social support effects. The results of Cutrona and Troutman (1986) indicate that, when social support does serve to reduce a stressful experience (parenting a difficult child), it primarily does so not only by affecting feelings of self-control, as previously argued, but also by bolstering self-esteem.

Self-disclosure

A second reason that social support improves our well-being appears to involve the benefits of self-disclosure. A series of provocative studies by Pennebaker and his associates involving college students and traumatized populations (e.g. Pennebaker *et al.* 1989; for a review, see Pennebaker 1997) indicate that simply having individuals write or talk about the traumatic events in their lives lowers their health risks in the months following such disclosure. Indeed, in one such study, individuals who engaged in this disclosure showed changes in immune function not shown by control participants (Pennebaker *et al.* 1988). One possible reason for this is that writing or talking about such events may help enable individuals to interpret such events without guilt or with an understanding that gives them some confidence that they can prevent recurrences of such events. Thus, it is likely that one reason social support is helpful is that support from those we care about often prompts us to talk about the events that trouble us. In accord with this, Pennebaker and O'Heeron (1984) found that those who reported discussing traumatic events with close friends had fewer health problems than those who did not engage in such disclosure. In addition, these individuals then spent less time repetitively thinking about the event.

Immune function

In addition to these helpful effects, research suggests that high social support may improve health-related outcomes due to its direct physiological effects in times of stress. For example, in one study, Baron *et al.* (1990) examined the immune responses of individuals whose spouses were hospitalized for treatment of serious cancers. Observing the side-effects of cancer treatment on a loved one is in itself quite stressful, as is the threat of losing one's mate to cancer, and as a result all participants were experiencing at least moderate to intense psychological distress. The researchers took blood samples from these spouses and found that those with high social support were better on two basic forms of immune functioning: the ability of blood lymphocytes to reproduce and the ability of the system to kill cancer cells. These results mirror those found in other populations, including people caring for spouses or relatives with Alzheimer's disease, college students and medical students during examinations, and cancer patients (for reviews, see Herbert and Cohen 1993; Uchino *et al.* 1996). Thus, there is converging evidence that the immune system may play a mediating role in the association between social support and health. There is also some evidence that elderly individuals with strong social support may have lower levels of stress-related hormones (Seeman *et al.* 1994). While many of these studies are non-experimental in nature, consistent evidence comes from experimental research on social support in which the presence or absence of social support is manipulated. For example, Gerin *et al.* (1992) varied whether or not individuals were in the presence of someone who agreed with them as they completed a debating task. The presence of this supportive person led to lower blood pressure and other signs of cardiac arousal. Thus, one reason social support is related to positive health outcomes appears to be because it has several beneficial physiological effects in stressful circumstances (Uchino *et al.* 1999).

THE BUFFERING HYPOTHESIS

Additional research is currently examining the kinds of actions (on the part of companions) that most effectively produce feelings of social support (e.g. Costanza *et al.* 1988) and under which circumstances different types of social support will provide the greatest benefit (Cutrona 1990). One intriguing idea, the 'buffering hypothesis', states that social support only provides benefit in times of stress. Although the buffering hypothesis has some support, other studies have found that high social support contributes to health even when stress is absent. The reason for these inconsistent outcomes may be that some forms of social support are generally beneficial even in times of low stress, whereas other forms only heighten well-being if stress is present (Cohen and Wills 1985). Karen Rook (1987) argued that, when social contact takes the form of shared recreation, humour and affection, it will have beneficial effects on well-being and psychological adjustment whether or not stress is present. She labelled this type of social contact 'companionship'. In contrast, more problem-oriented actions, such as offering guidance, material aid, reassurance and sympathy, are most likely to prove beneficial in stressful periods. Rook labelled this form of contact 'social support'. Thus, the inconsistent data regarding the buffering hypothesis may reflect differences in the way researchers measure or define social support.

CAN SOCIAL SUPPORT BE HARMFUL?

Although friends and relatives can offer aid, reassurance and love, they can also be a source of criticism, thoughtlessness, pity, disagreement and selfishness. Melamed and Brenner (1990), for example, found that married couples often do not even agree about which types of behaviours are supportive and which are not. In a similar vein, Dakof and Taylor (1990) documented the irritation cancer patients experience when well-meaning visitors and staff attempt to cheer them up by minimizing the extent of their illness. In short, sources of support often cause substantial upset and irritation (Rook 1998; Newsom 1999). Rook (1998) suggests that such situations provoke a 'negativity effect'. She argues that the harm done by social stress is generally greater than the harm provoked by non-social stress and that the negative effects of bad social interactions are more extreme than the benefits of supportive social situations. In accord with this view, in studies conducted with the elderly, negative social interactions affected psychological well-being more than positive episodes (Rook 1984; Pagel et al. 1985; Ingersoll-Dayton et al. 1997). For example, Pagel et al. (1985) found that when members of a social network managed to upset the spouses of Alzheimer patients, this led to increases in the spouses' depression. This was particularly true when the friends or relatives were materially helpful to the caregiver but also served as a source of irritation. Quite possibly, this result occurred because the caregiving spouse cannot easily avoid these upsetting personal contacts because she or he needs the help provided by the source of the irritation. Although some studies have only found this negativity effect in elderly populations (Ingersoll-Dayton et al. 1997), others have found such effects in younger groups (Vinokur and Von Ryn 1993). Kiecolt-Glaser et al. (1993) reported similar results when they asked newly married couples to discuss their relationship. When the discussion provoked conflict in the partners, immune reaction was poorer and blood pressure was higher in the next 24 hours. In contrast, when the marital discussion was positive, immunity and blood pressure were unaffected. Thus, here too, negative social support had a greater effect than positive social support. Not only are negative reactions more extreme when they occur; some data suggest that they last longer as well (Rook 1998).

It is increasingly apparent that inept 'social support' can do far more harm than good. What types of behaviours serve to undermine social support? Some researchers have found that social support can increase depressive symptoms if that support is characterized by behaviours such as criticism, micro-management, resentment or condescension (e.g. Clark and Stephens 1996). In one troubling article, Newsom (1999) reports that among impaired older adults, negative reactions to social support occur in at least one-third of cases (across studies). Obviously, being part of a strong social network does not necessarily imply that individuals will receive effective social support. As noted above, psychologically effective social support should bolster self-esteem and feelings of control, as well as providing advice, affection and tangible assistance. Clearly, some social networks do this more effectively than others. If, instead, social support leads the recipient to feel incompetent, guilty, weak or dependent, even needed support could have a negative effect on psychological well-being (Newsom 1999).

MATCHING THEORIES OF SOCIAL SUPPORT

The fact that social support sometimes backfires and occasionally does not have strong therapeutic effects has led social support researchers to try to gain a better understanding of what types of social support work best in various settings. Cutrona and Russell (1990) suggested that an optimal matching hypothesis might determine the effect of social support. Their view was that if people are faced with a controllable stressor, they are better off with material (i.e. tangible aid/information) forms of social support, whereas with uncontrollable stressors emotional support will have a greater soothing impact. The thinking here is that in uncontrollable settings, all one can hope for is reassurance and commiseration. Initial research on this idea has been mixed, however. For example, Cutrona and Suhr (1992, 1994) found, contrary to the optimal matching model, that in cases of controllable stress, stressed individuals appeared to resent it when their spouses offered them information. Indeed, these individuals reported greater satisfaction with their spouses when the spouse offered them emotional support. More importantly in these studies, the controllability of the stress did not generally affect how satisfied individuals were with offers of support that provided them with esteem and emotional reassurance (these forms of support provoked high satisfaction regardless of the situation). These results, for the most part, do not confirm the optimal matching view.

On the other hand, Martin et al. (1994) did find support for a closely related notion. These authors, like Cutrona and Russell, suggested that the nature of the stressor may affect how individuals react to different 'flavours' of social support. They pointed out that some forms of stress are socially embarrassing and certain types of social support may only serve to heighten the public humiliation involved. Martin *et al.* (1994) compared the reactions of chronic headache sufferers and individuals with irritable bowl syndrome to the reactions of cancer patients. The nature of the stress was indeed found to affect how individuals reacted to three basic forms of social support: information, tangible aid and emotional/esteem support. Cancer patients were equally interested in all three forms of support, whereas the embarrassing problems of irritable bowl patients led them to be particularly interested in emotional/esteem support. These results represent some support for the idea that particular forms of social support will be more sought after and satisfying with particular types of stress. A complementary notion is that the nature and effectiveness of social support will be different for various types of individuals. This work draws on attachment theory, which specifies that individuals have different 'styles' of interacting with intimate associates. For example, Collins and Feeney (2000) had dating couples discuss their personal problems. They found that individuals who generally used an avoidant ('don't smother me') attachment style were poor at directly requesting support from their partners. On the other hand, individuals characterized by an anxious ('please don't leave me') coping style were so attentive to their own needs that they were poor at providing support to their partner. Such intricacies may explain why the simple availability of a partner or a friend in times of stress does not always translate into psychologically helpful support.

RANDOM ASSIGNMENT AND SOCIAL SUPPORT RESEARCH

Studies with healthy humans and primates

One drawback to much of the research on social support is the fact that it is correlational. That is, in a typical study, individuals are categorized as being high or low in social support (based on their reports or their social memberships) and their response to stress or their health status is then assessed. The problem with such designs is that one cannot be sure whether it is low social support or some other 'hidden variable' that is really responsible for any differences between the high and low social support groups. Thus, it is possible that those who have low social support are unpopular because they are, say, lazy and that it is this laziness that really accounts for their poor reactions to stress. The way to avoid such interpretive problems is to rely on research designs in which participants are randomly assigned to high and low support groups and/or to high and low stress conditions. Such procedures, of course, make it highly unlikely that the (randomly selected) high support people are lazier (or smarter or taller or whatever, on average) than the low support people. In recent years, researchers have begun to use such strategies.

In one such study, Cohen *et al.* (1992) observed colonies of four to five male monkeys for 26 months in an enriched laboratory setting. One group of monkeys was left undisturbed and, as a result, could establish fairly stable friendship networks and status hierarchies (pecking orders). Here each monkey knew his place and who his friends and enemies were. A second group of monkeys, however, was randomly assigned to be rearranged into new colonies every month. This, of course, disrupted the social network of these colonies. These monkeys had to establish new friendships and, more crucially, had to go through the aggressive displays and behaviours needed to determine the new status hierarchy in each new colony. These animals found this rearrangement to be disturbing. In this sense, the disrupted social network served both as a manipulation of social support (stable *vs.* unstable) and as a stress manipulation. Cohen *et al.* (1992) observed that in the unstable conditions, monkeys engaged in more affiliative behaviour (playing, grooming, staying close to each other) than in the stable condition. Thus, as in Schachter's early work with humans, these monkeys reacted to stress by increasing their contact with others. Cohen and his team took blood samples at the end of this two-year study and found that the monkeys in the unstable condition also showed evidence of suppressed immunity. This suppressed immunity, however, was less likely among unstable animals if they had engaged in relatively high levels of affiliation in their colonies. In short, it would appear from this work that disrupting a naturally occurring social network is a stressful event among primates, but that affiliation can minimize the damage produced by this stress. Note that the negative effects with respect to immunity and cardiovascular functioning are quite consistent with other correlational findings discussed above, linking low social support to poor health outcomes.

Other studies have also begun to randomly manipulate the availability of social support. As noted above, Gerin *et al.* (1992) found that the physiological stress of public speaking was less pronounced among individuals who were permitted to participate with other people who agreed with their ideas (i.e. supportive others) (see also Kirschloaum *et al.* 1995). Allen *et al.* (1991) reported similar results, except that in this case the stressor was mathematical performance and the 'supportive other' was likely to have a wagging tail and a great sense of smell. In one interesting study, Olds *et al.* (1997) worked with unmarried, teenage mothers in Elmira, New York. Some of these low-income mothers were randomly assigned to receive home-visit advice and emotional support from a visiting nurse throughout their pregnancy until the infant's second birthday. This combination of education and social support lowered high-risk behaviours (e.g. smoking, drug use) by the mother during and after pregnancy, resulted in fewer health problems for the infant during pregnancy and during the child's first two years, and led to a lower likelihood of subsequent pregnancy and arrest that was evident up to 15 years later (Olds *et al.* 1997; for a review of single-person support interventions, see Eckenrode and Hamilton 2000).

Research with patient populations

Many studies have suggested that social support manipulations can have positive results under the right circumstances (for a review, see Cohen *et al.* 2000), but by far the most notable studies manipulating social support have concerned the stress of cancer. Spiegel *et al.* (1989) randomly assigned women with terminal stage breast cancer to either standard medical treatment or participation in weekly 'psycho-social' support groups for a year. The support groups were designed to create friendships, reduce fear and pain, and to help the women reorder their life values. Spiegel *et al.* found that women in the support groups had superior mood, better coping and twice the survival (36.6 months) of women in the normal medical treatment group (18.9 months). Similar results have been reported by other researchers who randomly manipulated support group membership while focusing on various forms of cancer (e.g. Richardson *et al.* 1990; Fawzy *et al.* 1993; for a review, see Fawzy and Fawzy 1998), cardiovascular disease (Linden *et al.* 1996) and HIV disease (Kelly *et al.* 1993). Similarly, Mittelman *et al.* (1995) reported less depression among spouse caregivers of Alzheimer patients if they had been randomly assigned to support groups.

The results on this topic, however, are not fully consistent (see Helgeson and Gottlieb 2000). For example, when Goodwin *et al.* (2001) carefully examined the impact of weekly support groups on 158 patients with metastatic breast cancers, she found, in contrast to Spiegel *et al.* (1989), that the survival of patients in support groups (mean = 17.9 months) did *not* significantly exceed that of 77 control patients (mean = 17.6 months). However, the patients in support groups did report less pain and better mood than control patients. Thus, although there is some controversy about whether social support groups actually prolong the life expectancy of cancer patients, results consistently support the idea that such groups have beneficial effects on mood and pain tolerance for such patients. Indeed, Meyer (1995) concluded after a meta-analysis of 45 cancer studies, that something about these psychosocial interventions has a powerful effect on coping with the stress of cancer. This strong effect is thought to be due to the fact that patients with life-threatening diseases feel reluctant to burden their family with their feelings and problems and, as a result, end up feeling isolated even if they have a strong 'pre-disease' social network. Thus, it is likely that the social support provided by these disease-specific support groups is a key ingredient in their effectiveness (Spiegel *et al.* 1989).

At present, research is being conducted to examine the specific role played by social support as opposed to the other components of 'psychosocial' treatment (e.g. pain control, clarified life goals, etc). Telch and Telch (1986) found that simply having cancer patients express feelings and emotions in a support group setting (with no other skills training) over six weeks had little therapeutic effect. In the same study, patients in another condition who received coping skills training (without emotional expression) did show an improvement in mood, activity and distress. This suggests that emotional/social support may not, on its own, be sufficient. It may have to be accompanied by various forms of skill and coping training if it is to have the powerful effects produced in the studies of Spiegel *et al.* (1989) and Fawzy *et al.* (1993). Helgeson *et al.* (1999) recently reported results congruent with this notion from a study of breast cancer patients. In this study, eight weeks of peer discussion alone had few theraputic effects. However, when the groups discussed various educational and coping issues, positive physical and psychological effects occurred and were maintained up to six months later. Clearly, we need to learn more about maximizing the impact of such support groups. We do not yet understand precisely what it is about such groups that is helpful or for whom they work best (Helgeson and Gottlieb 2000). However, even a sceptic would have to conclude that much of the available evidence indicates that providing patients with social support offers a potential means of lowering the stress of living with a life-threatening disease.

Social skills training

Much of the research randomly manipulating social support stems from research in health psychology. Research in clinical psychology offers an alternative strategy. Clinical psychologists have for some years been concerned with treating people who suffer from loneliness, social isolation and social anxiety. Data on such individuals indicate that they are more likely than others to have poor communication skills and high anxiety when it comes to meeting new people. Clinical psychologists have, therefore, put together treatment packages that attempt to strengthen such skills and ameliorate such feelings of shyness and anxiety. These treatments work on improving patients' skill at such things as body language (lean forward, maintain eye contact), reciprocal self-disclosure, how to express sympathy or understanding, and how to stay focused (Barlow and Lehman 1996; Nathan *et al.* 1999). Similarly, relaxation techniques such as pleasant imagery, deep breathing and progressive relaxation are used to reduce social anxiety (Heimberg and Juster 1995). A final strategy is to correct any irrational or maladaptive cognitive concerns that individuals have about asking for support (e.g. 'people will think I'm weak'). Barlow and Lehman (1996) reviewed the research on this topic and concluded that such a combination of social skills and anxiety reduction training does increase the social success of lonely individuals (see also Heimberg and Juster 1995). As a result, one means of testing the impact of social support is to randomly assign some socially phobic or isolated individuals to receive such training and to see whether this training leads to enhanced social support and improved stress resilience over time. There is some initial research on this topic (for a review, see Cutrona and Cole 2000). In this research, investigators try various strategies to improve the social functioning of the support network as a whole, the individuals providing support or the individuals who need support. For example, Hansell *et al.* (1998) found that randomly assigning parents and caregivers of children with HIV to receive monthly coaching sessions designed to improve the social support they (the parents) received did in fact improve their social support. El-Bassel *et al.* (1997) performed a similar randomized experiment with over 100 incarcerated female drug offenders who attended 16 two-hour sessions in which they learned social skills needed to elicit social support. This was designed to aid these women in establishing a non-criminal support network. This training not only increased their emotional support, but also heightened their post-release coping and use of safe sex techniques. Similarly, Brand (1995), using a randomized design, reported positive results of such coaching with divorced and recently bereaved adults who reported greater esteem and family social support following such training, compared with controls. It would appear, therefore, that social skills coaching is capable of reducing social anxiety (Barlow and Lehman 1996) and heightening the social support experienced by individuals (for a review, see Cutrona and Cole 2000). What has yet to be demonstrated, however, is that such 'coached' gains in social support also produce long-term gains in health or mental adjustment (Cutrona and Cole 2000).

The research just discussed has focused on treating the person in need of social support. Another research strategy is to work with those people who will, or could, provide the support. This can involve something as simple as improving communication within a support network, thereby heightening coordination and cooperation (e.g. 'I'll visit grandma on Monday and you can cover the weekend'). It can also take the form of coaching family and friends how to provide support in a helpful and non-stressful fashion, thereby avoiding some of the pitfalls of providing support discussed earlier. In this way, the risk of micro-management, criticism or threats to the autonomy and esteem of the aided individual can be minimized. Research following this strategy has been limited, but it holds promise as a means of maximizing the positive aspects of social support (see Cutrona and Cole 2000).

SUMMARY

Many researchers have indicated that the presence of others makes a variety of stressors easier to tolerate. Moreover, non-human species exhibit similar effects. These benefits occur most reliably when the stressed individual has companions who remain calm. In some of the earliest research on this issue, Schachter (1959) found that frightened people wished to be with others. He argued that this was because (a) frightened people wanted to engage in social comparison and (b) fear is reduced when with others. Research has supported both views, even in cases of simple affiliation (i.e. where group members are strangers to each other). However, the truly dramatic instances of stress reduction have been seen in studies of social support that examined the stress-reducing properties of receiving the support of friends, loved ones and family. These studies examined the effects of losing social support, as well as having it available in times of stress. Both approaches indicate that social support is an important factor not only in psychological adjustment, but in physical adjustment as well. Losing one's spouse increases one's likelihood of contracting a number of ailments and can substantially increase the risk of death, particularly among males. In contrast, those who report high social support appear less susceptible to such problems. Recent attempts to explain this relationship between social support and health have investigated variables such as perceived control, self-esteem and the possible effects of social support on the immune system. In addition, researchers have begun to examine ways in which social conditions can interfere with stress-related coping. Although much research on social support is correlational, some studies have randomly manipulated the level of either affiliation or social support and have found that such manipulations do indeed affect our ability to cope with various stressors (from mental math to cancer). Current work is focusing on various means of heightening the social support of individuals who lack social support. Although much remains to be learned, research is confirming what many of us know from personal experience to be true – that a life filled with the support of others is a happier and healthier life.

SUGGESTIONS FOR FURTHER READING

Cohen, S., Underwood, L.G. and Gottlieb, B.H. (2000) *Social Support Measurement and Intervention*. New York: Oxford University Press. An excellent recent review.

Goodwin, P.A. *et al.* (2001) The effect of group psychosocial support on survival in metastatic breast cancer. *New England Journal of Medicine*, 345: 1719–26. Do support groups help cancer patients live longer? Maybe not.

House, J.S., Landis, K.R. and Umberson, D. (1988) Social relationships and health. *Science*, 241: 540–5. Reviews large-scale research studies linking social support to lower mortality.

Janis, I.L. (1963) Group identification under conditions of external danger. *British Journal of Medical Psychology*, 36: 227–38. One of the earliest papers on social support.

Pennebaker, J.W. (1997) *Opening Up: The Healing Power of Expressing Emotions*, revised edn. New York: Guilford Press. Discusses how talking about trauma can have therapeutic results.

Stroebe, W. (2000) *Social Psychology and Health*, 2nd edn. Buckingham: Open University Press. A thorough review of this interesting literature.

ELEVEN

ELECTRONIC GROUPS

KEY CONCEPTS

- What are some of the similarities and differences between computer groups and face-to-face groups?
- When will electronic groups be better than worse than face-to-face groups, and why?
- What are some of the ways that we react differently to virtual others than real others?

BACKGROUND

The invention of the printing press made news, knowledge and political discourse available to the masses. As such, it not only was a technical advance in communication, but a key factor in changing the world's political structure, ushering in the age of democracy (and revolution). Other changes in communication techniques such as television and radio have had equally powerful effects on humankind. The closing years of the twentieth century witnessed the most recent revolutionary change in human communication, the use of computer networks and internet communication. This innovation in human communication, like those before it, also promises to have far-reaching political, social and psychological consequences. One such consequence, the creation of electronic groups, serves as the focus for this chapter. Electronic groups can take the form of e-mail networks, on-line chat groups or bulletin board type 'newsgroups' (where individuals can post or reply to messages or just quietly observe the interplay as 'lurkers', McKenna and Bargh 1998). The possibilities of effective electronic communication have led many organizations to create so-called *virtual teams*, in which people who may live and work all over the globe may communicate and collaborate electronically to complete a project (DeSanctis and Monge 1998; Cooper and Rousseau 1999). And even when such work groups are not widely distributed geographically, there are now many new tools for assisting groups to do their work, including access to large databases, links to other groups and software tools to assist in groupwork; the latter are variously referred to as *group performance support systems* (GPSS; McGrath and Hollingshead 1994), *group decision support systems* (GDSS), *computer supported collaborative work* (CSCW) or simply *groupware*, well illustrated by software to permit electronic brainstorming, discussed earlier. Not surprisingly, group researchers in many disciplines are beginning to show a great deal of interest in such computer-based groups and computer-mediated communication, often abbreviated as *cmc* (e.g. Hollingshead *et al.* 2002).

UNIQUE FEATURES OF COMPUTER GROUPS

Much of the social psychological research on electronic or computer groups has focused on the way in which more traditional, face-to-face groups differ from those relying on computer-based forms of communication and interaction. Below, we consider some of the research that has found that such differences can indeed alter group process and productivity.

Attenuation of information exchanged

Our usual mode of communication in face-to-face groups is verbal. Very few of us can express ourselves as spontaneously, as quickly or as fluently using the more common tools of electronic expression (e.g. a keyboard or a mouse). Hence, all else being equal, we might expect that one of the effects of switching from face-to-face to computer-linked groups will be that less information gets exchanged. Several studies have found this to be the case (e.g. Strauss and McGrath 1994; McLeod *et al.* 1997).

For example, Hollingshead (1996a) compared face-to-face with computer-mediated groups on a hidden-profile task (discussed in earlier chapters). On such tasks, vital information tends to be ignored by group members if only one person knows of it. Hollingshead found that, overall, much less information was shared in the computer-mediated groups. More importantly, a procedural remedy to avoid the hidden profile bias did not work well in computer groups. This remedy entails having groups rank order all options rather than just pick their top choice. Hollingshead (1996) found that this strategy worked well for the face-to-face groups but did not improve the amount of unshared information exchanged in the computer-mediated groups. Such findings suggest that face-to-face groups may still retain certain advantages over at least some types of electronic groups.

Loss of non-verbal and paralinguistic information

One distinct aspect of most current forms of computer-mediated interaction is that it is limited to written forms of communication. In particular, the most common means of inter-computer discourse (viz. sending typed notes, either synchronously, as in a chat room, or sequentially, as with e-mail) results in the loss of both non-verbal information (e.g. facial expressions, eye contact, hand gestures, interpersonal distancing) and paralinguistic information (e.g. vocal tone and emphases, pauses). Such information can serve several important functions, including regulating conversation (e.g. pauses may indicate when one speaker is finished and another may begin to speak) and expressing felt emotion (e.g. via facial expression). It is probable that the loss of such information may sometimes handicap members of computer work groups.

In one study, for example (Hollingshead 1998: experiment 1), pairs of strangers were compared with dating couples in their abilities to answer general knowledge questions. Half of the dyads communicated face-to-face; the remainder used a 'chat room', which precluded the exchange of any non-verbal or paralinguistic information. The dating couples did much better at the task when they could interact face-to-face than in the chat rooms, and also did much better than the pairs of strangers (regardless of which mode of communication they used). Dating couples interacting face-to-face looked at one another more and worked together more to effectively pool their knowledge. In a follow-up study, Hollingshead (1998: experiment 2) was able to show that providing dating couples either with paralinguistic information (allowing group members to hear one another) or non-verbal behaviour (allowing them to see but not hear one another) substantially improved their performance. Together, these results also suggest that group members who know each other well are most likely to be adversely affected by the restriction to simple written communication and that technologies that restore paralinguistic or non-verbal information (e.g. cameras that permit one to see the source of a message) can reduce these adverse effects.

Loss of status information

Although most current modes of electronic group interaction do not provide discussants with non-verbal information, this lack of information may contribute to group effectiveness under certain conditions. In particular, the relatively more anonymous conditions of computer-mediated interaction can reduce perceived status differences among group members and, for certain tasks, lead to more effective groups. This is particularly likely when low-status members might have highly relevant task information which they either are reluctant to offer to the group (cf. Bonito and Hollingshead 1997) or, if offered, are unable to get higher status members to accept. Recall the classic study by Torrance (1954), discussed in earlier chapters, in which low-status members of bomber crews who knew the correct answer were far less likely to get the rest of the group to adopt their solution than high-status members. This type of bias should be less apparent in computer-linked groups. Several researchers have explored this view.

As early as 1984, Kiesler and her colleagues recognized that computer groups could not only transcend geographic and temporal boundaries but that, in such groups, physical characteristics and non-verbal cues should be far less influential than in face-to-face groups. As Kiesler *et al.* (1984) pointed out, many of the stylistic features that contribute to forceful leader communication, such as confidence, commitment and sincerity, depend on the non-verbal aspects of direct face-to-face communication. In addition, given that status differences are often bolstered by such non-verbal cues (e.g. expensive clothing, regal demeanour, etc.), Kiesler *et al.* also suggested that status effects would be less pronounced in computer-based groups. Dubrovsky *et al.* (1991) reported just such effects in an early study on this topic. This tendency to be less affected by status differences in computerized groups can work to the group's advantage, especially in cases where democratic discourse is beneficial or where lower status individuals have key information as in the Torrance study. Note however, that, if group members are already aware of status differences before they enter their computer groups, the usual status effects (e.g. greater participation and influence by higher status members) may persist (e.g. Spears and Lea 1992; Saunders *et al.* 1994; Weisband *et al.* 1995).

This persistence of status effects may not be all that unfortunate, however. Although some status biases may be counterproductive for groups (e.g. ignoring good ideas from low-status members), in many instances status differences serve key functions for groups. First, status differences provide a reasonably accurate indication to both group members and outsiders of who in the group has greater experience, power or expertise. This, in turn, allows individuals to assess whose opinion is most likely to be credible or which person is most important to convince. In short, a total lack of information about member status during computer-mediated communication might make communications by group leaders or other experts less effective. Another possible drawback to eliminating status differences in real organizations is that group leaders may be more susceptible to interruption, complaints and second guessing of their decisions by low-status members. This leads us to consider a second key function provided by status.

A second function of status differences is that they often provide the most essential group members with enough freedom and power to maximize their productivity for the group. When such status differences are minimized, the productivity of these key individuals is likely to suffer. For example, with e-mail, high-status individuals can now be reached directly by a wide array of individuals, whereas in 'the good old days' the privacy of such individuals was protected by secretaries, assistants and other bureaucratic barriers. Thus, while this universal access to high-status individuals increases the democratic nature of group functioning, it also disrupts the concentration and work flow of these key individuals (for a review, see Hollingshead 2001). In addition, that individuals defer less to high-status individuals during computerized discussion will tend to give more 'voice' to those in the group who may have the least experience or expertise, thereby affecting the speed and quality of group solutions. The solution here may be to rely more on anonymous computerized communication in the early stages of a decision process where the goal is to maximize idea production by the group as a whole, regardless of status or popularity, and then return to a more status focused discussion procedure in later stages of the process where a final decision must be reached and the group wishes to attend more to the opinions of its most experienced and trusted members. This suggested strategy relies on the assumption that anonymous computer-mediated communication encourages group members to express a broader array of ideas, even unpopular ones. What is the evidence for this?

COMPUTER-MEDIATED COMMUNICATION AND ANONYMITY

That computer-mediated communication often provides individuals with high levels of anonymity has been noted by many commentators (e.g. Kiesler *et al.* 1984; Spears and Lea 1994; Zickmund 1997; McKenna and Bargh 2000), who have suggested that such anonymity could heighten impulsive, extreme, antisocial or aggressive behaviour that normally would be kept in check. This, of course, would apply to the expression of unpopular or extreme ideas. In accord with this, Siegel *et al.* (1986) found that group polarization on risk items was more pronounced when groups worked in computer-linked groups as opposed to face-to-face and that verbal hostility was higher in such groups.

McLeod *et al.* (1997) tested the notion that the anonymity associated with computer-mediated communication (cmc) might free individuals to express minority views (see also Spears and Lea 1994) by using a hidden-profile design. In this study, one randomly selected group member was given all the bits of information needed to successfully solve a business investment problem. The other group members had information that led them to favour a suboptimal choice. McLeod *et al.* found that, as they predicted, in anonymous cmc conditions, this 'all knowing' dissenter was far more likely to criticize and disagree with the majority view than in non-anonymous cmc and face-to-face conditions, thereby attempting to save the group from the usual hidden-profile effect. So far, so good. But there was a catch. Under the anonymous cmc condition, the dissenter was far less successful at convincing the other group members than under face-to-face conditions, but it must be said that this condition was effective at broadening the topics and arguments considered by the group. Douglas and McGarty (2001) offer a study that complements McLeod and co-workers' report that computer-mediated communication can lower adherence to normative pressure. Douglas and McGarty examined the extent to which group members directed verbal aggression (flamed) against an outgroup in accord with group norms. As in the study of McLeod *et al.*, individuals were more likely to disagree with the (aggressive) group norm when their identity was not known to other group members in the computer network. Thus, anonymity does not always lead to greater aggression, but it does seem to lead to less conformity during active group discussion in which at least certain group members have differing opinions.

GROUP COHESION AND IDENTITY

Spears, Postmes and their associates (e.g. Spears *et al.* 1990; Postmes *et al.* 2001) suggest another subtle effect of computer-mediated communication.

They argue that, without the personalizing cues provided by face-to-face communication, cmc groups often will feel greater social cohesion and entitativity – that is, be more aware of their common group based characteristics. If so, all else being equal, cmc-based groups should respond more to group norms than face-to-face groups. As we have seen in our chapter on group extremity (Chapter 6), both Postmes *et al.* (2001) and Spears *et al.* (1990) have reported such effects. Thus, when Postmes *et al.* primed groups to value either efficiency or social needs in hospital service, they adhered most to the primed norm under anonymous cmc conditions. This finding appears to contradict McLeod *et al.* (1997), who reported that less conformity occurred under the least personalized condition. In addition, the results reported by Postmes *et al.* (2001) contradict the findings of Douglas and McGarty (2001) reported just above. Importantly, in that study, the salience of social identity was high in that group members were reminded or told about the existence of outgroups during the procedure. This high group salience is a key condition according to the SIDE model of deindividuation we discussed in Chapter 6. Given that both the studies by Postmes and Douglas and McGarty purport to support the SIDE model, these results suggest that some future clarification of this model is needed, as well as continued research to disentangle precisely when cmc anonymity decreases conformity to group norms as many have suggested (e.g. Kiesler *et al.* 1984; Zickmund 1997) or heightens such conformity as Postmes *et al.* and Spears *et al.* contend. One key variable here may be how widely accepted the group norm is among group members. Specifically, cmc anonymity may decrease conformity when some members hold strong minority opinions, as found by McLeod *et al.* (1997), while it may increase conformity when all members of the group generally accept the norm.

SOCIAL CORROBORATION, SOCIAL SUPPORT AND LONELINESS

As we have seen, several writers have noted that one danger of electronic groups is their potential for escalating hate and aggression. This can be due to providing anonymity from outside groups or verbalizing norms that encourage outgroup aggression. In addition to these effects of computer communication, McKenna and Bargh (1998) highlight the fact that computer-mediated communication can provide social corroboration that can heighten such aggressive reactions. McKenna and Bargh emphasize that, in cmc groups, individuals with stigmatized attitudes or preferences can find corroboration for their ideas in anonymous Internet groups. Whether one has an unusual erotic preference, believes the world is flat or is a vicious racist, one can find literally thousands of individuals on the net who share one's perspective, whereas without the net you might think you are largely alone.

McKenna and Bargh documented that individuals with such 'marginal' beliefs or preferences (gays, skinheads, believers in extraterrestrials on earth), who also actively participated in like-minded computer newsgroups groups, felt greater social identification with such groups and, moreover, as a result, felt improved self-acceptance and less estrangement from others. In this inventive study, the authors posted their questionnaire on the newsgroup web site (inviting replies) and, in addition, solicited any individuals they could identify from such sites via e-mail. Indeed, McKenna and Bargh discovered that, after such Internet activity, these individuals were far more likely to reveal their feelings to friends and family members – an impressive indication of greater self-acceptance and also of greater confidence. This, of course, can be most beneficial to those who unfairly suffer from marginalized identities (individuals who are gay, obese, psychologically challenged, etc.), in that they can breach the limits of geography, status and culture to establish contact with others who can give them a sense of acceptance, identity and normalcy. On the other hand, the dark side of this picture concerns individuals who hold deeply prejudiced attitudes or who hold dysfunctional beliefs and preferences (e.g. terrorists, racists, child molesters) or who wish to persist in unhealthy behaviours (e.g. drug abusers, bulimics). As we have seen earlier in this volume, social corroboration from such likeminded others is likely to polarize attitude and action. Thus, Baron et al. (1996a) demonstrated that just finding out that others agree with you on some issue intensifies one's confidence and belief extremity regarding that issue. Similarly, active discussion of such issues leads to a biased flow of arguments, social competition and social identification, which are well-established sources of attitude polarization. Thus, with certain newsgroups, we can anticipate some very unfortunate outcomes.

Recently, Kraut et al. (1998) reported data from a sample of new Internet users in Pittsburgh, Pennsylvania, indicating that individuals who get 'caught up' in Internet use can experience heightened loneliness and depression. On the other hand, large national and international samples indicate very positive reactions from users regarding their Internet experience (e.g. Katz and Aspden 1997; cf. McKenna and Bargh 1999, 2000) in terms of its impact on their lives. For example, Parks and Roberts (1998) found that regular Internet interaction led to feelings of friendship among the participants in over 90 per cent of surveyed cases. Thus, whether or not Internet use does generally lead to greater loneliness is an issue that needs to be examined further. At a more specific level, however, when computer-linked groups are designed especially to serve as support groups for patient groups, they can be very effective at relieving stress for individuals who are geographically isolated or who desire anonymity (Dunham et al. 1998; see discussion below).

ELECTRONIC VIOLENCE ON AND OFF THE INTERNET

Another issue that has begun to concern social researchers is whether aggressive computer-based games somehow make young people more insensitive to violence, more willing to engage in aggression themselves and just, incidentally, very good shots. Thus, Anderson and Morrow (1995) reported that the competitive framework implicit in these games encourages aggression while playing a game like Mario Brothers. Moreover, in this study, the aggression took the form of detached, 'passionless' behaviour. Others (e.g. Schutte *et al.* 1988) have reported that playing computer and video games with aggressive themes heightens subsequent (post-game) aggression in children as well. Indeed, Cooper and Mackie (1986) found that just watching such games elevates subsequent aggression in children. Reviews of this expanding literature (e.g. Anderson and Bushman 2001) indicate that violent video games do increase aggressive behaviour in children and young adults, increase physiological arousal, increase aggression-related thoughts and feelings, and decrease prosocial behaviour. Although it is too early to be certain, investigators and social commentators have suggested that such reactions to violent video games may play some role in the rash of school shootings that have surfaced in the USA in the last ten years, in which young people have attacked fellow schoolmates in a dispassionate and detached manner, acting almost as if they were in a movie rather than in an event that will change – or end – their lives forever.

SIMILARITIES BETWEEN COMPUTER GROUPS AND FACE-TO-FACE GROUPS

Most of the research we have discussed above has focused on how our reactions in electronic groups may differ from our reactions in face-to-face groups. On the other hand, much research also shows that many group phenomena arise in similar ways in both types of group. Thus, for example:

- As we saw earlier, Williams *et al.* (2000) documented that (ring toss) ostracism on the internet produces many of the same negative reactions as it does in face-to-face groups.
- The Köhler motivation gain effect – less capable members persisting longer at conjunctive group tasks – has also been replicated in groups working collaboratively at a cognitive task over a computer network (Hertel *et al.*, in press).
- The well-known psychological benefits of face-to-face social support were replicated in a computer support group of teenage mothers (Dunham *et al.* 1998). Indeed, this particular use of the internet has exceptional potential for linking geographically isolated individuals or those who have an unusual source of stress not widely found in most communities. Thus, one could link individuals with rare illnesses or physical conditions (e.g. teenagers with kidney failure) or individuals who suffer from stressors that they wish to discuss anonymously (e.g. rape, torture), who otherwise would not have any practical means of sharing their experiences with similar others. This is an area of distinct promise.
- As noted earlier, several studies have suggested that computer-mediated communication can adversely affect interaction and performance in task groups. However, in most of these studies, the computer-mediated conditions were much more unfamiliar to participants than face-to-face interaction. What happens when group members become more familiar and practiced at interacting on-line? A series of studies by McGrath and

his colleagues (e.g. Hollingshead *et al.* 1993; Arrow *et al.* 1996) suggested that the disadvantages of computer-mediated communication fade as one becomes used to working in this environment. For example, in one study (Hollingshead *et al.* 1993), the initial inferiority of computer-mediated group task performance was eliminated by only 6 hours of experience working on the computers.

SOCIAL FACILITATION IN ELECTRONIC GROUPS

Social facilitation is another group phenomenon that has important implications for the age of the electronic group. Aiello and his associates (e.g. Aiello and Kolb 1995) have pointed out that, in work settings, supervisors now have the capacity to observe electronically the work and communication taking place on the networked computers of their subordinates. Aiello and his team (e.g. Aiello 1996; Douthitt and Aiello 2001) found that this form of electronic monitoring provokes many of the same reactions as 'live social evaluation', as documented in the social facilitation literature (see also Robinson-Staveley and Cooper 1990). Thus the work of highly skilled performers is socially facilitated by electronic monitoring, while poorly skilled workers, or those working on difficult tasks, respond with social impairment of performance (Aiello and Svec 1993; Aiello and Kolb 1995).

Much of Aiello's work has examined what conditions help minimize this drop in performance. One condition that appears to be beneficial is giving participants some feeling of control over work conditions or the ability to control when they are being monitored by their supervisor (Aiello and Svec 1993; Douthitt and Aiello 2001). Also, feeling that one is being evaluated in a group reduces the negative impact of performance monitoring (Aiello and Svec 1993). In addition, allowing monitored participants to inform their supervisor of their preferences in terms of on what basis they should be evaluated and how that evaluation should be communicated, heightened feelings of fairness and satisfaction (Douthitt and Aiello 2001). These results are similar to those reported for non-computer groups (Cawley *et al.* 1998).

SOCIAL INFLUENCE IN ELECTRONIC NETWORKS

One remarkable aspect of social influence in groups is that, despite all the social forces operating to create uniformity in opinion, opinion minorities often manage to survive. In his dynamic social impact model (e.g. Nowak *et al.* 1990), Latané has suggested that this can be understood in spatial terms – people tend to communicate with and influence those who are closest to them in space, and this can result in pockets or clusters of minority opinion (e.g. small Amish communities). More recently, Latané and his associates (Latané and Bourgeois 1996; Latané and L'Herrou 1996) examined such phenomena in groups that communicate electronically.

For example, Latané and L'Herrou (1996) asked members of moderate size e-mail groups or networks ($n = 26$) to play a 'conformity game'. The groups' goal was to try to figure out (and adopt) the preferences of the majority of group members. Groups were allowed to communicate in five sessions over a two-week period. Different groups used different communication 'geometries', to simulate different possibilities of mutual communication in the networks. For example, a random geometry permitted each person to communicate with four different, randomly chosen others in each session. This simulates a 'wide open' space where anyone might communicate with and influence anyone else. In this geometry, group members soon learned and adopted the majority position (few minority opinions survived). However, the dynamics were quite different in other, more 'closed' geometries. Consider, for example, the ribbon geometry which simulates people living along both sides of a street. In this space, one can only communicate with four of one's neighbours (e.g. on either side and across the street). Latané and L'Herrou found that large clusters of minority opinion routinely formed and survived in such a space. Or consider the family geometry, in which one can only communicate with three people in one's immediate 'family' and with one person in another family (e.g. each member of the family has a good friend in another family). Clusters of minority opinion were harder to form in this space, but once a 'family' adopted a minority opinion, its relative isolation made the resulting cluster hard to alter. Thus, as in more traditional groups, group members in these e-mail networks did grow more similar in their opinions over time and – depending upon the structure of their electronic space – broke into subgroups of different types, suggesting that these individuals were not reacting as disinterested or disconnected individuals, but rather as members of an emerging group with distinct norms and structure.

WORKING WITH VIRTUAL PARTNERS

Thus far, we have focused on the differences and similarities between traditional, face-to-face groups and groups that communicate through some type of electronic network. But there is quite another type of 'electronic group', one in which one or more members is not a human being at all, but literally a 'virtual' member. There is a tradition within certain areas of group research (e.g. research using experimental games like the Prisoner's Dilemma) to have the computer take the place of a group member, and play the game according to some preprogrammed strategy. But in such studies, real participants are usually led to believe falsely that the 'other' really is another person. What concerns us at present is how we interact with 'others' who we know are not humans, but some kind of artificial, simulated 'persons'. As anyone who has dealt with voice mail messengers, 'assistants' within software programs, or the like, such encounters are becoming increasingly common. And with improvements in technology, such human–computer interactions are becoming increasingly sophisticated. A good illustration are attempts to provide therapeutic virtual counsellors (e.g. O'Dell and Dickson 1984); you can try out ELIZA, an early version of computerized client-centred therapy on the Internet (at http://www-ai.ijs.si/eliza-cgi-bin/eliza_script).

In Chapter 8, we learned that members of groups that could discuss social dilemmas with one another were more likely to act cooperatively, and that this effect appears to be due, at least in part, to group members making and keeping promises to cooperate with each other (cf. Kerr and Kaufman-Gilliland 1994; Bicchieri 2002). But do group members do likewise with virtual group partners? This question was explored by Kiesler *et al.* (1996), whose participants played a Prisoner's Dilemma game with one of four partners: a human confederate, a computer that communicated through written text, a computer that communicated with synthesized speech or a computer that also had an animated face to accompany its synthesized speech. The striking result was that the human participants' responses to the computer were roughly similar to their responses to their live human partner. For example, on the initial round of the game, 80 per cent of the participants suggested to their human partner that they both cooperate; the corresponding figure for the computer conditions was 59 per cent. Even more impressively, most participants who suggested mutual cooperation kept their end of the bargain – 94 per cent when their partner was human, and although somewhat lower, still 62 per cent when the bargain was struck with a computer! Interestingly, such promises to the computers were less likely to be broken when the computer partner was simpler (90 per cent kept their promises for the text-only computer partner) than when it was more complex (e.g. only 41 per cent of the promises were kept to the computer with animated face and voice). Kiesler *et al.* plausibly attributed this to our reliance on facial cues to evaluate and build trust in others, and to negative reactions to any imperfections in facial displays of the computer face–voice combination. Whether one views these findings as revealing a half-empty glass (people are more likely to break a promise to a computer than to a live human, especially if the computer doesn't 'look right') or a half full one (most people keep their commitments, even if they are made to virtual partners) is a matter of perspective. Kiesler *et al.* chose the latter perspective and concluded that, 'people keep commitments, whether to a person, group, dog, or computer, not because they believe each of these is human, but because they, themselves, are human' (p. 63).

SUMMARY

In this chapter, we have only scratched the surface of an exciting new arena of group research – electronic groups. We have seen that unfamiliarity with new technology, loss of certain types of information (e.g. nonverbal or paralinguistic cues, group member status) can change the way groups communicate, influence one another and perform. On the other hand, there are also many indications that the dynamics of electronic groups will, in many important regards, be very similar to the dynamics of more familiar, face-to-face groups.

These studies on how individuals behave in electronic groups or while engaged in computer-mediated communication are obviously just the beginning of a growing surge of research on such topics in group processes. As we write this chapter, norms of Internet use are evolving (Kiesler *et al*. 1984; Kiesler 1997) and new technologies of human communication are being developed that will change fundamentally the way we work, play and maintain relationships. Such changes in communication technology will not only have far-reaching practical implications for human groups and for society at large, but should also offer fascinating opportunities to manipulate and study the ways in which humans behave in a variety of groups, and thereby to understand better what it really means to be human.

SUGGESTIONS FOR FURTHER READING AND LINKS

Douthitt, E.A. and Aiello, J.R. (2001) The role of participation and control in the effects of computer monitoring on fairness perceptions, task satisfaction, and performance. *Journal of Applied Psychology*, 86: 867–74.

Kiesler, S., Siegal, J. and McGuire, T. (1984) Social psychological aspects of computer-mediated communication. *American Psychologist*, 39: 1123–34.

McKenna, K.Y.A. and Bargh, J.A. (1998) Coming out in the age of the Internet: identity 'de-marginalization' through virtual group participation. *Journal of Personality and Social Psychology*, 75: 681–94.

Zickmund, S. (1997) Approaching the radical other: the discursive culture of cyberhate. In S.G. Jones (ed.) *Virtual Culture*. London: Sage.

http://www.usabilityfirst.com/groupware/index.txl for links to research and application of groupware.

TWELVE

CONCLUDING THOUGHTS

At one level, the findings generated by research on groups are full of apparent paradoxes. The social support literature shows that groups can have a soothing influence, whereas research on social facilitation suggests that other persons can elevate arousal and tension; sometimes group settings can enhance performance, whereas at other times social loafing and free riding are induced by groups; computer groups sometimes but not always work less effectively than face-to face groups; groups can dramatically elevate aggressive behaviour, yet cooperative group experiences represent one of the most powerful means of reducing prejudice and hostility. These superficial contradictions, however, appear less 'paradoxical' if one considers why each phenomenon occurs. So, for example, a careful consideration of task and situational variables makes it clear that social loafing occurs in some settings and social facilitation occurs in others because on some tasks co-workers enhance comparability and evaluative concerns, whereas on other tasks co-workers minimize these factors. Similarly, computer groups are less productive primarily on tasks that require a great deal of coordination and cooperation.

In short, if you ask how groups affect motivation, perception, performance, behaviour, aggression and problem-solving, you will not receive a simple answer. There are, however, a few conclusions that do seem valid. First, group settings can have dramatic effects on all these phenomena. Predicting precisely what type of effects these will be requires a careful analysis of situational and task features, as well as some understanding of the structure and composition of the group in question.

Second, it is clear that groups can have a profound impact on what we think is true and good; what we think we should do; indeed, even on what we think we are seeing and hearing. Not only can groups contribute to our initial impressions, under appropriate conditions group discussion can also produce polarization of those impressions. Major contributing factors to these social influence phenomena are our tendencies to trust a consensus of our peers and our reluctance to incur their wrath. These tendencies can lead us to suppress our private reservations (e.g. Janis 1972), to refrain from offering information that we feel is not commonly shared (e.g. Stasser and Titus 1987) and to perform extreme behaviours that violate our own private values (e.g. Milgram 1974).

Third, groups are a major source of comfort, orientation and sense of identity. This would appear to explain why even rejection and ridicule from total strangers are so avidly avoided. Our inclination to please those around us is apparently so overlearned that we reflexively avoid offending others with deviant opinions and actions, even when the consequences for doing so would be fairly minimal.

Fourth, it is clear that group process phenomena are highly significant for many contemporary world problems. Research on conformity, groupthink, social decision schemes and group polarization has direct relevance for problems ranging from the work of juries to international policy decision-making. Research on social support, social dilemmas, social loafing and free riding has obvious relevance for a variety of health, economic and environmental issues. For example, given the powerful therapeutic effect of social support, hospitals might consider providing a more structured means of incorporating family members into health treatment, and might even consider providing coaching to insure that the support that is provided is not undermined by psychologically harmful actions and attitudes. We should also consider how best to apply the principles developed in social dilemma research so that we, as a species, can act as more careful stewards of our dwindling planetary resources. Research on group aggression and cooperative problem-solving offers insights that should aid us in alleviating racial, ethnic, religious and nationalistic hostility. These, of course, are all large and complex applied problems that will not be solved by any single academic discipline. Nevertheless, research on group processes can make a significant and distinctive contribution to our understanding of, and our ability to meet, a number of these contemporary challenges.

GLOSSARY

Additive task: a task for which the group's potential productivity is the simple sum of the productivities of the group members

Affiliation research: examines the factors that lead other individuals to join or gather together with other people; it typically focuses on the stress-reducing effects of such affiliation

Attentional overload: created when an organism tries to attend to more inputs than they can process; leads to a focus on the narrower array of cues and the making of response priorities

Attentional theory of social facilitation: the idea that social facilitation/impairment is caused by attentional overload, which leads us to focus on a narrow array of cues, thereby screening out irrelevant stimuli or distractions on simple tasks but ignoring key cues on complex tasks

Audience paradigm: refers to studies in which research participants work on a task while thinking that their actions can be observed by others (e.g. an experimenter, passive observers)

Brainstorming: a form of group idea generation, stressing spontaneity, no criticism or evaluation of new ideas, and building on one another's suggestions; its proponents allege that it is more productive than comparable nominal groups

Broken heart effect: the fact that surviving spouses have a greater likelihood of illness and death following the death of their partner

Buffering hypothesis: the view that social support provides psychological benefits, primarily in times of stress

Challenge reaction: the physiological changes that occur when an individual feels that they have adequate resources to cope with a given stressor. This entails a substantial increase in cardiac output accompanied by a decrease in vascular resistance. There is no change in blood pressure (contrast with *Threat reaction*)

Co-action paradigm: refers to studies in which research participants work on a task in the presence of other participants who are working on the same task

Commitment norm: a norm that prescribes that one carry out those actions which one has promised or committed oneself to perform

Common ingroup identity model: a series of recommended procedures designed to lead individuals to recognize category memberships they hold in common

Comparison level: a term from exchange theory indicating the amount of profit from a relationship that is considered to be fair or equitable

Comparison level for alternatives: a term from exchange theory indicating the largest amount of profit an individual would obtain in their best alternative relationship

Computer-mediated communication (cmc): groups linked by online chat groups, e-mail or newsgroups

Conjunctive task: a task on which the group cannot perform any better than its least capable member

Contact hypothesis: the hypothesis that increased contact between members of antagonistic groups can, under certain conditions, reduce that antagonism

Convergent thought: Nemeth's view that majority influence prompts individuals to think primarily about why the majority may be correct

Conversion: a change in one's private beliefs following careful thought about an issue

Cross-categorization: a shift from viewing people as members of distinct groups ('us and them') to viewing them as members of many groups whose boundaries overlap and cross-cut

Decategorization: a shift from viewing people as members of distinct groups ('us and them') to viewing them as distinct individuals ('me and you')

Decision rule: the level of agreement or consensus among group members required to define a group choice

Deindividuation: the notion that crowds lead individuals to be less self-conscious and, therefore, more impulsive and willing to engage in anti-social behaviour

Demonstrability: capable of being shown to be correct within some shared conceptual system; depends upon both the opportunity and motivation to present the arguments favouring a solution

Disjunctive task: a task on which the group must select the contribution of a single member; hence, the group's potential productivity is defined by the productivity of its most capable member

Distraction/conflict (D/C) theory: holds that social facilitation is caused when individual performers split their attention between the experimental task and the reactions and performances of other people. It predicts that social facilitation is most likely when social comparison is likely and audience evaluation is present. Also predicts that non-social distractions cause social facilitation

Divergent thought: Nemeth's view that minority influence prompts individuals to think in a more creative and varied way; this includes considering disconfirming instances

Drive theory of social facilitation: the theory that the presence of others increases drive, which, in turn, facilitates well-learned and simple tasks while impairing performance of poorly learned and complex tasks

Dual identity: a shift from viewing people simply as members of distinct groups ('us and them') to viewing them as members of both distinct groups and of an inclusive, superordinate group

Dyad: a group of two persons

Emergent norm theory: a theory that contends that crowd behaviour is governed by temporary norms that evolve in the group; these norms may violate wider societal norms

Entitativity: the extent to which a collection of individuals is viewed as a distinct and intact group

Equalitarian model: the view that group problem-solving is slowed by the need to allow most members of the group to express their opinions (contrast with *Hierarchical model*)

Eureka task: a task for which one answer is self-evidently correct

Exceptional case bias: the tendency to dismiss instances that contradict a stereotype as being due to the behaviour of an outgroup member who is atypical for their group

Exchange theory: the view that individuals incur costs and gain rewards in relationships with other individuals and that their attraction to such relationships is a function of these factors

Expectancy value theory: the view that our efforts at a task are strongly affected by our beliefs about how likely it is that such effort will result in a reward and how much we value that reward

Expectancy violation theory: the notion that careful message processing follows social conditions in which the individual is surprised by the social information they receive

Framing: the particular way in which a problem is posed or described which often affects how the problem is solved

Free riding: a group motivation loss arising from the perception that one's efforts are dispensable for group performance

Functional size: refers to the amount of gross productivity generated by a group after correcting for the amount of process loss that occurs. Thus, if a group of ten people only produces as much as two people would acting without process loss, the functional size of the ten-person group is two

General reinforcer: a stimulus that has gained intense reinforcing power by being paired with an array of either primary reinforcements or primary punishments (e.g. money, social approval, rejection)

Group: a number of interdependent individuals who influence one another through social interaction (Forsyth 1999)

Group cohesion: the extent to which group members as a whole, or on average, value their group membership; it is generally thought to be a function of mutual respect, trust, attraction and group identification

Group motivation gain: an increase in the motivation of group members relative to the level of motivation exhibited by a comparable individual performer

Group motivation loss: a decline in the motivation of group members relative to the level of motivation exhibited by a comparable individual performer

Group performance support system (GPSS): technology (both hardware and software) designed to channel or modify a group's task performance process and/or task products; also referred to as *groupware*

Group polarization: the phenomenon whereby groups of likeminded individuals become more extreme in their beliefs after discussion of those beliefs

Groupthink: the tendency of groups to provoke self-censorship, stifle dissent and exaggerate their feelings of superiority and moral correctness, especially when the favoured group norm is apparent to all group members

Hidden profiles: the case when several bits of shared information favour one decision option and the unshared information favours another option and the latter outnumbers the former

Hierarchical model: the view that the most capable member of a group will dominate discussion during group problem-solving

Horizontal (versus vertical) cohesion: the amount of respect, attraction and trust felt by group members for each other within a given level of status or organization within a group

ID model of deindividuation: explains mob behaviour as a function of emergent group norms and lowered feelings of fear and guilt; ignores the role of self-awareness in the process

Identification/compliance/internalization: Kelman's distinction between agreeing with a group because of wanting to see oneself as similar to the group, fearing the group or being convinced by the group

Illusory correlation: the observation that people tend to see relationships between group membership and behaviours that are not justified by the facts

Information-reducing task: a task for which individual contributions to the group product cannot be individually identified

Information sampling theory: a theory that predicts that group members are more likely to discuss those ideas that they share in common, while tending to ignore ideas that are held only by a single group member

Informational social influence: refers to social influence based on our tendency to trust the information provided by others, especially when they are in agreement

Ingroup favouritism: a tendency to provide more resources to, or evaluate more favourably, members of one's ingroup than members of an outgroup

Intellective task: a task for which there is a solution or choice that is demonstrably correct within some shared conceptual system

Interdependence: one's own outcomes depend not just on one's own actions, but also upon the actions of another

Judgmental task: a task for which there is no demonstrably correct solution or choice, requiring some reliance upon social consensus to evaluate alternatives

Köhler effect: a group motivation gain exhibited by relatively low-capability members on a conjunctive group task

Leader categorization theory: the view that we have person-schemas that describe specific characteristics and behaviours of leaders in particular types of groups and that such schemas affect who is selected to serve as leader in such groups

Learned drive theory: the idea that other people elevate our drive because in certain settings they have been associated with rewards and punishments. In such settings, therefore, we experience 'anticipatory drive'. For humans, this is likely to be true in evaluative and competitive circumstances

Leniency bias: a tendency for jury factions favouring acquittal during deliberation to have more influence than comparably sized factions advocating conviction

Matching theory: the view that certain forms of social support are better suited to reducing stress in specific stressful settings, while other forms of support provide little benefit in such settings

Means rule: the idea that we consider our fellow group members' capabilities when evaluating the adequacy of their contribution to group goals

Mere presence hypothesis: Zajonc's assertion that simply having others around us elevates arousal, even in non-competitive, non-evaluative situations

Minimal groups: experimental groups based on trivial or random criteria, with no apparent prior or future basis for conflict

Nominal groups: sets of individuals who work independently and whose individual products are combined as permitted by the task demands; the resultant combination may serve as a reasonable potential productivity baseline for certain tasks (e.g. group brainstorming)

Normative social influence: refers to social influence based on the power of the group to reward and punish the individual

Norms: shared expectancies and standards within a culture or a group regarding what is normal, correct, moral and good

Optimal distinctiveness theory: the view that individuals work to balance their desire for social acceptance and belonging against their desire to be distinctive individuals

Ostracism: ignoring an individual in a setting in which social interaction is possible or likely

Persuasive arguments theory: a theory of group polarization that attributes polarization to group members hearing new, high-quality ideas during group discussion

Potential productivity: the maximum productivity one might reasonably expect from a group, based on the resources the members bring to the task, the demands of the task and the optimal use of member resources

Priming: presenting an individual with a stimulus that is related to a cognitive category

Prisoner's Dilemma: a two-person version of a social dilemma, the structure of which is sometimes illustrated by a scenario involving two prisoners being interrogated

Privatizing: giving group members personal access and control of some share of a common resource

Process loss: the difference between groups' potential productivity and their actual productivity, which can be attributed to faulty group performance processes

Prospective research design: a study in which a key variable, such as social support, is measured at one point in time and used to predict other target outcomes, such as health, in the future

Prototypic group norms: that position in the group that maximizes similarity to ingroup members while also minimizing similarity to outgroup members. According to self-categorization theory, this is the most desirable position for group members who wish to assert their identification with their group

Prototypic individuals: a term from self-categorization theory referring to group members who best exemplify the norms, behaviours and outlook of a given group

Realistic conflict theory: the view that intergroup hostility stems from groups competing for resources and having conflicting goals

Recategorization: a shift from viewing people as members of distinct groups ('us and them') to viewing them as members of an inclusive, superordinate group ('us all')

Reciprocity norm: a norm that prescribes that one return to another a benefit or harm equivalent to that received

Reference groups: social groups we identify with and admire; they are particularly important for socially validating our beliefs and values

Referent informational influence: refers to the process of using information from other group members to determine where the preferred group norm is

Relative deprivation: the belief that one's outcomes are inequitable relative to one's expected outcomes, either based on recent experience or by comparison with others (often members of some social group)

Releaser cues: acts performed in crowded settings that 'break the ice' regarding exuberant, aggressive or antisocial behaviour

Role conflict: instances in which an individual occupies two or more roles in a group or society and the demands of one such role contradict, or are inconsistent with, the demands of another

Scapegoating: redirecting hostility triggered by one agent to another target (often a whole social group) that is less able to retaliate, is distinctive or is authorized as a target by social norm or convention

Self-categorization theory: the view that our sense of identity is deeply affected by those social categories we belong to, provided that such categories are salient to us at the moment. An extension of social identity theory, it assumes that individuals wish to maximize their similarity to salient ingroup norms while maximizing differences to salient outgroup norms

Self-categorization view of polarization: the theory that group polarization is due to group members' desires to conform to prototypic group norms that differentiate them from outgroup members

Self-efficacy: a feeling of mastery and self-confidence in one's ability to meet a challenge or successfully complete a task

Self-efficacy theory: the theory that when we expect to perform well, audiences and co-actors improve our performance; when we expect to perform poorly, audiences and co-actors will harm our performance

SIDE model of deindividuation: a theory that explains mob action by contending that anonymity heightens conformity to group norms; it discounts the role of decreased fear and guilt in large crowd settings

SIM model of groupthink: a theory that argues that groupthink occurs when group salience and cohesion are high and group members feel that the group is under attack

Social attraction: a term from self-categorization theory that refers to the attraction felt for prototypic individuals; that is, those who come closest to embodying the norms and spirit of the group. Assumed to be a key factor in group cohesion

Social comparison theory: the view that when objective standards are unreliable or unavailable, we assess the correctness of our beliefs and the strengths of our abilities by comparing ourselves to other individuals

Social compensation: a group motivation gain arising when individuals increase their efforts on collective tasks to compensate for the anticipated poor performance of other group members

Social corroboration: created when others agree with our choices and judgments; generally a source of heightened confidence and opinion polarization

Social decision scheme: a probabilistic function, usually summarized in a matrix, that specifies the probability that each possible group decision will be reached for each possible initial distribution of group member preferences

Social dilemma: a situation in which the defecting choices that benefit oneself harm the group as a whole, and where universal defection leads to poorer collective outcomes than universal cooperation

Social facilitation: refers to improvements in performance that occur when individuals respond or work in the presence of either observers or co-workers; it typically occurs on well-learned or simple tasks

Social identity theory: the view that our sense of identity and self-esteem is due, in large part, to the groups we identify with. Assumes that this social identification process explains why we tend to favour our own groups over others even when we are unfamiliar with others in our own group

Social impairment: refers to the performance decrements that occur when individuals respond or work in the presence of either observers or co-workers; it typically occurs on poorly learned or complex tasks

Social loafing: (a) a group motivation loss attributable to a lack of individual identifiability on information-reducing group tasks; (b) more generally, a synonym for group motivation losses

Social monitoring view: the idea that social facilitation/impairment is caused when co-actors or audiences heighten our feelings of uncertainty; this is most likely when they are paying attention to us and we cannot observe them easily

Social motive or orientation: an individual difference in the relative weight placed upon one's own outcomes versus those of others. Usually classified into one of three types: *cooperators*, who give substantial weight to both; *individualists*, who lend most weight to their own outcomes; and *competitors*, who seek to maximize the difference self and other

Social roles: a set of expectancies, obligations and privileges associated with a particular position, status or job function in a group or society

Social support: the receipt of advice, material aid, love, acceptance and esteem from loved ones and acquaintances

Sociobiology: the view that many human preferences and reactions have been shaped in some way by natural selection

Stages of indoctrination: the *softening up stage* involves high stress and sleep loss; the *compliance stage* involves the individual paying lip service to group demands; the *internalization stage* is marked by the individual beginning tentatively to accept group policy; the *consolidation stage* occurs when the individual is deeply committed to the group position

Status: refers to the rank, privileges and respect accorded an individual who serves a given function within a group or organization

Strength in numbers: a feature of certain social decision schemes, whereby numerically larger factions exert more influence over the final group decision than one would expect based simply on their relative size

Stroop task: a task in which one must report the colour of ink that objects are printed in. On critical trials, the objects are colour name words that interfere with our ability to quickly complete the task because of our automatic tendency to process the semantic content of the words

Sucker effect: a group motivation loss arising from the perception that other capable group members are free riding on one's own efforts, resulting from attempts to achieve a fairer, more equitable ratio of individual effort to payoff

Superordinate goals: important goals that can only be met by cooperating with others; often used to induce cooperation between groups with a history of conflict

Task demands: the constraints that a task places upon performance, based on the criterion of performance, the processes that are permitted when performing the task (e.g. the rules of the task) and the processes that successful task performance requires

Threat reaction: the physiological changes that occur when individuals feel that they do not have adequate resources to cope with a given stressor. This entails a moderate increase in cardiac output accompanied by either an increase or no change in vascular resistance. A rise in blood pressure also occurs (contrast with *Challenge reaction*)

Tit-for-tat: a strategy for interacting in repeated cases of interdependence in which one reciprocates on the ith + 1 trial the response of one's partner on the ith trial

Trust: confidence that one will find what is desired from another, rather than what is feared

Truth wins: a social decision scheme in which a single advocate of a demonstrably correct, 'true' alternative is sufficient to insure that the group adopts this alternative

Transformational leader style: marked by an innovative selection of inspiring group goals, charismatic communication style, enthusiasm for innovation in subordinates, absence of manipulative strategies and the reinforcement of appropriate behaviour in followers

Two-process view of conversion: Moscovici's notion that minorities provoke thoughtful attitude change, whereas majorities provoke compliance

Ultimate attribution error: a tendency to attribute the undesirable behaviour of outgroup members to stable, personal characteristics while attributing desirable behaviours to unstable situational causes

Vertical cohesion: the extent to which rank-and-file members view their leader with respect and trust; assumed to be an important component of group cohesion

Virtual team: a group of geographically and/or organizationally dispersed co-workers that is assembled using a combination of telecommunications and information technologies to accomplish an organizational task

REFERENCES

Abrams, D. and Hogg, M.A. (1988) Comments on the motivational status of self-esteem in social identity and intergroup discrimination. *European Journal of Social Psychology*, 18: 317–34.

Abrams, D. and Hogg, M.A. (1990) Self-categorization, self identification and social influence. In W. Stroebe and M. Hewstone (eds) *European Review of Social Psychology*, Vol. 1. Chichester: Wiley.

Abrams, D., Wetherell, M., Cochrane, S. and Hogg, M.A. (1990) Knowing what to think by knowing who you are: self-categorization and the nature of norm formation, conformity and group polarization. *British Journal of Social Psychology*, 29(2): 97–119.

Acorn, D.A., Hamilton, D.L. and Sherman, S.J. (1988) Generalization of biased perceptions of groups based on illusory correlations. *Social Cognition*, 6: 345–72.

Adams, J.S. (1963) Toward an understanding of inequity. *Journal of Abnormal and Social Psychology*, 67: 422–36.

Adams, J.S. (1965) Inequity in social exchange. In L. Berkowitz (ed.) *Advances in Experimental Social Psychology*, Vol. 2. New York: Academic Press.

Ader, R. and Tatum, R. (1963) Free-operant avoidance conditioning in individual and paired human subjects. *Journal of the Experimental Analysis of Behavior*, 6: 357–9.

Aiello, J.R. (1996) The effects of electronic performance monitoring on stress: locus of control as a moderator variable. *Computers in Human Behavior*, 12: 407–23.

Aiello, J.R. and Douthitt, E.A. (2001) Social facilitation from Triplett to electronic performance monitoring. *Group Dynamics*, 5(3): 163–80.

Aiello, J.R. and Kolb, K.J. (1995) Electronic performance monitoring and social context: impact on productivity and stress. *Journal of Applied Psychology*, 80: 339–53.

Aiello, J.R. and Svec, C.M. (1993) Computer monitoring of work performance: extending the social facilitation framework to electronic presence. *Journal of Applied Social Psychology*, 23: 537–48.

Aldag, R.J. and Fuller, S.R. (1993) Beyond fiasco: a reappraisal of the groupthink phenomenon and a new model of group decision processes. *Psychological Bulletin*, 11: 533–52.

Allen, K.M., Blascovich, J., Tomaka, J. and Kelsey, R.M. (1991) The presence of human friends and pet dogs as moderators of autonomic responses to stress in women. *Journal of Personality and Social Psychology: Interpersonal Relations and Group Processes*, 61: 582–9.

Allison, S.T. and Messick, D.M. (1985) Effects of experience on performance in a replenishable resource trap. *Journal of Personality and Social Psychology*, 49: 943–8.

Allport, F.H. (1924) *Social Psychology*. Boston, MA: Houghton-Mifflin.

Allport, G.W. (1954) *The Nature of Prejudice*. Reading, MA: Addison-Wesley.

Alvaro, E.M. and Crano, W.D. (1996) Cognitive responses to minority- or majority-based communications: factors that underlie minority influence. *British Journal of Social Psychology*, 35(1): 105–21.

Alvaro, E.M. and Crano, W.D. (1997) Indirect minority influence: evidence for leniency in source evaluation and counterargumentation. *Journal of Personality and Social Psychology*, 72(5): 949–64.

Amoroso, D. and Walters, R. (1969) Effects of anxiety and socially mediated anxiety reduction on paired-associate learning. *Journal of Personality and Social Psychology*, 11: 388–96.

Anderson, C.A. and Bushman, B.J. (2001) Effects of violent video games on aggressive behavior, aggressive cognition, aggressive affect, physiological arousal, and prosocial behavior: a meta-analytic review of the scientific literature. *Psychological Science*, 12(5): 353–9.

Anderson, C. and Morrow, M. (1995) Competitive aggression without interaction: effect of competitive versus cooperative instructions on aggressive behavior in video games. *Personality and Social Psychology Bulletin*, 21: 1020–30.

Anshel, M.H. (1995) Examining social loafing among elite female rowers as a function of task duration and mood. *Journal of Sport Behavior*, 18(1): 39–49.

Argote, L., Devadas, R. and Melone, N. (1990) The base-rate fallacy: contrasting processes and outcomes of group and individual judgment. *Organizational Behavior and Human Decision Processes*, 46: 296–310.

Aronson, E. (1968) Dissonance theory: progress and problems. In R.P. Abelson, E. Aronson, W.J. McGuire, T.M. Newcomb, M.J. Rosenberg and P.H. Tanenbaum (eds) *Theories of Cognitive Consistency: A Sourcebook*. Chicago, IL: Rand McNally.

Aronson, E., Blaney, N., Stephan, C., Sikes, J. and Snapp, M. (1978) *The Jig-Saw Classroom*. London: Sage.

Arrow, H. (1997) Stability, bi-stability, and instability in small groups influence patterns. *Journal of Personality and Social Psychology*, 72: 75–85.

Arrow, H., Berdahl, J.L., Bouas, K. *et al.* (1996) Time, technology, and groups: an integration. *Computer Supported Cooperative Work*, 4: 253–61.

Asch, S.E. (1955) Opinions and social pressure. *Scientific American*, 193: 31–55.

Asch, S.E. (1956) Studies of independence and submission to group pressure: I. On minority of one against a unanimous majority. *Psychological Monographs*, 70(9) (Whole No. 417).

Atoum, A.O. and Farah, A.M. (1993) Social loafing and personal involvement among Jordanian college students. *Journal of Social Psychology*, 133(6): 785–9.

Axelrod, R. (1984) *The Evolution of Cooperation*. New York: Basic Books.

Back, K.W. (1951) Influence through social communication. *Journal of Abnormal and Social Psychology*, 46: 9–23.

Baker, S.M. and Petty, R.E. (1994) Majority and minority influence: source position imbalance as a determinant of message scrutiny. *Journal of Personality and Social Psychology*, 67(1): 5–19.

Bales, R.F. (1958) Task roles and social roles in problem-solving groups. In E.E. Maccoby, T.M. Newcomb and E.L. Hartley (eds) *Readings in Social Psychology*. New York: Holt.

Bales, R.F. and Strodtbeck, F.L. (1951) Phases in group problem-solving. *Journal of Abnormal and Social Psychology*, 46: 485–95.

Ballew vs. Georgia (1978) *United States Reports*, 435: 222–45.

Bandura, A. (2000) Exercise of human agency through collective efficacy. *Current Directions in Psychological Science*, 9(3): 75–8.

Bandura, A., Ross, D. and Ross, S.A. (1961) Transmission of aggression through imitation of aggressive models. *Journal of Abnormal and Social Psychology*, 63: 575–82.

Barlow, D.H. and Lehman, C. (1996) Advances in the psychosocial treatment of anxiety disorders: implications for national health care. *Archives of General Psychiatry*, 53: 727–35.

Baron, J. (1996) Do no harm. In D. Messick (ed.) *Codes of Conduct: Behavioral Research into Business Ethics*. New York: Sage.

Baron, R.S. (1986) Distraction-conflict theory: progress and problems. In L. Berkowitz (ed.) *Advances in Experimental Social Psychology*, Vol. 19. New York: Academic Press.

Baron, R.S. (2000) Arousal, capacity, and intense indoctrination. *Personality and Social Psychology Review*, 4: 238–54.

Baron, R.S. and Roper, G. (1976) Reaffirmation of social comparison views of choice shifts: averaging and extremity effects in an autokinetic situation. *Journal of Personality and Social Psychology*, 33: 521–30.

Baron, R.S., Roper, G. and Baron, P.H. (1974) Group discussion and the stingy shift. *Journal of Personality and Social Psychology*, 30: 538–45.

Baron, R.S., Moore, D.L. and Sanders, G.S. (1978) Distraction as a source of drive in social facilitation research. *Journal of Personality and Social Psychology*, 36: 816–24.

Baron, R.S., Cutrona, C.E., Hicklin, D., Russell, D.W. and Lubaroff, D.M. (1990) Social support and immune function among spouses of cancer patients. *Journal of Personality and Social Psychology*, 59: 344–52.

Baron, R.S., Inman, M., Kao, C.F. and Logan, H. (1992) Negative emotion and superficial social Processing. *Motivation and Emotion*, 16: 323–46.

Baron, R.S., Hoppe, S., Linneweh, B. and Rogers, D. (1996a) Social corroboration and opinion extremity. *Journal of Experimental Social Psychology*, 32: 537–60.

Baron, R.S., Vandello, J.A. and Brunsman, B. (1996b) The forgotten variable in conformity research: the impact of task importance on social influence. *Journal of Personality and Social Psychology*, 71: 915–27.

Baron, R.S., Crawley, K. and Paulina, D. (2003) Aberrations of power: leadership in totalist groups. In D. van Knippenberg and M.A. Hogg (eds) *Identity, Leadership, and Power*. London: Sage.

Bass, B.M. (1998) *Transformational Leadership: Industrial, Military and Educational Impact*. Mahwah, NJ: Lawrence Erlbaum Associates.

Bat-Chava, Y. (1994) Group identification and self-esteem of deaf adults. *Personality and Social Psychology Bulletin*, 23: 494–502.

Batson, C.D., Batson, J.G., Todd, R.M. and Brummett, B.H. (1995) Empathy and the collective good: caring for one of the others in a social dilemma. *Journal of Personality and Social Psychology*, 68: 619–31.

Baumeister, R.F. (1984) Choking under pressure: self-consciousness and para- doxical effects of incentives on skillful performance. *Journal of Personality and Social Psychology*, 46: 610–20.

Baumeister, R.F. and Leary, M.R. (1995) The need to belong: desire for inter- personal attachments as a fundamental human motivation. *Psychology Bulletin*, 117: 497–529.

Baun, M., Bergstrom, N., Langston, N. and Thoma, L. (1984) Physiological effects of human/companion animal bonding. *Nursing Research*, 33(3): 126–9.

Beaman, A.L., Klentz, B., Diener, E. and Syanum, S. (1979) Self-awareness and transgression in children: two field studies. *Journal of Personality and Social Psychology*, 37: 1835–46.

Beilock, S. and Carr, T.H. (2001) On the fragility of skilled performance: what governs choking under pressure? *Journal of Experimental Psychology: Gen- eral*, 130: 701–25.

Berger, J. and Zelditch, M. (1998) *Status, Power, and Legitimacy: Strategies & Theories*. New Brunswick, NJ: Transaction.

Berkman, L.F. and Syme, L.S. (1979) Social networks and mortality. *American Journal of Epidemiology*, 109: 186–204.

Berkowitz, L. (1972) Social norms, feelings, and other factors affecting helping and altruism. In L. Berkowitz (ed.) *Advances in Experimental Social Psycho- logy*, Vol. 6. New York: Academic Press.

Berkowitz, L. (1989) Frustration–aggression hypothesis: examination and re- formulation. *Psychological Bulletin*, 106: 59–73.

Berscheid, E. and Walster (Hatfield), E. (1978) *Interpersonal Attraction*. Reading, MA: Addison-Wesley.

Bettencourt, B.A. and Dorr, N. (1997) Collective self-esteem as a mediator of the relationship between allocentrism and subjective well-being. *Personal- ity and Social Psychology Bulletin*, 23: 301–19.

Bettencourt, B.A. and Dorr, N. (1998) Cooperative interaction and intergroup bias: effects of numerical representation and cross-cut role assignment. *Personality and Social Psychology Bulletin*, 24: 1276–93.

Bettencourt, B.A., Brewer, M.B., Croak, M.R. and Miller, N. (1992) Cooperation and the reduction of intergroup bias: the role of reward structure and social orientation. *Journal of Experimental Social Psychology*, 28: 201–309.

Bicchieri, C. (2002) Covenants without swords: group identity, norms, and communication in social dilemmas. *Rationality and Society*, 14: 187–222.

Bingham, H. (1988) *Selected Writings of Hiram Bingham 1814–1869: Missionary to the Hawaiian Islands, to Raise the Lord's Banner*. Lewiston, NY: E. Mellen Press.

Bishop, G.D. and Myers, D.G. (1974) Informational influence in group discus- sion. *Organizational Behavior and Human Performance*, 12: 92–104.

Blanchard, F.A., Adelman, L. and Cook, S.W. (1975) Effect of group success and failure upon interpersonal attraction in cooperating interracial groups. *Journal of Personality and Social Psychology*, 31: 1020–30.

Blascovich, J. (2001) Immersive virtual environmental technology as a tool in psychological science. *Psychological Science Agenda*, 14(6): 8–9.

Blascovich, J., Ginsburg, G.P. and Veach, T.L. (1975) A pluralistic explanation of choice shifts on the risk dimension. *Journal of Personality and Social Psychology*, 31: 422–9.

Blascovich, J., Mendes, W.B., Hunter, S.B. and Salomon, K. (1999) Social facilitation as challenge and threat. *Journal of Personality and Social Psychology*, 76: 68–77.

Boldry, J.G. and Kashy, D.A. (1999) Intergroup perception in naturally occurring groups of differential status: a social relations perspective. *Journal of Personality and Social Psychology*, 77: 1200–12.

Bond, C.F. (1982) Social facilitation: a self-presentational view. *Journal of Personality and Social Psychology*, 42: 1042–50.

Bond, C.F. and Titus, L.J. (1983) Social facilitation: a meta-analysis of 241 studies. *Psychological Bulletin*, 94: 265–92.

Bond, R. and Smith, P.B. (1996) Culture and conformity: a meta-analysis of studies using Asch's (1952b, 1956) line judgment task. *Psychological Bulletin*, 119(1): 111–37.

Bonito, J.A. and Hollingshead, A.B. (1997) Participation in small groups. *Communication Yearbook*, 20: 227–61.

Bouas, K.S. and Komorita, S.S. (1996) Group discussion and cooperation in social dilemmas. *Personality and Social Psychology Bulletin*, 22: 1144–50.

Bowlby, J. (1958) The nature of a child's tie to his mother. *International Journal of Psycho-Analysis*, 39: 350–73.

Brand, E.F., Lakey, B. and Berman, S. (1995) A preventive, psychoeducational approach to increase perceived social support. *American Journal of Community Psychology*, 23: 117–35.

Brann, P. and Foddy, M. (1988) Trust and the consumption of a deteriorating common resource. *Journal of Conflict Resolution*, 31: 615–30.

Brauer, M., Judd, C.M. and Gliner, M.D. (1995) The effects of repeated expressions on attitude polarization during group discussions. *Journal of Personality and Social Psychology*, 68(6): 1014–29.

Braver, S.L. (1995) Social contracts and the provision of public goods. In D. Schroeder (ed.) *Social Dilemmas: Social Psychological Perspectives*. New York: Praeger.

Braver, S.L. and Wilson, L. (1984) A laboratory study of social contracts as a solution to public goods problems: surviving on the lifeboat. Paper presented to the *Western Social Science Association*, San Diego, CA, April.

Bray, R.M. and Kerr, N.L. (1982) Methodological considerations in the study of the psychology of the courtroom. In N. Kerr and R. Bray (eds) *The Psychology of the Courtroom*. New York: Academic Press.

Bray, R.M., Kerr, N.L. and Atkin, R.S. (1978) Group size, problem difficulty, and group performance on unitary disjunctive tasks. *Journal of Personality and Social Psychology*, 36: 1224–40.

Brewer, M.B. (1979) In-group bias in the minimal intergroup situation: a cognitive-motivational analysis. *Psychological Bulletin*, 86(2): 307–24.

Brewer, M.B. (1981) Ethnocentrism and its role in interpersonal trust. In M. Brewer and B. Collins (eds) *Scientific Inquiry and the Social Sciences*. San Francisco, CA: Jossey-Bass.

Brewer, M.B. (1991) The social self: on being the same and different at the same time. *Personality and Social Psychology Bulletin*, 17: 475–82.

Brewer, M.B. (2000) Reducing prejudice through cross-categorization. In S. Oskamp (ed.) *Reducing Prejudice and Discrimination*. Mahway, NJ: Lawrence Erlbaum Associates.

Brewer, M.B. (in press) *Intergroup Relations*, 2nd edn. Buckingham: Open University Press.

Brewer, M.B. and Gardner, W. (1996) Who is this 'we'? Levels of collective identity self representations. *Journal of Personality and Social Psychology*, 71: 83–93.

Brewer, M.B. and Harasty, A.S. (1996) Seeing groups as entities: the role of perceiver motivation. In R. Sorrentino and E.T. Higgins (eds) *Handbook of Motivation and Cognition, Vol. 3. The Interpersonal Context*. New York: Guilford Press.

Brewer, M.B. and Kramer, R.M. (1986) Choice behavior in social dilemmas: effects of social identity, group size, and decision framing. *Journal of Personality and Social Psychology*, 50: 543–9.

Brewer, M.B. and Miller, N. (1984) Beyond the contact hypotheses: theoretical perspectives on desegregation. In N. Miller and M.B. Brewer (eds) *Groups in Contact: The Psychology of Desegregation*. New York: Academic Press.

Brewer, M.B. and Weber, J.G. (1994) Self-evaluation effects of interpersonal versus intergroup social comparison. *Journal of Personality and Social Psychology*, 66: 268–75.

Brickner, M.A. (1987) Locked into performance: goal setting as a moderator of the social loafing effect. Paper presented at the Annual Meeting of the Midwestern Psychological Association, Chicago, IL, May.

Brickner, M.A., Harkins, S. and Ostrom, T. (1986) Personal involvement: thought provoking implications for social loafing. *Journal of Personality and Social Psychology*, 51: 763–9.

Brown, R. (1988) *Group Processes: Dynamics Within and Between Groups*. New York: Blackwell.

Brown, R. and Wootton-Millward, L. (1993) Perceptions of group homogeneity during group formation and change. *Social Cognition*, 11: 126–49.

Brown, R.J. and Abrams, D. (1986) The effects of intergroup similarity and goal interdependence on intergroup attitudes and task performance. *Journal of Experimental Social Psychology*, 22: 78–92.

Brown, R.J. and Wade, G. (1987) Superordinate goals and intergroup behavior: the effect of role ambiguity and status in intergroup attitudes and task performance. *European Journal of Social Psychology*, 17: 131–42.

Brown, R.J., Vivian, J. and Hewstone, M. (1999) Changing attitudes through intergroup contact: the effects of group membership salience. *European Journal of Social Psychology*, 29: 741–64.

Bruning, J.L., Capage, J.E., Kozuh, J.F., Young, P.F. and Young, W.E. (1968) Socially induced drive and range of cue utilization. *Journal of Personality and Social Psychology*, 9: 242–4.

Buck, R., Losow, J.I., Murphy, M.M. and Costanzo, P. (1992) Social facilitation and inhibition of emotional expression and communication. *Journal of Personality and Social Psychology*, 63(6): 962–8.

Buehler, R. and Griffin, D. (1994) Change-of-meaning effects in conformity and dissent: observing construal processes over time. *Journal of Personality and Social Psychology*, 67(6): 984–96.

Burch vs. Louisiana (1979) *United States Reports*, 441: 130–9.

Burnstein, E. and Vinokur, A. (1973) Testing two classes of theories about group induced shifts in individual choice. *Journal of Experimental Social Psychology*, 9: 123–37.

Burnstein, E. and Vinokur, A. (1977) Persuasive argumentation and social comparison as determinants of attitude polarization. *Journal of Experimental Social Psychology*, 13: 315–32.

Butera, F., Mugny, G., Legrenzi, P. and Perez, J. (1996) Majority and minority influence, task representation and inductive reasoning. *British Journal of Social Psychology*, 135: 123–36.

Butler, J.L. and Baumeister, R.F. (1998) The trouble with friendly face: skilled performance with a supportive audience. *Journal of Personality and Social Psychology*, 75(5): 1213–30.

Cacioppo, J.T., Rourke, P., Tassinary, L., Marshall-Goodall, B. and Baron, R.S. (1990) Rudimentary physiological effects of mere observation. *Psychophysiology*, 27: 177–86.

Caddick, B. (1982) Perceived illegitimacy and intergroup relations. In H. Tajfel (ed.) *Social Identity and Intergroup Relations*. Cambridge: Cambridge University Press.

Cadinu, M.R. and Rothbart, M. (1996) Self-anchoring and differentiation processes in the minimal group setting. *Journal of Personality and Social Psychology*, 70: 661–77.

Callaway, M.R., Marriott, R.G. and Esser, J.K. (1985) Effects of dominance on group decision making: toward a stress-reduction explanation of groupthink. *Journal of Personality and Social Psychology*, 49: 949–52.

Camacho, L.M. and Paulus, P.B. (1995) The role of social anxiousness in group brainstorming. *Journal of Personality and Social Psychology*, 68: 1071–80.

Campbell, D.T. (1956) Enhancement of contrast as a compositive habit. *Journal of Abnormal and Social Psychology*, 53: 350–5.

Campbell, D.T. (1958) Common fate, similarity, and other indices of the status of aggregates of persons as social entities. *Behavioral Science*, 3: 14–25.

Campbell, J.D. and Fairey, P.J. (1989) Informational and normative routes to conformity: the effect of faction size as a function of norm extremity and attention to the stimulus. *Journal of Personality and Social Psychology*, 57(3): 457–68.

Cantor, J.R., Zillmann, D. and Einsiedel, E.F. (1978) Female responses to provocation after exposure to aggressive and erotic films. *Communication Research*, 9: 177–86.

Carlson, M. and Miller, N. (1988) The differential effects of social and nonsocial negative events on aggressiveness. *Sociology and Social Research*, 72: 155–8.

Cauce, A.M., Felner, R.D. and Primavera, J. (1982) Social support in high-risk adolescents: structural components and adaptive impact. *American Journal of Community Psychology*, 10: 417–28.

Cawley, B.D., Keeping, L.M. and Levy, P.E. (1998) Participation in the performance appraisal process and employee reaction: a metanalytic review of field investigations. *Journal of Applied Psychology*, 83: 615–63.

Chalk, F. and Jonassohn, K. (1990) *The History of Sociology of Genocide: Analyses and Case Studies*. New Haven, CT: Yale University Press.

Charbonnier, E., Huguet, P., Brauer, M. and Montiel, J.-M. (1998) Social loafing and self-beliefs: people's collective effort depends on the extent to which they distinguish themselves as better than others. *Social Behavior and Personality*, 26(4): 329–40.

Chen, X. and Komorita, S.S. (1994) The effects of communication and commitment in a public goods social dilemma. *Organizational Behavior and Human Decision Processes*, 60: 367–86.

Cheryan, S. and Bodenhausen, G.V. (2000) When positive stereotypes threaten intellectual performance: the psychological hazards of 'Model Minority' Status. *Psychological Science*, 11(5): 399–402.

Cialdini, R.B., Kallgren, C.A. and Reno, R.R. (1991) A focus theory of normative conduct: a theoretical refinement and reevaluation of the role of norms in human behavior. In M.P. Zanna (ed.) *Advances in Experimental Social Psychology*, Vol. 24. New York: Academic Press.

Cialdini, R.B., Wosinska, W., Barrett, D.W., Butner, J. and Gornik-Durose, M. (1999) Compliance with a request in two cultures. *Personality and Social Psychology Bulletin*, 25: 1242–53.

Clark, S.L. and Stephens, M.A.P. (1996) Stroke patients' well-being as a function of caregiving spouse's helpful and unhelpful actions. *Personal Relationships*, 3: 171–84.

Cobb, S. (1976) Social support as a moderator of life stress. *Psychosomatic Medicine*, 38: 300–14.

Cohen, S. and McKay, G. (1984) Social support, stress and the buffering hypothesis: a theoretical analysis. In A. Baum, J.E. Singer and S.E. Taylor (eds) *Handbook of Psychology and Health*, Vol. 4. Hillsdale, NJ: Lawrence Erlbaum Associates.

Cohen, S. and Syme, S.C. (1985) *Social Support and Health*. New York: Academic Press.

Cohen, S. and Wills, T. (1985) Stress, social support, and the buffering hypothesis. *Psychological Bulletin*, 98: 310–57.

Cohen, S., Kaplan, J.R., Cunnick, J.E. *et al.* (1992) Chronic social stress, affiliation, and cellular immune response in nonhuman primates. *Psychological Science*, 3(5): 301–4.

Cohen, S., Doyle, W.J., Skoner, D.P., Rabin, B.S. and Gwaltney, J.M. (1997) Social ties and susceptibility to the common cold. *Journal of the American Medical Association*, 277: 1940–4.

Cohen, S., Underwood, L.G. and Gottlieb, B.H. (2000) *Social Support Measurement and Intervention*. New York: Oxford University Press.

Collins, N.L. and Feeney, B.C. (2000) A safe haven: an attachment theory perspective on support seeking and caregiving in intimate relationships. *Journal of Personality and Social Psychology*, 78: 1053–73.

Comacho, L.M. and Paulus, P.B. (1995) The role of social anxiousness in group brainstorming. *Journal of Personality and Social Psychology*, 68: 1071–80.

Cooper, C.L. and Rousseau, D.M. (1999) The virtual organization. In C.L. Cooper and D.M. Rousseau (eds) *Trends in Organizational Behavior*, Vol. 6. New York: Wiley.

Cooper, J. and Mackie, D. (1986) Video games and aggression in children. *Journal of Applied Psychology*, 16: 726–44.

Costanza, R.S., Derlega, V.J. and Winstead, B.A. (1988) Positive and negative forms of social support: effects of conversational topics on coping with stress among same-sex friends. *Journal of Experimental Social Psychology*, 24: 182–93.

Cota, A.A., Evans, C.R., Dion, K.L. *et al.* (1995) The structure of group cohesion. *Personality and Social Psychology Bulletin*, 21(6): 572–80.

Cotton, J.L. and Baron, R.S. (1980) Anonymity, persuasive arguments, and choice shifts. *Social Psychology Quarterly*, 43(4): 391–404.

Cottrell, N.B. (1972) Social facilitation. In C.G. McClintock (ed.) *Experimental Social Psychology*. New York: Holt.

Cottrell, N.B., Wack, D.L., Sekerak, G.J. and Rittle, R.H. (1968) Social facilitation of dominant responses by the presence of an audience and the mere presence of others. *Journal of Personality and Social Psychology*, 9: 245–50.

Craighead, W.E., Kimball, .W.H. and Rehak, P.J. (1979) Mood changes, physiological responses, and self-statements during social rejection imagery. *Journal of Consulting and Clinical Psychology*, 47: 385–96.

Crano, W.D. and Chen, X. (1998) The leniency contract and persistence of majority and minority influence. *Journal of Personality and Social Psychology*, 74(6): 1437–50.

Crocker, J. and Luhtanen, R. (1990) Collective self esteem and ingroup bias. *Journal of Personality and Social Psychology*, 58: 60–7.

Crocker, J., Luhtanen, R., Blaine, B. and Broadnax, S. (1994) Collective self esteem and psychological well-being among White, Black and Asian college students. *Personality and Social Psychology Bulletin*, 20: 503–13.

Crosby, F. (1976) A model of egotistical relative deprivation. *Psychological Review*, 83: 85–113.

Crott, H.W. and Werner, J. (1994) The norm-information-distance model: a stochastic approach to preference change in group interaction. *Journal of Experimental Social Psychology*, 30: 68–95.

Crott, H.W., Giesel, M. and Hoffmann, C. (1998) The process of inductive inference in groups: the use of positive and negative hypothesis and target testing in sequential rule discovery tasks. *Journal of Personality and Social Psychology*, 75: 938–52.

Cunha, D. (1985) Interpersonal trust as a function of social orientation. Unpublished doctoral dissertation, University of Delaware, Delaware, OH.

Cutrona, C.E. (1990) Stress and social support: in search of optimal matching. *Journal of Social and Clinical Psychology*, 9(1): 3–14.

Cutrona, C.E. and Cole, V. (2000) Optimizing support in the natural network. In S. Cohen, L.G. Underwood and B.H. Gottlieb (eds) *Social Support Measurement and Intervention*. Oxford: Oxford University Press.

Cutrona, C.E. and Russell, D.W. (1990) Type of social support and specific stress: toward a theory of optimal matching. In B.R. Sarason and I.G. Irwin (eds) *Social Support: An Interactional View*, pp. 319–66. New York: Wiley.

Cutrona, C.E. and Suhr, J.A. (1992) Controllability of stressful events and satisfaction with spouse support behaviors. *Communication Research*, 19: 154–74.

Cutrona, C.E. and Suhr, J.A. (1994) Social support communication in the context of marriage: an analysis of couples' supportive interactions. In B. Burleson, T. Albrecht and I. Sarason (eds) *The Communication of Social Support: Messages, Interactions, Relationships, and Community*. Newbury Park, CA: Sage.

Cutrona, C.E. and Troutman, E. (1986) Social support, infant temperament, and parenting self-efficacy. *Child Development*, 57: 1507–18.

Dakof, G.A. and Taylor, S.E. (1990) Victims' perceptions of social support: what is helpful from whom? *Journal of Personality and Social Psychology*, 58(1): 80–9.

Darley, J.M. (1966) Fear and social comparison as determinants of conformity behavior. *Journal of Personality and Social Psychology*, 4: 73–8.

Darley, J.M. and Latané, B. (1968) Bystander intervention in emergencies: diffusion of responsibility. *Journal of Personality and Social Psychology*, 8: 377–83.

David, B. and Turner, J.C. (1996) Studies in self-categorization and minority conversion: is being a member of the out-group an advantage? *British Journal of Social Psychology*, 35: 179–99.

Davies, J.C. (1969) The J-curve of rising and declining satisfaction as a cause of some great revolutions and a contained rebellion. In H. Graham and T. Gurr (eds) *The History of Violence in America: Historical and Comparative Perspectives*. New York: Praeger.

Davis, J.H. (1969) *Group Performance*. Reading, MA: Addison-Wesley.

Davis, J.H. (1973) Group decision and social interaction: a theory of social decision schemes. *Psychological Review*, 80: 97–125.

Davis, J.H. (1982) Social interaction as a combinational process in group decision. In H. Brandstatter, J.H. Davis and G. Stocker-Kreichgauer (eds) *Group Decision Making*. London: Academic Press.

Davis, J.H. (1996) Group decision making and quantitative judgments: a consensus model. In E.H. Witte and J.H. Davis (eds) *Understanding Group Behavior, Vol. 1: Consensual Action by Small Groups*. Hillsdale, NJ: Lawrence Erlbaum Associates.

Davis, J.H. and Kerr, N.L. (1986) Thought experiments and the problem of sparse data in small-group performance research. In P. Goodman (ed.) *Designing Effective Work Groups*. New York: Jossey-Bass.

Davis, J.H. and Restle, F. (1963) The analysis of problems and prediction of group problem solving. *Journal of Abnormal and Social Psychology*, 66: 103–16.

Davis, J.H., Kerr, N.L., Atkin, R., Holt, R. and Meek, D. (1975) The decision processes of 6- and 12-person mock juries assigned unanimous and 2/3 majority rules. *Journal of Personality and Social Psychology*, 32: 1–14.

Davis, J.H., Stasson, M.F., Parks, C.D. *et al*. (1993) Quantitative decisions by groups and individuals: voting procedures and monetary awards by mock civil juries. *Journal of Experimental Social Psychology*, 29: 326–46.

Davis, J.H., Hulbert, L., Au, W.T., Chen, X. and Zarnoth, P. (1997) Effects of group size and procedural influence on consensual judgments of quantity: the examples of damage awards and mock civil juries. *Journal of Personality and Social Psychology*, 73(4): 703–18.

De Dreu, C.K. and McCusker, C. (1997) Gain loss frames and cooperation in two person social dilemmas: a transformational analysis. *Journal of Personality and Social Psychology*, 72: 1093–1106.

De Dreu, C.K.W. and De Vries, N.K. (1993) Numerical support, information processing and attitude change. *European Journal of Social Psychology*, 23(6): 647–62.

De Dreu, C.K.W. and De Vries, N.K. (1996) Differential processing and attitude change following majority versus minority arguments. *British Journal of Social Psychology*, 35(1): 77–90.

Dennis, A.R. and Valacich, J.S. (1993) Computer brainstorms: more heads are better than one. *Journal of Applied Psychology*, 78: 531–7.

DeSanctis, G. and Monge, P. (1998) Communication processes for virtual organizations. *Journal of Computer Mediated Communication*, 4 (http://www.ascusc.org/jcmc/vol3/issue4/ahuja.html).

Deutsch, M. (1973) *The Resolution of Conflict: Constructive and Destructive Processes*. New Haven, CT: Yale University Press.

Deutsch, M. and Gerard, H.B. (1955) A study of normative and informational social influence upon individual judgment. *Journal of Abnormal and Social Psychology*, 51: 629–36.

Diehl, M. and Stoebe, W. (1987) Productivity loss in brainstorming groups: toward solution of a riddle. *Journal of Personality and Social Psychology*, 53: 497–509.

Diehl, M. and Stroebe, W. (1991) Productivity loss in idea-generating groups: tracking down the blocking effect. *Journal of Personality and Social Psychology*, 61: 392–403.

Diener, E. (1976) Effects of prior destructive behavior, anonymity, and group presence on deindividuation and aggression. *Journal of Personality and Social Psychology*, 33: 497–507.

Diener, E. (1980) Deindividuation: the absence of self-awareness and self-regulation in group members. In P. Paulus (ed.) *The Psychology of Group Influence*. Hillsdale, NJ: Lawrence Erlbaum Associates.

Diener, E. and Wallboom, M. (1976) Effects of self-awareness on antinormative behavior. *Journal of Research in Personality*, 10: 107–11.

Diener, E., Fraser, S.C., Beaman, A.L. and Kelem, R.T. (1976) Effects of de-individuating variables on stealing by Halloween trick-or-treaters. *Journal of Personality and Social Psychology*, 33: 178–83.

Dion, K.L. (2000) Group cohesion: from 'field of forces' to multidimensional construct. *Group Dynamics: Theory, Research, & Practice*, 4(1): 7–26.

Dion, K.L., Baron, R.S. and Miller, N. (1970) Why do groups make riskier decisions than individuals? In L. Berkowitz (ed.) *Advances in Experimental Social Psychology*, Vol. 5. New York: Academic Press.

Dolinski, D. and Nawrat, R. (1998) 'Fear-then-relief' procedure for producing compliance: beware when the danger is over. *Journal of Experimental Social Psychology*, 34: 27–50.

Dollard, J. (1938) Hostility and fear in social life. *Social Forces*, 17: 15–25.

Dollard, J., Doob, L.W., Miller, N.E., Mowrer, O.H. and Sears, R.R. (1939) *Frustration and Aggression*. New Haven, CT: Yale University Press.

Doms, M. and van Avermaet, E. (1980) Majority influence, minority influence, and conversion behavior: a replication. *Journal of Experimental Social Psychology*, 16: 283–92.

Douglas, K.M. and McGarty, C. (2001) Identifiability and self-presentation: computer-mediated communication and intergroup interaction. *British Journal of Social Psychology*, 40: 399–416.

Douthitt, E.A. and Aiello, J.R. (2001) The role of participation and control in the effects of computer monitoring on fairness perceptions, task satisfaction, and performance. *Journal of Applied Psychology*, 86: 867–74.

Dovidio, J.F., Gaertner, S.L. and Validzic, A. (1998) Intergroup bias: status, differentiation, and a common in-group identity. *Journal of Personality and Social Psychology*, 75, 109–20.

Dubrovsky, V.J., Kiesler, S. and Sethna, B.N. (1991) The equalization phenomenon: status effects in computer-mediated and fact-to-face decision-making groups. *Human–Computer Interaction*, 6: 119–46.

Dunham, P.J., Hurshman, A., Litwin, E. *et al.* (1998) Computer-mediated social support: single young mothers as a model system. *American Journal of Community Psychology*, 25: 281–306.

Eagly, A.H. (1978) Sex differences in influenceability. *Psychological Bulletin*, 85: 86–116.

Eagly, A.H. and Steffen, V.J. (1986) Gender and aggressive behavior: a meta-analytic review of the social psychological literature. *Psychological Bulletin*, 100: 309–30.

Eagly, A.H., Wood, W. and Fishbaugh, L. (1981) Sex differences in conformity: surveillance by the group as a determinant of male nonconformity. *Journal of Personality and Social Psychology*, 40: 384–94.

Earley, P.C. (1989) Social loafing and collectivism: a comparison of the United States and the People's Republic of China. *Administrative Science Quarterly*, 34(4): 565–81.

Easterbrook, J.A. (1959) The effects of emotion on cue-utilization and the organization of behavior. *Psychological Review*, 66: 183–201.

Eckenrode, J. and Hamilton, J. (2000) One to one support interventions: home visitation and monitoring. In S. Cohen, L.G. Underwood and B.H. Gottlieb (eds) *Social Support Measurement and Intervention*. Oxford: Oxford University Press.

El-Bassel, N., Ivanoff, A., Schilloing, R.F., Borne, D. and Gilbert, L. (1997) Skills building and social support enhancement to reduce HIV risk among women in jail. *Criminal Justice and Behavior*, 25: 205–23.

Epley, N. and Gilovich, T. (1999) Just going along: nonconscious priming and conformity to social pressure. *Journal of Experimental Social Psychology*, 35(6): 578–89.

Epley, S.W. (1974) Reduction of the behavioral effects of aversive stimulation by the presence of companions. *Psychological Bulletin*, 81: 271–83.

Erev, I., Bornstein, G. and Galili, R. (1993) Constructive intragroup competition as a solution to the free rider problem: a field experiment. *Journal of Experimental Social Psychology*, 29: 463–78.

Erez, M. and Somech, A. (1996) Is group productivity loss the rule or the exception? Effects of culture and group-based motivation. *Academy of Management Journal*, 39(6): 1513–37.

Esser, J.K. (1998) Alive and well after 25 years: a review of group think research. *Organizational Behavior and Human Decision Processes*, 73: 116–41.

Evan, W.M. and Simmons, R.G. (1969) Organizational effects of inequitable rewards: two experiments in status inconsistency. *Administrative Science Quarterly*, 14: 224–37.

Evans, C.R. and Dion, K.L. (1991) Group cohesion and performance: a meta-analysis. *Small Group Research*, 22(2): 175–86.

Everett, J.J., Smith, R.E. and Williams, K.D. (1992) Effects of team cohesion and identifiability on social loafing in relay swimming performance. *International Journal of Sport Psychology*, 23: 311–24.

Eysenck, M.W. (1977) *Human Memory: Theory, Research, and Individual Differences*. Elmsford, NY: Pergamon Press.

Fawzy, F.F. and Fawzy, N.W. (1998) Group therapy in the cancer setting. *Journal of Psychosomatic Research*, 45(3): 191–200.

Fawzy, F.I., Fawzy, N.W., Hyun, C.S. *et al.* (1993) Malignant melanoma: effects of an early structured psychiatric intervention, coping and affective state on recurrence and survival 6 years later. *Archives of General Psychiatry*, 50: 681–9.

Festinger, L. (1954) A theory of social comparison processes. *Human Relations*, 7: 117–40.

Fiedler, F.E. (1967) *A Theory of Leadership Effectiveness*. New York: McGraw-Hill.

Finney, B. and Houston, J. (1996) *Surfing: A History of the Ancient Hawaiin Sport*. Rohnert Park, CA: Pomegranate Communications.

Florian, V. and Mukulincer, M. (1997) Fear of death and the judgment of social transgressions: a multidimensional test of terror management theory. *Journal of Personality and Social Psychology*, 73, 369–80.

Fodor, E.M. (1978) Stimulated work climate as an influence on choice of leadership style. *Personality and Social Psychology Bulletin*, 4: 111–14.

Fodor, E.M. and Smith, T. (1982) The power motive as an influence on group decision making. *Journal of Personality and Social Psychology*, 42(1): 178–85.

Forgas, J.P., Brennan, G., Howe, S., Kane, J.F. and Sweet, S. (1980) Audience effects on squash players' performance. *Journal of Social Psychology*, 111: 41–7.

Forsyth, D. (1999) *Group Dynamics*, 3rd edn. Belmont, CA: Brooks/Cole Wadsworth.

Foster, M.D. and Matheson, K. (1995) Double relative deprivation: combining the personal and political. *Personality and Social Psychology Bulletin*, 21: 1167–77.

Fox, D.R. (1985) Psychology, ideology, utopia, and the commons. *American Psychologist*, 40: 48–58.

Freedman, J.L. and Doob, A.N. (1968) *Deviancy: The Psychology of Being Different*. New York: Academic Press.

Friedmann, E., Katcher, A.H., Lynch, J.J. and Thomas, S.A. (1980) Animal comparisons and one year survival of patients after discharge from a coronary care unit. *Public Health Reports*, 95: 307–12.

Friedmann, E., Katcher, A., Thomas, S., Lynch, J. and Messent, P. (1983) Social interaction and blood pressure: influence of animal companions. *Journal of Nervous and Mental Disease*, 171(8): 461–5.

Gabrenya, W.K., Jr., Wang, Y.E. and Latané, B. (1981) Social loafing among Chinese overseas and U.S. students. Paper presented at the *Asian Conference of the International Association for Cross-Cultural Psychology*, Taipei, Taiwan, June.

Gaertner, S.L. and Dovidio, J.F. (2000) *Reducing Intergroup Bias: The Common Ingroup Identity Model*. Philadelphia, PA: Psychology Press.

Gaerther, S.L. and Insko, C.A. (2000) Intergroup discrimination in the minimal group paradigm: categorization, reciprocation, or fear? *Journal of Personality and Social Psychology*, 79(1): 77–94.

Gaertner, S.L., Mann, J.A., Dovidio, J.F., Murrell, A.J. and Pomare, M. (1990) How does cooperation reduce intergroup bias? *Journal of Personality and Social Psychology*, 59: 692–704.

Gagne, M. and Zuckerman, M. (1999) Performance and learning goal orientations as moderators of social loafing and social facilitation. *Small Group Research*, 30: 524–41.

Gagnon, A. and Bourhis, R.Y. (1996) Discrimination in the minimal group paradigm: social identity or self-interest? *Personality and Social Psychology Bulletin*, 22: 1289–1301.

Gallupe, R.B., Bastianutti, L.M. and Cooper, W.H. (1991) Unblocking brainstorms. *Journal of Applied Psychology*, 76(1): 137–42.

Gardham, K. and Brown, R. (2001) Two forms of intergroup discrimination with positive and negative outcomes: explaining the positive–negative asymmetry effect. *British Journal of Social Psychology*, 40: 23–34.

Gardner, W., Pickett, C.L. and Brewer, M.B. (2000) Social exclusion and selective memory: how the need to belong influences memory for social events. *Personality and Social Psychology Bulletin*, 26: 486–96.

Garrity, T.F., Stallones, L., Marx, M.B. and Johnson, T.P. (1989) Pet ownership and attachment as supportive factors in the health of the elderly. *Anthrozoos*, 3: 35–44.

Gastorf, J.W., Suls, J. and Sanders, G.S. (1980) Type A coronary-prone behavior pattern and social facilitation. *Journal of Personality and Social Psychology*, 38: 773–80.

Geen, R.G. (1976) Test anxiety, observation, and range of cue utilization. *British Journal of Social and Clinical Psychology*, 15: 253–9.

Geen, R.G. (1979) Effects of being observed on learning following success and failure experiences. *Motivation and Emotion*, 3: 355–71.

Geen, R.G. (1985) Evaluation apprehension and response withholding in solution of anagrams. *Personality and Individual Differences*, 6: 293–8.

Geen, R.G. (1989) Alternative conceptions of social facilitation. In P. Paulus (ed.) *Psychology of Group Influence*, 2nd edn. Hillsdale, NJ: Lawrence Erlbaum Associates.

Geen, R.G. and Gange, J.J. (1977) Drive theory of social facilitation: twelve years of theory and research. *Psychological Bulletin*, 84: 1267–88.

Geer, J.H., Davison, G.C. and Gatchel, R.I. (1970) Reduction of stress in humans through nonveridical perceived control of aversive stimulation. *Journal of Personality and Social Psychology*, 16: 731–8.

Gerard, H.B. (1963) Emotional uncertainty and social comparison. *Journal of Abnormal and Social Psychology*, 66: 568–73.

Gerard, H.B. (1983) School desegregation: the social science role. *American Psychologist*, 38: 869–77.

Gerard, H.B. and Miller, N. (1975) *School Desegregation*. New York: Plenum Press.

Gergen, K.J., Morse, S.J. and Bode, K. (1974) Overpaid or overworked? Cognitive and behavioral reactions to inequitable rewards. *Journal of Applied Social Psychology*, 4: 259–74.

Gergen, K.J., Ellsworth, P., Maslach, C. and Seipel, M. (1975) Obligation, donor resources, and reactions to aid in three cultures. *Journal of Personality and Social Psychology*, 31: 390–400.

Gerin, W., Pieper, C., Levy, R. and Pickering, T.G. (1992) Social support in social interaction: a moderator of cardiovascular reactivity. *Psychosomatic Medicine*, 54(3): 324–36.

Gibb, J.R. (1951) The effects of group size and of threat reduction upon creativity in a problem solving situation. *American Psychologist*, 6: 324 (abstract).

Gigone, D. and Hastie, R. (1993) The common knowledge effect: information sharing and group judgment. *Journal of Personality and Social Psychology*, 65(5): 959–74.

Glaser, A.N. (1982) Drive theory of social facilitation: a critical reappraisal. *British Journal of Social Psychology*, 21: 265–82.

Glass, D.C. and Singer, J.E. (1972) *Urban Stress*. New York: Academic Press.

Goethals, G.R., Messick, M.M. and Allison, S.T. (1990) The uniqueness bias: studies of constructive social comparison. In J. Suls and T. Wills (eds) *Social Comparison: Contemporary Theory and Research*. Hillsdale, NJ: Lawrence Erlbaum Associates.

Gonzales, D. (2000) *Manhattan Project & the Atomic Bomb in American History*. Berkely Hights, NJ: Enslow Publishers.

Goodwin, P.A. *et al.* (2001) The effect of group psychosocial support on survival in metastatic breast cancer. *New England Journal of Medicine*, 345: 1719–26.

Gore, S. (1978) The effect of social support in moderating the health consequences of unemployment. *Journal of Health and Social Behavior*, 19: 157–65.

Gouldner, A.W. (1960) The norm of reciprocity: a preliminary statement. *American Sociological Review*, 25: 161–78.

Greenberg, J., Simon, L., Jones, E.A. *et al.* (1995) Testing alternative explanations for mortality salience effects: terror management, value accessibility, or worrisome thoughts? *European Journal of Social Psychology*, 25: 417–33.

Grieve, P. and Hogg, M.A. (1999) Subjective uncertainty and intergroup discrimination in the minimal groups situation. *Personality and Social Psychology Bulletin*, 25: 926–40.

Griffin, D. and Buehler, R. (1993) Role of construal processes in conformity and dissent. *Journal of Personality and Social Psychology*, 65: 657–69.

Groff, B.D., Baron, R.S. and Moore, D.L. (1983) Distraction, attentional conflict, and drivelike behavior. *Journal of Experimental Social Psychology*, 19: 359–80.

Gross, S.R., Holtz, R. and Miller, N. (1995) Attitude certainty. In R.E. Petty and J.A. Krosnick (eds) *Attitude Strength*. Mahwah, NJ: Lawrence Erlbaum Associates.

Groueff, S. (2000) *Manhattan Project*. Boulder, CO: Lightning Source.

Gruenfeld, D.H., Thomas-Hunt, M.C. and Kim, P.H. (1998) Cognitive flexibility, communication strategy, and integrative complexity in groups: public versus private reactions to majority and minority status. *Journal of Experimental Social Psychology*, 34(2): 202–26.

Guerin, B. (1983) Social facilitation and social monitoring: a test of three models. *British Journal of Social Psychology*, 22: 203–14.

Guerin, B. (1986) Mere presence effects in humans: a review. *Journal of Experimental Social Psychology*, 22: 38–77.

Guerin, B. (1993) *Social Facilitation*. European Monographs in Social Psychology. Cambridge: Cambridge University Press.

Guerin, B. (1999) Social behaviors as determined by different arrangements of social consequences: social loafing, social facilitation, deindividuation, and a modified social loafing. *Psychological Record*, 49: 565–78.

Guerin, B. and Innes, J.M. (1982) Social facilitation and social monitoring: a new look at Zajonc's mere presence hypothesis. *British Journal of Social Psychology*, 21, 7–18.

Gump, B.G. and Kulik, J.A. (1997) Stress, affiliation and emotional contagion. *Journal of Personality and Social Psychology*, 72: 305–19.

Hackman, J.R. and Morris, C.G. (1975) Group tasks, group interaction process and group performance effectiveness: a review and proposed integration. In L. Berkowitz (ed.) *Advances in Experimental Social Psychology*, Vol. 8. New York: Academic Press.

Hains, S.C., Hogg, M.A. and Duck, J.M. (1997) Self-categorization and leadership: effects of group prototypicality and leader stereotypicality. *Personality and Social Psychology Bulletin*, 23(10): 1087–99.

Hamilton, D.L. and Gifford, R.K. (1976) Illusory correlation and the maintenance of stereotypic beliefs. *Journal of Experimental Social Psychology*, 12: 392–407.

Hamilton, D.L., Sherman, S.J. and Lickel, B. (1998) Perceiving social groups: the importance of the entitativity continuum. In C. Sedikides, J. Schopler and C.A. Insko (eds) *Intergroup Cognition and Intergroup Behavior*. Mahwah, NJ: Lawrence Erlbaum Associates.

Hans, V.P. and Doob, A.N. (1976) Section 12 of the Canada Evidence Act and the deliberations of simulated juries. *Criminal Law Quarterly*, 18: 235–54.

Hans, V. and Vidmar, N. (1986) *Judging the Jury*. New York: Plenum Press.

Hansell, P.S., Hughes, C.B., Caliandro, G. *et al.* (1998) The effect of a social support boosting intervention on stress, coping, and social support in caregivers of children with HIV/AIDs. *Nursing Research*, 47: 79–86.

Hardin, G. (1968) The tragedy of the commons. *Science*, 162: 1243–8.

Harkins, S. (1987) Social loafing and social facilitation. *Journal of Experimental Social Psychology*, 23: 1–18.

Harkins, S. and Jackson, J. (1985) The role of evaluation in eliminating social loafing. *Personality and Social Psychology Bulletin*, 11: 457–65.

Harkins, S. and Petty, R.E. (1982) Effects of task difficulty and task uniqueness on social loafing. *Journal of Personality and Social Psychology*, 43: 1214–30.

Harkins, S. and Szymanski, K. (1987a) Social loafing and social facilitation: new wine in old bottles. In C. Hendrick (ed.) *Group Processes and Intergroup Relations*. Newbury Park, CA: Sage.

Harkins, S. and Szymanski, K. (1987b) Social loafing and self-evaluation with an objective standard. *Journal of Experimental Social Psychology*, 24: 354–65.

Harkins, S. and Szymanski, K. (1989) Social loafing and group evaluation. *Journal of Personality and Social Psychology*, 56: 934–41.

Hart, P. (1998) Preventing groupthink revisited: evaluating and reforming groups in government. *Organizational Behavior and Human Decision Processes*, 73: 306–26.

Harvey, O.J. and Consalvi, C. (1960) Status and conformity to pressures in informal groups. *Journal of Abnormal and Social Psychology*, 60: 182–7.

Hastie, R., Penrod, S.D. and Pennington, N. (1983) *Inside the Jury*. Cambridge, MA: Harvard University Press.

Hastorf, A.H. and Cantril, H. (1954) They saw a game: a case study. *Journal of Abnormal and Social Psychology*, 49: 129–34.

Hawkins, C. (1962) Interaction rates of jurors aligned in factions. *American Sociological Review*, 27: 689–91.

Hearst, P.C. (1982) *Every Secret Thing*. Garden City, NY: Doubleday.

Heimberg, R.G. and Juster, H.R. (1995) Cognitive behavior treatments: literature review. In R.G. Heimberg, M.R. Liebowitz, D.A. Hope and F.R. Scheier (eds) *Social Phobia: Diagnosis, Assessment and Treatment*. New York: Guilford Press.

Helgeson, V.S. and Gottlieb, B.H. (2000) Support groups. In S. Cohen, L.G. Underwood and B.H. Gottlieb (eds) *Social Support Measurement and Intervention*. Oxford: Oxford University Press.

Helgeson, V.S., Cohen, S., Schulz, R. and Yasko, J. (1999) Effects of education and peer discussion of group interventions in 6 month adjustment to breast cancer. *Archives of General Psychiatry*, 56: 340–7.

Hepworth, J.T. and West, S.G. (1988) Lynchings and the economy: a time series reanalysis of Hovland and Sears (1940). *Journal of Personality and Social Psychology*, 55: 239–47.

Herbert, T.B. and Cohen, S. (1993) Stress and immunity in humans: a meta analytic review. *Psychosomatic Medicine*, 55: 364–79.

Herek, G., Janis, I.L. and Huth, P. (1987) Decision making during international crisis: is quality of process related to outcome? *Journal of Conflict Resolution*, 31: 203–26.

Hertel, G. and Kerr, N.L. (2001) Priming in-group favoritism: the impact of normative scripts in the minimal group paradigm. *Journal of Experimental Social Psychology*, 37: 316–24.

Hertel, G., Kerr, N.L. and Messé, L.A. (2000) Motivation gains in groups: paradigmatic and theoretical advances on the Koehler effect. *Journal of Personality and Social Psychology*, 79: 580–601.

Hertel, G., Deter, C. and Konradt, U. (in press) Motivation gains in computer-supported groups. *Journal of Applied Social Psychology*.

Hewstone, M. (1990) The 'ultimate attribution error'? A review of the literature on intergroup causal attribution. *European Journal of Social Psychology*, 20(4): 311–35.

Hewstone, M. and Brown, R.J. (1986) Contact is not enough: an intergroup perspective on the 'contact hypothesis'. In M. Hewstone and R.J. Brown (eds) *Contact and Conflict in Intergroup Encounters*. Oxford: Blackwell.

Hewstone, M., Fincham, F. and Jaspans, J. (1981) Social categorization and similarity in intergroup behaviour: a replication with 'penalties'. *European Journal of Social Psychology*, 11(1): 101–7.

Hilbert, G.A. and Allen, L.R. (1985) The effect of social support on educational outcomes. *Journal of Nursing Education*, 24: 48–52.

Hill, G.W. (1982) Group versus individual performance: are $N + 1$ heads better than one? *Psychological Bulletin*, 91, 517–39.

Hinkle, L.E. and Wolff, H.G. (1956) Communist interrogation and indoctrination. *Archives of Neurology and Psychiatry*, 76: 115–74.

Hinsz, V. (1990) Cognitive and consensus processes in group recognition memory performance. *Journal of Personality and Social Psychology*, 59: 705–18.

Hinsz, V.B. (1999) Group decision making with responses of a quantitative nature: the theory of social decision schemes for quantities. *Organizational Behavior and Human Decision Processes*, 80: 28–49.

Hobbes, T. ([1651] 1974) *Leviathan*. London: Kent.

Hodson, G. and Sorrentino, R.M. (1997) Groupthink and uncertainty orientation: personality differences in reactivity to the group situation. *Group Dynamics: Theory, Research and Practice*, 1: 144–55.

Hoeksema van Orden, C.Y.D., Gaillard, A.W.K. and Buunk, B.P. (1998) Social loafing under fatigue. *Journal of Personality and Social Psychology*, 75: 1179–90.

Hogg, M.A. (1993) Group cohesiveness: a critical review and some new directions. In W. Strobe and M. Hewstone (eds) *European Review of Social Psychology*, Vol. 4. Chichester: Wiley.

Hogg, M.A. (2001) A social identity theory of leadership. *Personality and Psychology Review*, 5: 184–200.

Hogg, M.A. and Abrams, D. (1993) Towards a single process uncertainty reduction model of social motivation in groups. In M.A. Hogg and D. Abrams (eds) *Group Motivation: Social Psychological Perspectives*. New York: Harvester-Wheatsheaf.

Hogg, M.A. and Hains, S.C. (1996) Intergroup relations and group solidarity: effects of group identification and social beliefs on depersonalized attraction. *Journal of Personality and Social Psychology*, 70(2): 295–309.

Hogg, M.A. and Hains, S.C. (1998) Friendship and group identification: a new look at the role of cohesiveness in groupthink. *European Journal of Social Psychology*, 28(3): 323–41.

Hogg, M.A. and Hardie, E.A. (1991) Social attraction, personal attraction and self-categorization: a field study. *Personality and Social Psychology Bulletin*, 17(2): 175–80.

Hogg, M.A. and Hardie, E.A. (1992) Prototypicality, conformity and depersonalized attraction: a self-categorization analysis of group cohesiveness. *British Journal of Social Psychology*, 31(1): 41–56.

Hogg, M.A. and Mullin, B.A. (1999) Joining groups to reduce uncertainty: subjective uncertainty reduction and group identification. In D. Abrams and M. Hogg (eds) *Social Identity and Social Cognition*. Malden, MA: Blackwell.

Hogg, M.A. and Sunderland, J. (1991) Self-esteem and intergroup discrimination in the minimal groups paradigm. *British Journal of Social Psychology*, 30: 51–62.

Hogg, M.A. and Turner, J.C. (1987) Social identity and conformity: a theory of referent informational influence. In W. Doise and S. Moscovici (eds) *Current Issues in European Social Psychology*, Vol. 2. Cambridge: Cambridge University Press.

Hogg, M.A., Turner, J.C. and Davidson, B. (1990) Polarized norms and social frames of reference: a test of the self-categorization theory of group polarization. *Basic and Applied Social Psychology*, 11: 77–100.

Hogg, M.A., Copper-Shaw, L. and Holzworth, D.W. (1993) Group prototypicality and depersonalized attraction in small interactive groups. *Personality and Social Psychology Bulletin*, 19(4): 452–65.

Hogg, M.A., Hains, S.C. and Mason, I. (1998a) Friendship and group identification: a new look at the role of cohesiveness in groupthink. *European Journal of Social Psychology*, 28(3): 323–41.

Hogg, M.A., Hains, S.C. and Mason, I. (1998b) Identification and leadership in small groups: salience, frame of reference, and leader stereotypicality effects on leader evaluations. *Journal of Personality and Social Psychology*, 75(45): 1248–63.

Hollingshead, A.B. (1996a) Information suppression and status persistence in group decision making: the effects of communication media. *Human Communication Research*, 23(2): 193–219.

Hollingshead, A.B. (1996b) The rank order effect: decision procedure, communication technology and group decisions. *Organizational Behavior and Human Decision Processes*, 68(3): 1–13.

Hollingshead, A.B. (1998) Retrieval processes in transactive memory systems. *Journal of Personality and Social Psychology*, 74: 659–71.

Hollingshead, A.B. (2001) Communication technologies, the Internet, and group research. In M. Hogg and S. Tindale (eds) *Blackwell Handbook of Social Psychology, Vol. 4: Groups*. Malden, MA: Blackwell.

Hollingshead, A.B., McGrath, J.E. and O'Connor, K.M. (1993) Group task performance and communication technology: a longitudinal study of computer-mediated versus fact-to-face work groups. *Small Group Research*, 24(3): 307–33.

Hollingshead, A.B., Fulk, J. and Monge, P. (2002) Fostering intranet knowledge sharing: an integration of transactive memory and public goods approaches, in P. Hinds and S. Kiesler (eds) *Distributed Work*, pp. 335–55. Cambridge, MA: MIT Press.

House, J.S., Landis, K.R. and Umberson, D. (1988) Social relationships and health. *Science*, 241: 540–5.

House, R.J. and Shamir, B. (1993) Toward the integration of transformational, charismatic and visionary theories. In M.M. Chemers and R. Aymans (eds) *Leadership Theory and Research: Perspectives and Directions*. San Diego, CA: Academic Press.

Hovland, C. and Sears, R.R. (1940) Minor studies in aggression: VI. Correlation of lynchings with economic indices. *Journal of Psychology*, 9: 301–10.

Huguet, P., Charbonnier, E. and Montiel, J.M. (1999a) Productivity loss in performance groups: people who see themselves as average do not engage in social loafing. *Group Dynamics*, 3(2): 118–31.

Huguet, P., Galvaing, M.P., Monteil, J.M. and Dumas, F. (1999b) Social presence effects in the Stroop task: further evidence for an attentional view of social facilitation. *Journal of Personality and Social Psychology*, 77: 1011–25.

Hunter, J.A., Platow, M.J., Bell, L.M., Kypri, K. and Lewis, C.A. (1997) Intergroup bias and domain specific self-esteem, threats to identity and dimensional importance. *British Journal of Social Psychology*, 36: 405–26.

Ingersoll-Dayton, B., Morgan, D. and Antonucci, T.C. (1997) The effects of positive and negative social exchanges on aging adults. *Journal of Gerontology: Social Sciences*, 52: S190–S200.

Ingham, A.G., Levinger, G., Graves, J. and Peckham, V. (1974) The Ringelmann effect: studies of group size and group performance. *Journal of Experimental Social Psychology*, 10: 371–84.

Insko, C.A. and Schopler, J. (1998) Differential distrust of groups and individuals. In C. Sedikides, J. Schopler and C.A. Insko (eds) *Intergroup Cognition and Intergroup Behavior*. Mahwah, NJ: Lawrence Erlbaum Associates.

Jacobs, R. and Campbell, D.T. (1961) The perpetuation of an arbitrary tradition through several generations of a laboratory microculture. *Journal of Abnormal and Social Psychology*, 62: 649–58.

Janes, L.M. and Olson, J.M. (2000) Jeer pressures: the behavioral effects of observing ridicule of others. *Personality and Social Psychology Bulletin*, 26(4): 474–85.

Janis, I.L. (1963) Group identification under conditions of external danger. *British Journal of Medical Psychology*, 36: 227–38.

Janis, I.L. (1972) *Victims of Groupthink*. Boston, MA: Houghton-Mifflin.

Janis, I.L. (1982) *Groupthink*, 2nd edn. Boston, MA: Houghton-Mifflin.

Jetten, J., Spears, R. and Manstead, A.S.R. (1996) Intergroup norms and intergroup discrimination: distinctive self-categorization and social identity effects. *Journal of Personality and Social Psychology*, 71: 1222–33.

Jetten, J., Spears, R. and Manstead, A.S.R. (1997) Strength of identification and intergroup differentiation: the influence of group norms. *European Journal of Social Psychology*, 27: 603–9.

Johnson vs. Louisiana (1972) *United States Reports*, 406: 356–403.

Johnson, D.W. and Johnson, R.T. (1981) Effects of cooperative and individualistic learning experiences on interethnic interaction. *Journal of Educational Psychology*, 73: 444–9.

Johnson, D.W., Maruyama, G., Johnson, R., Nelson, D. and Skon, L. (1981) Effects of cooperative, competitive, and individualistic goal structures on achievement: a meta-analysis. *Psychological Bulletin*, 89: 47–62.

Johnson, H.H. and Torcivia, J.M. (1967) Group and individual performance on a single-stage task as a function of distribution of individual performance. *Journal of Experimental Social Psychology*, 3: 266–73.

Johnson, R.D. and Downing, L.J. (1979) Deindividuation and valence of cues: effects of pro-social and anti-social behavior. *Journal of Personality and Social Psychology*, 37: 1532–8.

Johnston, L. and Hewstone, M. (1992) Cognitive models of stereotype change: III. Subtyping and the perceived typicality of disconfirming group members. *Journal of Experimental Social Psychology*, 28: 360–86.

Kahan, J.P. and Rapoport, A. (1984) *Theories of Coalition Formation*. Hillsdale, NJ: Lawrence Erlbaum Associates.

Kahneman, D. and Tversky, A. (1984) Choices, values and frames. *American Psychologist*, 39: 341–50.

Kalven, H. and Zeisel, H. (1966) *The American Jury*. Boston, MA: Little-Brown.

Kaplan, M.F. and Miller, L.E. (1978) Reducing the effects of juror bias. *Journal of Personality and Social Psychology*, 36: 1443–55.

Kaplan, M.F. and Miller, L.E. (1987) Group decision making and normative versus information influence: effects of type of issue and assigned decision rule. *Journal of Personality and Social Psychology*, 53: 306–13.

Karau, S.J. and Hart, J.W. (1998) Group cohesiveness and social loafing: effects of a social interaction manipulation on individual motivation within groups. *US: Educational Publishing Foundation*, 2(3): 185–91.

Karau, S.J. and Williams, K.D. (1993) Social loafing: a meta-analytic review and theoretical integration. *Journal of Personality and Social Psychology*, 65: 681–706.

Karau, S.J. and Williams, K.D. (1997) The effects of group cohesiveness on social loafing and social compensation. *US: Educational Publishing Foundation*, 1(2): 156–68.

Katz, J.E. and Aspden, P. (1997) A nation of strangers? *Communications of the ACM*, 40: 81–6.

Kelley, H.H., Condry, J.C., Jr., Dahlke, A.E. and Hill, A.H. (1965) Collective behavior in a simulated panic situation. *Journal of Experimental Social Psychology*, 1: 20–54.

Kelly, J.A., Murphy, D.A., Bahr, R. *et al.* (1993) Outcome of cognitive-behavioral and support group brief therapies for depressed, HIV-infected persons. *American Journal of Psychiatry*, 150: 1679–86.

Kelly, J.R., Jackson, J.W. and Hutson-Comeaux, S.L. (1997) The effects of time pressure and task differences on influence modes and accuracy in decision-making groups. *Personality and Social Psychology Bulletin*, 23: 10–22.

Kelman, H.C. (1958) Compliance, identification and internalization: three processes of attitude change. *Journal of Conflict Resolution*, 2: 51–60.

Kerr, N.L. (1981) Social transition schemes: charting the group's road to agreement. *Journal of Personality and Social Psychology*, 41: 684–702.

Kerr, N.L. (1983) Motivation losses in task-performing groups: a social dilemma analysis. *Journal of Personality and Social Psychology*, 45: 819–28.

Kerr, N.L. (1986) Motivational choices in task groups: a paradigm for social dilemma research. In H. Wilke, D. Messick and C. Rutte (eds) *Experimental Social Dilemmas*. Frankfurt-am-Main: Lang GmbH.

Kerr, N.L. (1989) Illusions of efficacy: the effects of group size on perceived efficacy in social dilemmas. *Journal of Experimental Social Psychology*, 25: 287–313.

Kerr, N.L. (1992a) Issue importance and group decision making. In S. Worchel, W. Wood and J. Simpson (eds) *Group Process and Productivity*. Newbury Park, CA: Sage.

Kerr, N.L. (1992b) Group decision making at a multialternative task: extremity, interfaction distance, pluralities, and issue importance. *Organizational Behavior and Human Decision Processes*, 52: 64–95.

Kerr, N.L. (1999) Anonymity and social control in social dilemmas. In M. Foddy *et al.* (eds) *Resolving Social Dilemmas*. Philadelphia, PA: Psychology Press.

Kerr, N.L. (2000) On the virtues of assuming minimal differences in information processing between individuals and groups. *Group Processes and Intergroup Relations*, 3: 203–17.

Kerr, N.L. (2001a) Is it what one says or how one says it? Style *vs.* substance from an SDS perspective. In C. De Dreu and N. De Vries (eds) *Group*

Consensus and Minority Influence: Implications for Innovation. Oxford: Blackwell.

Kerr, N.L. (2001b) Motivational processes task performing groups. In J. Forgas, K. Williams and L. Wheeler (eds) *The Social Mind: Cognitive and Motivational Aspects of Interpersonal Behavior.* Cambridge: Cambridge University Press.

Kerr, N.L. (in press) When is a minority a minority? Active *vs.* passive minority advocacy and social influence. *European Journal of Social Psychology.*

Kerr, N.L. and Bruun, S. (1981) Ringelmann revisited: alternative explanations for the social loafing effect. *Journal of Personality and Social Psychology,* 7: 224–31.

Kerr, N.L. and Bruun, S. (1983) The dispensability of member effort and group motivation losses: free rider effects. *Personality and Social Psychology Bulletin,* 44: 78–94.

Kerr, N.L. and Kaufman-Gilliland, C.M. (1994) Communication, commitment, and cooperation in social dilemmas. *Journal of Personality and Social Psychology,* 48: 349–63.

Kerr, N.L. and Kaufman-Gilliland, C.M. (1997) '...and besides, I probably couldn't have made a difference anyway': justification of social dilemma defection via perceived self-inefficacy. *Journal of Experimental Social Psychology,* 33: 211–30.

Kerr, N.L. and MacCoun, R. (1984) Sex composition of groups and member motivation II: effects of relative member ability. *Basic and Applied Social Psychology,* 5: 255–71.

Kerr, N.L. and MacCoun, R.J. (1985) The effects of jury size and polling method on the process and product of jury deliberation. *Journal of Personality and Social Psychology,* 48: 349–63.

Kerr, N.L. and Stanfel, J.A. (1993) Role schemata and member motivation in task groups. *Personality and Social Psychology Bulletin,* 19(4): 432–42.

Kerr, N.L. and Sullaway, M.E. (1983) Group sex composition and member motivation. *Sex Roles,* 91: 413–17.

Kerr, N.L., Atkin, R., Stasser, G. *et al.* (1976) Guilt beyond a reasonable doubt: effects of concept definition and assigned decision rule on the judgments of mock jurors. *Journal of Personality and Social Psychology,* 34: 282–94.

Kerr, N.L., Stasser, G. and Davis, J.H. (1979) Model-testing, model-fitting, and social decision schemes. *Organizational Behavior and Human Performance,* 23: 399–410.

Kerr, N.L., MacCoun, R., Hansen, C.H. and Hymes, J.A. (1987) Gaining and losing social support: momentum in decision-making groups. *Journal of Experimental Social Psychology,* 23: 119–45.

Kerr, N.L., MacCoun, R. and Kramer, G.P. (1996) Bias in judgment: comparing individuals and groups. *Psychological Review,* 103: 687–719.

Kerr, N.L., Niedermeier, K. and Kaplan, M. (1999) Bias in jurors *vs.* juries: new evidence from the SDS perspective. *Organizational Behavior and Human Decision Processes,* 80: 70–86.

Kerr, N.L., Messé, L.A., Park, E., Sambolec, E. and Baird, B. (2002) Identifiability and performance feedback and the Köhler effect. Unpublished manuscript, Michigan State University.

Kerwin, J. and Shaffer, D.R. (1994) Mock jurors versus mock juries: the role of deliberations in reactions to inadmissible testimony. *Personality and Social Psychology Bulletin,* 20: 153–62.

Kessler, J.J. and Wiener, Y. (1972) Self-consistency and inequity dissonance as factors in undercompensation. *Organizational Behavior and Human Performance*, 8: 456–66.

Kiecolt-Glaser, J.K., Malarkey, W.B., Chee, M. *et al.* (1993) Negative behavior during marital conflict is associated with immunological down regulation. *Psychosomatic Medicine*, 55: 395–409.

Kiesler, S. (1997) *Culture of the Internet*. Mahwah, NJ: Lawrence Erlbaum Associates.

Kiesler, S., Siegal, J. and McGuire, T. (1984) Social psychological aspects of computer-mediated communication. *American Psychologist*, 39: 1123–34.

Kiesler, S., Sproull, L. and Waters, K. (1996) A prisoner's dilemma experiment on cooperation with people and human-like computers. *Journal of Personality and Social Psychology*, 70: 47–65.

Kim, H. and Markus, H.R. (1999) Deviance or uniqueness, harmony or conformity? A cultural analysis. *Journal of Personality and Social Psychology*, 77(4): 785–800.

Kim, H.S. and Baron, R.S. (1988) Exercise and the illusory correlation: does arousal heighten stereotypic processing? *Journal of Experimental Social Psychology*, 24: 366–80.

Kimble, C.E. and Rezabek, J.S. (1993) Playing games before an audience: social facilitation or choking. *Social Behavior and Personality*, 20: 115–20.

Kirschbaum, C., Klauer, T., Filipp, S. and Hellhammer, D.H. (1995) Sex-specific effects of social support on cortisol and subjective responses to acute psychological stress. *Psychosomatic Medicine*, 57(1): 23–31.

Knox, R.E. and Stafford, R.K. (1976) Group caution at the race track. *Journal of Experimental Social Psychology*, 12: 317–24.

Kohlfeld, D.L. and Weitzel, W. (1969) Some relations between personality factors and social facilitation. *Journal of Experimental Research in Personality*, 3: 287–92.

Köhler, O. (1926) Kraftleistungen bei Einzel- und Gruppenabeit [Physcial performance in individual and group situations]. *Industrielle Psychotechnik*, 4: 209–26.

Köhler, O. (1927) Über den Gruppenwirkungsgrad der menschilchen Körperarbeit und die Bedingung optimaler Kollektivkraftreaktion [On group efficiency of physical labor and the conditions of optimal collective performance]. *Industrielle Psychotechnik*, 4: 209–26.

Komorita, S.S. (1987) Cooperative choice in decomposed social dilemmas. *Personality and Social Psychology Bulletin*, 13: 53–63.

Komorita, S.S. and Parks, C.D. (1994) *Social Dilemmas*. Dubuque, IA: Brown & Benchmark.

Komorita, S.S. and Parks, C.D. (1995) Interpersonal relations: mixed-motive interaction. *Annual Review of Psychology*, 46: 183–207.

Komorita, S.S. and Parks, C.D. (1999) Reciprocity and cooperation in social dilemmas: review and future directions. In D.V. Budescu *et al.* (eds) *Games and Human Behavior: Essays in Honor of Amnon Rapoport*. Mahwah, NJ: Lawrence Erlbaum Associates.

Komorita, S.S., Sweeney, J. and Kravitz, D.A. (1980) Cooperative choice in N-person dilemma situation. *Journal of Personality and Social Psychology*, 38(3): 504–16.

Komorita, S.S., Parks, C.D. and Hulbert, L.G. (1992) Reciprocity and the induction of cooperation in social dilemmas. *Journal of Personality and Social Psychology*, 62: 607–17.

Komorita, S.S., Chan, D.K. and Parks, C.D. (1993) The effects of reward structure and reciprocity in social dilemmas. *Journal of Experimental and Social Psychology*, 29: 252–67.

Koszakai, T., Moscovici, S. and Personnaz, B. (1994) Contrary effects of group cohesiveness in minority influence: intergroup categorization of the source and levels of influence. *European Journal of Social Psychology*, 24: 713–18.

Kowalski, R.M. (1997) *Aversive Interpersonal Behaviors*. New York: Plenum Press.

Kowalski, R.M. (2000) 'I was only kidding': victims' and perpetrators' perceptions of teasing. *Personality and Social Psychology Bulletin*, 26: 231–41.

Kramer, G.P., Kerr, N.L. and Carroll, J.S. (1990) Pretrial publicity, judicial remedies, and jury bias. *Law and Human Behavior*, 14: 409–38.

Kramer, R.M. (1998) Revisiting the Bay of Pigs and Vietnam decisions 25 years later: how well has the groupthink hypothesis stood the test of time. *Organizational Behavior and Human Decision Processes*, 73: 236–71.

Kramer, R.M. and Brewer, M.B. (1986) Social group identity and the emergence of cooperation in resource conservation dilemmas. In H. Wilke, D.M. Messick and C.G. Rutte (eds) *Experimental Social Dilemmas*. Frankfurt-am-Main: Verlag Peter Lang.

Kramer, R.M., Messick, D.M. and McClintock, C.G. (1986) Social values and cooperative response to a simulated resource conservation crisis. *Journal of Personality*, 54: 576–92.

Krantz, D., Grundberg, N. and Baum, A. (1985) Health psychology. *Annual Review of Psychology*, 36: 349–83.

Kraut, R., Patterson, M., Lundmark, V. *et al.* (1998) Internet paradox: a social technology that reduces social involvement and psychological well-being? *American Psychologist*, 53: 1017–31.

Kravitz, D.A. and Martin, B. (1986) Ringelmann rediscovered: the original article. *Journal of Personality and Social Psychology*, 50: 936–41.

Kruglanski, A.W. and Mackie, D.M. (1990) Majority and minority influence: a judgmental process analysis. In W. Strobe and M. Hewstone (eds) *European Review of Social Psychology*, Vol. 1. Chichester: Wiley.

Kugihara, N. (1999) Gender and social loafing in Japan. *Journal of Social Psychology*, 139(4): 516–26.

Kuhlman, D.M. and Marshello, A. (1975) Individual differences in game motivation as moderators of preprogrammed strategic effects in prisoner's dilemma. *Journal of Personality and Social Psychology*, 32: 922–31.

Kulik, J.A., Mahler, H.I.M. and Moore, P.J. (1996) Social comparison and affiliation under threat: effects on recovery from major surgery. *Journal of Personality and Social Psychology*, 71: 967–79.

Lago, D., Connell, C.M. and Knight, B. (1983) A companion animal program. In M.A. Smyer and M. Gatz (eds) *Mental Health and Aging*. Beverly Hills, CA: Sage.

Lamm, H. and Trommsdorff, G. (1973) Group versus individual performance on tasks requiring ideational proficiency (brainstorming). *European Journal of Social Psychology*, 3: 361–87.

Larson Jr., J.R., Christensen, C., Franz, T.M. and Abbott, A.S. (1998) Diagnosing groups: the pooling, management, and impact of shared and unshared case information on team-based medical decision-making. *Journal of Personality and Social Psychology*, 75: 93–108.

Larsson, K. (1956) *Conditioning and Sexual Behavior in the Male Albino Rat*. Stockholm: Almqvist & Wiksell.

Latané, B. (1981) The psychology of social impact. *American Psychologist*, 36: 343–56.

Latané, B. and Bourgeois, M.J. (1996) Experimental evidence for dynamic social impact: the emergence of subcultures in electronic groups. *Journal of Communication*, 46(4): 35–47.

Latané, B. and L'Herrou, T. (1996) Spatial clustering in the conformity game: dynamic social impact in electronic groups. *Journal of Personality and Social Psychology*, 70(6): 1218–30.

Latané, B. and Nida, S. (1981) Ten years of research on group size and helping. *Psychological Bulletin*, 89: 308–24.

Latané, B., Eckman, J. and Joy, V. (1966) Shared stress and interpersonal attraction. *Journal of Experimental Social Psychology, Supplement*, 1: 92–102.

Latané, B., Williams, K. and Harkins, S. (1979a) Many hands make light the work: the causes and consequences of social loafing. *Journal of Personality and Social Psychology*, 37: 822–32.

Latané, B., Williams, K. and Harkins, S. (1979b) Social loafing. *Psychology Today*, 13: 104–10.

Laughlin, P.R. (1980) Social combination process of cooperative, problem-solving groups at verbal intellective tasks. In M. Fishbein (ed.) *Progress in Social Psychology*, Vol. 1. Hillsdale, NJ: Lawrence Erlbaum Associates.

Laughlin, P.R. (1996) Group decision making and collective induction. In E. Witte and J.H. Davis (eds) *Understanding Group Behavior: Consensual Action by Small Groups*, Vol. 1. Mahwah, NJ: Lawrence Erlbaum Associates.

Laughlin, P.R. (1999) Collective induction: twelve postulates. *Organizational Behavior and Human Decision Processes*, 80: 50–69.

Laughlin, P.R. and Ellis, A.L. (1986) Demonstrability and social combination processes on mathematical intellective tasks. *Journal of Experimental Social Psychology*, 22: 177–89.

Laughlin, P.R. *et al.* (1975) Group size, member ability, and social decision schemes on an intellective task. *Journal of Personality and Social Psychology*, 31: 522–35.

Laughlin, P.R., Kerr, N.L., Munch, M. and Haggerty, C.A. (1976) Social decision schemes of the same four-person groups on two different intellective tasks. *Journal of Personality and Social Psychology*, 33: 80–88.

Laughlin, P.R., VanderStoep, S.W. and Hollingshead, A.B. (1991) Collective versus individual induction: recognition of truth, rejection of error, and collective information processing. *Journal of Personality and Social Psychology*, 61: 50–67.

Laughlin, P.R., Bonner, B.L. and Altermatt, T.W. (1998) Collective versus individual induction with single versus multiple hypotheses. *Journal of Personality and Social Psychology*, 75: 1481–9.

Lea, M., Spears, R. and deGroot, D. (2001) Knowing me, knowing you: anonymity effects on social identity processes within groups. *Personality and Social Psychology Bulletin*, 27: 526–37.

Leary, M.R., Springer, C., Negel, L., Ansell, E. and Evans, K. (1998) The causes of phenomenology and consequences of hurt feelings. *Journal of Personality and Social Psychology*, 74: 1225–37.

Leavitt, H.J. (1951) Some effects of certain communication patterns on group performance. *Journal of Abnormal and Social Psychology*, 46: 38–50.

LeBon, G. ([1895] 1960) *The Crowd: A Study of the Popular Mind*. New York: Viking Press.

Lemyre, L. and Smith, P.M. (1985) Intergroup discrimination and self esteem in the Minimal Groups Paradigm. *Journal of Personality of Social Psychology*, 49: 660–70.

Levine, J.M. (1989) Reaction to opinion deviance in small groups, in P.B. Paulus (ed.) *Psychology of Group Influence*, 2nd edn. Hillsdale, NJ: Lawrence Erlbaum.

Levine, J.M. (1999) Transforming individuals into groups: some hallmarks of the SDS approach to small group research. *Organizational Behavior and Human Decision Processes*, 80: 21–7.

Lewis, B. and Linder, D. (1997) Thinking about choking? Attentional processes and paradoxical performance. *Personality and Social Psychology Bulletin*, 23: 937–44.

Lickel, B., Hamilton, D.L., Wieczorkowska, G. *et al.* (1998) Varieties of social groups: differing bases of perceived entitativity. Unpublished manuscript, University of California, Santa Barbara, CA.

Liebrand, W.B.G. (1983) A classification of social dilemma games. *Simulation and Games*, 14: 123–38.

Liebrand, W.B.G. and van Run, G.J. (1985) The effect of social motives across two cultures on behavior in social dilemmas. *Journal of Experimental Social Psychology*, 21: 86–102.

Liebrand, W.B.G., Messick, D.M. and Wolters, F.J.M. (1986a) Why we are fairer than others: a cross-cultural replication and extension. *Journal of Experimental Social Psychology*, 22: 590–604.

Liebrand, W.B.G., Jansen, R.W.T.L., Rijken, V.M. and Suhre, C.J.M. (1986b) Might over morality: social values and the perception of other players in experimental games. *Journal of Experimental Social Psychology*, 22: 203–15.

Lifton, R.J. (1961) *Thought Reform and the Psychology of Totalism*. New York: W.W. Norton.

Lightdale, J.R. and Prentice, D.A. (1994) Rethinking sex differences in aggression: aggressive behavior in the absence of social roles. *Personality and Social Psychology Bulletin*, 20(1): 34–44.

Linden, W., Stossel, C. and Maurice, J. (1996) Psychosocial interventions for patients with coronary heart disease. *Archives of Internal Medicine*, 156: 745–52.

Linn, M.W., Sandifer, R. and Stein, S. (1985) Effects of unemployment on mental and physical health. *American Journal of Public Health*, 75: 502–6.

Linville, P.W. and Fischer, G.W. (1998) Group variability and covariation: effects on intergroup judgment and behavior. In C. Sedikides, J. Schopler and C.A. Insko (eds) *Intergroup Cognition and Intergroup Behavior*. Mahwah, NJ: Lawrence Erlbaum Associates.

Linville, P.W., Fischer, G.W. and Salovey, P. (1989) Perceived distributions of the characteristics of in-group and out-group members: empirical evidence and a computer simulation. *Journal of Personality and Social Psychology*, 57(2): 165–88.

Long, K.M. and Spears, R. (1998) Opposing effects of personal and collective self-esteem on interpersonal and intergroup comparisons. *European Journal of Social Psychology*, 28(6): 913–30.

Long, K.M., Spears, R. and Manstead, A.S.R. (1994) The influence of personal and collective self-esteem on strategies of social differentiation. *British Journal of Social Psychology*, 33: 313–29.

Longley, J. and Pruitt, D. (1980) Groupthink: a critique of Janis' theory. In L. Wheeler (ed.) *Review of Personality and Social Psychology*, Vol. 1. Beverly Hills, CA: Sage.

Loomis, J.M., Blascovich, J.J. and Beall, A.C. (1999) Immersive virtual environment technology as a basic research tool in psychology. *Behavior Research Methods, Instruments, and Computers*, 31: 557–64.

Lord, R.G., Foti, R.J. and Devader, C.L. (1984) A test of leader categorization theory: internal structure, information processing and leadership perceptions. *Organizational Behavior and Human Performance*, 34: 343–78.

Lorge, I. and Solomon, H. (1955) Two models of group behavior in the solution of eureka-type problems. *Psychometrika*, 20: 139–48.

Lorge, I., Fox, D., Davitz, J. and Brenner, M. (1958) A survey of studies contrasting the quality of group performance and individual performance, 1920–1957. *Psychological Bulletin*, 55: 337–72.

Lount, R., Messé, L.A. and Kerr, N.L. (2000) Trying harder for different reasons: conjunctivity and sex composition as bases for motivation gains in performing groups. *Zeitschrift für Socialpsychologie*, 31: 221–30.

Luce, R.D. and Raiffa, H. (1957) *Games and Decisions*. New York: Wiley.

Luus, E. and Wells, G.L. (1994) The malleability of eyewitness confidence: co-witness and perseverance effects. *Journal of Applied Psychology*, 79(5): 714–23.

Lynch, J.J., Flaherty, L., Emrich, C. and Mills, M.E. (1974) Effects of human contact on the heart activity of curarized patients in a shock-trauma unit. *American Heart Journal*, 88(2): 160–9.

Maass, A. and Clark, R.D. (1983) Internalization versus compliance: differential processes underlying minority influence and conformity. *European Journal of Social Psychology*, 13: 197–215.

Maass, A. and Clark, R.D. (1984) Hidden impact of minorities: fifteen years of minority influence research. *Psychological Bulletin*, 95: 428–50.

Maass, A., Clark, R.D. and Haberkorn, G. (1982) The effects of differential ascribed category membership and norms on minority influence. *European Journal of Social Psychology*, 12: 89–104.

MacCoun, R.J. (1990) The emergence of extralegal bias during jury deliberation. *Criminal Justice and Behavior*, 17: 303–14.

MacCoun, R.J. and Kerr, N.L. (1988) Asymmetric influence in mock jury deliberations: jurors' bias for leniency. *Journal of Personality and Social Psychology*, 54: 21–33.

Mackie, D.M. (1986) Social identification effects in group polarization. *Journal of Personality and Social Psychology*, 50(4): 720–8.

Mackie, D.M. (1987) Systematic and nonsystematic processing of majority and minority persuasive communications. *Journal of Personality and Social Psychology*, 53: 41–52.

Mackie, D.M. and Cooper, J. (1984) Attitude polarization: effects of group membership. *Journal of Personality and Social Psychology*, 46(3): 575–85.

Mackie, D., Gastardo-Conaco, M.C. and Skelly, J.J. (1992) Knowledge of the advocated position and the processing of intergroup and out-group persuasive messages. *Personality and Social Psychology Bulletin*, 18: 145–51.

MacKinnon, D.P., Geiselman, R.E. and Woodward, J.A. (1985) The effects of effort on Stroop interference. *Acta Psychologica*, 58: 225–35.

MacNeil, M.K. and Sherif, M. (1976) Norm change over subject generations as a function of arbitrariness of prescribed norms. *Journal of Personality and Social Psychology*, 34: 762–73.

Maier, N.R.F. and Solem, A.R. (1952) The contribution of a discussion leader to the quality of group thinking: the effective use of minority opinions. *Human Relations*, 5: 277–88.

Manstead, A.S.R. and Semin, G.R. (1980) Social facilitation effects: mere enhancement of dominant responses? *British Journal of Social and Clinical Psychology*, 19: 119–36.

Maoz, I., Ward, A., Katz, M. and Ross, L. (2002) Reactive devaluation of an 'Israeli' vs. 'Palestinian' peace proposal. *Journal of Conflict Resolution*, 46(4): 515–46.

Marcus-Newhall, A., Miller, N., Holtz, R. and Brewer, M.B. (1993) Cross cutting category membership with role assignment: a means of reducing intergroup bias. *British Journal of Social Psychology*, 32: 125–46.

Marcus-Newhall, A., Pedersen, W.C., Carlson, M. and Miller, N. (2000) Cross-cutting category membership with role assignment. *Journal of Personality and Social Psychology*, 78: 670–89.

Marks, G. and Miller, N. (1987) The 'false consensus effect': an empirical and theoretical view. *Psychological Bulletin*, 102: 72–90.

Martin, R. (1995) Majority and minority influence using the afterimage paradigm: a replication with an unambiguous blue slide. *European Journal of Social Psychology*, 12(4): 373–81.

Martin, R. (1998) Majority and minority influence using the afterimage paradigm: a series of attempted replications. *Journal of Experimental Social Psychology*, 34(1): 1–26.

Martin, R. and Hewstone, M. (2001) Determinants and consequences of cognitive processes in majority and minority influence. In J.P. Forgas and K.D. Williams (eds) *Social Influence: Direct and Indirect Processes. The Sydney Symposium of Social Psychology*. Philadelphia, PA: Psychology Press/Taylor & Francis.

Martin, R. and Young, B.P. (1979) *Escape*. Denver, CO: Accent Books.

Martin, R., Davis, G.M., Baron, R.S., Suls, J. and Blanchard, J. (1994) Specificity in social support: perceptions of helpful and unhelpful provider behaviors among irritable bowel syndrome, headache, and cancer patients. *Health Psychology*, 13(5): 432–9.

Matsui, T., Kakuyama, I. and Onglatco, M.L.U. (1987) Effects of goals and feedback on performance in groups. *Journals of Applied Psychology*, 72: 407–15.

McCauley, C. (1989) The nature of social influence in groupthink: compliance and internalization. *Journal of Personality and Social Psychology*, 57(2): 250–60.

McCauley, C., Stitt, C.L., Woods, K. and Lipton, D. (1973) Group shift to caution at the race track. *Journal of Experimental Social Psychology*, 9(1): 80–6.

McClintock, C.G. (1972) Social motivation: a set of propositions. *Behavioral Science*, 17: 438–54.

McGarty, C., Turner, J.C., Oakes, P.J. and Haslam, S.A. (1993) The creation of uncertainty in the influence process: the roles of stimulus information and disagreement with similar others. *European Journal of Social Psychology*, 23(1): 17–38.

McGarty, C., Haslam, S.A., Hutchinson, K.J. and Turner, J.C. (1994) The effects of salient group memberships on persuasion. *Small Group Research*, 25(2): 267–93.

McGarty, C., Haslam, S.A., Hutchinson, K.J. and Grace, D.M. (1995) Determinants of perceived consistency: the relationships between group entitativity and the meaningfulness of categories. *British Journal of Social Psychology*, 34: 237–56.

McGrath, J.E. (1984) *Groups: Interaction and Performance*. Englewood Cliffs, NJ: Prentice-Hall.

McGrath, J.E. and Hollingshead, A.B. (1994) *Groups Interacting with Technology: Ideas, Evidence, Issues, and an Agenda*. Thousand Oaks, CA: Sage.

McKelvey, W. and Kerr, N.H. (1988) Difference in conformity among friends and strangers. *Psychological Reports*, 62: 759–62.

McKenna, K.Y.A. and Bargh, J.A. (1998) Coming out in the age of the Internet: identity 'de-marginalization' through virtual group participation. *Journal of Personality and Social Psychology*, 75: 681–94.

McKenna, K.Y.A. and Bargh, J.A. (1999) Causes and consequences of social interaction on the Internet: a conceptual framework. *Media Psychology*, 1: 249–69.

McKenna, K.Y.A. and Bargh, J.A. (2000) Plan 9 from cyberspace: the implications of the Internet for personality and social psychology. *Personality and Social Psychology Review*, 4: 57–75.

McLeod, P., Baron, R.S., Marti, M.W. and Yoon, K. (1997) The eyes have it: minority influence in face to face and computer mediated group discussion. *Journal of Applied Psychology*, 82(5): 706–18.

Melamed, B.G. and Brenner, G.F. (1990) Social support and chronic medical stress: an interaction-based approach. *Journal of Social and Clinical Psychology*, 9(1): 104–17.

Messé, L.A., Kerr, N.L., Hertel, G., Lount, R. and Park, E. (2002) Knowledge of partner's ability as a moderator of group motivation gains: an exploration of the Köhler effect. *Journal of Personality and Social Psychology*, 82(6): 935–46.

Messick, D.M. (1973) To join or not to join: an approach to the unionization decision. *Organizational Behavior and Human Performance*, 10: 145–56.

Messick, D.M. (1984) Solving social dilemmas: individual and collective approaches. *Representative Research in Social Psychology*, 14: 72–87.

Messick, D.M. and Brewer, M.B. (1983) Solving social dilemmas: a review. In L. Wheeler and P. Shaver (eds) *Annual Review of Personality and Social Psychology*, Vol. 3. Beverly Hills, CA: Sage.

Messick, D.M. and McClelland, C.L. (1983) Social traps and temporal traps. *Personality and Social Psychology Bulletin*, 9: 105–10.

Messick, D.M. and McClintock, C.G. (1968) Motivational basis of choice in experimental games. *Journal of Experimental Social Psychology*, 4: 1–25.

Messick, D.M., Wilke, H., Brewer, M.B. *et al.* (1983) Individual adaptations and structural change as solutions to social dilemmas. *Journal of Personality and Social Psychology*, 44: 294–309.

Meuman, L. (1904) Haus-und Schularbeit: Experimente on Kindern der Volkschule. *Die Deutsche Schule*, 8: 278–303, 337–59, 416–31.

Meyer, T.J. (1995) Effects of psycho-social interventions with cancer patients: a meta-analysis of randomized experiments. *Health Psychology*, 14: 101–8.

Michaels, S.W., Blommel, J.M., Brocato, R.M., Linkous, R.A. and Rowe, J.S. (1982) Social facilitation in a natural setting. *Replications in Social Psychology*, 2: 21–4.

Miles, J.A. and Greenberg, J. (1993) Using punishment threats to attenuate social loafing effects among swimmers. *Organizational Behavior and Human Decision Processes*, 56: 246–65.

Milgram, S. (1974) *Obedience to Authority*. New York: Harper & Row.

Miller, C.E. (1989) The social psychological effects of group decision rules. In P. Paulus (ed.) *Psychology of Group Influence*, 2nd edn. Hillsdale, NJ: Lawrence Erlbaum Associates.

Miller, N. (1981) Changing views about the effects of school desegregation: *Brown* then and now. In M.B. Brewer and B.E. Collins (eds) *Scientific Inquiry in the Social Sciences*. San Francisco, CA: Jossey-Bass.

Miller, N., Brewer, M.B. and Edwards, K. (1985) Cooperative interaction in desegregated settings: a laboratory analogue. *Journal of Social Issues*, 41: 63–79.

Miller, N.E. and Bugelski, R. (1948) Minor studies in aggression: the influence of frustrations imposed by the ingroup on attitudes toward out-groups. *Journal of Psychology*, 25: 437–42.

Mills, J. and Mintz, P.M. (1972) Effect of unexplained arousal on affiliation. *Journal of Personality and Social Psychology*, 24: 11–13.

Mittelman, M.S. *et al.* (1995) A comprehensive support program: effect on depression in spouse-caregivers of AD patients. *Gerontologist*, 35: 792–802.

Mohammed, S. and Ringseis, E. (2001) Cognitive diversity and consensus in group decision making: the role of inputs, processes, and outcomes. *Organizational Behavior and Human Decision Processes*, 85: 310–35.

Moore, D.L. and Baron, R.S. (1983) Social facilitation: a psychophysiological analysis. In J. Cacioppo and R. Petty (eds) *Social Psychophysiology: A Sourcebook*. New York: Guilford Press.

Moore, D.L., Byers, D. and Baron, R.S. (1981) Socially mediated fear reduction in rodents: distraction, communication, or mere presence? *Journal of Experimental Social Psychology*, 17: 485–505.

Moore, D.L., Baron, R.S., Logel, M.L., Sanders, G.S. and Weerts, T.C. (1988) Methodological note: assessment of attentional processing using a parallel phenomenon strategy. *Personality and Social Psychological Bulletin*, 14(3): 565–72.

Morrow, G.R., Carpenter, P.J. and Hoagland, A.C. (1984) The role of social support in parental adjustment to pediatric cancer. *Journal of Pediatric Psychology*, 9: 317–29.

Moscovici, S. (1980) Toward a theory of conversion behavior. In L. Berkowitz (ed.) *Advances in Experimental Social Psychology*, Vol. 13. New York: Academic Press.

Moscovici, S. (1985) Social influence and conformity. In G. Lindzey and E. Aronson (eds) *The Handbook of Social Psychology*, Vol. 2, 3rd edn. New York: Random House.

Moscovici, S. and Lage, E. (1976) Studies in social influence: III. Majority *vs.* minority influence in a group. *European Journal of Social Psychology*, 6: 149–74.

Moscovici, S. and Personnaz, B. (1980) Studies on social influence: V. Minority influence and conversion behavior in a perceptual task. *Journal of Experimental Social Psychology*, 16: 270–82.

Moscovici, S. and Personnaz, B. (1986) Studies on latent influence by the spectrometer method I: The impact of psychologization in the case of conversion by a minority or a majority. *European Journal of Social Psychology*, 16: 345–60.

Moscovici, S. and Zavalloni, M. (1969) The group as a polarizer of attitudes. *Journal of Personality and Social Psychology*, 12: 125–35.

Moscovici, S., Lage, E. and Naffrechoux, M. (1969) Influence of a consistent minority on the responses of a majority in a colour perception task. *Sociometry*, 32: 365–79.

Moscovici, S., Mucchi-Faina, A. and Maass, A. (eds) (1994) *Minority Influence*. Chicago, IL: Nelson Hall.

Muehleman, J.T., Bruker, C. and Ingram, C.M. (1976) The generosity shift. *Journal of Personality and Social Psychology*, 34: 344–51.

Mugford, R.A. and McComisky, J.G. (1975) Therapeutic value of cage birds with old people. In R.S. Anderson (ed.) *Pet Animals and Society*. London: Baillière & Tindall.

Mugny, G. (1975) Negotiations, image of the other and the process of minority influence. *European Journal of Social Psychology*, 5: 209–28.

Mugny, G. and Papastamou, S. (1975–76) A propos du 'credit idiosynchrasique' chez Hollander: conformisme initial ou negociation? *Bulletin de Psychologie*, 29: 970–6.

Mugny, G. and Perez, J.A. (1991) *The Social Psychology of Minority Group Influence*. Cambridge: Cambridge University Press.

Mullen, B. (1986) Atrocity as a function of lynch mob composition: a self-attention perspective. *Personality and Social Psychology Bulletin*, 12: 187–97.

Mullen, B. and Hogg, M.A. (1999) Motivations for group membership: the role of subjective importance and uncertainty reduction. *Basic and Applied Social Psychology*, 21: 91–102.

Mullen, B. and Johnson, C. (1990) Distinctiveness based illusory correlations and stereotyping: a meta-analytic integration. *British Journal of Social Psychology*, 29(1): 11–27.

Mullen, B., Salas, E. and Driskell, J.E. (1989) Salience, motivation and artifact as contributions to the relation between participation rate and leadership. *Journal of Experimental Social Psychology*, 25(6): 545–59.

Mullen, B., Brown, R. and Smith, C. (1992) Ingroup bias as a function of salience, relevance, and status: an integration. *European Journal of Social Psychology*, 22(2): 103–22.

Mullen, B., Anthony, T., Salas, E. and Driscoll, J.E. (1994) Group cohesiveness and quality of group decision making: an integration of tests of the groupthink hypothesis. *Small Group Research*, 25: 189–204.

Mummendey, A., Simon, B. and Dietze, C. *et al.* (1992) Categorization is not enough: intergroup discrimination in negative outcome allocation. *Journal of Experimental Social Psychology*, 28(2): 125–44.

Muschel, I. (1984) Pet therapy with terminal cancer patients. *Journal of Contemporary Social Work*, 64: 451–8.

Myers, D.G. (1982) Polarizing effects of social interaction. In H. Brandstatter, J.H. Davis and G. Stocker-Kreichgauer (eds) *Group Decision Making*. New York: Academic Press.

Myers, D.G. and Bishop, G.D. (1970) Discussion effects on racial attitudes. *Science*, 169: 778–9.

Myers, D.G. and Lamm, H. (1976) The group polarization phenomenon. *Psychological Bulletin*, 83: 602–27.

Myers, D.G., Schreiber, B.J. and Veil, D.J. (1974) Effects of discussion on opinions concerning illegal behavior. *Journal of Social Psychology*, 92: 77–84.

Nail, P.R., Macdonald, G. and Levy, D.A. (2000) Proposal of a four dimensional model of social response. *Psychological Bulletin*, 126(3): 454–70.

Nash, E.B., Edwards, G.W., Thompson, J.A. and Barfield, W. (2000) A review of presence and performance in virtual environments. *International Journal of Human–Computer Interaction*, 12: 1–41.

Nathan, P.E., Gorman, J.M. and Salkind, N.J. (1999) *Treating Mental Disorders: A Guide to What Works*. New York: Oxford University Press.

Nemeth, C. (1977) Interactions between jurors as a function of majority *vs.* unanimity decision rules. *Journal of Applied Social Psychology*, 7: 38–56.

Nemeth, C.J. and Kwan, J. (1987) Minority influence, divergent thinking and detection of correct solutions. *Journal of Applied Social Psychology*, 17: 786–97.

Nemeth, C.J. and Rogers, J. (1996) Dissent and the search for information. *British Journal of Social Psychology*, 35: 67–76.

Newcomb, T.M. (1943) *Personality and Social Change*. New York: Dryden.

Newsom, J.T. (1999) Another side to caregiving: negative reactions to being helped. *Current Directions in Psychological Science*, 8: 183–7.

Nezlek, J., Kowalski, R., Leary, M., Blevins, T. and Holgate, S. (1997) Personality moderators of reactions to interpersonal rejection: depression and trail self-esteem. *Personality and Social Psychology Bulletin*, 23: 1235–44.

Ng, S.H. (1986) Equity, intergroup bias and interpersonal bias in reward allocation. *European Journal of Social Psychology*, 16: 239–53.

Nijstad, B.A. (2000) *How the Group Affects the Mind*. Utrecht: ICS University of Utrecht.

Nowak, A., Szamrej, J. and Latané, B. (1990) From private attitude to public opinion: a dynamic theory of social impact. *Psychological Review*, 97: 362–76.

Nuckolls, K.B., Cassel, J. and Kaplan, B.H. (1972) Psychosocial assets, life crisis and the prognosis of pregnancy. *American Journal of Epidemiology*, 5: 431–41.

O'Dell, J. and Dickson, J. (1984) ELIZA as a 'therapeutic' tool. *Journal of Clinical Psychology*, 40: 942–5.

O'Malley, J.J. and Poplawsky, A. (1971) Noise-induced arousal and breadth of attention. *Perceptual and Motor Skills*, 33: 887–90.

Offner, A.K., Kramer, T.J. and Winter, J.P. (1996) The effects of facilitation, recording, and pauses on group brainstorming. *Small Group Research*, 27: 283–98.

Olds, D., Eckenrode, J., Henderson, C.R., Jr. *et al.* (1997) Long-term effects of home visitation on maternal life course and child abuse and neglect: 15 year follow-up of a randomized trial. *Journal of the American Medical Association*, 278: 637–43.

Olson, M. (1965) *The Logic of Collective Action: Public Goods and the Theory of Groups*. Cambridge, MA: Harvard University Press.

Orbell, J.M. and Dawes, R.M. (1981) Social dilemmas. In G. Stephenson and J.H. Davis (eds) *Progress in Applied Social Psychology*, Vol. 1. Chichester: Wiley.

Orbell, J.M. and Dawes, R.M. (1993) Social welfare, cooperators' advantage, and the option of not playing the game. *American Sociological Review*, 58: 787–800.

Orbell, J.M., Schwartz-Shea, P. and Simmons, R. (1984) Do cooperators exit more readily than defectors? *American Political Science Review*, 78: 147–62.

Orbell, J., Dawes, R. and van de Kragt, A. (1988) Explaining discussion induced cooperation. *Journal of Personality and Social Psychology*, 54: 811–19.

Orive, R. (1988) Group consensus, action immediacy, and opinion confidence. *Personality and Social Psychology Bulletin*, 14: 573–7.

Osbourn, A.F. (1957) *Applied Imagination*. New York: Scribners.

Osgood, C.E. (1979) GRIT for MBFR: a proposal for unfreezing force-level postures in Europe. *Peace Research Reviews*, 8(2): 77–92.

Otten, S., Mummendey, A. and Blanz, M. (1996) Intergroup discrimination in positive and negative outcome allocations: impact of stimulus valence, relative group status, and relative group size. *Personality and Social Bulletin*, 22(6): 568–81.

Ouwerkerk, J.W., van Lange, P.A.M. and van Vugt, M. (2001) Avoiding the social death penalty: threat of exclusion and cooperation in a public good. Paper presented at the *Ninth International Conference on Social Dilemmas*, Chicago, IL, July.

Oxley, N.L., Dzindolet, M.T. and Paulus, P.B. (1996) The effects of facilitators on the performance of brainstorming groups. *Journal of Social Behavior and Personality*, 11: 633–46.

Pagel, M.D., Becker, J. and Coppel, D. (1985) Loss of control, self-blame, and depression: an investigation of spouse caregivers of Alzheimer's disease patients. *Journal of Abnormal Psychology*, 94: 169–82.

Palestis, B.G. and Burger, J. (1998) Evidence for social facilitation of preening in the common term. *Animal Behaviour*, 56(5): 1107–111.

Park, B. and Rothbart, M. (1982) Perception of out-group homogeneity and levels of social categorization: memory of the subordinate attributes of in-group and out-group members. *Journal of Personality and Social Psychology*, 42: 1051–68.

Park, E.S., Locunt, R.B., Kerr, N.L. and Messé, L.A. (2002) 'Stand by your man': sex role attitudes and the Köhler effect. Paper presented at the Third Annual Conference of the Society of Personality and Social Psychology, Savannah, GA, 31 January–2 February.

Parks, C.D. (1994) The predictive ability of social values in resource dilemmas and public goods games. *Personality and Social Psychology Bulletin*, 20: 431–8.

Parks, C.D. and Hulbert, L.G. (1995) High and low trusters' responses to fear in a payoff matrix. *Journal of Conflict Resolution*, 39: 718–30.

Parks, C.D. and Nelson, N.L. (1999) Discussion and decision: the inter-relationship between initial preference distribution and group discussion content. *Organizational Behavior and Human Decision Processes*, 80: 87–101.

Parks, C.D. and Sanna, R.J. (1998) *Group Performance and Interaction*. Denver, CO: Westview Press.

Parks, C.D., Menager, R.F. and Scamahorn, S.D. (1996) Trust and reactions to messages of intent in social dilemmas. *Journal of Conflict Resolution*, 40: 134–51.

Parks, M.R. and Roberts, L.D. (1998) 'Making moosic': the development of personal relationships on line and a comparison to their off-line counter-parts. *Journal of Social and Personal Relationships*, 15: 517–37.

Patnoe, S. (1988) *A Narrative History of Experimental Social Psychology: The Lewinian Tradition*. New York: Springer-Verlag.

Paulus, P.B. (1989) *Psychology of Group Influence*, 2nd edn. Hillsdale, NJ: Lawrence Erlbaum Associates.

Paulus, P. (1998) Developing consensus about group think after all these years. *Organizational Behavior and Human Decision Processes*, 73: 362–73.

Paulus, P.B. and Cornelius, W.L. (1974) An analysis of gymnastic performance under conditions of practice and spectator observation. *Research Quarterly*, 45: 56–63.

Paulus, P.B. and Dzindolet, M.T. (1993) Social influence processes in group brainstorming. *Journal of Personality and Social Psychology*, 64: 575–86.

Pedersen, W.C., Gonzales, C. and Miller, N. (2000) The moderating effect of trivial triggering provocation on displaced aggression. *Journal of Personality and Social Psychology*, 78: 913–27.

Pendry, L. and Carrick, R. (2001) Doing what the mob do: priming effects on conformity. *European Journal of Social Psychology*, 31(1): 83–92.

Pennebaker, J.W. (1997) *Opening Up: The Healing Power of Expressing Emotions*, revised edn. New York: Guilford Press.

Pennebaker, J. and O'Heeron, R. (1984) Confiding in others and illness rate among spouses of suicide and accidental death victims. *Journal of Abnormal Psychology*, 93: 473–6.

Pennebaker, J.W., Kiecolt-Glaser, J.K. and Glaser, R. (1988) Disclosure of traumas and immune function: health implications for psychotherapy. *Journal of Consulting and Clinical Psychology*, 56(2): 239–45.

Pennebaker, J.W., Barger, S.D. and Tiebout, J. (1989) Disclosure of traumas and health among Holocaust survivors. *Psychosomatic Medicine*, 51(5): 577–89.

Pessin, J. (1933) The comparative effects of social and mechanical stimulation on memorizing. *American Journal of Psychology*, 45: 263–70.

Peterson, R.S. (1997) A directive leadership style in group decision making can be both a virtue and vice: evidence from elite and experimental groups. *Journal of Experimental and Social Psychology*, 72: 1107–21.

Peterson, R.S. and Nemeth, C.J. (1996) Focus versus flexibility: majority and minority influence can both improve performance. *Personality and Social Psychology Bulletin*, 22(1): 14–23.

Pettigrew, T.F. (1979) The ultimate attribution error: extending Allport's cognitive analysis of prejudice. *Personality and Social Psychology Bulletin*, 5: 461–76.

Pettigrew, T.F. (1997) Generalized intergroup contact effects on prejudice. *Personality and Social Psychology Bulletin*, 23: 173–85.

Pettigrew, T.F. (1998) Intergroup contact theory. *Annual Review of Psychology*, 49: 65–85.

Pettigrew, T.F. and Tropp, L.R. (2000) Does intergroup contact reduce prejudice: recent meta-analytic findings. In S. Oskamp (ed.) *Reducing Prejudice and Discrimination: The Claremont Symposium on Applied Social Psychology*. Mahwah, NJ: Lawrence Erlbaum Associates.

Petty, R., Harkins, S. and Williams, K. (1980) The effects of diffusion of cognitive effort on attitudes: an information processing view. *Journal of Personality and Social Psychology*, 38: 81–92.

Platow, M.J., McClintock, C.G. and Liebrand, W.B. (1990) Predicting intergroup fairness and ingroup bias in the minimal group paradigm. *European Journal of Social Psychology*, 20: 221–39.

Pool, G.J., Wood, W. and Leck, K. (1998) The self-esteem motive in social influence: agreement with valued majorities and disagreement with derogated minorities. *Journal of Personality and Social Psychology*, 75: 967–75.

Postmes, T. and Spears, R. (1998) Deindividuation and antinormative behavior: a meta-analysis. *Psychological Bulletin*, 123: 238–59.

Postmes, T., Spears, R., Sakhel, K. and deGroot, D. (2001) Social influence in computer mediated communication: the effects of anonymity on group behavior. *Personality and Social Psychology Bulletin*, 27: 1243–54.

Pratkanis, A.R. and Aronson, E. (2000) *Age of Propaganda*, 2nd edn. New York: Freeman.

Prentice-Dunn, S. and Rogers, R.W. (1989) Deindividuation and the self-regulation of behavior. In P.B. Paulus (ed.) *Psychology of Group Influence*, 2nd edn. Hillsdale, NJ: Lawrence Erlbaum Associates.

Pritchard, R.D., Dunnette, M.D. and Jorgenson, D.O. (1972) Effects of perceptions of equity and inequity on worker performance and satisfaction.
Journal of Applied Psychology Monograph, 56: 75–94.

Pruitt, D. and Carnevale, P. (1993) *Negotiation in Social Conflict*. Pacific Grove,
CA: Brooks/Cole.

Quattrone, G.A. and Jones, E.E. (1980) The perception of variability within ingroups and out-groups: implications for the law of small numbers. *Journal
of Personality and Social Psychology*, 38: 141–52.

Rabbie, J.M. and Horwitz, M. (1969) Arousal of ingroup–outgroup bias by a
chance win or loss. *Journal of Personality and Social Psychology*, 13: 269–77.

Rabbie, J.M., Lodewijkx, H. and Broeze, M. (1985) Individual and group aggression under the cover of darkness. Paper presented to the *Symposium on
Psychology of Peace at the Third European Congress of the International Society
for Research on Aggression (ISRA)*, devoted to multidisciplinary approaches
to conflict and appeasements in animals and men, Parma, Italy, 3–7
September.

Rabbie, J.M., Schot, J.C. and Visser, L. (1989) Social identity theory: a conceptual and empirical critique from the perspective of a behavioral interaction model. *European Journal of Social Psychology*, 19: 171–202.

Rajecki, D.W., Ickes, W., Corcoran, C. and Lenerz, K. (1977) Social facilitation
of human performance: mere presence effects. *Journal of Social Psychology*,
102: 297–310.

Rapoport, An. (1973) *Experimental Games and Their Uses in Psychology*.
Morristown, NJ: General Learning Press.

Rapoport, An. (1974) Prisoner's dilemma: recollections and observations. In
An. Rapaport (ed.) *Game Theory as a Theory of Conflict Resolution*. Dordrect:
Reidel.

Rapoport, An. and Chammah, A.M. (1965) *Prisoner's Dilemma: A Study in Conflict and Cooperation*. Ann Arbor, MI: University of Michigan Press.

Redd, M. and de Castro, J.M. (1992) Social facilitation of eating: effects of
social instruction on food intake. *Physiology and Behavior*, 52(4): 749–54.

Rees, W. and Lutkins, S. (1967) Mortality of bereavement. *British Medical Journal*, 4: 13–16.

Reich, P. (1983) How much does stress contribute to cardiovascular disease.
Journal of Cardiovascular Medicine, 8: 825.

Reicher, S.D., Spears, R. and Postmes, T. (1995) A social identity model of the
deindividuation phenomenon. In W. Strobe and M. Hewstone (eds) *European Review of Social Psychology*, Vol. 6. Chichester: Wiley.

Reis, H.T. (1998) Gender differences in intimacy and related behaviors: con-
text and process. In D.J. Canary and K. Dindia (eds) *Sex Differences and
Similarities in Communication: Critical Essays and Empirical Investigations of
Sex and Gender in Interaction*. Mahwah, NJ: Lawrence Erlbaum Associates.

Restle, F. and Davis, J.H. (1962) Success and speed of problem solving by
individuals and groups. *Psychological Review*, 69: 520–36.

Richardson, J.L., Shelton, D.R., Krailo, M. and Levine, A.M. (1990) The effect
of compliance with treatment on survival among patients with hematologic
malignancies. *Journal of Clinical Oncology*, 8: 356–64.

Ringelmann, M. (1913) Research on animate sources of power: the work of
man. *Annales de l'Institut National Agronomique, 2e serie-tome*, XI: 1–40.

Robb, S. and Stegman, C. (1983) Companion animals and elderly people:
a challenge for evaluators of social support. *The Gerontologist*, 23(3): 277–
82.

Robert, C. and Carnevale, P.J. (1997) Group choice in ultimatum bargaining. *Organizational Behavior and Human Decision Processes*, 72: 256–79.

Robinson-Staveley, K. and Cooper, J. (1990) Mere presence, gender, and reactions to computers: studying human–computer interaction in the social context. *Journal of Experimental Social Psychology*, 26(2): 168–83.

Rogers, R.W. and Prentice-Dunn, S. (1981) Deindividuation and anger-mediated interracial aggression: unmasking regressive racism. *Journal of Personality and Social Psychology*, 41: 63–73.

Rohrer, J.H., Baron, S.H., Hoffman, E.L. and Swander, D.V. (1954) The stability of autokinetic judgments. *Journal of Abnormal and Social Psychology*, 49: 595–7.

Rook, K. (1984) The negative side of social interaction: impact on psychological well being. *Journal of Personality and Social Psychology*, 46: 1097–1108.

Rook, K. (1987) Social support *vs.* companionship: effects on life stress, loneliness and evaluations by others. *Journal of Personality and Social Psychology*, 52: 1132–47.

Rook, K. (1998) Investigating the positive and negative sides of personal relationships: through a lens darkly? In B.H. Spitzberg *et al.* (eds) *The Dark Side of Close Relationships*. Mahwah, NJ: Lawrence Erlbaum Associates.

Rosenbaum, L.L. and Rosenbaum, W.B. (1971) Morale and productivity consequences of group leadership style, stress, and type of task. *Journal of Applied Psychology*, 55: 343–8.

Ross, L., Greene, D. and House, P. (1977) The 'false consensus effect': an egocentric bias in social perception and attributional processes. *Journal of Experimental Social Psychology*, 13: 279–301.

Rothbart, M. and Hallmark, W. (1988) In-group/out-group differences in the perceived efficacy of coercion and conciliation in resolving social conflict. *Journal of Personality and Social Psychology*, 55: 248–57.

Rothgerber, H. (1997) External intergroup threat as an antecedent to perceptions in in-group and out-group homogeneity. *Journal of Personality and Social Psychology*, 73: 1206–12.

Rubin, J.Z. and Brown, B.R. (1975) *The Social Psychology of Bargaining and Negotiation*. New York: Academic Press.

Rubin, M. and Hewstone, M. (1998) Social identity theory's self-esteem hypothesis: a review and some suggestions for clarification. *Personality and Social Psychology Review*, 2: 40–62.

Rule, B.G., Nesdale, A.R. and Dyck, R. (1975) Objective self-awareness and differing standards of aggression. *Representative Research in Social Psychology*, 6: 82–8.

Runciman, W.G. (1966) *Relative Deprivation and Social Justice*. London: Routledge & Kegan Paul.

Rutte, C.G. and Wilke, H.A.M. (1984) Social dilemmas and leadership. *European Journal of Social Psychology*, 14: 105–21.

Rutte, C.G. and Wilke, H.A.M. (1992) Goals, expectations and behavior in a social dilemma situation. In W. Liebrand and D.M. Messick (eds) *Social Dilemmas: Theoretical Issues and Research Findings*. Elmsford, NY: Pergamon Press.

Saks, M.J. (1977) *Jury Verdicts: The Role of Group Size and Social Decision Rule*. Lexington, MA: Heath.

Saks, M.J. and Baron, C. (eds) (1982) *The Use/Nonuse/Misuse of Applied Social Research in the Courts*. Cambridge, MA: Abt Books.

Sanders, G.S. (1981) Driven by distraction: an integrative review of social facilitation theory and research. *Journal of Experimental Social Psychology*, 17: 227–51.

Sanders, G.S. (1984) Self presentation and drive in social facilitation. *Journal of Experimental Social Psychology*, 20: 312–22.

Sanders, G.S. and Baron, R.S. (1975) The motivating effects of distraction on task performance. *Journal of Personality and Social Psychology*, 32: 956–63.

Sanders, G.S. and Baron, R.S. (1977) Is social comparison irrelevant for producing choice shifts? *Journal of Experimental Social Psychology*, 13: 303–14.

Sanders, G.S., Baron, R.S. and Moore, D.L. (1978) Distraction and social comparison as mediators of social facilitation effects. *Journal of Experimental Social Psychology*, 14: 291–303.

Sanna, L.J. (1992) Self efficacy theory: implications for social facilitation and social loafing. *Journal of Personality and Social Psychology*, 62: 774–86.

Sanna, L.J. and Pusecker, P.A. (1994) Self efficacy, valence of self evaluation and performance. *Personality and Social Psychology Bulletin*, 20: 82–92.

Sanna, L.J. and Shotland, L.R. (1990) Valence of anticipated evaluation and social facilitation. *Journal of Experimental Social Psychology*, 26: 82–92.

Saunders, C., Robey, D. and Vaverek, K. (1994) The persistence of status differentials in computer conferencing. *Human Communication Research*, 20: 443–72.

Schachter, S. (1951) Deviation, rejection and communication. *Journal of Abnormal and Social Psychology*, 46: 190–207.

Schachter, S. (1959) *The Psychology of Affiliation*. Stanford, CA: Stanford University Press.

Schachter, S., Nuttin, J., de Monchaux, C. *et al.* (1954) Cross-cultural experiments on threat and rejection. *Human Relations*, 7: 403–39.

Schafer, M. and Crichlow, S. (1996) Antecedents of groupthink: a quantitative study. *Journal of Conflict Resolution*, 40: 415–35.

Schmitt, B.H., Gilovich, T., Goore, N. and Joseph, L. (1986) Mere presence and social facilitation: one more time. *Journal of Experimental Social Psychology*, 22: 242–8.

Schroeder, D.A., Jensen, T.D., Reed, A.J., Sullivan, D.K. and Schwab, M. (1983) The actions of others as determinants of behavior in social trap situations. *Journal of Experimental Social Psychology*, 19: 522–39.

Schofield, J.W. and Sagar, H.A. (1977) Peer interaction patterns in an integrated middle school. *Sociometry*, 40: 130–8.

Schopler, J. and Insko, C.A. (1992) The discontinuity effect in interpersonal and intergroup relations: generality and mediation. In S. Stroebe and M. Hewstone (eds) *European Review of Social Psychology*, Vol. 3. New York: Wiley.

Schulz-Hardt, F.D., Luthgens, C. and Moscovici, S. (2000) Biased information search in group decision making. *Journal of Personality and Social Psychology*, 78: 655–69.

Schutte, N.S., Malouff, J.M., Post-Gordon, J.C. and Rodasta, A. (1988) Effects of playing video games on children's aggressive and other behaviors. *Journal of Applied Psychology*, 18: 454–60.

Seeman, T.E., Berkman, L.F., Blazer, D. and Rowe, J.W. (1994) Social ties and support and neuroendicrine function: the MacArthur studies of successful aging. *Annals of Behavioral Medicine*, 16: 95–106.

Seidman, O., Bensen, S.B., Miller, I. and Meeland, T. (1957) Influence of a partner on tolerance for a self-administered electric shock. *Journal of Abnormal and Social Psychology*, 54: 210–12.

Seta, J.J., Seta, C.E. and Donaldson, S. (1991) The impact of comparison processes on coactors' frustration and willingness to expend effort. *Personality and Social Psychology Bulletin*, 17: 560–8.

Shaver, P. and Liebling, B.A. (1976) Explorations in the drive theory of social facilitation. *Journal of Social Psychology*, 99: 259–71.

Shaw, M.E. (1932) Comparison of individuals and small groups in the rational solution of complex problems. *American Journal of Psychology*, 44: 491–504.

Shaw, M.E. (1981) *Group Dynamics*, 3rd edn. New York: McGraw-Hill.

Shepperd, J.A. (1995) Productivity loss in performance groups: a motivation analysis. *Psychology Bulletin*, 113: 67–81.

Sherif, M. (1935) A study of some social factors in perception. *Archives of Psychology*, 27: No. 187.

Sherif, M. (1936) *The Psychology of Social Norms*. New York: Harper & Row.

Sherif, M., Harvey, O.J., White, B.J., Hood, W.R. and Sherif, C.W. (1961) *Intergroup Conflict and Cooperation: The Robber's Cave Experiment*. Norman, OK: Institute of Group Relations.

Sherman, S.J., Hamilton, D.L. and Lewis, A.C. (1999) Perceived entitativity and the social identity value of group memberships. In D. Abrams and M.A. Hogg (eds) *Social Identity and Social Cognition*. Oxford: Blackwell.

Siegel, J.M. (1990) Stressful life events and use of physician services among the elderly: the moderating role of pet ownership. *Journal of Personality and Social Psychology*, 58: 1081–6.

Siegel, J.M., Dubrovosky, V., Kiesler, S. and McGuire, T.W. (1986) Group processes in computer-mediated communication. *Organizational Behavior and Human Decision Processes*, 37(2): 157–87.

Simon, B. and Brown, R.J. (1987) Perceived intragroup homogeneity in minority–majority contexts. *Journal of Personality and Social Psychology*, 53: 703–11.

Skinner, B.F. (1969) *Contingencies of Reinforcement*. New York: Appleton-Century-Crofts.

Slavin, R.E. (1985) Cooperative learning: applying contact theory in desegregated schools. *Journal of Social Issues*, 16: 169–80.

Smith, A. ([1776] 1976) *The Wealth of Nations*. Chicago, IL: University of Chicago Press.

Smith, B.N., Kerr, N.A., Marcus, M.J. and Stasson, M.F. (2001) Individual differences in social loafing: need for cognition as a motivator in collective performance. *Group Dynamics*, 5(2): 150–8.

Smith, C.M., Tindale, R.S. and Steiner, L. (1998) Investment decisions by individuals and groups in 'sunk cost' situations: the potential impact of shared representations. *Group Processes and Intergroup Relations*, 1: 175–89.

Smith, J.P. and Welch, F. (1984) Affirmative action and labor markets. *Journal of Labor Economics*, 2: 269–301.

Sniezek, J.A. (1992) Groups under uncertainty: an examination of confidence in group decision making. *Organizational Behavior and Human Decision Processes*, 52(1): 124–55.

Sokill, G.R. and Mynatt, C.R. (1984) Arousal and free throw shooting. Paper presented to the *Midwestern Psychology Association*, Chicago, IL, May.

Sommer, R., Wynes, M. and Brinkley, G. (1992) Social facilitation effects in shopping behavior. *Environment and Behavior*, 24(3): 285–97.

Sorrentino, R.M. and Boutillier, R.G. (1975) The effect of quantity and quality of verbal interaction on ratings of leadership ability. *Journal of Experimental Social Psychology*, 11: 403–11.

Sorrentino, R.M., King, G. and Leo, G. (1980) The influence of the minority on perception: a note on a possible alternative explanation. *Journal of Experimental Social Psychology*, 16: 293–301.

Spears, R. and Lea, M. (1992) Social influence and the influence of the 'social' in computer-mediated communication. In M. Lea (ed.) *Contexts of Computer-mediated Communication*. London: Harvester-Wheatsheaf.

Spears, R. and Lea, M. (1994) Panacea or panopticon? The hidden power in computer-mediated communication. *Communication Research*, 21: 427–59.

Spears, R., Lea, M. and Lee, S. (1990) Deindividuation and group polarization in computer-mediated communication. *British Journal of Social Psychology*, 29(2): 121–34.

Spence, K.W. (1956) *Behavior, Theory and Conditioning*. New Haven, CT: Yale University Press.

Spiegel, D., Bloom, J.R., Kraemer, H.C. and Gottheil, E. (1989) The effects of psychosocial treatment on survival of patients with metastatic breast cancer. *Lancet*, 334: 888–91.

Stahlberg, D., Eller, F., Maass, A. and Frey, D. (1995) We knew it all along: hindsight bias in groups. *Organizational Behavior and Human Decision Processes*, 63: 46–58.

Stasser, G. (1988) Computer simulation as a research tool: the DICUSS model of group decision making. *Journal of Experimental and Social Psychology*, 24: 393–422.

Stasser, G. (1999) A primer of social decision scheme theory: models of group influence, competitive model-testing, and prospective modeling. *Organizational Behavior and Human Decision Processes*, 80: 3–20.

Stasser, G. and Stewart, D.D. (1992) Discovery of hidden profiles by decision-making groups: solving a problem versus making a judgment. *Journal of Personality and Social Psychology*, 63: 426–34.

Stasser, G. and Titus, W. (1985) Pooling of unshared information in group decision making: biased information sampling during group discussion. *Journal of Personality and Social Psychology*, 48: 1467–78.

Stasser, G. and Titus, W. (1987) Effects of information load and percentage shared information on the dissemination of unshared information during discussion. *Journal of Personality and Social Psychology*, 53: 81–93.

Stasser, G., Kerr, N.L. and Bray, R. (1982) The social psychology of jury deliberations: structure, process, and product. In N. Kerr and R. Bray (eds) *The Psychology of the Courtroom*. New York: Academic Press.

Stasser, G., Kerr, N.L. and Davis, J.H. (1989a) Influence processes and consensus models in decision-making groups. In P. Paulus (ed.) *Psychology of Group Influence*, 2nd edn. Hillsdale, NJ: Lawrence Erlbaum Associates.

Stasser, G., Taylor, L.A. and Hanna, C. (1989b) Information sampling in structured and unstructured discussions of three- and six-person groups. *Journal of Personality and Social Psychology*, 57: 67–78.

Stasser, G., Stewart, D.D. and Wittenbaum, G.M. (1995) Expert roles and information exchange during discussion: the importance of knowing who knows what. *Journal of Experimental Social Psychology*, 31: 244–65.

Steele, C.M. (1997) A threat in the air: how stereotypes shape intellectual identity and performance. *American Psychologist*, 52(6): 613–29.

Steiner, I.D. (1966) Models for inferring relationships between group size and potential group productivity. *Behavioral Science*, 11: 273–83.

Steiner, I.D. (1972) *Group Process and Productivity*. New York: Academic Press.

Stephan, F.F. and Mishler, E.G. (1952) The distribution of participation in small groups: an exponential approximation. *American Sociological Review*, 17: 598–608.

Stewart, D.D. and Stasser, G. (1995) Expert role assignment and information sampling during collective recall and decision making. *Journal of Personality and Social Psychology*, 69: 619–28.

Stewart, D.D. and Stasser, G. (1998) The sampling of critical, unshared information in decision-making groups: the role of an informed minority. *European Journal of Social Psychology*, 28: 95–113.

Stewart, D.D., Billings, R.S. and Stasser, G. (1998) Accountability and the discussion of unshared, critical information in decision-making groups. *Group Dynamics*, 2: 18–23.

Stoner, J.A.F. (1961) A comparison of individual and group decisions including risk. Unpublished thesis, Massachusetts Institute of Technology, School of Management, Cambridge, MA.

Strauss, M.A. and McGrath, J.E. (1994) Does the medium matter? The interaction of task type and technology on group performance and member reactions. *Journal of Applied Psychology*, 79(1): 87–97.

Strodtbeck, F.L. and Mann, R. (1956) Sex role differentiation in jury deliberation. *Sociometry*, 19: 3–11.

Stroebe, W. (2000) *Social Psychology and Health*, 2nd edn. Buckingham: Open University Press.

Stroebe, W. and Diehl, M. (1994) Why groups are less effective than their members: on productivity losses in idea-generating groups. In W. Stroebe and M. Hewstone (eds) *European Review of Social Psychology*, Vol. 5. London: Wiley.

Stroebe, W. and Frey, B.S. (1982) Self-interest and collective action: the economics and psychology of public goods. *British Journal of Social Psychology*, 21: 121–37.

Stroebe, W., Stroebe, M.S., Gergen, K.J. and Gergen, M. (1982) The effects of bereavement on mortality: a social psychological analysis. In J.R. Eiser (ed.) *Social Psychology and Behavioral Medicine*. Chichester: Wiley.

Stroebe, M., Stroebe, W. and Hansson, R.E. (1993) *Handbook of Bereavement: Theory, Research and Intervention*. Cambridge: Cambridge University Press.

Stroebe, W., Diehl, M. and Abakoumkin, G. (1996) Social compensation and the Köhler effect: toward a theoretical explanation of motivation gains in group productivity. In E. Witte and J. Davis (eds) *Understanding Group Behavior: Consensual Action by Small Groups*, Vol. 2. Mahwah, NJ: Lawrence Erlbaum Associates.

Stroessner, S.J. and Plaks, J.E. (2001) Illusory correlation and stereotype formation: tracing the arc of research over a quarter century. In G. Moskowitz (ed.) *Cognitive Social Psychology: The Princeton Symposium on the Legacy and Future of Social Cognition*. Mahwah, NJ: Lawrence Erlbaum Associates.

Strube, M.J., Miles, M.E. and Finch, W.H. (1981) The social facilitation of a simple task: field tests of alternative explanations. *Personality and Social Psychology Bulletin*, 7: 701–7.

Stryker, S. (1972) Coalition behavior. In C.G. McClintock (ed.) *Experimental Social Psychology*. New York: Holt.

Suedfeld, P. and Rank, A.D. (1976) Revolutionary leaders: long-term success as a function of changes in conceptual complexity. *Journal of Personality and Social Psychology*, 34: 169–78.

Suls, J. and Wheeler, L. (2000) *Handbook of Social Comparison: Theory and Research*. New York: Kluwer Academic/Plenum Publishers.

Suls, J., Martin, R. and Wheeler, L. (2000) Three kinds of opinion comparison: the triadic model. *Personality and Social Psychology Bulletin*, 4: 219–37.

Szniezek, J.A. (1992) Groups under uncertainly: an examination of confidence in group decision making. *Organizational Behavior and Human Decision Processes*, 52: 124–55.

Szymanski, K. and Harkins, S. (1987) Social loafing and self-evaluation with a social standard. *Journal of Personality and Social Psychology*, 53: 891–7.

Tajfel, H. (1970) Experiments in intergroup discrimination. *Scientific American*, 223: 96–102.

Tajfel, H. (1982) Social psychology of intergroup relations. *Annual Review of Psychology*, 33: 1–39.

Tajfel, H. and Turner, J.C. (1979) An integrative theory of intergroup conflict. In W.G. Austin and S. Worchel (eds) *The Social Psychology of Intragroup Relations*. Monterey, CA: Brooks/Cole.

Tajfel, H. and Turner, J.C. (1986) The social identity theory of intergroup behavior. In S. Worchel and W.G. Austin (eds) *Psychology of Intergroup Relations*. Chicago, IL: Nelson Hall.

Tajfel, H. and Wilkes, A.L. (1963) Classification and quantitative judgment. *British Journal of Psychology*, 54: 101–13.

Tanford, S. and Penrod, S. (1984) Social influence model: a formal integration of research on majority and minority influence processes. *Psychological Bulletin*, 95: 189–225.

Tarde, G. (1895) *Essais et me langes socialogigues*. Lyon: Storck.

Taylor, D.W. (1954) Problem solving by groups. In *Proceedings of the XIV International Congress of Psychology*. Amsterdam: North-Holland.

Taylor, D.W. and Faust, W.L. (1952) Twenty questions: efficiency in problem solving as a function of size of group. *Journal of Experimental Psychology*, 44: 360–8.

Telch, C.F. and Telch, M.J. (1986) Group coping skills instruction and supportive group therapy for cancer patients: a comparison of strategies. *Journal of Consulting Clinical Psychiatry*, 54: 802–8.

Tesser, A., Campbell, J. and Mickler, S. (1983) The role of social pressure, attention to the stimulus, and self-doubt in conformity. *European Journal of Social Psychology*, 13: 217–34.

Tetlock, P.E. (1979) Identifying victims of groupthink from public statements of decision makers. *Journal of Personality and Social Psychology*, 37(8): 1314–24.

Tetlock, P.E., Peterson, R.S., McGuire, C. *et al.* (1992) Assessing political group dynamics: a test of the groupthink model. *Journal of Personality and Social Psychology*, 63(3): 403–25.

Thaler, R. (1985) Mental accounting and consumer choice. *Marketing Science*, 4: 199–214.

Thibaut, J.W. and Kelley, H.H. (1959) *The Social Psychology of Groups*. New York: Wiley.

Thomas, E.J. and Fink, C.F. (1961) Models of group problem solving. *Journal of Abnormal and Social Psychology*, 63: 53–63.

Thomas, E.J. and Fink, C.F. (1963) Effects of group size. *Psychological Bulletin*, 60: 371–84.

Thompson, S.C. and Kyle, D.J. (2000) The role of perceived control in coping with the losses associated with chronic illness. In J.H. Harvey and E.D. Miller (eds) *Loss and Trauma: General and Close Relationship Perspectives*. Philadelphia, PA: Brunner-Routledge.

Thompson, W.C. (1989) Death qualification after Wainwright *vs.* Witt and Lockhart *vs.* McCree. *Law and Human Behavior*, 13: 185–216.

Tibblin, G. *et al.* (1986) *Social Support, Health and Disease*. Stockholm: Almqvist & Wiksell.

Tindale, R.S., Smith, C.M., Thomas, L.S., Filkins, J. and Sheffey, S. (1996) Shared representations and asymmetric social influence processes in small groups. In E.H. Witte and J.H. Davis (eds) *Understanding Group Behavior: Consensual Action by Small Groups*, Vol. 1. Hillsdale, NJ: Lawrence Erlbaum Associates.

Torrance, E.P. (1954) Some consequences of power differences on decision making in permanent and temporary three-man groups. *Research Studies, State College of Washington*, 22: 130–40.

Triplett, N. (1898) The dynamogenic factors in pacemaking and competition. *Journal of Psychology*, 9: 507–33.

Trost, M. and Kenrick, D. (1994) Ego involvement in the minority influence paradigm: the double-edged sword of minority advocacy. In S. Moscovici, A. Mucchi-Faina and A. Maass (eds) *Minority Influence*. Chicago, IL: Nelson Hall.

Trost, M.R., Maass, A. and Kenrick, D.T. (1992) Minority influence: personal relevance biases cognitive processes and reverses private acceptance. *Journal of Experimental Social Psychology*, 28(3): 234–54.

Tuckman, B.W. (1965) Developmental sequences in small groups. *Psychological Bulletin*, 63: 384–99.

Tuckman, B.W. and Jensen, M.A.C. (1977) Stages of small group development revisited. *Group and Organizational Studies*, 2: 419–27.

Turner, J.C. (1991) *Social Influence*. Buckingham: Open University Press.

Turner, J.C., Wetherell, M.A. and Hogg, M.A. (1989) Referent informational influence and group polarization. *British Journal of Social Psychology*, 28(2): 135–47.

Turner, M.E. and Pratkanis, A.R. (1998a) Twenty-five years of groupthink theory and research: lessons from the evaluation of a theory. *Organizational Behavior and Human Decision Processes*, 73: 105–15.

Turner, M.E. and Pratkanis, A.R. (1998b) A social identity maintenance model of groupthink. *Organizational Behavior and Human Decision Processes*, 73: 210–35.

Turner, M.E., Pratkanis, A.R., Porbasco, P. and Leve, C. (1992) Threat, cohesion and group effectiveness: testing a social identity maintenance perspective on groupthink. *Journal of Personality and Social Psychology*, 63: 781–96.

Turner, R.H. and Killian, L.M. (1972) *Collective Behavior*, 2nd edn. Englewood Cliffs, NJ: Prentice-Hall.

Uchino, B.N., Cacioppo, J.T. and Kiecolt-Glaser, J.K. (1996) The relationship between social support and physiological processes: a review with emphasis on underlying mechanisms and implications for health. *Psychological Bulletin*, 119(3): 488–531.

Uchino, B., Uno, D. and Holt-Lunstad, J. (1999) Social support, physiological processes and health. *Current Directions in Psychological Science*, 8: 145–8.

Umberson, D., Chen, M.D., House, J.S. and Hopkins, K. (1996) The effect of social relationships on psychological well-being: are men and women really so different? *American Sociological Review*, 61: 837–57.

Urban, L.M. and Miller, N. (1998) A theoretical analysis of crossed categorization effects: a meta-analysis. *Journal of Personality and Social Psychology*, 74: 894–908.

Valacich, J.S., Dennis, A.R. and Connolly, T. (1994) Idea generation in computer-based groups: a new ending to an old story. *Organizational Behavior and Human Decision Processes*, 57: 448–67.

Valenzi, E.R. and Andrews, I.R. (1971) Effect of hourly overpay and underpay inequity when tested with a new induction procedure. *Journal of Applied Psychology*, 55: 22–7.

Vallone, R.P., Ross, L. and Lepper, M.R. (1985) The hostile media phenomenon: biased perception and perceptions of media bias in coverage of the Beirut massacre. *Journal of Personality & Social Psychology*, 49(3): 577–85.

van de Kragt, A., Dawes, R.M., Orbell, J., Braver, S. and Wilson, L. (1986) Doing well and doing good as ways of resolving social dilemmas. In H. Wilke, D. Messick and C. Rutte (eds) *Experimental Social Dilemmas*. Frankfurt-am-Main: P. Lang.

van Dijk, E. and Wilke, H. (1997) Is it mine or is it ours? Framing property rights and decision making in social dilemmas. *Organizational Behavior and Human Decision Processes*, 71: 195–209.

van Dijk, E., Wilke, H.A.M. and Wit, A. (in press) Preferences for leadership in social dilemmas: public good dilemmas versus common resource dilemmas. *Journal of Experimental Social Psychology*.

van Lange, P.A.M. and Kuhlman, D.M. (1994) Social value orientations and impressions of partner's honesty and intelligence: a test of the might versus morality effect. *Journal of Personality and Social Psychology*, 67(1): 126–41.

van Lange, P.A.M. and Semin-Goosens, A. (1998) The boundaries of reciprocal cooperation. *European Journal of Social Psychology*, 28: 847–54.

van Lange, P.A.M. and Visser, K. (1999) Locomotion in social dilemmas: how people adapt to cooperative, tit-for-tat, and noncooperative partners. *Journal of Personality and Social Psychology*, 77: 762–73.

van Lange, P.A.M., van Vugt, M., Meertens, R.M. and Ruiter, R.A.C. (1998) A social dilemma analysis of commuting preferences: the roles of social value orientation and trust. *Journal of Applied Social Psychology*, 28: 796–820.

Vanneman, R.D. and Pettigrew, T.F. (1972) Race and relative deprivation in the urban United States. *Race*, 13: 461–86.

van Vugt, M. (1997) Concerns about the privatization of public goods: a social dilemma analysis. *Social Psychology Quarterly*, 60(4): 355–67.

van Vugt, M. and Samuelson, C.D. (1999) The impact of personal metering in the management of a natural resource crisis: a social dilemma analysis. *Personality and Social Psychology Bulletin*, 25: 731–45.

van Vugt, M., Snyder, M., Tyler, T. and Biel, A. (2001) *Co-operation in Modern Society: Promoting the Welfare of Communities, States and Organizations*. London: Routledge.

Vinokur, A.D. and von Ryn, M. (1993) Social support and undermining in close relationships: their independent effects on the mental health of unemployed persons. *Journal of Personality and Social Psychology*, 65(2): 350–9.

Vroom, V.H. (1964) *Work and Motivation*. New York: Wiley.

Wagner, J.A. (1995) Studies in individualism and collectivism: effects on co-operation in groups. *Academy of Management Journal*, 38(1): 152–72.

Walster, E., Walster, G.W. and Berscheid, E. (1978) *Equity: Theory and Research*. Boston, MA: Allyn & Bacon.

Weiner, N., Pandy, J. and Latané, B. (1981) Individual and group productivity in the United States and India. Paper presented to the *American Psychological Association*, Los Angeles, CA, August.

Weisband, S.P., Schneider, S.K. and Connolly, T. (1995) Electronic communication and social information: status salience and status differences. *Academy of Management Journal*, 38: 1124–51.

Weiss, R. (1974) The provisions of social relationships. In Z. Rubin (ed.) *Doing Unto Others*. Englewood Cliffs, NJ: Prentice-Hall.

Weldon, E. and Gargano, G.M. (1988) Cognitive loafing: the effects of accountability and shared responsibility on cognitive effort. *Personality and Social Psychology Bulletin*, 14(1): 159–71.

Wheelan, S.A. (1994) *Group Process: A Developmental Perspective*. Boston, MA: Allyn & Bacon.

Wheeler, L. (1966) Toward a theory of behavioral contagion. *Psychological Review*, 73(2): 179–92.

Whyte, G. (1993) Escalating commitment in individual and group decision making: a prospect theory approach. *Organizational Behavior and Human Decision Processes*, 54: 430–55.

Wilder, D.A. (1977) Perception of groups, size of opposition, and social influence. *Journal of Experimental Social Psychology*, 13: 253–68.

Wilder, D.A. (1981) Perceiving persons as a group. In D. Hamilton (ed.) *Cognitive Processes in Stereotyping and Intergroup Behavior*. Hillsdale, NJ: Lawrence Erlbaum Associates.

Wilder, D.A. (1986) Social categorization: implications for creation and reduction of intergroup bias. In L. Berkowitz (ed.) *Advances in Experimental Social Psychology*, Vol. 19. New York: Academic Press.

Wilder, D.A. and Allen, V.L. (1977) Social support, extreme social support and conformity. *Representative Research in Social Psychology*, 8: 33–41.

Wilder, D.A. and Shapiro, P. (1988) Effects of anxiety on impression formation in a group context: an anxiety-assimilation hypothesis. *Journal of Experimental and Social Psychology*, 25: 481–99.

Wilder, D.A. and Shapiro, P. (1989) Role of competition-induced anxiety in limiting the beneficial impact of positive behavior by an out-group member. *Journal of Personality and Social Psychology*, 56(1): 60–9.

Wilder, D.A. and Thompson, J.E. (1980) Intergroup contact with independent manipulations of in-group and out-group interaction. *Journal of Personality and Social Psychology*, 38: 589–603.

Wilder, D.A., Simon, A.F. and Faith, M. (1996) Enhancing the impact of counterstereotypic information: dispositional attributions for deviance. *Journal of Personality and Social Psychology*, 71: 276–87.

Williams, K.D. (1997) Social ostracism. In R. Kowalski (ed.) *Aversive Interpersonal Behaviors*. New York: Plenum Press.

Williams, K.D. and Karau, S.J. (1991) Social loafing and social compensation: the effects of expectations of co-worker performance. *Journal of Personality and Social Psychology*, 61: 570–81.

Williams, K.D. and Sommer, K.L. (1997) Social ostracism by co-workers: does rejection lead to social loafing or compensation? *Personality and Social Psychology Bulletin*, 23: 693–706.

Williams, K.D. and Williams, K.B. (1984) Social loafing in Japan: a cross-cultural developmental study. Paper presented to the *Midwestern Psychological Association*, Chicago, IL, May.

Williams, K.D., Harkins, S. and Latané, B. (1981) Identifiability as a deterrent to social loafing: two cheering experiments. *Journal of Personality and Social Psychology*, 40: 303–11.

Williams, K.D., Shore, W.J. and Grahe, J.E. (1998) The silent treatment: perceptions of its behaviors and associated feelings. *Group Processes and Intergroup Relations*, 1: 117–41.

Williams, K.D., Cheung, C.K.T. and Choi, W. (2000) Cyberostracism: effects of being ignored over the internet. *Journal of Personality and Social Psychology*, 79(5): 746–62.

Williams, S. and Taormina, R.J. (1993) Unanimous versus majority influences on group polarization in business decision making. *Journal of Personality and Social Psychology*, 125: 355–63.

Williams vs. Florida (1970) *United States Reports*, 399: 78–145.

Wills, T.A. (1997) Social support and health. In A. Baum, S. Newman, J. Weinman, R. West and C. McManus (eds) *Cambridge Handbook of Psychology, Health and Medicine*. New York: Cambridge University Press.

Wit, A. and Wilke, H.A. (1990) The presentation of rewards and punishments in a simulated social dilemma. *Social Behaviour*, 5(4): 231–45.

Witte, E.H. (1989) Köhler rediscovered: the anti-Ringelmann effect. *European Journal of Social Psychology*, 19: 147–54.

Wittenbaum, G.M. and Stasser, G. (1995) The role of prior expectancy and group discussion in the attribution of attitudes. *Journal of Experimental Social Psychology*, 31: 82–105.

Wittenbaum, G., Hubbell, A.P. and Zuckerman, C. (1999) Mutual enhancement: toward an understanding of the collective preference for shared information. *Journal of Personality and Social Psychology*, 77: 967–78.

Wolf, S. (1979) Behavioral style and group cohesiveness as sources of minority influence. *European Journal of Social Psychology*, 9: 381–95.

Wood, W. (2000) Attitude change: persuasion and social influence. *Annual Review of Psychology*, 51: 539–70.

Wood, W., Lundgren, S., Ouellette, J.A., Busceme, S. and Blackstone, T. (1994) Minority influence: a meta-analytic review of social influence processes. *Psychological Bulletin*, 115(3): 323–45.

Wood, W., Pool, G.J., Leck, K. and Purvis, D. (1996) Self-definition, defensive processing, and influence: the normative impact of majority and minority groups. *Journal of Personality and Social Psychology*, 71(6): 1181–93.

Worchel, S., Andreoli, V.A. and Folger, R. (1977) Intergroup cooperation and intergroup attraction: the effect of previous interaction and outcome of combined effort. *Journal of Experimental Social Psychology*, 13: 131–40.

Worchel, S., Rothgerber, H., Day, E.A., Hart, D. and Butemeyer, J. (1998) Social identity and individual productivity within groups. *British Journal of Social Psychology*, 37: 389–413.

Worringham, C.J. and Messick, D.M. (1983) Social facilitation of running: an unobtrusive study. *Journal of Social Psychology*, 121: 23–9.

Wright, E.F., Lüüs, C.E. and Christie, S.D. (1990) Does group discussion facilitate the use of consensus information in making causal attributions? *Journal of Personality and Social Psychology*, 59: 261–9.

Wright, S.C., Aron, A., McLaughlin-Volpe, T. and Ropp, S.A. (1997) The extended contact effect: knowledge of cross-group friendships and prejudice. *Journal of Personality and Social Psychology*, 73: 73–90.

Yamagishi, T. (1986) The provision of a sanctioning system as a public good. *Journal of Personality and Social Psychology*, 51: 110–16.

Yamagishi, T., Jin, N. and Kiyonari, T. (1999) Bounded generalized reciprocity: in-group boasting and in-group favoritism. *Advances in Group Processes*, 16: 161–97.

Zaccaro, S.J. (1984) Social loafing: the role of task attractiveness. *Personality and Social Psychology Bulletin*, 10: 99–106.

Zajonc, R.B. (1965) Social facilitation. *Science*, 149: 269–74.

Zajonc, R.B. (1980) Compresence. In P. Paulus (ed.) *Psychology of Group Influence*, 2nd edn. Hillsdale, NJ: Lawrence Erlbaum Associates.

Zajonc, R.B., Heingartner, A. and Herman, E.M. (1969) Social enhancement and impairment of performance in the cockroach. *Journal of Personality and Social Psychology*, 13: 83–92.

Zdaniuk, B. and Levine, J.M. (1996) Anticipated interaction and thought generation: the role of faction size. *British Journal of Social Psychology*, 35: 201–18.

Zeisel, H. and Diamond, S. (1978) The effect of peremptory challenges on jury and verdict: an experiment in a federal district court. *Stanford Law Review*, 30: 491–531.

Zickmund, S. (1997) Approaching the radical other: the discursive culture of cyberhate. In S.G. Jones (ed.) *Virtual Culture*. London: Sage.

Ziller, R.C. (1957) Group size: a determinant of the quality and stability of group decisions. *Sociometry*, 20: 165–73.

Zillmannn, D. (1979) *Hostility and Aggression*. Hillsdale, NJ: Lawrence Erlbaum Associates.

Zillmannn, D. (1998) *Connections Between Sexuality and Aggression*, 2nd edn. Hillsdale, NJ: Lawrence Erlbaum Associates.

Zillmannn, D., Johnson, R.C. and Day, K.D. (1974) Attribution of apparent arousal and proficiency of recovery from sympathetic activation affecting excitation transfer to aggressive behavior. *Journal of Experimental Social Psychology*, 10: 503–15.

Zimbardo, P. (1969) The human choice: individuation, reason, and order versus deindividuation, impulse, and chaos. In W.J. Arnold and D. Levine (eds) *Nebraska Symposium on Motivation*, Vol. 17. Lincoln, NE: University of Nebraska Press.

INDEX

Abrams, Dominic, 3
additive task, 207
Ader, R., 177
adjournment, group development, 17
affiliation, 176–8, 207
afterimage study, 84–6
aggression
  computer games, 199–200
  displaced aggression, 157
  emergent norm theory, 115
  see also conflict
Aiello, J.R., 201
Allen, K.M., 183, 188
Allen, V.L., 76
Allport, F.H., 21
Allport, G.W., 167, 169
Alvaro, E.M., 86
Amoroso, D., 176, 177
Anderson, C., 199–200
anonymity
  computer-mediated communication,
   197, 198
  emergent norm theory, 115
  integrated deindividuation model,
   117–18
  mob behaviour, 111, 113–15
  social identity view of
   deindividuation effects, 116–17
  see also deindividuation;
   identification
Aronson, E., 168
arousal
  social facilitation, 23, 24
  see also drive theory of social facilitation

Asch, Solomon, 74–5, 76, 79, 80
attachment theory, 175, 187
attentional conflict, 25–7
attentional overload, 31, 207
attentional theories, 31–3, 207
audience paradigms, 207
  social facilitation, 21
autokinetic effect, 6

Back, K.W., 12
'bad apple' effect in social dilemmas,
  152
Baker, S.M., 90
Balkans conflict, 156
Bargh, J.A., 198–9
Barlow, D.H., 190
Baron, J., 145
Baron, R.S.
  attentional overload, 31
  conformity, 79
  distraction/conflict theory, 25–6
  drive theory, 27
  health and social support, 184
  indoctrination, 109
  social corroboration, 69–70, 199
Bass, B.M., 16
Baumeister, R.F., 175
Beaman, A.L., 114
beliefs, as social constructions, 68–9
Berkman, L.F., 181–2
Bettencourt, B.A., 170
biases
  intergroup relations, 163–6
  judgmental biases, 131–3

leniency bias in jury decisions, 127–9, 210
reduction of
  gradual and reciprocal concession technique, 171–3
  intergroup contact, 167
  manipulation of categorization, 169–71
  superordinate goals, 168–9
Bishop, G.D., 99
Blascovich, J.
  competitive social comparison, 100
  drive theory, 28–9
  group polarization, 103
  self-efficacy theory, 31
  threat reactions, 29
Bodenhausen, G.V., 32
Bond, Charles F.
  drive theory, 28
  self-efficacy theory, 31
  self-presentation theory, 29
  social facilitation, 25
Bond, R., 75, 77
brainstorming, 207
  group performance, 44–7
  social compensation, 64
Brand, E.F., 191
Brauer, M., 100
Braver, S.L., 149
Bray, R.M., 49
Brenner, G.F., 185
Brewer, M.B., 144, 149
'broken heart' effect, 179, 207
Brown, R., 162
Bruning, J.L., 32–3
Buehler, R., 82
buffering hypothesis, 184–5, 207
Burnstein, E., 99, 102
Butera, F., 89

Cacioppo, J.T., 24, 28
Callaway, M.R., 95
Campbell, Donald T., 18, 73–4
Campbell, J.D., 76
Cantril, H., 157
Carrick, R., 78
categorization, manipulation of to reduce conflict, 169–73
Catherine, Queen, 8
challenge pattern, drive theory, 28
challenge reaction, 207
Chen, X., 88
Cheryan, S., 32
choice, see social dilemmas
Clark, R.D., 84

co-action paradigms, 21, 207
Cobb, S., 180
cockroach experiment, social facilitation, 20, 22
cognitive dissonance, 110
Cohen, S., 175, 187–8
cohesion, 11–15, 209
  computer-mediated communication, 197–8
  horizontal cohesion, 14, 210
  multidimensional views, 14–15
  social identity view, 12–14
  see also conformity; norms
collective induction, group decision-making, 133–5
Collins, N.L., 187
commitment
  commitment norm, 207
  social dilemmas, 149
common ingroup identity model, 170, 208
communication
  communication networks, 10–11
  face-to-face and computer-mediated, 194
  non-verbal communication
    lost in computer-mediated communication, 194–5, 196
  paralinguistic information
    lost in computer-mediated communication, 195
  social dilemmas, 149–50
  see also computer-mediated communication
comparison level, 208
  comparison level for alternatives (CLalt) (exchange level), 4, 208
  comparison level (CL) (exchange level), 4
  see also social comparison theory
competitive social comparison, group polarization, 99–100
compliance, 74, 80
  indoctrination, 108–11
  obedience studies, 8–9
  see also conformity
computer supported collaborative work (CSCW), 194
computer-mediated communication (cmc), 193–204, 208
  anonymity, 197, 198
  computerized brainstorming groups, 46
  dating, 195
  group cohesion, 197–8

identity, 198–9
Köhler effect, 200
leadership, 196
loneliness, 199
minority influences, 87
non-verbal and paralinguistic
    information lost, 194–5
social corroboration, 198–9
social facilitation/impairment, 201
social influence, 201–2
social support, 200
status information lost, 195–7
violence in computer games, 199–200
virtual partners, 202–3
see also communication
conditioning theory, 2
confidence
    computer-mediated communication,
        199
    consensus, 107
    group member characteristics, 44
conflict
    and aggression, 155–73
    contact hypothesis, reducing
        intergroup prejudice, 167
    discontinuity effect, distrust of
        outgroups, 164–5
    displaced aggression, 157
    distraction/conflict theory, 25–7
    emergent norm theory, 115
    fundamental attribution error, 166
    illusory correlation effect, 164–5
    ingroup favoritism, 160–3
    outgroup homogeneity, 163–4
    perceived injustice, 157–8
    realistic conflict theory, 155–6
    reduction of
        gradual and reciprocal concession
            technique, 171–3
        intergroup contact, 167
        manipulation of categorization,
            169–71
        superordinate goals, 168–9
    relative deprivation, 158–9
    'Robbers Cave' study, 156, 160, 167,
        168
    scapegoat theory, 156–7
    superordinate goals as reducing
        intergroup conflict, 168–9
    triggering events, 159–60
    ultimate attribution error, 166
    see also aggression
conformity, 73–83
    computer-mediated communication,
        198

gender, 77–8
group identification, 79–83
priming, impact, 78
self-categorization theory, 101
social identity view of
    deindividuation effects (SIDE),
    116–17
societal function, 75–6
task importance, relevance of, 78–9
see also cohesion; norms
conjunctive tasks, 62, 208
Consalvi, C., 9
consensus, feelings of confidence,
    107
contact hypothesis, 167, 208
convergent thought, 89, 208
conversion theory, 83–4, 208
    divergent thought, 89
    expectancy violation view, 90–1
    two-process model, 87–8
Cooper, J., 102, 200
cooperative tasks, 37
    early research on, 37–8
    Steiner's model, 38–43
    see also communication; social
        dilemmas
coordination loss, Steiner's model of
    group performance, 39
Cornelius, W.L., 22
costs, exchange theory, 3–4
Cottrell, N.B., 24–5, 55
counterculture, 3
Crano, W.D., 86, 88
Crocker, J., 15
cross-categorization, 208
Cuba, Bay of Pigs invasion, 96
Cutrona, C.E., 183, 186

Dakof, G.A., 185
Darley, J.M., 109
Darwin, Charles, 5
dating, computer-mediated
    communication, 195
David, B., 81, 87
Davis, J.H.
    group performance, 41, 42, 49
    information-reducing task, 54
    social decision scheme (SDS), 122,
        125, 126, 129
Dawes, R.M., 153
De Dreu, C.K.W., 88
De Vries, N.K., 88
decategorization, 208
    see also categorization
decision rule, 208

decision-making (group)
   collective induction, 133–5
   faction size, deliberation and
      decision-making, 135–6
   judgmental biases, 131–3
   juries, 125–9
   leniency bias in jury decisions,
      127–9
   social combination, 120–37
   social decision scheme (SDS), 122–5,
      129–31
   status, 10
   see also extremism
Dederich, Chuck, 17
Defreeze, Donald, 6
deindividuation, 208
   integrated deindividuation model
      (ID model), 117–18
   mob behaviour, 111–12, 113–15
   social identity view of
      deindividuation effects (SIDE),
      116–17
   see also anonymity
demonstrability, 208
Dennis, A.R., 46
Deutsch, M., 146
deviates
   and competitive social comparison,
      99
   impact on conformity, 76
   social influence, 83
   social rejection, 71
   see also outgroups
Diamond, S., 124–5
Diehl, M., 45
Diener, E., 114
dilemmas, *see* social dilemmas
Dion, K.L., 14
discontinuity effect, 164–5
discrimination, *see* ingroup favoritism
disengagement, social rejection, 73
disjunctive task, 208
dispensibility, free riding, 56–7
displacement, scapegoat theory, 156–7
distinctiveness, *see* optimal
      distinctiveness theory
distraction/conflict (D/C) theory, 25–7,
   208
divergent thought, 89, 208
Dolinski, D., 109
dominant response, social facilitation,
   22, 23, 26, 27
Doob, A.N., 71
Dorr, N., 170
Douglas, K.M., 197, 198

Dovidio, J.F., 170
Downing, L.J., 115
drive theory of social facilitation, 21–3,
   27–9, 208
dual identities, 170–1, 208
Dubrovsky, V.J., 196
dyad, 208

Eagly, A.H., 77–8
East Germany, dissatisfaction, 4
El-Bassel, N., 190
electronic groups, *see* computer-
      mediated communication
emergent norm theory, 115, 208
enforcement, social dilemmas, 151–2
entitativity, 18, 209
Epley, N., 78
equalitarian model, 209
equity
   inequity-based motivation loss, 58–9
   perceived injustice, 157–8
   relative deprivation, 158–9
eureka task, 37, 209
European Union, dual identities, 171
evaluation
   evaluation apprehension, process
      loss in brainstorming, 45
   identifiability-mediated motivation
      loss, 54–5
Evans, C.R., 14
exceptional case bias, 209
exchange theory, 3–4, 209
expectancy value theory, 61, 209
expectancy violation theory, 90–1, 209
extremism, 93–119
   deindividuation, 113–15
   emergent norm theory, 115
   group polarization, 98–108
   groupthink, 94–8
   indoctrination, 108–11
   mob action, 111–18
   social identity view of
      deindividuation effects (SIDE),
      116–17

Fairey, P.J., 76
false consensus effect, 70
favoritism, ingroup favoritism, 160–3,
   210
Fawzy, F.F., 189
fear
   and affiliation, 176, 191
   indoctrination, 109
feedback, impact on social dilemmas,
   145–6

Feeney, B.C., 187
Festinger, Leon, 69, 70
Fink, C.F., 44, 47
flexibility, leadership, 15–16
Forgas, J.P., 22
forming, group development, 17
Forsyth, D., 2
framing, 209
free riding, 55–8, 209
  inequity-based motivation loss, 58–9
  see also social loafing
Freedman, J.L., 71
Friedmann, E., 182
functional size, 209
fundamental attribution error, 166

Gaertner, S.L., 170
Gardham, K., 162
Gardner, W., 73
Geen, R.G., 29, 31
gender
  and conformity, 77–8
  Köhler effect, 63
general reinforcer, 209
Gerard, H.B., 178
Gerin, W., 184, 188
Gigone, D., 105–6
Gilovich, T., 78
Ginsberg, G.P., 103
Glaser, A.N., 28
Goodwin, P.A., 189
Gorbachev, Mikhail, 172
Gore, S., 181
gradual and reciprocal concession
    technique (GRIT)
  conflict reduction, 171–3
  social dilemmas, 146
grief, 179
Griffin, D., 82
Groff, B.D., 26–7
group, definition, 1–2, 209
group decision support system (GDSS),
    194
group performance support system
    (GPSS), 194, 209
groupthink, 107–8, 209
  avoiding, 97–8
  extreme views/decisions, 94–8
  social identity maintenance, 97
Guerin, B., 24
Guyana, mass suicide, 93

Hains, S.C., 12–13
Halloween, self-awareness and mob
    behaviour, 114

Hansell, P.S., 190
Hardie, M.A., 12–13
Hardin, Garrett, 140, 145
Harkins, S., 54–5, 57
Harvey, O.J., 9
Hastie, R., 105–6
Hastorf, A.H., 157
Hawaiians, early Christians and social
    comparison, 70
Hawkins, C., 135
health, and social support, 181–91
Hearst, Patricia, 6, 14, 108–9, 110
Helgeson, V.S., 189–90
Henry VIII, King, 8
Herek, G., 96–7
Hertel, G., 60–1, 62
hidden profiles, 209
hierarchical model, 41, 209
Hobbes, Thomas, 141
Hogg, Michael A., 3
  ingroup/outgroup norms, 102
  leadership, 16
  prototypic norms, 80–1
  social identity view of group
    cohesion, 12–13
Hollingshead, A.B., 194, 195
horizontal cohesion, 14, 210
Horse Trader Problem, 43, 44
House, J.S., 182
Hovland, C., 157
Huguet, P., 33
Husbands and Wives problem, 37, 50,
    56, 57

ID model of deindividuation, 117–18,
    210
identifiability
  free riding, 57–8
  Köhler effect, 62–3
  motivation loss, 53–5
identification (group), 210
  and anonymity, 116–17
  and conformity, 79–83
  see also anonymity
identity
  computer-mediated communication,
    198–9
  indoctrination, 110
  see also social identity
illness, and social support, 175
illusory correlation, 164–5, 210
immune responses, social support, 184
individual, and social dilemmas, 146–7
individuality, optimal distinctiveness
    theory, 5

indoctrination, 108–11
  Patricia Hearst, 6, 14, 108–9, 110
influence
  afterimage study, 84–6
  computer-mediated communication,
    201–2
  conversion theory, 83–4
  see also conformity; majority
    influence; minority influence;
    norms
information sampling theory, 210
  group polarization, 104–7
information-reducing task, 54, 210
informational social influence, 74, 210
Ingham, A.G., 52, 66
ingroup favoritism, 160–3, 210
ingroup/outgroup norms, 101–2
Insko, C.A., 164
instrumentality theory, 61
integrated deindividuation model
    (ID model), 117–18, 210
intellective task, 210
interdependence, 210
internalization, indoctrination, 109–10
internet, see computer-mediated
    communication
isolation, and anxiety, 176

Jackson, J., 54–5
Jacobs, R., 73–4
Jakarta, anti-Chinese riots, 111
Janes, L.M., 78
Janis, I.L.
  groupthink, 94–5, 96, 108
  social support, 180
Jensen, M.A.C., 17
Jetten, J., 162
jigsaw technique, intergroup contact,
    168
Johnson, H.H., 44
Johnson, Lyndon, 94, 95
Johnson, R.D., 115
Jones, E.E., 163, 164
Jones, Rev.Jim, 17, 93
judgement
  effect of group norms, 6
  judgmental biases, juries, 131–3
  judgmental task, 210
juries
  decision-making, 125–9
  judgmental biases, 131–3
justice, perceived injustice, 157–8

Kaplan, M.F., 131, 132, 133
Karau, S.J., 64–5

Kelley, Harold H., 4, 48
Kelman, H.C., 80
Kennedy, John F., 96
Kerr, N.L.
  free riding, 56, 58, 59
  judgmental biases, 133
  leniency bias in jury decisions,
    128–9
KGB, 108
Kiecolt-Glaser, J.K., 185
Kiesler, S., 195–6, 203
Kimble, C.E., 22
Knox, R.E., 103
Köhler effect, 210
  computer-mediated communication,
    200
  motivation gains, 60–3
  and social compensation, 64–5
Köhler, Otto, 60–3
Koszakai, T., 90
Kramer, R.M.
  communication in social dilemmas,
    149
  groupthink, 96
  social dilemmas, 144, 149
  social identity, 151
Kraut, R., 199
Kruglanski, A.W., 90
Ku Klux Klan, 115
Kulik, J.A., 178
Kwan, J., 89

Lage, E., 87
Larson Jr., J.R., 105
Larsson, K., 21
Latané, B.
  groups as demotivating, 66
  influence in computer-mediated
    communication, 201–2
  social loafing, 52–3, 54
Laughlin, P.R., 129–31, 134–5
Le Bon, G., 112
Lea, M., 116
leader categorization theory, 16, 210
leadership, 15–17
  computer-mediated communication,
    196
  social dilemmas, 145
learned drive theory, 24–5, 55, 210
Leary, M.R., 175
Leavitt, H.J., 10
Lehman, C., 190
leniency bias, 210
  jury decision-making, 127–9
Levine, J.M., 104

Lewin, Kurt, 11–12
L'Herrou, T., 202
Liebling, B.A., 177
Liebrand, W.B.G., 158
Linville, P.W., 164
loneliness, computer-mediated
    communication, 199
Lord, R.G., 16
Lorge, I., 37, 47
Lount, R., 63
Lutkins, S., 179
Luus, E., 70
Lynch, J.J., 176
lynchings
    displaced aggression, 157
    mob behaviour, 114, 118

Maass, A., 84
McCauley, C., 103
MacCoun, R., 128–9
McGarty, C., 197, 198
McGrath, J.E., 37, 200–1
McKenna, K.Y.A., 198–9
Mackie, D.M.
    aggression in computer games, 200
    expectancy violation view, 90
    group salience and polarization, 103
    ingroup/outgroup norms and
        polarization, 101, 102
    two-process model of conversion, 88
McLeod, P.
    anonymity, 197
    conformity, 198
    expectancy violation view, 90
    information sampling theory, 107
    minority influence, 87
Maier, N.R.F., 43
majority influence
    and conformity, 76
    convergent thought pattern, 89
    and minority influence, 83–91
    see also decision-making (group);
        influence; minority influence
Manhattan Project, 36–7, 38, 39, 40,
    42, 48
Manstead, A.S.R., 28, 31–2, 33
Marcus-Newhall, A., 170
Martin, R., 85, 186, 187
matching theories of social support,
    186–7, 210
means rule, 210
Melamed, B.G., 185
memory, and social rejection, 73
mere presence hypothesis, 23–5, 28,
    34, 210

Messé, L.A., 60
Messick, D.M., 144
Meyer, T.J., 189
Middle East
    conflict, 156, 157
    Sharon's escalation of tensions, 173
Milgram, S., 8
Miller, L.E., 131, 132, 133
Mills, J., 178
minimal groups, 160–3, 210
minority influence
    afterimage study, 84–6
    conversion theory, 83–4
    divergent thought, 89
    expectancy violation view, 90–1
    and majority influence, 83–91
    meta-analyses of minority influence
        studies, 86
    and social decision scheme, 130
    two-process model of conversion,
        87–8
    variables affecting, 86–7
    see also decision-making (group);
        deviates; influence; majority
        influence
Mintz, P.M., 178
Mishler, E.G., 49
Mittelman, M.S., 189
mob action, 111–18
    deindividuation, 113–15
    emergent norm theory, 115
    integrated deindividuation model
        (ID model), 117–18
    social identity view of
        deindividuation effects (SIDE),
        116–17
modeling, mob action, 112–13
Moore, D.L., 26, 27
More, Sir Thomas, 8
Morrow, M., 199–200
mortality, broken heart effect, 179
Moscovici, Serge
    afterimage study, 85–6
    conversion theory, 83–4, 87, 88
    minority influence, 83–6, 87, 88,
        130
motivation (group)
    free riding, 55–8
    gain, 209
    inequity-based motivation loss, 58–9
    Köhler effect, 60–3
    loss, 52, 54–5, 58–9, 66, 209
    motivation gains
        Köhler effect, 60–3
        social compensation, 63–5

motivation loss, social loafing, 52–9
social compensation, 63–5
Steiner's model of group
    performance, 39, 42
sucker effect, inequity-based
    motivation loss, 58–9
Mugny, G., 87
Mullen, B., 95, 114
multidimensional views, group
    cohesion, 14–15
Myers, D.G., 99
Mynatt, C.R., 22–3

Nail, P.R., 80
Nature of Paradise, The (Allport), 167
Nawrat, R., 109
Nemeth, Charlan J., 89
Newcomb, T.M., 69, 74
Newsom, J.T., 186
Nijstad, B.A., 45
nominal groups, 210–11
nonverbal communication, loss
    of in computer-mediated
    communication, 194–5, 196
normative social influence, 74, 211
norming, group development, 17
norms, 211
    conformity, 73–83
    cultural rules, 68–9
    emergent norm theory, mob
        behaviour, 115
    enforcement in social dilemmas, 151
    group norms, 6–7
    ingroup favoritism, 161–2
    ostracism, 71–3
    reciprocity in social dilemmas, 148–9
    social comparison theory, 69–71
    social dilemmas, 144
    see also cohesion; conformity
Nuckolls, K.B., 181

obedience studies, 8–9
    see also compliance
O'Heeron, R., 184
Olds, D., 188
Olson, J.M., 78
omission, acts of, 162
Oppenheimer, J.Robert, 37, 38, 39, 42
optimal distinctiveness theory, 5, 211
Orbell, J.M., 152–3
Osbourn, A.F., 45
Osgood, C.E., 171
ostracism, 71–3, 200, 211
outcome expectancy, self-efficacy
    theory, 30

outgroups
    discontinuity effect, 164–5
    outgroup homogeneity, conflict,
        163–4
    see also deviates; ingroup/outgroup
        norms
Ouwerkerk, J.W., 152

Pagel, M.D., 185
Pakistan, creation of, 158
Papastamou, S., 87
paralinguistic information, lost
    in computer-mediated
    communication, 195
Parks, M.R., 199
Paulus, P.B., 22, 46
Pendry, L., 78
Pennebaker, J., 184
People's Temple, 17
performance choking, 32
performance (group)
    brainstorming, 44–7
    early research, 37–8
    process loss, 39, 43–9
    size, 47–9
    Steiner's model, 38–43
performing, group development, 17
Personnaz, B., 85
persuasive arguments theory, 99–100,
    102, 211
Pessin, J., 26
Peterson, R.S., 89
pets, as social support, 182–3
Pettigrew, T.F., 167
Petty, R.E., 57, 90
polarization (group), 98–108, 209
    anonymity in computer-mediated
        communication, 197
    competitive social comparison,
        99–100
    group salience, 102–3
    groups with real consequences, 103–4
    information sampling theory, 104–7
    ingroup/outgroup norms, 101–2
    persuasive arguments theory, 99–100
    self-categorization, 100–1
Polynesians, as easy-going, 68–9
Pool, G.J., 82–3
Postmes, T.
    anonymity and group identification,
        116–17
    cohesion in computer-mediated
        communication, 197–8
    deindividuation, 113–14
    self-awareness, 114

potential, Steiner's model of group
    performance, 38–43
potential productivity, 211
Prentice-Dunn, S., 113
priming, 78, 211
Prisoner's Dilemma, 211
    discontinuity effect, 164
    social dilemmas, 141–3, 144
    virtual partners, 203
privatization, structural solutions to
    social dilemmas, 150–1
privatizing, 211
problem-solving
    collective induction, 133–5
    hierarchical model, 41
process loss, group performance, 39,
    43–9, 52, 211
production blocking, process loss in
    brainstorming, 45–6
productivity, and degree of cohesion,
    14
prospective research design, 211
    health and social support, 181
prototypic group members
    group cohesion, 12–14
    prototypic group norms, 80–1, 101,
        211
prototypic individuals, 211
Pusecker, P.A., 30–1

Quattrone, G.A., 163, 164

Rabbie, J.M., 115
race
    displaced aggression, 157
    jigsaw technique, intergroup contact,
        168
    lynchings, 114, 118, 157
    outgroup homogeneity, 164
    relative deprivation and conflict,
        158–9
    rioting, 111
Rank, A.D., 15
rats, social facilitation, 21
realistic conflict theory, 155–6, 211
recategorization, 211
reciprocity
    gradual and reciprocal concession
        technique (GRIT), 146, 171–3
    reciprocal strategy, social dilemmas,
        148–9
    reciprocity norm, 211
Rees, W., 179
reference groups, 211
referent informational influence, 211

reflection, conversion theory, 84
Reich, P., 179
reinforcement, social approval, 72
relative deprivation, 211
    conflict, 158–9
releaser cues, 212
resources
    scarcity and conflict, 156
    Steiner's model of group
        performance, 38–43
responsibility, deindividuation and
    mob action, 112
Restle, F., 41, 42, 49
rewards, exchange theory, 3–4
Rezabek, J.S., 22
Ringelmann, Max, 47, 52, 60
'Robbers Cave' study, 156, 160, 167,
    168
Roberts, L.D., 199
Rogers, R.W., 113
Rohrer, J.H., 73
roles, 7–9
    role conflict, 8, 212
Rook, Karen, 185
Roosevelt, President Franklin, 69
rope-pulling team, process loss, 47, 52
Russell, D.W., 186

salience
    group polarization, 102–3
    self-categorization theory, 3
Sanders, G.S., 26
Sanna, Larry, 26, 29, 30–1
scapegoating, 156–7, 212
Schachter, Stanley, 70–1, 176, 178, 191
Schmitt, B.H., 23
Schopler, J., 164
Schultz-Hardt, F.D., 107
Sears, R.R., 157
Seidman, O., 177
self-awareness, and deindividuation,
    114–15, 118
self-categorization theory, 212
    group identification, 80–1
    group polarization, 100–1
    group salience and polarization,
        102–3
    ingroup/outgroup norms and
        polarization, 101–2
    social identity theory, 3
self-categorization view of polarization,
    212
self-censorship, group cohesion, 13
self-disclosure, social support and
    health, 183–4

self-efficacy theory, 30–1, 212
self-esteem
  collective self-esteem, 15
  group identification, 82
  ingroup favoritism, 161
  social support and health, 183
self-presentation theory, 29–31
Semin, G.R., 28, 31–2, 33
sexual excitement, and mob action,
    112
Sharon, Ariel, 173
Shaver, P., 177
Shaw, M.E., 37, 41
Sherif, Muzafer
  autokinetic effect, 6, 73, 74
  conformity, 73, 79, 80
  contact hypothesis, 167
  'Robbers Cave' study, 156, 160, 167,
    168
Sherman, S.J., 18
Shotland, L.R., 30
SIDE (social identity view of
    deindividuation effects), 116–17,
    198, 212
Siegel, J.M., 182, 197
SIM model of groupthink, 97, 212
size (group), 7
  group performance, 47–9
  structural solutions to social
    dilemmas, 151
Skinner, B.F., 72
Smith, Adam, 141
Smith, P.B., 75, 77
social attraction, 212
  group cohesion, 12–14
social comparison theory, 69–70, 212
  conditioning theory, 2
social compensation, 212
  motivation gains, 63–5
  social rejection, 72–3
social constructions, beliefs as, 68–9
social corroboration, 212
social decision scheme (SDS), 122–5,
    129–31, 212
  judgmental biases, 132–3
  jury decision-making, 126
social dilemmas, 139–54, 142t, 212
  communication, 149–50
  enforcement, 151–2
  and the individual, 146–7
  leadership, 145
  privatization as structural solution,
    150–1
social exclusion, 72
  see also ostracism

social facilitation/impairment, 20–34,
    212, 213
  attentional theories, 31–3, 207
  computer-mediated communication,
    201
  distraction/conflict theory, 25–7
  drive theory, 21–3, 27–9
  learned drive view, 24–5
  mere presence hypothesis, 23–4
  self-presentation theory, 29
social identity
  group cohesion, 12–14
  ingroup favoritism, 161
  leadership, 16–17
  self-categorization theory, 3
  and social dilemmas, 151
  social identity maintenance (SIM),
    97, 212
  social identity theory, 3, 161–2,
    212–13
  social identity view of
    deindividuation effects (SIDE),
    116–17
social interaction, definition of group, 2
social loafing, 52–9, 213
social matching, process loss in
    brainstorming, 45–6
social monitoring view, 213
  uncertainty, 24
social motive, 213
social rejection, 70–1
  ostracism, 71–3
social roles, 213
social skills training, 190–1
social support, 180–1, 213
  broken heart and mortality, 179
  buffering hypothesis, 184–5
  computer-mediated communication,
    200
  as harmful to health, 185–6
  and health, 181–91
  optimal matching hypothesis, 186–7
  pets as, 182–3
sociobiology, 4–5, 213
Sokill, G.R., 22–3
Solem, A.R., 43
Solomon, H., 47
Sommer, K.L., 73
Sorrentino, R.M., 85
Soviet Union, de-escalation of world
    tension under Gorbachev, 172
Spears, R.
  anonymity, 116, 117
  cohesion in computer-mediated
    communication, 197–8

deindividuation, 113–14
    group salience, 102
    self-awareness, 114
Spiegel, D., 189
Stafford, R.K., 103
Stasser, G.
    hidden profile, 105
    information sampling theory, 104–5,
        106, 107
    shared information, 135
status, 9–10, 213
    and communication networks, 10–11
    group member characteristics, 43–4
    loss of information in computer-
        mediated communication, 195–7
Steiner, I.D.
    group size, process loss, 48, 49, 52
    model of group performance, 38–43,
        47
Stephan, F.F., 49
Stewart, D.D., 97, 106, 107
Stoner, J.A.F., 98
storming, group development, 17
strength in numbers, 213
stress
    health and social support, 179–91
    impact of affiliation, 176–8, 191
    impact of social support, 178–84
    indoctrination, 108–10
    pets as social support, 182–3
    social skills training, 190–1
    social support as harmful, 185–6
Stroebe, W., 45, 62, 179
Stroop task, 33, 213
Strube, M.J., 25
structure
    group structure, 7
    structural solutions to social
        dilemmas, 150–3
subgroups, 10
sucker effect, 213
    inequity-based motivation loss, 58–9
Suedfeld, P., 15
Suhr, J.A., 186
superordinate goals, 213
    recategorization, 170
    as reducing intergroup conflict,
        168–9
survival
    norms, 7
    sociobiological theory, 5
Symbionese Liberation Army (SLA),
        6–7, 14, 108–9
Syme, L.S., 181–2
Synanon, 17

Tajfel, H., 160–2
task demands, 213
task-oriented leadership, 15
Tatum, R., 177
Taylor, S.E., 185
Telch, C.F., 189
Telch, M.J., 189
Tetlock, P.E., 96
therapy, negotiating rewards and costs,
        4
Thibaut, John, 4
Thomas, E.J., 44, 47
Thompson, J.E., 172
threat reactions, 28, 29, 213
tit-for-tat, 214
Titus, L.J., 25, 28, 29
Titus, W., 105
Torcivia, J.M., 44
Torrance, E.P., 10, 43–4, 195
transformational leadership, 16–17,
        214
Triplett, Milton, 20
Triplett, N., 47
Trost, M.R., 86
Troutman, E., 183
trust, 146, 214
    and distrust of outgroups, 164–5
truth wins, 214
Tuckman, B.W., 17
Turner, J.C., 81, 87
Turner, M.E., 95–6
two-process view of conversion, 87–8,
        214
typing experiment, social facilitation,
        23

ultimate attribution error, 166,
        214
unanimity, jury decision-making,
        125–7
uncertainty
    and social facilitation, 23
    social monitoring, 24
    social rejection, 71, 72
USA
    jigsaw technique, intergroup contact,
        168
    lynchings, 114, 118, 157
    relative deprivation and conflict,
        158–9
    rioting, 111
    school shootings and computer
        games, 200
    Soviet Union's de-escalation of world
        tension, 172

triggering events for conflict, 157,
    159–60

Valacich, Joseph S., 46
Van Dijk, E., 144–5
vertical cohesion, 14, 214
Vietnam War, 94, 95
Vinokur, A., 99, 102
violence
    computer games, 199–200
    see also conflict
virtual team, 214

Wallboom, M., 114
Walters, R., 176, 177
Weiss, R., 180–1
Wells, G.L., 70
Wilder, D.A., 76, 169, 172
Wilke, H., 144–5

Williams, K.D.
    motivation loss, 54
    ostracism and social rejection, 72,
        73, 200
    social compensation, 64–5
witnesses, social corroboration,
    70
Wood, Wendy, 81–3, 86
World Trade Center, terrorist attack,
    51, 170
Wright, S.C., 167

Zajonc, Robert B., 33
    drive theory, 28
    social facilitation, 20, 21–4
Zdaniuk, B., 104
Zeisel, H., 124–5
Zillmannn, D., 112
Zimbardo, P., 113, 115

INTERGROUP RELATIONS
Second Edition

Marilynn Brewer

Praise for the first edition:

> ...manages to integrate theory, research, and illustration very nicely...all in all an excellent piece of work.
> Michael Hogg, University of Queensland

> ...extremely contemporary in its coverage and yet it introduces the classic works as well. The balance here is perfect.
> Samuel Gaertner, University of Delaware

- What are the origins of individuals' identification with groups?
- What are the causes and consequences of the distinction between different groups?
- How can intergroup conflict be reduced, whilst maintaining group loyalty and community?

The first edition of *Intergroup Relations*, co-authored with Norman Miller, received considerable critical acclaim. In this fully revised edition, Marilynn Brewer has added new research and ideas to provide an up-to-date and invaluable resource for all those concerned with this key area of social psychology. It is clearer than ever that group identities play a major role in human behaviour, impelling heroic action on behalf of ingroups, as well as horrific atrocities against designated outgroups. Revisions have been made that reflect the relevance of recent international events and the social psychological approaches that can illuminate and explain them. Social psychological understanding of these processes has grown as the study of intergroup relations takes centre stage within the discipline, making this a topical and timely new edition for undergraduate courses in social psychology and the wider social sciences.

Contents
Preface – From basic psychological processes to intergroup behaviour – Ethnocentrism and ingroup identity: the need for 'we-ness' – Intergroup discrimination: what is just to us is unfair to them – Outgroup prejudice: negative affect and hostility – Intergroup contact, cooperation, and competition: does togetherness make friends? – International conflict: what makes war possible? – Glossary – References – Index.

c.224pp   0 335 20989 0 (Paperback)   0 335 20990 4 (Hardback)

SOCIAL PSYCHOLOGY AND HEALTH
Second Edition

Wolfgang Stroebe

If you are a student of social or health psychology, or if you are working in one of the health professions, you are likely at some point to address questions such as the following:

- Which behaviour patterns are detrimental to health?
- Why do people engage in such behaviour, even if they know about its negative effects?
- How can people be influenced to changed their behaviour?
- What do we mean by stressful life events and how can their impact on health be mediated?

In *Social Psychology and Health* you will find these major health topics discussed from a social psychological perspective. During recent decades there have been significant changes in conceptions of health and illness, with a move towards a broader conception of health to include physical, mental and social well-being. In line with these changes, health psychology has become a dominant force in the health sciences. This relatively new field of psychology is much influenced by social psychological theory and research, and the focus of the book reflects this.

Social Psychology and Health gives an up-to-date perspective on these key health psychology questions. The book argues for an integrative approach that combines psychological, economic and environmental interventions in order to reduce the potential risks to health arising from behaviour or stressful life events.

The second edition of this highly successful textbook has been extensively revised, expanded and updated. Much new material has been added base on research done in the last five years, in particular drawing on the author's own research into obesity and sexual risk behaviour. Many of the epidemiological examples and more than a third of the references have been updated. It is essentially a new book which will make an important contribution to the literature.

Contents
Changing conceptions of health and illness – Determinants of health behaviour: a social psychological analysis – Beyond persuasion: the modification of health behaviour – Behaviour and health: excessive appetites – Behaviour and health: self-protection – Stress and health – Moderators of the stress-health relationship – The role of social psychology in health promotion – Glossary – References – Author index – Subject index.

352pp   0 335 19921 6 (Paperback)   0 335 19922 4 (Hardback)

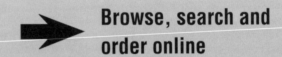
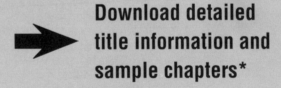